THE LIVES OF THE SAINTS

Originally Compiled by the
REV. ALBAN BUTLER

Now Edited, Revised, and Copiously Supplemented by
HERBERT THURSTON, S.J.
AND
DONALD ATTWATER

VOL. IX
SEPTEMBER

P. J. KENEDY & SONS
NEW YORK

NIHIL OBSTAT:

Thomas McLaughlin, S.Th.D.,
Censor deputatus.

IMPRIMATUR:

✠ Joseph Butt,
Vicarius generalis.

Westmonasterii,
die 18a Januarii, 1934.

Made and Printed in Great Britain
1934

NOTE

AS in the two preceding volumes, July and August, the text
of Butler's *Lives* has been revised and additional notices
written by Mr. Attwater, Father Thurston being responsible
only for the bibliographies and notes accompanying them.

The following *beati*, omitted from this volume, will be dealt
with in the supplementary and index volume: BB. Liberatus a
Lauro, Peregrinus a Falerone, and Mark Crisin and his
companions.

THE EDITORS.

CONTENTS OF VOLUME IX

(The entries marked with an asterisk are additions to Butler's text. A few of his notices have been discarded and written anew; many have been supplemented, and all have been revised.)

CONTENTS OF VOLUME IX

CONTENTS OF VOLUME IX

CONTENTS OF VOLUME IX

x

CONTENTS OF VOLUME IX

xi

CONTENTS OF VOLUME IX

THE LIVES OF THE SAINTS

SEPTEMBER 1

ST GILES, ABBOT AND CONF.

c. A.D. 712

THE legend of St Giles (Aegidius), one of the most famous of the Middle Ages, was derived chiefly from a biography written in Latin in the tenth century. According to this work he was an Athenian by birth, the son of distinguished parents, Theodore and Pelagia, and during his youth cured a sick beggar by giving him his own cloak, after the manner of St Martin. Giles's piety and learning drew admiration in such a manner that it was impossible for him to enjoy in his own country that obscurity and retirement which were the chief object of his desires on earth ; he dreaded temporal prosperity and the applause of men, which after the death of his parents was showered on him because of the liberality of his alms and his numerous miracles. He therefore took ship for the west, landed at Marseilles, and, after passing two years with St Caesarius at Arles, eventually made his hermitage in a wood near the mouth of the Rhone. He lived three years in this solitude, with no other subsistence than wild herbs or roots and water, conversing only with God, and living rather like an angel than a man. He was for some time nourished with the milk of a hind, which was eventually pursued by a certain king, Flavius, who was hunting in the forest. The beast took refuge with St Giles in his cave, and the hounds gave up their chase and refused to approach nearer than a stone's throw ; on the following day the hind was found again and the same thing happened ; and again on the third day, when the King had brought with him the Bishop of Nîmes to watch the peculiar behaviour of his hounds. This time one of the huntsmen shot an arrow at a venture into the dense bushes which screened the cave, and when they had forced their way through they found Giles, wounded by the arrow, sitting with the hind between his knees. Flavius and the Bishop approached and asked the hermit to give an account of himself and of how he came to be wounded, and

I

when they heard his story they humbly begged his pardon and promised at once to send physicians to attend him. Giles begged them to leave him alone and refused all the gifts they pressed upon him, so that the King and his retinue departed marvelling. When they had gone, " the holy confessor, finding that his earthly frame was suffering from the wound he had received, remembered the heavenly saying that virtue is perfected by infirmity. He therefore prayed the Lord that he might never regain his former health so long as he should live in this world."

King Flavius continued frequently to visit St. Giles, who eventually asked him to devote his proffered alms to founding a monastery ; this the King agreed to do provided Giles would become its first abbot. In due course the monastery was built near the cave, a community gathered round, and the reputation of the austerities of the monks and of the holiness of their abbot reached the ears of Charles, King of France (whom medieval romancers identified as Charlemagne). Giles was sent for to the court at Orleans, where the King consulted him on spiritual matters but was ashamed to name a grievous sin that was on his conscience. " On the following Sunday, when the holy man was celebrating Mass according to custom and praying to God for the King during the canon, an angel of the Lord appeared to him and laid on the altar a scroll on which was written the sin which the King had committed, and which further said that he would be forgiven at Giles's intercession, provided he did penance and desisted from that sin in the future. . . . When Mass was ended Giles gave the scroll to the King to read, who fell at the saint's feet, begging him to intercede with the Lord for him. And so the man of the Lord commended him to God in prayer and gently admonished him to refrain from that sin in the future." St Giles then returned to his monastery and afterwards went to Rome to commend his monks to the Holy See. The Pope granted them many privileges and made a present of two carved doors of cedar-wood ; to emphasise his trust in divine providence St Giles threw these doors into the Tiber, and they safely preceded him to France. After being warned of his approaching end in a dream, he died on a Sunday, September 1, " leaving the world sadder for his bodily absence but giving joy in Heaven by his happy arrival." Before he died he prophesied that his monastery would be destroyed by an enemy before very long time had elapsed (the Saracens in fact invaded southern France in 719).

This and other medieval accounts of St Giles, our sole source of information, are utterly untrustworthy and some of their statements are obviously self-contradictory. For example, Giles could not have met both St Caesarius of Arles and Charlemagne, for the one died in 542 and the other became king of the Franks in 768 ; nor is this difficulty overcome by seeing in King Charles of France Charles Martel.   On the other hand, though the legend must be rejected, St Giles was certainly an historical person ; not a Greek but a Provençal, for the name Aegidius was in use in Gaul long after its original form had ceased to be current in Greece in the fourth century.   A Visigothic king of Spain, Flavius Wamba, made an expedition so far as the Rhone in 673, and, according to a papal bull of the ninth century, founded an abbey there for St Giles ; this abbey was offered by the saint to Benedict II, who, it is alleged, granted it a charter.   As that pope reigned only from June 684 till May 685 St Giles may have visited Rome during that year.   He was, therefore, a contemporary neither of St Caesarius nor of any King Charles, who were doubtless introduced into the narrative to enhance the reputation of the saint and his abbey with their great names.   In the same way the story of the hind, variations of which are found in the lives of several saints, was probably borrowed by the biographer from the legends of St Emilian Cucullatus or of St Carilefus.   But that of St Giles is the most famous and for many centuries he was one of the most popular of saints.   He is numbered among the Fourteen Holy Helpers (the only one of them who is not a martyr) and his tomb at his monastery became a place of pilgrimage of the first importance.   Around it grew up the flourishing town of Saint-Gilles, whose prosperity, however, was ruined by the crusade against the Albigensians in the thirteenth century ; there was some revival of the pilgrimage after the return of a part of the saint's relics (which had been removed to Toulouse to save them from the Huguenots) to the town in 1862.   Other crusaders named another town Saint-Gilles (now Sinjil), on the borders of Benjamin and Ephraim, and his cult spread throughout western Europe ; England had so many as 160 parish churches dedicated in his honour, and he was invoked as the patron of cripples, beggars, and blacksmiths.   John Lydgate, monk of Bury in the fifteenth century, invokes him in a poem as

> " Gracious Giles, of poor folk chief patron,
>   Medicine to sick in their distress,
> To all needy shield and protection,
>   Refuge to wretches, their damage to redress,
>   Folk that were dead restoring to quickness. . . ."

On this day are also commemorated the Spanish ST GILES, who with St Arcanus is said to have founded the town of Borgo San Sepolcro in Umbria during the tenth century ; BD. GILES, abbot of the Cistercian monastery of Castañeda in the Asturias, who died about the year 1203 ; and BD. GILES, a Dominican who died at Ghent in the middle of the thirteenth century and is honoured at Saint-Omer.

Complete and uninterrupted solitude is a state which few are able to bear with unabated fervour and without fatal relaxation. A man in solitude whom sloth warps or whose conversation is not always with God and His angels is his own most dangerous tempter and worst company. Aristotle having defined man as a social creature, or one born for society, added that he who lives alone must either be a god or a beast. But the Philosopher was unacquainted with the happiness of religious contemplation. The old Christian proverb is more exact : that he who lives always alone is either an angel or a devil. This state therefore is not without snares and dangers, nor does an hermitage necessarily make a saint. But when a person, by an extraordinary call, embraces it with fervour and strenuously applies himself to all the exercises of retirement and penance, such an one, being disengaged in his affections from all earthly ties, exchanges the society of a vain and sinful world for that of God and holy spirits, and has certainly attained the highest degree of happiness under Heaven ; this state is its novitiate, and in some degree an anticipation of its eternal sweet and noble employment. He who accompanies the exercise of contemplation and divine love with zealous and undaunted endeavours to conduct others to the same glorious end shall be truly " great in the kingdom of Heaven."

The text of the Latin Life of St Giles is printed in the *Acta Sanctorum*, September, vol. i, and another recension in the *Analecta Bollandiana*, viii (1889), pp. 103–120. There is also a metrical version and an adaptation in old French. For these last consult the careful study of Miss E. C. Jones, *Saint Gilles, Essai d'Histoire littéraire* (1914). The genuineness of the supposed bull of Benedict II can hardly be maintained ; it is asterisked by Jaffé, n. 2127. For the folklore which has gathered round the name of St Giles see Bächtold-Stäubli, *Handwörterbuch des deutschen Aberglaubens*, vol. i, pp. 212 *seq.*, and, for the treatment in art, Künstle, *Ikonographie*, vol. ii, pp. 32–34. This Saint's distinctive emblem, as might be expected, is a hind with an arrow. For English readers an excellent account of St Giles and his cultus is provided in the illustrated booklet of F. Brittain, *Saint Giles*, Cambridge, 1928.

ST VERENA, VIRG.

A.D. 344 (?)

The Roman Martyrology mentions on this day the death of Verena the Virgin at " Aquae Durae " in the neighbourhood of

Constance, of whom nothing at all, not even the era of her life, is known. She has been drawn into the legend of the Theban Legion (September 22) and her fictitious " acts " represent her as a native of the Thebaid and a relative of St Victor, who had been her preceptor. She came to Milan and thence to Agaunum to venerate the relics of the martyrs there and search for traces of Victor, and settled at Solothurn, where SS. Victor and Ursus had been put to death. There is still shown the cave in which she lived and from whence she would go out on errands of mercy among the peasants of the district, for whose personal cleanliness she had a particular care. The devil in vain tried to frighten her away by terrifying physical assaults. Later Verena visited Coblenz in Switzerland and ended her days in a cell built for her by a priest at Zurzach in the Aargau, where her tomb shows her holding a comb and a bowl, emblems of her charitable works. St Verena is held in great honour throughout Switzerland.

The legendary Life of St Verena is printed in the *Acta Sanctorum*, September, vol. i. A certain respectability attaches to the cult of the saint from the fact that the name appears in the additions to the *Hieronymianum*, e.g. in the MS. of Reichenau and also in the Munich martyrologium of the ninth century (MS. Latin 15818). See also Huber, *Das Leben der h. Jungfrau Verena* (1870) ; A. Lütolf, *Glaubensboten der Schweiz* (1871), pp. 182–92, and especially E. A. Stückelberg in his *Schweizerischen Heiligen des Mittelalters*, pp. 127–134, and other publications.

ST FIRMINUS II, Bp. of Amiens, Conf.
Fourth Century

He is honoured as the third bishop of Amiens. His father Faustinian, a senator of Gaul, had been baptised by St Firminus I and in his honour gave him his name. Eulogius, the second bishop of Amiens (the first known to history), who had assisted at the Council of Cologne in 346 and at that of Sardica in 343, died about the year 350, and St Firminus II was placed in that see, being consecrated by John, Bishop of Lyons. After visiting Rome he returned to his charge, which he administered with great zeal and sanctity during forty years. He was buried in the church of our Lady, now called of St Acheul, which he had built, from which St Salvius in the seventh century translated his relics into the cathedral. All information available about this saint is late and unreliable. He may be the same as St Firminus I (September 25).

See the *Acta Sanctorum*, September, vol. i, but more especially Duchesne, *Fastes Épiscopaux*, vol. iii, pp. 122–127. A popular account is provided in Corblet *Hagiographie du diocèse d'Amiens* (1870), vol. ii, pp. 189–216.

THE TWELVE BROTHERS, Marts.

A.D. 303 (?)

The twelve martyred brothers mentioned in the Roman Martyrology on this day were, according to their legend, natives of Adrumetum in proconsular Africa and the children of SS. Boniface and Thecla, whose passion is commemorated on August 30. They were seized at Adrumetum, brought to Carthage and tortured, and then sent into Italy chained together by the neck as they refused to apostatise. Four of them, Honoratus, Fortunatus, Orontius, and Savinian, were put to death by beheading at Potenza on August 27 ; Septimius, Januarius, and Felix at Venosa on the 28th ; Vitalis, Satyrus, and Repositus at Velleianum on the 29th ; and another Felix and Donatus at Sentianum on September 1. These martyrs of Apulia were not in fact related to one another nor to SS. Boniface and Thecla, and were probably not Africans. But after their relics had been taken up by the duke Arechis, in the year 760, and enshrined in the church of St Sophia at Benevento they became associated together in the general mind and the story grew up that they were brothers from across the seas. They are also known as the Martyrs of the South.

What purports to be a brief history of these martyrs will be found in the *Acta Sanctorum*, September, vol. i ; but for an adequate investigation of the composition of this group we must have recourse to Père Delehaye's commentary on the *Hieronymianum* in the *Acta Sanctorum*, November, vol. ii, part 2, pp. 471–472 and 480–482. *Cf.* also Lanzoni, *Le Diocesi d'Italia*, pp. 285–288.

ST AMMON, Mart.

c. A.D. 322

The Roman Martyrology mentions to-day the passion at Heraclea in Thrace " of St Ammon the deacon and forty holy virgins, whom he instructed in the faith and took with him to the glory of martyrdom under the tyrant Licinius." He was put to death by having a red-hot helmet forced on to his head. It would seem that the number of his maiden disciples was four, not forty. On September 8 are named the holy martyrs at Alexandria, Ammon, Theophilus, Neoterius, and twenty-two others. The traditional names of these twenty-two have come down to us, but nothing is known of the circumstances or date of their passion. A St Ammon martyred under Diocletian at Nicomedia is commemorated on the 12th, and

another Ammon is among the sons of St Rebecca, whose martyrdom with their mother at Alexandria is celebrated by the Copts on
the 7th.

See the *Acta Sanctorum*, September, vol. i, and the *Synaxarium Cp.* in
the *Propylæum* to the *Acta Sanctorum*, November, col. 3.

ST LUPUS, or LEU, ABP. OF SENS, CONF.
A.D. 623

He was a saint from the cradle, and brought up in the sanctuary,
like another Samuel, in learning and piety among the clergy of
Orleans, where his brother, Austrenius, was bishop. His mother
Austregildis was herself a saint and is commemorated on this same
day. It was always a favourite devotion with him to visit the tombs
of the martyrs, honouring God in His faithful servants who had
glorified His name by the sacrifice of their lives. Desiring to walk
in their spirit, he subdued his flesh by austere fasts, watching in
prayer, humiliations, and penance, and became a monk at Lérins.
Having succeeded St Artemius in the archbishopric of Sens in 609
he distinguished himself by the most zealous discharge of every
branch of the pastoral duty, and showed that, as no dignity could
inspire him with pride, so no application to public employment
could divert him from constant attention to God. When the safety
of his country demanded his assistance he was active in maintaining
public order, and after the death of King Theodericus II he supported the party of his son Sigebert to the utmost of his power.
Afterwards King Clotaire became master of Burgundy and sent
Farulphus thither to take care of his affairs. This minister proceeded against St Lupus, who when Sens was besieged had escaped
the swords of Clotaire only by ringing the church bell and thereby
frightening them off. The Archbishop neglected the precaution of
buying his safety from Farulphus, who accused him falsely to the
King, and was seconded in his calumnies by Medegislus, abbot of
St Remigius's in the suburbs of Sens, whose aim it was to supplant
St Lupus in his see. The wages of the success of this unscrupulous
prelate was that the people of Sens broke into his church and there
slew him.

Clotaire had not learned how dangerous a thing it is for a prince
to listen to or encourage informers, and, being deceived by the
slanderers, banished St Lupus, and gave orders to an officer to conduct
him to Ausène, a village not far from Lyons. The holy Bishop on his

arrival found temples in which the people of the country worshipped false gods. He believed he was sent by God for their conversion, which he undertook by his zealous preaching and example. By restoring sight to a blind man he converted Landegislus, the governor, and baptised him with several other pagans in the armies of the Franks. In the meantime St Winebald, abbot of Troyes, and the citizens of Sens asked King Clotaire to recall St Lupus. That prince, who was then near Rouen, realised the injury he had done the man and the slanders of his accusers. He therefore disgraced them, sent for St Lupus to ask his forgiveness, entertained him at his table, and sent him back to his church. The saint never showed the least resentment against his enemies, sought no other revenge than by conferring benefits on his calumniators, and by the evenness of temper with which he bore his disgrace gave the highest mark of true heroism and sincere virtue. The King granted him the right to mint money within the limits of his diocese, where Lupus founded a monastery in honour of St Columba, a local martyr and patron of Sens. Among the marvels told of this saint is that one day while singing Mass a precious stone dropped miraculously into the chalice. This is referred to in the Roman Martyrology, with the guarded word *refertur*, " it is reported," which is certainly called for when we consider how easily a jewel might become detached from a vestment. Nevertheless it was kept as a relic in the treasury of the cathedral of Sens, where also was preserved the archbishop's episcopal ring, one of the many in legend that were dropped into water and recovered in the belly of a fish. St Lupus died in the year 623 at Brinon, and was buried according to his directions at the church of St Columba in Sens.

On the 25th of this month, on which day is commemorated St Aunacharius of Auxerre, brother to St Lupus of Sens, the Roman Martyrology names another ST LUPUS, " who from being an anchorite was made bishop " of Lyons. He was monk and abbot of the monastery of St Barbara in the Saône, near that city, of which he was elected bishop about the year 523. After the murder of King St Sigismund, Burgundy was devastated by fighting between Burgundians and Franks, in which troubles St Lupus was involved. He presided at an important synod held at Orléans in 538 to restore discipline and order, and died four years later.

The earliest Latin biography of St Lupus of Sens has been critically edited in the *Monumenta Germaniæ, SS. rerum Meroving*, vol. iv, pp. 176–178. B. Krusch assigns it no higher date than the ninth century and thinks it historically unreliable. See, however, G. Vielhaber in *Analecta Bollandiana*, xxvi (1907), pp. 43–44 ; and *cf.* H. Bouvier, *Histoire de l'Eglise de Sens*, vol. i, pp. 101–106, with Duchesne, *Fastes Épiscopaux*, vol. ii, p. 392.

ST DRITHELM, Conf.

c. A.D. 700

St Bede in the fifth book of his *Ecclesiastical History* relates what he calls " a memorable miracle, like to those of former days." It concerns a man called Drithelm, who was a householder at Cuningham in Northumbria and a person of virtuous life, father of a God-fearing family. Somewhere about the year 693 he was seized with an illness and one evening appeared to be dead, but the next morning he suddenly sat up, to the fear of those mourning around his body, who all fled except his wife. To her he said : " Be not afraid, for I am now truly risen from death and allowed again to live among men. But hereafter I am not to live as I have been wont but rather in a very different manner." He then went to pray in the church of the village and afterwards returned to his house where he made a division of his goods, one-third to his wife, one-third to his children, and the remaining third to the poor. He then made his way to King Aldfrid and told him his story, and at the King's request St Ethelwold, who was then abbot of Melrose, tonsured Drithelm and admitted him among his monks. Now the things which Drithelm had seen, and which " he would not tell to tepid persons and such as lived negligently, but only to those who, being feared with the dread of Hell or delighted with the hope of heavenly joys, would make use of his words to advance in religion," were these : After he was dead he had been met by one with a shining countenance and bright garments who led him towards the north-east, where sunrise is at midsummer. There was a valley of great extent, whereof one side was burning with flames and the other frozen with ice and snow, and everywhere were men's souls which seemed to be tossed from one side to the other as it were by a storm. Drithelm thought that this might be the Hell of which he had been so often warned, but his guide said it was not so and led him on till they came to a great fiery pit, on the edge of which Drithelm was left alone. The souls of folk were cast about in this pit and Drithelm could discern a priest, a layman, and a woman ; cries and lamentations and a horrible stench rose from the flames, and evil spirits of repulsive aspect were about to push Drithelm in. But his guide appeared again and led him forward, now towards the south-east to the quarter where the sun rises in winter, and they came out into an atmosphere of clear light where there was an endless unpierced wall. He found himself on the top of this wall, and within was a large and delightful field, " so full of fragrant flowers that the smell of their sweetness at once

9

dispelled the stink of the dark furnace, which had pierced me through and through." In this field were innumerable men and women, clothed in white and rejoicing together in groups, so that Drithelm thought that perhaps this was the kingdom of Heaven, of which also he had heard much. But his guide said : " This is not the kingdom of Heaven as you suppose." Then they went yet further and came to a place of light and singing and delight, beside which the first field was dull and bleak, and Drithelm was hoping that they would enter into that place, when his guide suddenly stopped, turned round, and led him back by the way they had come to the first field. Here he turned to Drithelm and said : " The valley of flames and cutting cold is the place where are tried the souls of those who have delayed to repent and confess their sins, but have done so at the point of death. And they shall be delivered at the day of Judgement, and some before then because of the prayers and alms-deeds and Masses of the living. The fiery and stinking pit which you saw is the mouth of Hell, into which whosoever is cast shall not be delivered for all eternity. This flowery place, in which you see these beautiful young people so shining and merry, is that into which are received for a space the souls who depart the body in good works but are not so perfect that they may at once be taken into Heaven. Whoever leave life perfect in thought, word, and deed are called at once into the kingdom of Heaven, of which you heard the singing, smelled the fragrance, and saw the light. As for you, who are now to return to your body and live among men again, if you will try nicely to examine your actions and direct your speech and behaviour in righteousness and simplicity, you shall have a place among the blessed souls. For when I left you for a while it was to learn what was to be your doom." Then Drithelm, fearing to ask any more questions, found himself living and among men once more.

St Drithelm lived for the rest of his days in a special cell provided for him on the banks of the Tweed, into the freezing waters of which he would sometimes cast himself by way of penance, and stand reciting his office with ice floating around him. At which some would say : " It is wonderful, Brother Drithelm, that you can stand such cold." And he, being a man " of much simplicity and indifferent wit," would reply simply : " I have seen greater cold." Or if they said, " It is strange how you can endure such hardship," he would answer, " I have seen greater hardship." In such ways. he continued to mortify his body till the day of his death and forwarded the salvation of many by his words and example. One such was a priest and monk called Hemgils, of whom St Bede wrote : " He is still living, and leading a solitary life in Ireland where he supports his declining years with coarse bread and cold water. He often went to Drithelm and heard of him all the particulars of what he had seen when separated from his body ; by whose relation we also came to the knowledge of the few particulars which we have briefly set down."

There has been no known *cultus* of St Drithelm, but Blessed Alcuin refers to him in his poem on the Saints of the Church of York. Bishop Challoner mentions him under this date in his *Memorials of Ancient British Piety*.

We know little of Drithelm beyond what is contained in Bede's *Historia Ecclesiastica* (see Plummer's edition and notes) ; but Abbot Ælfric devotes a homily to the vision (*Ed.* B. Thorpe, ii, pp. 348–356). *Cf.* also Archdeacon St John Seymour, *Irish Visions of the other World* (1930), especially pp. 154–156.

BD. JOAN SODERINI, Virg.

A.D. 1367

The Soderini were a noble family of Florence and Blessed Joan was born in that city in the year 1301. From a very early age she showed herself remarkably good and devoted to God, so much so that when she told her governess, Felicia Tonia, that she knew by a revelation that she, Felicia, would shortly die, she is said to have been believed, and the governess began to look around for a successor to take charge of her pupil. As soon as she was adolescent Joan's parents arranged a marriage for her, but the child protested that she had chosen our Lord for her only spouse. Her father and mother were not too well pleased, for she was their only child, but reluctantly gave their consent to her becoming a nun. At this time St Juliana Falconieri was organising the Servite third order regular (" Mantellate ") in Florence, and Blessed Joan elected to join this new community. She was soon distinguished by her corporal austerities and perseverance in prayer, but at the same time was active in the work of the house and the care of the sick who came to it for attention and medicine. She voluntarily undertook the most distasteful tasks, and endeared herself to her sisters by her equability and cheerfulness. Blessed Joan was visited with hard trials and grievous temptations which she triumphed over, attaining by her faithfulness to a certain gift of prophecy. She was the constant personal attendant of St Juliana during her last long illness, when she was almost continually sick and could digest no food. To Blessed Joan is attributed the first discovery of the image of a crucifix, alleged to have been found imprinted on the chest of St Juliana after her death. She survived her beloved prioress for twenty-six years and succeeded her in the government of the community, which she also sought to direct according to the example and wishes of St Juliana. Blessed Joan died on September 1, 1367, and was buried in the Annunziata at Florence, where her tomb at once became a place of pilgrimage. In 1827 Count Soderini, chamberlain to the King of Bavaria and a relative of Blessed Joan, petitioned Pope Leo XII for confirmation of this *cultus*, which was duly granted.

See the *Acta Sanctorum*, October, vol. xii, pp. 398–404 ; and also A. Gianni, *Annales Ordinis Servorum*, vol. i, pp. 320–321.

BD. BERNARD OF OFFIDA, Conf.

A.D. 1694

He was born at Appignano in the Marches in the year 1604 of humble parents, and when he was seven years old was set to tend sheep. But he heard the call of God to the religious life, and in 1626 was accepted as a lay-brother by the Capuchins at Offida. When he had made his profession he was sent to Fermo and put in charge of the infirmary, and afterwards to other houses of his order, in all of which he laboured with fervour and zeal. Sometimes, some of his brethren thought, with too much zeal, for on one occasion he was reported to the provincial for imprudent lavishness in the distribution of alms, whereby his community suffered damage. The provincial called him before a chapter of the house and administered a severe rebuke in the presence of them all, which was a matter of great satisfaction to the Franciscan heart of Blessed Bernard. When he was sixty years old he was appointed *quæstor*, to beg alms in the streets and from door to door for the friary at Offida, and in this duty he gave more than he received ; people came to him for advice and consolation and help, for his wisdom could not be hid. He had an especial gift for composing quarrels and restoring peace to distracted families, and the most hardened sinners would listen to him and be converted. Blessed Bernard's reputation among the people was such that they would come to him and quite simply and confidently ask for a miracle. This sometimes caused difficulties for him. It is said that once a woman came with a very sick baby to be cured, so sick that it died in Bernard's arms. The mother seized his habit and begged and implored him to restore it to life, or she would not let him go. Bernard led her

into the church, lay the body on the altar dedicated in honour of
St Felix of Cantalice, and exclaiming, " Now, my good St Felix,
this is the time to help me," set himself to prayer. And the child
became alive and well. It is also said that our Lady appeared to
him one day and told him that all his faults had been forgiven.

Blessed Bernard died when he was ninety years old, having spent
the last years of his life as door-keeper to his convent, where the
poor and unhappy never ceased to crowd to him, on August 22,
1694. He was beatified by Pope Pius VI in 1795 and his feast is
kept on this day by the Capuchin Friars Minor.

See Léon, *Auréole Séraphique* (Eng. Trans.), vol. iii, pp. 121–123 ;
and E. M. de Beaulieu, *Deux émules de S Félix de Cantalice*, Toulouse, 1919.

BD. MICHAEL GHEBRE, Mart.

A.D. 1855

The story of the Church of Abyssinia is one of the saddest in
Christian history. In the fifth century it followed its mother Church
of Alexandria into the Monophysite heresy, and from the seventh it
was almost unknown to the rest of Christendom until the end of
the fifteenth, when the country was " rediscovered " by Portuguese
traders and adventurers. For the following hundred and twenty-
five years ecclesiastical and political negotiations of varying fortune
took place between Abyssinia, Portugal, and Rome, but these came
to a violent end in 1634, when the Emperor Susneyos, who had
tried to impose reunion on his people by force, died, and his successor Basilides banished the European clergy who had seconded
Susneyos. For two hundred years Abyssinia was a closed country
to Catholic missionaries (needless to say this did not deter them
from going there secretly, and they had their martyrs, *e.g.* BB.
Agathangelo and Cassian), till in 1839 the famous Irish-French
traveller Arnauld d'Abbadie d'Arrast used his influence to get
another mission sent thither. The Lazarists established themselves
at Adowa with Father Justin de Jacobis at their head, and later the
Capuchins in the Galla country, under Mgr. (afterwards Cardinal)
William Massaia.

Father de Jacobis soon came to know Aba Ghebre Michael (*i.e.*
the servant of St Michael), a dissident Abyssinian monk of some
fifty years of age, who was renowned for his holiness and learning
and also very properly suspected of an inclination towards Catholi-
cism, which his fellow-monks stigmatised as a taint of Arianism !

In 1840 Aba Michael wished to visit Jerusalem in pursuance of his studies, and he was attached to a delegation from Tigre to the Coptic Patriarch of Alexandria ; for their safety on the journey they joined the caravan of Father de Jacobis, who accepted the charge on condition that the delegates be also accredited to the Holy See. The results of these visits to the Monophysite patriarch, to Pope Gregory XVI, and to various schismatical prelates in Jerusalem were that one delegate became a Catholic and that Aba Michael was convinced that Catholic teaching on the two natures in Christ was of the true faith. He set himself to purge the church of his country of heresy, and induced the Coptic patriarch to issue a decree forbidding the Abyssinian metropolitan, Abuna Salama,* to teach that the divinity of our Lord had absorbed and assimilated His humanity. He went to Gondar and won the young King John (who had been his pupil) to his views ; the decree was tendered to Salama, who refused it and was forced to flee. But the triumph of orthodoxy was only apparent ; Aba Michael had brought not peace and truth but dissension and bitter quarrelling to his Church ; he retired to the Lazarists at Adowa and in 1844 submitted himself to the Holy See.

The learned Abyssinian was a most valuable auxiliary for Father de Jacobis, especially in the training of native aspirants for the priesthood. Together they drew up a catechism of Christian doctrine adapted to local needs and translated Gury's moral theology into Amharic, and established a college of which Aba Michael was put in charge. This was an opportunity for Abuna Salama, still exiled in Tigre, to stir up feeling against " the Franks " which led to the ruler banishing their two leaders, who took refuge in the island of Massowa. Here Mgr. Massaia consecrated Father de Jacobis bishop ; he returned secretly to the scene of his mission, and his first episcopal act was to ordain Michael Ghebre to the priesthood in 1851. At once Aba Michael with two companions, an Italian Lazarist, Biancheri, and an Abyssinian monk, went to Gondar, and reconciled the king (*negus*), John, himself, followed by a number of clergy, monks, and lay people. But this success was short lived. In 1854 John was deposed by a vigorous soldier, Cassa, who seized the throne with the name of Theodore II, and bought the support of Salama by recalling him and threatening penalties for the repudiation of Monophysism. Aba Michael and four of his fellow-countrymen were

* *Abuna*, "Our father," is the title of the Abyssinian primate, derived from St Frumentius, their apostle, who was called *Abuna* or *Aba Salama*, "Father of peace." But Salama seems really to have been the name of this metropolitan.

thrown into prison and threatened with torture in order to make them apostatise. They refused to follow the example of the ex-king in this matter, and at intervals over a period of nine months they were dragged from their filthy cell into the presence of Theodore and his metropolitan to be browbeaten and cajoled ; and each time when they stood firm they were lashed with a giraffe's tail (whose hair is like steel wire) and otherwise tortured. " In matters of faith," said Blessed Michael to Salama, " I cannot be other than opposed to you. But so far as Christian charity is concerned I think I have never done you anything but good "—and indeed it was due to Michael's intervention that Salama had been exiled instead of executed when he refused the Coptic patriarch's decree. In March 1855 Theodore set out on an expedition against the ruler of Shoa, Blessed Michael was taken with him in chains, and on May 31 a last attempt was made to induce him to submit to the king by repudiating the true faith. He refused and was condemned to death. Among those present was the British consul, Walter Chichele Plowden, who had supported Theodore in his usurpation ; he now came forward with others and begged a reprieve for Blessed Michael, which was granted, but he was to be a prisoner for life. By the mouth of a friend he sent a message to the other prisoners at Gondar : " Be steadfast to death in your faith. I have no hope of seeing you again on this earth. If they kill me, I shall die testifying to my faith ; if they spare me, I shall go on preaching it." For three more months, decrepit with age and ill-treatment, Blessed Michael was dragged from place to place in the train of the king ; he caught cholera and recovered, giving away his pittance of food to other sufferers and earning the esteem even of his guards ; at last on August 28, 1855, he lay down by the side of the road and died. Blessed Ghebre Michael was beatified as a martyr by Pope Pius XI in 1926.

The decree for the beatification of Bd. Ghebre Michael, containing a biographical synopsis, is printed in the *Acta Apostolicæ Sedis*, xviii (1926), pp. 407–411. There is a French Life of this martyr by J. B. Coulbeaux (Paris, 1926) and one in Italian by E. Cassinari (Rome, 1926). See also the sketch by G. Goyau in M. Vaussard, *La Légende Dorée au delà des mers* (1930) (English translation : *The Golden Legend Overseas*, B.O.W.).

SEPTEMBER 2

ST STEPHEN, King of Hungary, Conf.

A.D. 1038

THE people whom we call Magyars came into the country of
Hungary during the last years of the ninth century. Their
racial origin is not determined, but they settled in the land
around the Danube from several districts to the east of it, under the
general leadership of a chief called Arpád. They were a fierce and
marauding people and first met Christianity in the course of their
raids into Italy, France, and westward generally. St Methodius
had already planted the faith firmly in Pannonia, but it was not
until the second half of the tenth century that the Magyars themselves began to pay any serious consideration to the Church. Géza,
the third duke (*voivode*) after Arpád, saw the political necessity of
Christianity to his country, and married Adelaide, sister of the Duke
of Poland, through whom St Adalbert of Prague came on a mission
into Hungary. Géza was baptised and a number of his nobles followed his example. But it was largely a conversion of expediency,
and had the usual result of such conversions : the Christianity of
the converts was merely nominal. An exception to this was Géza's
son, Vaik, who had been baptised at the same time as his father and
been given the name of Stephen (Istvan). He was then only about
ten and so had not yet acquired pagan ways and fixed habits of
mind, and doubtless his Catholic mother took special care in his
upbringing that he should properly assimilate his religion. In the
year 995, when he was twenty, he married Gisela, sister of Henry,
the Duke of Bavaria, better known as the Emperor St Henry II,
and two years later he succeeded his father as governor of the
Magyars. Being at peace with all the neighbouring nations, he
turned his thoughts wholly to root out idolatry, and as much as in
him lay to make Christ reign in the hearts of all his subjects. Performing himself the part of a missionary, he often accompanied the
preachers, but he was not always sufficiently prompt to suppress
efforts to spread the faith by coercive measures. There had come
to his assistance on his marriage numbers of German knights and
priests who settled in the country and made many converts. Many

16

others, however, were so obstinately attached to the superstitions
of their ancestors as to take up arms in defence of idolatry ; not
only that, but they were very alarmed by the presence of the German
strangers, who were a menace to their own interests.   The rebels
had at their head a count of great valour named Koppány, and with
a numerous army they laid siege to Veszprem.   St Stephen prepared
himself for the engagement by fasting, almsdeeds, and prayer, in-
voking particularly the intercession of St Martin and St George.
Though inferior to the rebels in the number of his forces he had
the advantage of German help, gave them a total overthrow, and
slew their leader.   To give to God the entire glory of this victory
he completed near the place where the battle was fought a great
monastery in honour of St Martin, called " the Holy Hill " ; and
besides estates in land he bestowed on it one-third of the spoils.
This monastery, known as the archabbey of Martinsberg, or Pannon-
halma, still flourishes ; it is the mother house of the Hungarian
Benedictine congregations and an abbey-*nullius* immediately subject
to the Holy See.   St Stephen having quelled the rebels found himself
at liberty to follow up his plans, which he did by inviting into his
dominions many priests and religious from Germany, France, and
Italy.   These by their exemplary lives and zealous preaching sowed
the seed of faith, civilised that savage nation by the precepts of the
gospel, built churches and monasteries, and some of them obtained
the crown of martyrdom.

   Hitherto Hungary had had no ecclesiastical organisation, so
St Stephen founded the archbishopric of Gran (Esztergom) with
five suffragan sees, and later the archbishopric of Kalocsa with three
suffragans.   He sent St Astericus or Anastasius to Rome to obtain of
Pope Sylvester II the confirmation of these foundations and of many
other things which he had done for the honour of God and the exaltation of His holy Church ; and at the same time to ask his Holiness to
confer upon him the title of king, which his nobles had long pressed
him to assume and which he now asked that he might with more
majesty and authority accomplish his great designs for promoting the
glory of God and the good of his people.   Boleslaus, Duke of Poland,
had at the same time sent an embassy to Rome to obtain the title of
king confirmed to him by the authority of the Apostolic See.   Sylvester II was disposed to grant his request, and prepared a royal
crown to send him with his blessing.   But the zeal, piety, and wisdom
of St Stephen deserving the preference (and perhaps not unmoved
by political representations from the Emperor Otto III who was
then in Rome) the Pope delivered this crown for him to his ambassador St Astericus.   At the same time he by a bull confirmed all the

religious foundations which the prince had made and the elections of bishops. St Stephen went to meet his ambassador upon his return, listened, standing with great respect, to the Pope's bulls whilst they were read, and bent his knee as often as the name of his Holiness was repeated. To express his own sense of religion and to inspire all his subjects with awe for whatever belonged to divine worship, he treated the pastors of the Church with great honour and respect. The same prelate who had brought the crown from Rome anointed and crowned him king with great solemnity and pomp in the year 1001.*

Firmly to root Christianity in his kingdom and to provide for its progress after his own time, St Stephen filled Hungary with pious foundations. At Stuhlweissenburg (Székes Fehervàr) he built a stately church in honour of the Mother of God, in which the kings of Hungary were afterwards both crowned and buried. This city St Stephen made his usual residence, whence it is called Alba Regalis to distinguish it from Alba Julia or Weissemberg in Transylvania. He founded in Buda the monastery of SS. Peter and Paul, and in Rome, Ravenna, and Constantinople hospices for pilgrims. He peopled Martinsberg with Benedictines and founded four other monasteries for that order as well as one for nuns of the Byzantine rite at Veszprem and other convents. The conversion of the Hungarians enabled the way for pilgrims to the Holy Land to be made more safe and convenient, and Stephen is said to have established a church and hospice at Jerusalem itself. For the support of the churches and their pastors and the relief of the poor throughout all his dominions he commanded tithes to be paid. Every tenth town had to build a church and support a priest ; the King himself furnished the churches and the bishops appointed the clergy. He abolished, not without violence, barbarous and superstitious customs derived from the former religion and by severe punishments repressed blasphemy, murder, theft, adultery, and other public crimes. He commanded all persons to marry except religious and churchmen, and forbade all marriages of Christians with idolaters. He was of easy access to people of all ranks, and listened to everyone's complaints without distinction or preference, but was most willing to hear the poor, knowing them to be more easily oppressed and considering that in them we honour

* The alleged bull of Pope Sylvester granting the title of Apostolic King and Apostolic Legate to St Stephen, with the right to have a primatial cross borne before him, is a forgery of the seventeenth century. The upper part of the crown sent by the Pope, fitted on to the lower part of a crown given to King Géza I by the Emperor Michael VII, is preserved at Budapest.

Christ who, being no longer among men on earth in His mortal state, has recommended to us the poor in His place and right. The good King provided for their subsistence throughout his kingdom, and took them, especially helpless orphans and widows, under his special protection. Not content with his general charities and care for the indigent, he frequently went about privately to discover the necessities of any that might be overlooked by his officers. One day it happened that, whilst he was dealing out his plentiful alms in disguise, a troop of beggars crowding round him knocked him down, hustled him, pulled at his beard and hair, and took away his purse, seizing for themselves what he intended for the relief of many others. The King took this indignity humbly and with good humour, happy to suffer in the service of his Saviour, and he said to our Lady : " See, O Queen of Heaven, in what manner I am rewarded by those that belong to your Son. As they are His friends, I am content." His nobles, when they heard of this, were amused and chaffed him about it ; but they were also disturbed and insisted that he should no more expose his person ; but he renewed his resolution never to refuse an alms to any poor person that asked him. The shining example of his virtue was a continual and most powerful sermon to those who came under his influence, and in no one was it better exemplified than in his son, Blessed Emeric, to whom St Stephen's code of laws was inscribed. These laws he caused to be promulgated throughout his dominions, and they were well suited to a fierce and rough people newly converted to Christianity. But they were not calculated to allay the discontent and alarm of those who who were still opposed to the new religion, and the wars which St Stephen had to undertake had a religious as well as a political significance.

In 1003 his uncle Gyula, Prince of Transylvania, invaded his dominions ; St Stephen defeated him in battle, and made him prisoner. He offered him his liberty and his dominions, requiring only that the gospel should be allowed to be freely preached in them, and that the Prince himself should cease to repudiate his baptism, for his father had been a Christian. But this Gyula refused. When Stephen had overcome an irruption of the Bulgarians he undertook the political organisation of his people. He abolished tribal divisions and divided the land into counties, with a system of governors and magistrates. Thus, and by means of a limited application of feudal ideas, making the nobles vassals of the crown, he welded the Magyars into a unity ; and by retaining direct control over all the common people he prevented undue accumulation of power into the hands of the lords. In 1025 he had to meet a revolt headed by a noble called Ajton, who was inclined to transfer his allegiance to the Eastern Emperor at Constantinople. Stephen mobilised his forces at Kalocsa and was enabled to gain a crushing victory by the treachery of Ajton's chief-of-staff, who deserted to the King at the last moment. Shortly after he had to drive out an invasion of the Bessi from Bulgaria. After their defeat some of the leaders returned to Hungary with the intention of settling peaceably there, but were set on and plundered by Magyars. St Stephen at once vindicated justice by hanging a number of his subjects along the frontier as a warning that strangers were to be properly treated. In 1024 his brother-in-law the Emperor St Henry II had died and been succeeded by Conrad II who, with his brother Bruno, Bishop of Augsburg, was intent on disendowing Henry's new see of Bamberg for their own personal benefit. Bruno proposed to make Emeric the heir of his share of these ill-gotten estates, but St Stephen refused to allow such a thing and urged that Bamberg should not be despoiled. Shortly after he refused to give a passage through his dominions to the imperial ambassador to Constantinople, and Conrad, who was beginning to fear the growing power and influence of Hungary on the Bavarian border, in 1031 marched against St Stephen. Hostilities were, however, avoided. A parley was arranged, terms of agreement settled, and Conrad retired; a bloodless campaign which the followers of Stephen attributed to the sanctity and peace-loving disposition of their leader. He was now anxious to entrust a greater part in the government to his only son, but in the autumn of the same year Emeric was killed while hunting. " God loved him, and therefore He has taken him away early," cried St Stephen in his grief. The death of Emeric left him without an heir, and the last years of his life were embittered by family disputes about the succession, with which he had to cope while suffering continually from painful illness. There were four or five claimants, of whom one, Peter, was the son of his sister Gisela, an ambitious and cruel woman who since the death of her husband, the Doge of Venice, had lived at the Hungarian court. She had made up her mind that her son should have the throne, and shamelessly took advantage of St Stephen's ill-health to forward her ends.

Two of the candidates, his cousins Andrew and Bela, entered into a conspiracy to kill him, and an assassin one night entered his bedroom with that object. But he dropped his dagger and so wakened the King, who calmly observed : " If God be for me, who shall be against me ? " The murderer accused Andrew and Bela, who were arrested, but St Stephen pardoned and released all three. It has been suggested that he recognised the plot to have been staged by Gisela in order to prejudice him against his two cousins. In any case she removed the Duke Basil from her path by violence and eventually procured the nomination of Peter as Stephen's successor, after he had recommended the other claimants to seek safety from his sister in flight. St Stephen died at the age of sixty-three on the feast of the Assumption 1038, and was buried beside Bd. Emeric at Stuhlweissenburg. His tomb was the scene of miracles, and forty-five years after his death, by an order of Pope St Gregory VII, at the request of the holy King St Ladislaus, his relics were enshrined and placed in a rich chapel which bears his name within the great church of our Lady at Buda. Innocent XI appointed his festival for September 2 in 1686, the Emperor Leopold having on that day recovered Buda from the hands of the Turks. In Hungary his chief feast is kept on August 20, the day of the translation of his relics.

Virtue is the most excellent dignity and the only good of rational beings, as St Augustine observes. Genius, learning, power, riches, and whatever else a man enjoys are only good when made subservient to virtue. Hence the Stoics called such external goods conveniences, not good things, because, said they, virtue alone deserves the name of good. This is our glory, our riches, and our happiness in time and eternity. To acquire and continually improve in virtue is the great business of our lives, but the generality of mankind is careless about it. Many spare no pains to cultivate their minds with science, or to excel in accomplishments of the body and in every other qualification for the world, yet neglect to reform and regulate their heart. Half that attention which they give to their body or studies would make them perfect in virtue. An hour, or half an hour, a day, employed in meditation, spiritual reading, and self-examination, would be of infinite service. It would teach us the ways of virtue, inspire us with its sublime sentiments, and instruct us in its exercises ; and a constant watchfulness in all our actions would inure us to its practice and ground us in good habits. Were we but to learn well one virtue every year, we should all soon be saints.

There are two early Lives of St Stephen, both dating apparently from the eleventh century, and known as the *Vita major* and the *Vita minor*. These texts have been edited in Pertz, *Monumenta Germaniæ*, SS., vol. xi. A certain Hartwick, Bishop of Veszprem (?), early in the twelfth century, compiled from these materials a biography which is printed in the *Acta Sanctorum*, September, vol. ii. Other facts concerning the saint may be gleaned from the *Chronica Ungarorum* edited in Endlicher's *Monumenta*, vol. i. Although the supposed bull of Sylvester II is certainly spurious, and although very serious doubts have been raised as to the genuineness of the crown alleged to have been sent by the Pope, still there does seem to be evidence of special powers conferred by papal authority which were equivalent to those of a legate *a latere*. The belief, however, that St Stephen was invested with the title of "Apostolic King" is altogether without foundation. See *e.g.* the article of L. Kropf in the *English Historical Review*, April, 1898, pp. 290–295. A very readable, but rather uncritical, Life (*Saint Etienne, Roi apostolique de Hongrie*, par. E. Horn, 1899) has appeared in the series "Les Saints." For more reliable and detailed information we have to go to such Hungarian authorities as J. Paulers, Mgr. Fraknoi, and Dr. Karácsonyi. In a later volume of the *Acta Sanctorum*, November, vol. ii, pp. 477–487, the Bollandists, when dealing with the life of St Emeric, have discussed many points which have a bearing on the history of the King, his father.

ST ANTONINUS, Mart.

Date Unknown

According to the eastern legend Antoninus was a Syrian stone-mason who, with an especially disinterested zeal, rebuked the idolaters of his native place for worshipping images of stone. He then lived with a hermit called Theotinus for two years, at the end of which time he came back to the town and found the people still worshipping their false gods. So he went into a temple and threw down the idol therein, whereupon he was driven from the place and came to Apamæa. Here the bishop engaged him to build a church, an undertaking which so angered the pagans that they raised a riot, in the course of which St Antoninus was killed by them.

This appears to be the Antoninus the martyr who, probably by a confusion of *Apamæa* with *Pamia*, is stated by the Roman Martyrology to have suffered at Pamiers. The story told in Languedoc is that he was born near Pamiers during the second half of the first century, lived a solitary for some years, and then went to Rome where he was ordained priest. On his return he evangelised the Rouergue and was martyred at the place now called Saint-Antonin. His relics were taken to Palencia in Spain, of which he is the patron, and which has its own version of the Pamiers legend. The name of St Antoninus is associated with those of SS. Almachius and John, who are supposed to have suffered with him, and has by another error become connected also with Capua, where "Antoninus, a boy," is venerated with St Aristæus, bishop and martyr, on September 3.

A great deal of confusion has undoubtedly grown up around the mention of this martyr in the ancient martyrology known as the *Hieronymianum*. Père Delehaye in his commentary published in the *Acta Sanctorum*, November, vol. ii, part 2, pp. 484–486, points out that there was an unquestionably authentic cultus of the Apamæan Antoninus, which is vouched for amongst others by Theodoret. The martyr is honoured, however, in the Greek Synaxaries on November 9.

ST CASTOR, Bp. of Apt, Conf.

c. A.D. 425

He was a native of Nîmes and probably brother to St Leontius of Fréjus. He had a good education and began a secular career, having married the daughter of a rich widow from Marseilles. But both were drawn to the life of the cloister, and St Castor founded, near Apt in Provence, the monastery of Manauque under the rules of St John Cassian, himself becoming the first abbot. His success in this office caused him to be called to the episcopal chair of Apt, an office he undertook unwillingly but discharged unwaveringly. He bent all his energies to the saving of souls, calling on them to love God with all their hearts, to join with the Church in serving Him who is all-lovely and all-worshipful. St Castor maintained the closest interest in the welfare of his monks, and it was at his request for them that Cassian wrote his work on the monastic life, *de Institutis Cœnobiorum*, which was dedicated to St Castor. His feast has been observed on various days in September ; the 2nd is the date of his death.

See the *Acta Sanctorum*, September, vol. vi ; *Gallia Christiana Novissima*, vol. i, pp. 192–195 ; and Duchesne, *Fastes Épiscopaux*, vol. i, p. 282. The feast is kept on this day at Nîmes because September 21, to which it is usually assigned in the calendars, is the feast of St Matthew, Apostle and Evangelist.

ST AGRICOLUS, Bp. of Avignon, Conf.

A.D. 700

Information about this saint is very unreliable, for it is obtained from no documents earlier than the fifteenth century, at which time a popular devotion towards him began to grow up. He has been officially recognised as the patron of the city of Avignon only since 1647. These late traditions say that Agricolus was born about the year 630, the son of St Magnus, a Gallo-Roman senator of the *gens*

Albina, who after the death of his wife became first a monk at Lérins and then bishop of Avignon. Agricolus himself went to Lérins when he was fourteen and, making great progress in learning and virtue, was advanced to the priesthood. After sixteen years as a monk his father summoned him to the episcopal city. Here he was appointed archdeacon and distinguished himself by his preaching, by his powers of administration, and by his care for the poor, the oppressed, and the sick. In 660 St Magnus was summoned to a synod at Chalon-sur-Saône, and before going there consecrated his son bishop as his coadjutor. Ten years later Magnus died and St Agricolus succeeded both to his father's see and to the success with which he administered it. The one church at Avignon was soon insufficient for its needs, and Agricolus built a second, to be served by monks from Lérins. The foundation of other churches soon followed, and he established a monastery of Benedictine nuns.

The armorial bearings of the see of Avignon display a stork, holding a snake in its beak, and this device is referred to an alleged incident during the episcopate of St Agricolus. Storks were numerous about the city and fed themselves on snakes, whose half-eaten corpses they were in the habit of dropping upon the roofs of the houses. There they decomposed and stank in the sun, and caused an epidemic of sickness among the inhabitants. Agricolus put an end to this nuisance by prayer and making the sign of the cross over the storks, which thereupon withdrew to the fields and did not return. St Agricolus died on September 2 in the year 700, and his relics were transferred to new shrines in the church of St Stephen four times between 1321 and 1612. He is invoked locally to bring both rain and fair weather.

In the *Acta Sanctorum*, September, vol. i, and more particularly Duprat, *Les Origines de l'Eglise d'Avignon* (1909), pp. 73 *seq.* A full bibliography may be found in the *Dictionnaire d'Histoire Ecclés.*, vol. i, *c.* 1019.

ST WILLIAM, Bp. of Roeskilde, Conf.

A.D. 1076

The historians of Denmark relate that St William was an English priest of eminent sanctity and zeal, and chaplain to King Canute. In one of the voyages which that prince made from England to Denmark, the zealous servant of God who attended him was so moved with compassion at the sight of the ignorance, idolatry, and superstition in which so many of the Danes lived that he decided to stay behind to preach Christ and His gospel. He gained innumerable souls to God, and was advanced to the episcopal see of Roeskilde in the island of Zealand. He was not the first Englishman to rule a Danish see, for Canute some twenty-five years before had got into trouble with the Archbishop of Hamburg-Bremen for appointing bishops in his province who had been consecrated in England, and another Englishman was bishop of Funen at this same time. Canute had been succeeded by King Sweyn Estridsen, who upon the death of his wife had married his stepdaughter, Guda. St William protested against this incestuous union, and appealed to the Archbishop of Hamburg-Bremen, who endeavoured in vain to remove so pernicious a scandal by remonstrances, and at length threatened a sentence of excommunication, which severity failed to bring the King to his duty. The matter was referred to the Holy See, and both the Pope and the Emperor wrote to Sweyn. St William again added his remonstrances, and in 1055 the King separated from Guda. The same King having once caused some persons to be put to death not only without a public or legal trial but also within the bounds of a church, the saint met him at the church door the next day and, holding out his pastoral staff, forbade him to enter the house of God till his hands were cleansed from the blood he had unjustly spilt; and seeing some of the courtiers draw their swords, he presented his neck, saying he was ready to die in defence of the Church of God. The King, who had always the highest veneration for the holy prelate, came to himself, bitterly bewailed his sin, and, after doing penance and making satisfaction, was conducted into the church by the Bishop himself; here he publicly confessed his crime at the high altar, and later gave some land to the church of Roeskilde as a peace offering. St William had a most sincere regard and warm affection for his troublesome sovereign, and for some years the saint and the penitent concurred with all their strength in a perfect union of hearts to promote the cause of piety and religion. But Sweyn could not forget the Archbishop of Hamburg-Bremen's threat of excommunication, and he tried hard but without success to rid himself of his jurisdiction by having William's see made metropolitan. Upon the death of the King his body was temporarily buried in the Benedictine abbey he had founded at Ringsted, till the cathedral of Roeskilde should be ready for its reception. At the same time a tomb was prepared there for St William, and it is said that, while Sweyn's body was being conveyed from Ringsted to Roeskilde, St William came out to meet it and himself died at its approach, so that the two friends were borne together to burial. St William is named in Danish calendars but he has never had a liturgical feast

25

in his honour. He has been confused with St William of Eskill, sometimes called in error " of Roeskilde," a French canon regular who came to Zealand in the twelfth century.

There is no separate biography of St William ; and his history has to be gleaned from such unsatisfactory chroniclers as Saxo Grammaticus in his *Gesta Danorum*. See Stanton's *Menology*, p. 434.

BD. MARGARET OF LOUVAIN, Virg. and Mart.

A.D. 1225

In the sixth book of his *Dialogue on Miracles*, dealing with Single-ness of Heart, the Cistercian monk, Caesarius of Heisterbach, tells the story of this young girl whose *cultus* in the diocese of Malines was confirmed by Pope Pius X in 1905. She was born at Louvain about the year 1207 and went into domestic service with a relative named Aubert. He was an innkeeper and a good and charitable man, who would entertain pilgrims and necessitous travellers free of charge. Margaret entered whole-heartedly into these good works, but the recollected way with which she went about them and her indifference to the attentions of men got her the nickname of " the proud Margaret." About the year 1225 Aubert and his wife deter-mined to become religious. Having sold their business and made the necessary preparations, they were spending their last night at home when they were visited by some evil-disposed men under the pretence of saying good-bye. Margaret was sent out to get some wine for the visitors, and while she was gone they set on Aubert and his wife, murdered them, and seized their money which they had by them to take to the monasteries to which they were going. On her return with the wine the robbers carried off Margaret and at a lonely spot near the river Dyle proposed to kill her too, as a witness to their crime. One of them offered to marry her if she would keep silence, but she refused, and thereupon an extra ten marks was added to the share of one of them to make away with her. "He, taking the innocent lamb like a cruel butcher, cut her throat, stabbed her in the side, and threw her into the river." The body was found and, in consequence of the supernatural light and angelic voices that were reported to accompany it, was taken in procession by the clergy of St Peter's collegiate church at Louvain and buried in a special chapel in their churchyard. Miracles were vouchsafed at this tomb and there Blessed Margaret has been vener-ated from that day to this. Concerning this story the novice in the

Dialogue asks : " What would you say was the cause of martyrdom in the case of this girl ? " To which his preceptor replies : " Simplicity and an innocent life, as I have already said. There are different kinds of martyrdom, namely, innocence, as in Abel ; uprightness, as in the Prophets and St John Baptist ; love of the law, as in the Machabees ; confession of the faith, as in the Apostles. For all these different causes Christ the Lamb is said to have been ' slain from the beginning of the world.' " All Christian virtues, being protestations of our faith and proofs of our fidelity to God, are a true motive of martyrdom.

The Bollandists, in the *Acta Sanctorum*, September, vol. i, find nothing to add to the account given by Caesarius, but they supply evidence regarding the later *cultus*, and translate from the Flemish a relation of a number of miracles wrought at the shrine. Several pious booklets of a popular kind have been printed about Bd. Margaret in modern times, the most noteworthy of which, by M. G. Ollivier, originally appeared as an article in the *Revue Thomiste*, vol. iv, 1896.

ST BROCARD, CONF.

A.D. 1231

On the death of St Berthold about the year 1195 he was succeeded as superior of the Frankish hermits on Mount Carmel by this Brocard or Burchard, who was a Frenchman perhaps born in Jerusalem. As these hermits had no fixed rule of life Brocard asked for instructions from St Albert, a canon regular who was Latin patriarch and papal legate in Palestine. About 1210 Albert gave them a short rule, which St Brocard imposed on his subjects. It bound them to live alone in separate cells, to recite the Divine Office or other prayers, to work with their hands, and to meet together daily for Mass ; to observe perfect poverty, perpetual abstinence, and long silences. They were to give obedience to St Brocard as prior during his life, and afterwards to his successors. After the fourth Council of the Lateran had passed a decree against new religious orders these hermits, who had begun to spread in Palestine, were attacked on the ground that they contravened this canon, not having been approved by the Holy See but only by its legate. According to the tradition of the Carmelite Order Pope Honorius III was going to suppress them, but warned by a vision of our Lady he confirmed their rule instead, about the year 1226. St Brocard directed his community with virtue and prudence during these difficulties, and died after being prior for some thirty-five years. One of the few events recorded in his life is that he miraculously restored to health a Mohammedan emir and converted him to the faith. It is said that St Albert intended to take St Brocard to the Lateran Council, as one well versed in Eastern affairs, understanding Islam, and respected by schismatics and infidels. But Albert was murdered the year before the Council assembled.

See the *Acta Sanctorum*, September, vol. i, and more especially the *Monumenta Historica Carmelitana* of Father Benedict Zimmerman, pp. 276–279. Some account of St Brocard may also be found in Lezana, *Annales*, iv, p. 244, and in the *Speculum Carmelitanum*, ii, p. 661. Fr. Zimmerman seems to think it improbable that St Brocard was born in Jerusalem.

BB. JOHN-MARY DU LAU, ABP. OF ARLES, AND HIS COMPANIONS
THE MARTYRS OF SEPTEMBER

A.D. 1792

There can be no doubt that at the time of the French Revolution there were conditions in the Church in France which, to phrase it mildly, were regrettable : worldly and domineering bishops and higher clergy who were indifferent to the sufferings of the people, numbers of self-seeking and ignorant rectors and curates who in the hour of trial did not refuse to accept an oath and constitution condemned by the Holy See and their own bishops, and many lay people who were, more or less culpably, indifferent or openly hostile to religion. The other, better, and larger side of the picture may be represented by those *émigré* priests and people who made so good an impression and helped on the cause of Catholic emancipation in our own country, and by those many others who gave their lives rather than co-operate with the forces of irreligion. Such, for example, were the martyrs who suffered in Paris on September 2 and 3, 1792. In 1790 the Constituent Assembly had passed the Civil Constitution of the Clergy, which the hierarchy at once condemned as unlawful : all the diocesan bishops except four and most of the urban clergy refused to take the oath imposed by it. In the following year Pope Pius VI confirmed this condemnation of the Constitution as " heretical, contrary to Catholic teaching, sacrilegious, and opposed to the rights of the Church." At the end of August 1792 the revolutionaries throughout France were infuriated by the rising of the peasants in La Vendée and the success of the arms of Prussia, Austria, and Sweden at Longwy and Verdun, and, inflamed by the fierce rhetoric of Danton against the royalists and clergy who upheld their country's foes, over fifteen hundred clergy, laymen, and women were massacred with the approval of the Legislative Assembly. Of these victims 191 individuals were beatified as martyrs by Pope Pius XI in 1926.

Early in the afternoon of September 2 the mob attacked the Abbaye, the former monastery where priests, loyal soldiers, and other disaffected persons were imprisoned. Led by a ruffian called Maillard, they tendered the constitutional oath to twenty-four priests, all of whom refused it and were killed on the spot. A mock tribunal then condemned the rest of the prisoners *en masse*, including fifty-four survivors of the King's Swiss Guard. They were all shot, cut down, or clubbed. Among the martyrs here was the ex-Jesuit (the Society was at that time suppressed throughout the world except in Russia and Silesia) BLESSED ALEXANDER LENFANT. He had preached several times before the King and his court at Versailles in less troubled times, and had been a devoted friend of the royal family in its misfortunes. This led to his arrest and, in spite of the efforts of an apostate priest to get him released, he suffered martyrdom at the Abbaye. The Abbé de Salamon tells in his memoirs how he actually saw Père Lenfant quietly hearing the confession of another priest in a court of the prison five minutes before both confessor and penitent were dragged out and slain.

Having been refreshed with wine and encouraged with *pourboires* by the Mayor of Paris, Maillard and his gang then made for the Carmelite church in the Rue de Rennes. Here were imprisoned over one hundred and fifty ecclesiastics, with one layman, BLESSED CHARLES DE LA CALMETTE, Comte de Valfons, an officer in the cavalry who had voluntarily accompanied his parish priest into confinement. This noble company, led by BLESSED JOHN-MARY DU LAU, Archbishop of Arles, BLESSED FRANCIS-JOSEPH DE LA ROCHEFOUCAULD, Bishop of Beauvais, and his brother BLESSED PETER-LOUIS, Bishop of Saintes, led a life of almost monastic regularity and astounded their gaolers by their cheerfulness and good temper. It was a sultry Sunday afternoon and the prisoners were allowed, on this day ordered, to take the air in the garden. While the bishops and some other clergy were saying Vespers in a chapel the murderers broke into the garden and killed the first priest they met. In the resulting panic Mgr. du Lau came quietly out of the chapel. " Are you the archbishop ? " he was asked. " Yes, sirs. I am the archbishop." He was cut down by a sword stroke and killed by the thrust of a pike as he lay on the ground. Amid howls of execration shooting began right and left : several were killed and wounded

and the Bishop of Beauvais's leg was shattered by a bullet. But
Maillard's sense of good order was outraged. A "judge" was
appointed, who sat in a passage between the church and the sacristy,
and two by two the confessors were brought in and had the constitutional oath tendered to them. Every one refused it without
hesitation, and as each recalcitrant couple passed down the narrow
staircase they were hacked to pieces. The Bishop of Beauvais was
called for. He replied from where he lay : " I do not refuse to die
with the others, but I cannot walk. I beg you to have the kindness
to carry me where you wish me to go." There could have been no
more telling rebuke than that courteous speech : it did not save
him, but silence fell on the murderers as he was brought forward
and rejected the proffered oath. The Abbé GALAIS, who had been
in charge of the feeding arrangements of the prisoners, handed to
the "judge" 325 francs which he owed the caterer ; BLESSED
JAMES FRITEYRE-DURVÉ, ex-Jesuit, was killed by a neighbour whom
he knew in his own birthplace ; three other ex-Jesuits and four
secular priests were aged men who had only recently been turned
out of a house of rest at Issy and made to walk to the Carmelite
church ; the Comte de Valfons and his confessor, the Abbé GUILLE-
MINET, met death side by side. Thus perished 120 martyrs, who
from their place of martyrdom are called " des Carmes " : the
remaining thirty or so were able to make their escape unseen or were
allowed to slip away by conscience-stricken soldiers. Among the
victims were BLESSED AMBROSE-AUGUSTINE CHEPREUX, superior of
the Maurist Benedictines at Paris, and two other monks ; BLESSED
FRANCIS-LOUIS HÉBERT, confessor of Louis XVI ; three Franciscans ; thirteen ex-Jesuits ; ten episcopal vicars general ; three
deacons ; an acolyte ; and a Christian Brother. The bodies were
buried some in a pit in the cemetery of Vaugirard and some in a
well in the garden of the Carmes.

On the night of September 3 the band of murderers came to
the famous Lazarist seminary of Saint-Firmin, also used as a prison,
where their first victim was BLESSED PETER GUÉRIN DU ROCHER, an
ex-Jesuit sixty years old. He was asked to choose between the oath
and death, and on his replying was thrown out of the nearest window
and stabbed in the courtyard below. His brother BLESSED ROBERT
was also a victim, and there were five other ex-Jesuits among the
ninety clerics there, of whom only four escaped. The superior of
the seminary was BLESSED LOUIS-JOSEPH FRANÇOIS, who in his
official capacity had advised that the oath was unlawful for the
clergy. He was so well loved in Paris that during the preparation
for the massacres an official had warned him of the danger and

offered to help him to escape. He refused to desert his fellow-prisoners, many of whom he knew had taken refuge at Saint-Firmin out of regard for his own reliability, confidence, and example. Among those who died with him were BLESSED HENRY GRUYER and other Lazarists, BLESSED YVES GUILLON DE KERANRUN, vice-chancellor of the University of Paris, and BLESSED MICHAEL LEBER, rector of the Madeleine. At the prison of La Force in the Rue Saint-Antoine there was not one survivor to describe the last moments of any of his fellows. Among those who were martyred here were BLESSED JOHN-BAPTIST BOTTEX, a priest from Belley who had been a deputy to the States General in 1789, and BLESSED HYACINTH LE LIVEC DE TRÉSURIN, once a Jesuit and chaplain at the convent of the Daughters of Calvary.

The brief of beatification, in which the names of the martyrs are individually recorded, is printed in the *Acta Apostolicæ Sedis*, vol. xviii (1926), pp. 415–425. Some account of these massacres may be found in most histories of the French Revolution, but the subject of the martyrdoms is dealt with in detail in many separate books, for example, in Lenôtre, *Les Massacres de septembre* (Paris, 1907) ; Sabatié, *Les Massacres de Septembre ; les Martyrs du Clergé* (Paris, 1912) ; Dom H. Leclercq, *Les Martyrs*, vol. xi ; and more concisely in F. Mourret, *Histoire générale de l'Eglise*, vol. vii, *l'Eglise et la Révolution* (Paris, 1913). There are also books devoted to special individuals or groups ; for example, G. Barbotin, *Le dernier évêque de Saintes, le Bienheureux Pierre de la Rochefoucauld* (La Rochelle, 1927) ; H. Fouqueray, *Un groupe des Martyrs du Septembre, 1792, vingt-trois anciens Jésuites* (Paris, 1927), and an anonymous booklet, *Martyrs Franciscains des Carmes* (Gembloux, 1926).

SEPTEMBER 3

ST PHOEBE, Deaconess

First Century A.D.

IN the last chapter of his epistle to the Christians of Rome St Paul sends his greetings to many of his friends there, but first of all refers to one Phoebe, of whom he writes : "And I commend to you Phoebe, our sister, who is in the ministry of the church that is in Cenchrae, that you receive her in the Lord as becometh saints and that you assist her in whatsoever business she shall have need of you. For she also hath assisted many, and myself also." Cenchrae was the port of Corinth from whence the Epistle to the Romans was written about the year 55, and it would appear that St Phoebe was the bearer of the letter. Beyond what St Paul tells us in his testimonial nothing is known of her ; she is named in the Roman Martyrology on this day and St John Crysostom eulogised her merits.

The Bollandists devote a few pages to St Phœbe, refuting in particular the allegation that she had been the wife of St Paul, but ministered to him afterwards as a dear sister. The notion that St Paul had been married seems to have been suggested by a phrase in the interpolated letter of St Ignatius to the Philadelphians, and by a remark of Clement of Alexandria. The insertion of Phœbe's name (as well as that of other New Testament characters) in the Martyrologium, is due to Ado in the ninth century. See Dom H. Quentin, *Les Martyrologes historiques*, p. 665.

ST MACANISIUS, Bp. and Conf.

Early Sixth Century

The records of St Macanisius (Aengus Macnisse) consist chiefly of miracles, many of them fantastic, and conflicting references. He is said to have been baptised by St Patrick and to have been brought up by St Olcan, a bishop in Antrim. He was eventually taken from Olcan's care by St Patrick, who in due course consecrated him bishop. It is related that he made a pilgrimage to the Holy Land and on the way back made a stay at Rome, where as an honoured guest he was asked to perform certain ordinations, assisted by the clergy of the city. He was given many valuable gifts there, and with these and a number of relics from Palestine he returned to Ireland, where he established a church and monastery which developed into the diocese of Connor, of which see he is venerated as the first bishop. The original foundation was probably not at Connor itself but at Kells, close by, where, according to a Latin Life, he changed the course of the river Curi, probably by natural means later regarded as miraculous, for the convenience of his monks. While journeying through Munster with St Patrick and St Brigid, Macanisius had a vision of angels at Lynally in Offaly, in consequence of which St Patrick wished to establish a monastery there. But St Macanisius dissuaded him, prophesying that that was to be the work of a bishop who would follow them sixty years after. This prophecy was duly verified in the person of St Colman Elo, who is venerated on the 26th of this month. Among the more incredible legends about St Macanisius is that his reverence for the Scriptures was so great that it would not allow him to carry them in a wallet when on his journey ; instead he proceeded on all fours, balancing the precious book on his back ! He is also alleged to have saved the life of the child who was to become St Colman of Kilruaidh. Colman's father was guilty of parricide and was sentenced to lose his own son. Macanisius in vain interceded for his innocent life, so when the child was tossed into the air to be caught on the spear-points of the waiting tribesmen, the saint, standing on an adjacent hillock, prayed with such fervour that Colman's body was blown by the wind safely into his arms, at which miracle the executioners abandoned their purpose. The feast of St Macanisius is kept on this day throughout Ireland.

The Latin legend of St Macnise has been printed by the Bollandists in the *Acta Sanctorum*, September, vol. i, and again in their edition of the *Codex Salmanticensis*, pp. 925–930. The saint is commemorated on this day in the *Félire* of Oengus. See also O'Hanlon, *Lives of the Irish Saints*, vol. ix, pp. 62 seq.

ST SIMEON STYLITES THE YOUNGER, Conf.

A.D. 597

This saint was born at Antioch in 521, the son of an Edessene and of a mother who is venerated as St Martha in the East. While yet a child he joined a community of hermits near Antioch, and for several years he served one of them, named John, who lived among the

BUTLER'S LIVES OF THE SAINTS [*Sept.* 3

community upon a pillar. Simeon laboured to be a faithful imitator of his master who, having had sufficient experience of his fervour, told him to make a pillar and live upon it. The youth obeyed as if it had been the voice of God, and lived thus close to John during the remaining eight years of his life. Simeon himself lived on in this extraordinary but indubitably historically true fashion for another sixty years; from time to time he moved to another pillar, and without coming down to the ground he was ordained deacon and priest. Apparently there was a platform on his pillar sufficiently large to enable him to celebrate the holy Mysteries there, and his disciples climbed up by a ladder to receive communion at his hands. It is recorded that God manifested his sanctity by a number of miracles, which he performed chiefly in curing the sick, foretelling things to come, and knowing the secret thoughts of others. Evagrius, a Syrian historian, was an eye-witness to many and assures us that he had experienced Simeon's knowledge of the thoughts of others in himself, when he visited him for spiritual advice.

Crowds of people of many races flocked to St Simeon for his spiritual advice and hoping to witness or be healed by a miracle. After the death of St John Stylites there was no one who could or would restrain his austerities, and Evagrius says that he supported life entirely on one sort of fruit or herb. He wrote to the Emperor Justin II in defence of the respect which is due to holy images, and this letter is quoted by St John Damascene and by the second Council of Nicæa; there are a number of other writings, spiritual treatises, hymns, etc., attributed to him. During the last years of his life St Simeon's pillar was on a mountain which was named from his miracles the " Hill of Wonders." Here he fell ill about the year 597, and Gregory, Patriarch of Antioch, being informed that he was at the point of death went in haste to assist at his last moments; but before he arrived St Simeon was dead.

The fervour of the saints in bewailing their sins, in singing the divine praises, and in contemplating the glorious society of the heavenly spirits made them seem to forget the world; in these exercises they found the greatest delights and the most pure joy. The great St Antony, having spent the whole night in prayer and the morning calling him to other duties, was heard to lament that the rising sun interrupted the converse of his soul with God, though by recollection and frequent aspirations at his manual labour and other work he continued his prayer the whole day. The ardour of the saints is a reproach to our laziness and self-love, and the pillar of St Simeon loudly condemns our indolence and not the less because we are not called to follow the same extraordinary path. Nature, it is true, is weak, and stands in need of some relief; but if a lazy unwilling mind is to be judge of its want of strength the judgement will itself be in favour of our inertia and self-indulgence.

The more systematic research of recent years has added vastly to our knowledge of such Oriental Saints as St Simeon the Younger. If Alban Butler had had before him the materials now accessible he would certainly have provided a more detailed notice of this interesting ascetic than he was able to compile in the eighteenth century. Although the full Greek text of the contemporary Life, which Dr. Van den Ven has long been preparing for the press, has not yet seen the light, still Père Delehaye has edited the more historical portions in his *Saints Stylites* (1923), pp. 238–271, and an early Georgian translation of the same document has been printed by C. Kekelidze in the *Monumenta hagiographica Georgica*, i (Tiflis, 1918), pp. 215–340. Besides these materials we have the Greek Life of St Martha the mother of the Stylite, which, with the biography of Simeon himself by Nicephorus Ouramus, will be found in the *Acta Sanctorum*, May, vol. v. In the preface to *Les Saints Stylites*, Delehaye has furnished (pp. lix–lxxv) an excellent account of Simeon's history. It is extraordinary to find all our authorities insisting that the boy ascetic had already taken up his abode on a column when he was ten years old, " before he had lost his first teeth "; and also to learn that he was ordained upon a still higher column at the age of thirty-three, the consecrating bishop climbing up to the top of the pillar in order to impose hands upon him. The authorship of the long Greek Life has been attributed to Arcadius, Bishop of Constantia in Cyprus, but Delehaye thinks this less probable. See also the article of Père Peeters on the " Clibanion du Mont Admirable " in the *Analecta Bollandiana*, vol. xlvi (1928), pp. 241–286. Simeon is also the reputed author of certain pious discourses and liturgical *troparia*, but evidence is lacking to establish this attribution satisfactorily.

ST REMACLUS, BP. OF MAESTRICHT, CONF.

c. A.D. 668

Remaclus, a native of Aquitaine, was a man of good family and was given a post at the court of Clotaire. He became a priest, and after, it is said, having spent some time in the study of the holy Scriptures under St Sulpicius of Bourges, was appointed by St Eligius first abbot of the monastery and seminary which he founded at Solignac, near Limoges. The saint was afterwards obliged to take upon him the government of the abbey of Cougnon, in the duchy of Luxemburg, but was soon after called to the court of King Sigebert, who in 645 had succeeded his father, Dagobert I, in Austrasia. Sigebert followed the advice of St Remaclus in founding the royal abbey of Stavelot and also that of Malmédy, both in the Ardennes, to help forward the evangelisation of that still pagan district. The direction of both these foundations was committed to St Remaclus,

35

till upon the resignation of St Amandus in 652 he was chosen Bishop of Maestricht, in which charge he laboured with great humility and zeal in preaching to his flock and relieving the poor. One day there came to him a youth, who said he was the son of a nobleman at the Austrasian court and that he had run away from home because he wished to lead a religious life. The bishop handed the boy over to the care of his staff, who because of his ragged clothes and dishevelled appearance treated him with scant respect. St Remaclus rebuked them, telling them to judge a man by his heart and not by his looks. Subsequently he sent the boy on to St Clodulphus, Bishop of Metz, and he became known as St Trudo, or Trond, an apostle of part of Brabant. After ten years Remaclus found his responsibilities too much for him, and, fearing that amid so many distractions he would become immersed in activities to his own detriment, he procured the consent of his clergy and of King Childeric II to resign his see to St Theodardus and to retire to Stavelot. The reputation of his sanctity moved many noblemen and others to embrace a penitential monastic state under his direction in that house. Remaclus walked before them in the narrow paths of true Christian perfection, encouraging them both by words and example to fervour in all religious exercises. He modified nothing of his austerities on account of his old age, but rather strove continually to increase his pace as he drew nearer to the end of his course, lest by sloth at the last he should forfeit his crown. He strongly exhorted his religious brethren to the love and practice of perfect self-denial, obedience, poverty, patience in adversity, and constant peace and union, virtues in which he had been to them a shining example, and died about the year 668. He was buried at Stavelot, and a monk of that monastery wrote down his life in the ninth century from the traditions current in the house. Several of these are common to another bishop of Maestricht, St Lambert, and are of no worth. There are a number of local legends and places still connected with the name of St Remaclus in the province of Liége.

No confidence can be placed in any of the medieval biographies which purport to describe the career of St Remaclus. A list of them will be found in the *Bibliotheca hagiographica Latina*, nn. 7113–7141. The more important have been printed by Mabillon and the Bollandists (*Acta Sanctorum*, September, vol. i). G. Kurth seems to have been the first to reveal the untrustworthy character of the principal document. His paper is printed in the *Bulletin de la Commission roy. d'hist. de Belgique*, 4 série, vol. iii. See also Van der Essen, *Étude critique sur les Vies des Saints méroving.*, pp. 96–105.

ST AIGULPHUS, ABBOT, AND HIS COMPANIONS, MARTS.
A.D. 676

Aigulphus (*Ayou*) was born at Blois, and at about the age of twenty became a monk at Fleury, then in its first fervour of Benedictine observance. About the year 670 a new abbot was required at Lérins, where the passage of time and the ravages of the Moors had somewhat impaired discipline, and Aigulphus, now a monk of twenty years' experience with a reputation for solid virtue and stability, was sent to fill the office. He is said to have introduced with his reforms the Rule of St Benedict itself into that house. But as is usual in such circumstances some of the religious were well content with the old ways and willing to go to a good deal of trouble to frustrate the efforts to improve their observance. In this case two of them, Arcadius and Columbus, went too far. They appealed to the Bishop of Uzès against their abbot, and when he sent a company of soldiers to keep order they used them to kidnap St Aigulphus and four of his chief supporters and carry them off to sea. They were landed on the island of Capraija, between Corsica and the coast of Tuscany, where their eyes and tongues were torn out and they were put to death. But one of the monks escaped and brought word to Lérins of what had taken place.

This account is given in an early Life of St Aigulphus, but it has been suggested, not without reason, that even were the abbot and his companions carried off by the bishop's soldiers, it is more likely that they were massacred by some marauding party of Moors. The bodies were brought back to Lérins and their transportation was the occasion of many miracles. Later, a bitter controversy arose between Lérins and Fleury as to which abbey really possessed the body of St Aigulphus.

According to a biography of St Aigulphus written by a monk of Fleury about the year 850 the saint was put in charge of the party of monks from Fleury and Le Mans which St Mommolus, abbot of the first named, sent to Italy in 652 to save the relics of St Benedict from the hands of the Lombards. Having arrived at Monte Cassino they were guided by a miraculous light which led them to the tombs of St Benedict and his sister, whence they removed their relics with infinite care and respect. As Paul the Deacon describes it : " At that time Monte Cassino, where the sacred body of St Benedict reposed, was but a vast solitude, when Franks came from the country of Maine and Orleans pretending to watch over and pass the night near the holy body. They took the bones of that venerable Father and those of his sister, St Scholastica, and brought them into their own country." Pope St Martin I heard of what had happened too late ; the armed messengers he sent after the French monks failed to catch them up. A hundred years later Pope St Zacharias and St Petronax, restorer and abbot of Monte Cassino, begged the Fleury monks to return the relics, which they continued to maintain had been stolen. The rights of this affair and the true resting-place or places of the relics of St Benedict do not concern us here. It is sufficient to notice that St Aigulphus almost certainly had nothing to do with it. In 652 he had been a monk only for a couple of years and was surely too young to be entrusted with so delicate a mission ; moreover the ninth-century Adrebaldus is the only early writer who mentions his name in connection with the mission of St Mommolus.

A somewhat lyrical account of Aigulphus written by Adrevaldus, a monk of Fleury, who lived two centuries later, does not inspire confidence. The Bollandists print it in the *Acta Sanctorum*, September, vol. i, together with a shorter narrative which they believe to be of earlier date and more reliable. See also H. Moris, *L'Abbaye de Lérins* (1909), and the *Dict. d'Hist. et Géog. Ecclésiastique*, i, cc. 1141–1142.

BB. JOHN OF PERUGIA AND PETER OF SASSOFERRATO, MARTS.

A.D. 1231

Among the Friars Minor whom St Francis of Assisi sent into Spain to preach the gospel to the Moors were Brother John, a priest of Perugia, and Brother Peter, a lay-brother from Sassoferrato in Piceno. These two friars established themselves at Teruel in Aragon, living in cells near the church of St Bartholomew, and there for some time prepared themselves for their apostolate. Their poverty and lowliness won the love and attention of the people of the place, and their lives and preaching bore much fruit. They then went on to Valencia, which was completely under the dominion of the Moors, and took up their quarters quietly at the church of the Holy Sepulchre, with the help of two Castilian gentlemen who admired their courage and evangelical fervour. But directly the friars attempted to preach in public the Mohammedans turned against them ; they were arrested in a mosque and brought before the emir, Azot. He asked what had brought them to Valencia, and Blessed John replied that they came to convert the Moors from the errors of Islam. They were then offered the usual alternatives of apostasy or death, and when they chose death were condemned to be beheaded. The sentence was carried out then and there in the emir's garden, the martyrs praying aloud for the conversion of their persecutor. This was on August 29, 1231. Seven years later James I the Conqueror, King of Aragon, drove the Moors from Valencia with the help of his English and other mercenaries, and in accordance with the martyrs' prayer Azot became a Christian. He gave his house to the Franciscans for a friary, saying to them : " While I was an infidel I killed your brethren from Teruel, and I want to make reparation for my crime. Here, then, is my house at your disposal, consecrated already by the blood of martyrs." The bodies of BB. John and Peter had been taken to Teruel, where miracles were reported at their tomb, and so a church was erected at the new friary at Valencia in their honour. This veneration was approved by Pope Clement XI and they were beatified by Pius VI in 1783.

An account of these martyrs is given in the *Acta Sanctorum*, August, vol. vi, where their story is reproduced as told by St Antoninus of Florence. An older narrative of the martyrdom has been printed in the *Analecta Franciscana*, vol. iii, pp. 186–187. See also Léon, *Auréole Séraphique* (Eng. Tr.), vol. iii, pp. 96–97.

BD. GUALA ROMANONI, Bp. of Brescia, Conf.

A.D. 1244

When St Dominic came to Bergamo towards the end of the year 1217 the first there to offer themselves as his disciples and to receive the habit of his new order from his hands were Guala Romanoni, a man already over thirty years of age, and his brother Roger. Guala went with St Dominic to Bologna, where he helped in the foundation of a house of nuns, and afterwards to Brescia for the establishment of the friars there, and of that house he became prior. While he was fulfilling that office St Dominic was struck down by his last sickness, and on August 6, 1221, Blessed Guala was praying for his recovery in the church, believing him to be still alive. Falling asleep, he seemed to see two ladders let down from the heavens, at the top of one of which stood our Lord and of the other His holy Mother. Angels were going up and down the ladders, and at their foot there sat between them a figure in the Dominican habit, his face covered with his hood as if for burial. Then the ladders were drawn up and with them the friar, borne up by the angels to the feet of Christ. This vision would seem to have only one possible meaning, and Guala went in great haste and alarm to Bologna, where he learned that at the very hour of his dream St Dominic had gone

to God. The third antiphon at Lauds in the office of St Dominic
refers to this : *Scala cælo prominens fratri revelatur, per quam pater
transiens sursum ferebatur :* " A brother was shown a ladder hanging
from Heaven, on which our dying Father was carried up." When
this office was solemnly sung for the first time, after the canonisation
of St Dominic in 1234, Blessed Guala was present in the choir at
Bologna and himself precented this antiphon. He was, we are told,
a man of remarkable prudence and of much experience in the world ;
a good religious and eloquent preacher and of impressive personality,
qualities sufficiently strong to get him noticed at both the papal and
imperial courts. While he was still a simple friar Pope Gregory IX
made him his legate to Savoy, and he took part in the negotiations
which led up to the treaty between the Holy See and the Emperor
Frederick II at San Germano. It was probably owing to the good
opinion that he had earned in these affairs that Blessed Guala was
about 1230 promoted to the see of Brescia, which he governed
successfully for some twelve years, the beloved father of the poor
and unfortunate. But the strife of Guelf and Ghibelline continued
to distract Lombardy, and in 1242 Blessed Guala resigned his
onerous charge and retired to a monastery of the Vallumbrosan
Benedictines at Astino. Here he lived in prayer and study till his
death two years later. The ancient *cultus* of Blessed Guala was
confirmed by Pope Pius IX in 1868.

See the *Acta Sanctorum*, September, vol. i ; Masetti, *Memorie storico-
biografico-critiche del B. Guala Romanoni* (*Rome*, 1868), and a Life in French
by J. Kuczynski (Fribourg, 1916). This last writer seems to have been
successful in exonerating Bd. Guala from the charge of having prompted
Pope Gregory IX to enforce throughout Lombardy the death penalty
against heretics, *cf*. the *Analecta Bollandiana*, vol. xxxix (1921), p. 223.
A short account of the career of this holy bishop will be found in Procter,
Dominican Saints, pp. 247-249.

BD. ANDREW DOTTI, Conf.

A.D. 1315

Was born at Borgo San Sepolcro in Tuscany about the year 1250.
His family was distinguished (Andrew's brother was a captain in
the bodyguard of King Philip the Fair), and the young man was
brought up accordingly, with no thought of the religious life. When
he was seventeen he became a secular tertiary of the Servites, and
when, a few years afterwards, a general chapter of that order was
held at Borgo San Sepolcro, Andrew naturally went to hear the

prior general, St Philip Benizi, preach. His text was, " Every one of you that doth not renounce all that he possesseth cannot be my disciple," and his eloquence and fire touched Andrew's heart ; he offered himself to St Philip, was accepted, and became a Servite friar. After he was ordained he was attached to a monastery governed by St Gerard Sostegni, one of the seven founders of the order, and from thence he preached with success throughout the surrounding country and accompanied St Philip Benizi on several of his missionary journeys. By his virtue and persuasion he induced a number of hermits who were living a rather go-as-you-please life at Vallucola to affiliate themselves to the Servites and submit to their discipline, and over these he was appointed superior for a time until his services were again required for preaching and as prior of various houses. In 1310 he was present at the death of St Alexis Falconieri, the principal founder of the Servites, at Montesenario, and so great was the impression made on him that he asked permission to retire to a hermitage and prepare for his own end, though he was barely sixty. Blessed Andrew lived with great penance and was the recipient of many visions, including a forewarning of his own death ; when the day came he was apparently in good health, and he went out to a certain rock where he was wont to give conferences to his brethren. When they assembled there they found their beloved father kneeling motionless on the rock, apparently in ecstasy ; but he was dead. He was buried in the church at Borgo San Sepolcro, where the popular veneration for his holiness was confirmed by miracles, and in 1806 Pope Pius VII approved the ancient *cultus.*

A full account of this Beato is given in A. Giani, *Annales Ordinis Servorum B.V.M.,* vol. i, especially pp. 230–231 ; and see also *Dict. d'Hist. et Géog. Ecclésiastique,* vol. ii, *c.* 1663.

BB. ANTONY IXIDA AND HIS COMPANIONS, MARTS.

A.D. 1632

These were the last in order of time of the 205 martyrs in Japan, beatified in 1867. Antony was a native of Japan, born there in 1569, was educated by the Jesuits, and became a novice of the Society at the age of twenty. After his ordination to the priesthood he played a big part by his eloquence, energy, and knowledge of his people, in reconciling apostates and making new conversions after the persecution of 1597. During the great persecution that began in 1614 he continued to work among its victims in the province of Arima

41

until the end of 1629, when, going on a sick-call to Nagasaki, he was there captured. When brought before the governor Blessed Antony was treated with consideration and respect : he was given a seat in court and listened to patiently while he defended and expounded the Christian religion. His words made an impression on the governor, who would have released him had he had the authority to do so. A few days later he arranged a conference between the priest and the bonzes, at which Blessed Antony was again profoundly impressive. On the following day he was sent to Omura, but was then apparently forgotten, for he remained in gaol there for two years. At the end of that time he was taken back with some companions to Nagasaki and examined by the chief bonze of the Buddhist sect Yodo. It was then decided to make a determined effort to induce these men to apostatise by the application of a quite ferocious form of torture. There lies between Nagasaki and Simabara a volcanic mountain called Unsen, water from the sulphurous hot-springs of which produces ulceration of the human flesh. The bodies of the confessors were sprinkled with this corrosive water until they were covered with virulent sores, and they were then laid on beds of prickly straw. When they remained firm, the ulcers were carefully dressed by physicians, and when they had gained some degree of ease their flesh was again sprinkled. And so on. This went on for thirty-three days, until, in despair of bringing about apostasy, the persecutors slew their victims by burning, on September 3, 1632. The five blessed companions of Blessed Antony Ixida were three Augustinian friars, a Japanese Franciscan priest, and a Spanish laybrother. On the 6th of this month the Society of Jesus keeps the feast of BLESSED THOMAS TZUGHI with his companions who received the crown of martyrdom at Nagasaki, on September 7, 1627.

See G. Boero, *Relazione della gloriosa Morte di 205 B. Martiri nel Giappone* (1867), pp. 151–162 ; L. Delplace, *Le Catholicisme au Japon*, vol. ii ; Profillet, *Le Martyrologe de l'Église du Japon* (1897, 3 vols.) ; L. Pagès, *Histoire de la Religion chrétienne au Japon* (1869, 2 vols.). The name Ixida is also variously spelt Ishida and Ichida. For Bd. Thomas Tzughi (or Tsouji) see Boero, pp. 138–140. He was a Japanese of noble family, and was burnt alive after thirty-four years of zealous ministry in the priesthood.

SEPTEMBER 4

SS. MARCELLUS AND VALERIAN, MARTS.

c. A.D. 178

THE massacre of the forty-eight martyrs of Lyons with their bishop, St Photinus, took place during the persecution of Marcus Aurelius in the year 177. Marcellus, a priest, was imprisoned but managed to escape to Chalon-sur-Saône, where he was given shelter. His host was a pagan, and seeing him offer incense before images of Mars, Mercury, and Minerva, Marcellus remonstrated with and converted him. While journeying towards the north the priest fell in with the governor Priscus, who asked him to a meal at his house. Marcellus accepted the invitation, but when he found that Priscus was preparing to fulfil religious rites he asked to be excused on the ground that he was a Christian. This raised an outcry, and the bystanders wanted to kill Marcellus there and then by tying him to the tops of two young poplars in tension and then letting them fly apart. The governor forbade this, but brought Marcellus before his court and ordered him to make an act of worship before an image of Saturn. He refused peremptorily, whereupon he was buried up to his middle in the earth on the banks of the Saône, and died in three days of exposure and starvation. Alban Butler mentions with this martyr St Valerian, who is named in the Roman Martyrology on September 15. He escaped from prison about the same time as Marcellus, and was beheaded for the faith at Tournus, near Autun.

Another MARCELLUS is mentioned in the Roman Martyrology to-day, whom it states to have been a bishop and martyr at Trier. He is also claimed by Tongres, but nothing is known about him. A ST MARCELLUS, bishop and martyr, is venerated at Le Puy in Haute Loire on the 11th, and on the 12th the Roman Martyrology has a ST VALERIAN, along with others, martyrs who were drowned in the sea at Alexandria under the Emperor Maximian.

The martyrs whom we have just named made the whole of their lives a preparation for martyrdom because they devoted it entirely to God by constant virtue. To be able to stand our ground in the time of trial and to make the necessary acts of virtue in the hour of death, we must be thoroughly grounded in good habits : we shall not otherwise exert them readily on sudden and difficult occasions. He whose soul is well regulated and in whose heart virtue has taken deep root finds its practice easy and, as it were, natural in times of sickness, persecution, or any other occasion, for he makes everything that occurs matter for its exercise. He subjects obstacles to himself and converts them into occasions of exerting the noble and heroic habits of resignation, patience, charity, and goodwill toward those who oppose or persecute him.

It is difficult to say how much confidence can be placed in the two sets of Acts (printed in the *Acta Sanctorum*, September, vol. ii) which record the martyrdom of St Marcellus. The eighteenth-century Bollandists seem inclined to defend them from the criticisms of Tillemont. In the second set the name of Valerian is associated with Marcellus, and an inscription in a church near Bagnols (Gar) couples together certain relics of the two saints. The cult of both was certainly early and is indirectly attested by Gregory of Tours ; see Delehaye, *Origines du Culte des Martyrs*, p. 401. Dom Quentin in his *Martyrologes historiques*, pp. 179–180, provides an interesting illustration of how the long elogium of Marcellus in the Roman martyrology originated.

ST MARINUS, Conf.

Fourth Century

Between the Italian provinces of Forli, Pesaro, and Urbino lies an area of land of less than forty square miles in extent, having only some 10,000 inhabitants, and yet forming an independent republic, which has retained its sovereignty against all assaults for nigh a thousand years. On the highest of seven hills, Il Titano, is built the capital city of this tiny state, called San Marino ; from this city the whole republic takes its name, and the San Marino referred to is St Marinus the Deacon, named in the Roman Martyrology on this day. His legend, unhappily fabulous, is as follows.

Marinus was born on the Dalmatian coast and was by trade a stonemason. Hearing that the walls and town of Rimini were being rebuilt, he went there to find work in company with another mason, St Leo. They were employed at squaring and working stone in the quarries of Monte Titano in what is now San Marino, and met among their fellow-workmen a number of Christians of gentle birth who had been sentenced to labour in the quarries because of their adherence to the faith. Marinus and Leo did their best to alleviate the hardships of these unfortunate people, helping them in their work and encouraging them to persevere ; and also made a number of new converts. At the end of three years St Leo was ordained priest by St Gaudentius, Bishop of Rimini, and went to live at

Montefeltro (where he is now titular of the cathedral) ; St Marinus was made deacon, and returned to his work that he might continue to look after the confessors and converts. For twelve years he was working on an aqueduct, and was known as a skilled and indefatigable mason and a good man, a model Christian workman. But then a misfortune happened to him. A Dalmatian woman turned up one day at Rimini, saw Marinus, and claimed him as her deserting husband. He lost his head. Escaping out of the city, he made his way to Monte Titano and there hid himself. The woman pursued him and for a week he had to barricade himself into a cave, until she retired for lack of food. Marinus took the opportunity to penetrate further up the mountain, the woman did not find him again, and he chose to pass the rest of his life there as a hermit. On the site of the hermitage the town of San Marino afterwards arose, and in 1586 there were discovered his alleged relics, which are now venerated there in the church of his name.

The Bollandists print this fabulous story from Mombritius (*Acta Sanctorum*, September, vol. ii ; and *cf.* August, vol. i, the priest Leo being honoured on August 1). See also L. A. Gentili, *Compendio della Vita di S. Marino*, etc., Bologna, 1864.

ST BONIFACE I, POPE AND CONF.

A.D. 422

Boniface was a priest of unblemished character, experienced in the discipline of the Church, and advanced in years when he succeeded St Zosimus in the pontificate on December 28 in 418. His election was made much against his will, as the relation of it, which was sent by the clergy and people of Rome and by the neighbouring bishops to the Emperor Honorius at Ravenna, shows ; in it concurred seventy priests, nine bishops, and the greater part of the people. But three bishops and others chose one Eulalius, who was archdeacon of the city, and consecrated him in the Lateran basilica. Symmachus, prefect of Rome, sent an account of this division or schism to the Emperor, who ordered that the election of Eulalius, which had the support of the prefect, should stand. St Boniface was thereupon expelled from Rome, but his supporters asked Honorius that a synod be assembled to determine the matter. The council which met desired that a greater number of prelates should be called, and made certain provisional decrees, including the temporary banishment of Eulalius also. As Easter was approaching Achilleus, Bishop of Spoleto, was deputed to celebrate the paschal services in the City, but Eulalius boldly returned and seized the Lateran with the intention of celebrating himself. On Holy Saturday he had to be expelled therefrom by soldiers, and the Emperor, indignant at this flouting of his own and ecclesiastical authority, directed that Boniface be recognised as legitimate pope. He was thereupon able to take quiet possession of his see fifteen weeks after election.

This pope was a lover of peace and remarkable for his mildness, yet he would not suffer the bishops of Constantinople to extend their patriarchate into Illyricum or the other western provinces which were then subject to the Eastern empire but had always belonged to the Western patriarchate. He strenuously maintained the rights of Rufus, Bishop of Thessalonica, who was his vicar in Thessaly and Greece, and would allow no election of bishops to be made in those countries which were not confirmed by him, according to the ancient discipline. When Peregrinus had been ordained bishop of Patras and the people of the place would not have him, St Boniface ordered him to be appointed to Corinth instead, and the ensuing trouble was used by the Eastern Emperor, Theodosius II, as a pretext for submitting Illyricum to Constantinople. The Pope induced Honorius to persuade Theodosius to suspend the enactment. Thus energetically did he set himself against the growing ambition of the bishops of Constantinople. " Study the sanctions of the canons," he writes to Rufus, " and you will find which are the second and third sees after Rome. Let the great churches, namely Alexandria and Antioch, keep their dignity. . . . The blessed apostle Peter received by our Lord's word and commission the care of the whole Church, which was founded on him." St Boniface had also to uphold the jurisdiction of the Holy See in the Church of Africa, and heard the appeal of a Numidian bishop who had been deposed from his see. In Gaul he diminished the primatial authority granted by his predecessor to the see of Arles and supported the metropolitan rights of Narbonne and Vienne, thus vindicating bishops against the encroachments of papal vicars. He was a strong supporter of St Augustine in his opposition to Pelagianism, and when letters were sent him by Pelagians slandering the Bishop of Hippo, he forwarded them to him for his information. As a mark of his respect and gratitude St Augustine dedicated his reply, in four books, to the Pope and sent it to him by the hand of St Alipius. He renewed and enforced the law that slaves and debtors were not to be admitted to holy orders and that women were not to handle altar linen or minister at sacred rites.

St Boniface died on September 4, 422, after being pope for not quite four years. He was buried in the cemetery of Maximus on the New Salarian Way, close to the chapel he had built over the grave of St Felicitas, to whose intercession he attributed the happy ending of the Eulalian schism and for whom in consequence he had a deep devotion.

The *Liber Pontificalis* with Duchesne's notes (i, 227–229 and *cf.* p. lxii), and the letters calendared by Jaffé-Kaltenbrunner (i, 52–54) form our most direct source of information. See also the *Acta Sanctorum*, September, vol. ii; the *Dictionnaire de Théologie cath.*, vol. ii, cc. 988–989, with appended bibliography; and Grisar, *History of Rome and the Papacy* (Eng. Trans.), nn. 219, 226, 466, 471.

ST ULTAN, Bp. and Conf.
c. A.D. 657 (?)

This Ultan is said to have been a disciple of St Declan of Ardmore and maternal uncle to St Brigid, but this cannot have been the case if, as is usually recorded, he died in the middle of the seventh century, for this would make him at least 150 years old. The uncertainty is made worse by confusion with other saints of the name, for instance, the St Ultan who was abbot of Fosse in Belgium in the seventh century. He is supposed to have succeeded St Brecan as bishop in Ardbraccan, whence he evangelised and ministered to the Dal Conchubhair branch of the Desi of Meath; on the other hand, he is entered in some calendars as a priest only. An old quatrain refers to his particular care for children, especially orphans and those sick (he was sometimes responsible for " fifty and thrice fifty " children at a time), and to his fondness for bathing in cold water on a windy day. He also educated and fed numerous poor students, and was a man of letters himself. He is said to have collected the writings of St Brigid, to have written the " third Life " of her, and to have supplied to St Tirechan the materials for his annotations on the life of St Patrick in the Book of Armagh. The hymn in honour of St Brigid, beginning *Christus in nostra insula, Quae vocatur Hibernia*, is often attributed to St Ultan, but was probably written by his disciple, St Brogan of Rosstuirc. He also, we are told, illuminated his own manuscripts. St Ultan is no longer commemorated liturgically in Ireland, but a holy well at Ardbraccan bears his name. Another Ultan is mentioned in some calendars on the 7th of this month.

There is no formal Life of St Ultan, either in Latin or Irish, but an unusually copious gloss is appended to his notice in the *Félire* of Oengus (p. 201). This deals more especially with the proverbial phrase " Ultan's left hand against evil." The saint was feeding children with his right hand when an appeal reached him to exert his power against the Norse marauders then infesting Ireland. Even with his left hand he put them to flight, and an early Irish poet wrote : " Had it been the right hand that noble Ultan raised against them, no foreigner would ever have come into the land of Erin." A Latin poem in praise of Ultan has been printed by Dümmler, *Poetæ Latini medii ævi*, i, 589. See also the references in *The Irish Liber Hymnorum* (Henry Bradshaw Society) ; *Dictionary of Nat. Biogr.*, vol. lviii, p. 21 ; and O'Hanlon, *Lives of the Irish Saints*, vol. ix, pp. 83 *seq.*

ST IDA OF HERZFELD, Widow

c. A.D. 813

This noble lady was a great-granddaughter of Charles Martel, and so came of a family distinguished as much by the sanctity of some of its members as by its secular dignity. Ida was born in Alsace, and her father, Duke Theodericus, was in great favour with Charlemagne, in whose court she had her upbringing ; she was strengthened by the example and conversation of her mother, Theodrada, who became abbess of Soissons, and of her uncles, St Adelhard and St Wala, both of whom were monks. The Emperor gave her in marriage to a lord of his court named Egbert, and bestowed on her a great fortune in estates, not only on account of her merit but also to recompense her father's services. The couple lived in perfect union of hearts, and encouraged each other to the practice of all good works, till the death of her husband left Ida a widow whilst she was yet very young. This state she sanctified by redoubling her devotions, self-denials, and austerities. The great revenues of her estate she chiefly employed in relieving the poor, and felt no greater pleasure than in clothing and feeding Jesus Christ in his members. She surpassed in the world the penitential practices of cloisters, and that she might prolong her prayers and wait on God before His altar with greater recollection and unobserved by men, she built herself a little chapel within a church which she had founded near her own seat at Hofstadt in Westphalia. Her exercises of piety and the heavenly favours she received in prayer were generally known only to God, so carefully did she conceal them as much as possible from the eyes of men.

When her son Warin, moved by his mother's example, went to be a monk at Corvey, of which house he became abbot, St Ida changed her residence to Herzfeld, where she lived for the remainder of her life, continuing always in good works. It is said that, to remind her both of her earthly end and of her duty to her neighbour, she had a stone coffin made for herself, which was daily filled up with food for distribution to the needy. During her last years she was afflicted with a painful and unremitting illness, which she bore with patience and turned to advantage. St Ida was buried at Herzfeld in the cemetery of the convent she had founded there ; in the year 980 the Bishop of Münster enshrined the relics and some were translated to Verdun on the Ruhr. Her feast is observed at Münster and Paderborn.

Her Life, written a century and a half after her death by Uffine, a monk of Werden, is full of improbable miracles. It is printed in the *Acta Sanctorum*, September, vol. ii. For a modern biography see A. Hüsing, *Die h. Ida, Gräfin von Herzfeld*, Münster, 1880.

ST ROSALIA, Virg.
A.D. 1160 (?)

There were churches dedicated in honour of St Rosalia in Sicily in the thirteenth century, but she was not mentioned in any of the ancient martyrologies and there are no accounts of her life older than the end of the sixteenth century. Her history, says Father Stilting, the Bollandist, is put together from the evidence of local tradition, inscriptions, and paintings. According to these she was the daughter of Sinibald, lord of Quisquina and Rosae, of the royal blood of Charlemagne, and while yet young left her home to live as a recluse in a cave on Mount Coschina, near Bivona in Sicily. Later she migrated to a damp, stalagmitic grotto on Monte Pellegrino, three miles from Palermo ; here she died, and in due course a stalactitic deposit completely covered her remains. The inscription to which Father Stilting referred was found carved on the walls of the cave at Coschina, ostensibly by her own hand : *Ego Rosalia Sinibaldi Quisquine et Rosarum domini filia amore Domini mei Iesu Christi in hoc antro habitare decrevi :* " I, Rosalia, daughter of Sinibald, lord of Quisquina and Rosae, disappeared to live in this cave for the love of my Lord Jesus Christ." St Rosalia has been claimed as a nun both by the Benedictines and by the Greek religious who formerly flourished in Sicily, and in the former Byzantine archabbey of St Saviour at Messina was a wooden crucifix with the inscription, " I, Sister Rosalia Sinibaldi, place this wood of my Lord, which I have ever followed, in this monastery." This relic is now at Palermo.

In the year 1624 an epidemic of plague broke out at Palermo.

In accordance, it is said, with a vision of St Rosalia that appeared to one of the victims, search was made in the cave on Monte Pellegrino and the bones of the maiden were found. They were put into a reliquary and carried in procession through the city, at the beginning of the holy year of jubilee 1625, and the pestilence was stayed. In their gratitude the people of Palermo made St Rosalia their principal patron and built a church over her hermitage. Pope Urban VIII entered her name in the Roman Martyrology, wherein she is mentioned twice, on this date (said to be of her death) and on July 15, the anniversary of the finding of her relics. With the bones were found a crucifix of terra-cotta, a Greek cross of silver, and a string of beads, twelve small and a large one, which was doubtless a rosary in one of its many early forms. The feast of St Rosalia on September 4 is still the principal popular *festa* among the Palermitans, who always look for a cleansing rain on the preceding days.

A multitude of small Italian biographies have been written to do honour to the patroness of Palermo, but they add nothing of value to the account, compiled by the Bollandists and illustrated with several engravings, in the *Acta Sanctorum*, September, vol. ii. See, however, D. M. Sparacio, *S Rosalia, Vergine Panormitana*, Foligno, 1924.

ST ROSE OF VITERBO, Virg.

c. A.D. 1252

It was the ambition of the Emperor Frederick II to make Rome the civil as well as the ecclesiastical capital of the world, with himself as overlord of all, and after a prolonged political struggle with Pope Gregory IX he took up arms against the Lombards, with whom and the Venetians, Tuscans, and Umbrians the Pope had entered into a defensive alliance. Gregory excommunicated Frederick, whereupon the Emperor set out to conquer the papal states themselves, and in 1240 occupied Viterbo in the Romagna. A few years previously there had been born in this city, to parents of lowly station, a girl child, who was called Rose. From babyhood she displayed a far from usual goodness and her childish virtue and devotion made such an impression that in after years a legend grew up that she had, when three years old, raised her aunt from death by her prayers. At the age of seven she wanted to live alone in a small room at her home, but in the following year she was taken seriously ill and it seemed for a time that she would not live. On the vigil of St John Baptist she had a vision or dream of our Lady, who told her that she was to be clothed in the habit of St Francis, but that she was to continue to live at home and to set a good example to her neighbours by both word and work. Rose soon recovered her health, received the dress of a Franciscan tertiary in due course, and thought more and more about the sufferings of our Lord and the thoughtless ingratitude of sinners. Perhaps inspired by some sermon she heard or the burning words of some indignant Guelf, she began when she was about twelve years old to preach up and down the streets, upbraiding the people for their supineness in submitting to Frederick and urging them to overthrow the Ghibelline garrison. Her simple words could not fail of effect, which was heightened by the rumours of marvels attending her speeches which circulated among the citizens. Crowds would gather outside her house to get a glimpse of her, till her father became frightened, and forbade her to show herself in public ; if she disobeyed she would be beaten. Rose replied gently : " If Jesus could be beaten for me, I can be beaten for Him. I do what He has told me to do, and I must not disobey Him." At the instance of their parish priest her father withdrew his prohibition and for about two years the Pope's cause continued to be preached in public by this young girl. Then the partisans of the Emperor became alarmed and clamoured that Rose should be put to death as a danger to the state. The *podestà* of the city would not hear of this : he was a just man, and moreover he feared the people ; but instead he passed a sentence of banishment against St Rose and her parents.

They took refuge at Soriano, and here, in the beginning of December 1250, St Rose is said to have announced the approaching death of the Emperor Frederick II. He in fact died in Apulia on the 13th of the month ; the papal party thereupon got the upper hand in Viterbo, and St Rose returned thither. There is a story that before doing so she confuted a zealous female Ghibelline at Vitorchiano by a successful appeal to the ordeal by fire. She now went to the convent of St Mary of the Roses at Viterbo and asked to be received as a postulant. The abbess refused. " Very well," said St Rose smilingly. " You will not have me now, but perhaps you will be more willing when I am dead." Her parish priest took it upon himself to open a chapel close by the convent, with a house attached wherein St Rose and a few companions might lead a religious life ; but the nuns got an order from Pope Innocent IV for it to be closed, on the ground that they had the privilege of having no other community of women within a given distance of their own. St Rose therefore returned to her parents' house, where she died on March 6, 1252, about the age of seventeen. She was buried in the church of Santa Maria in Podio, but her body was on this date in 1258 translated to the church of the convent of St Mary of the Roses, as she had foretold. This church was burnt down in 1357 but her incorrupt body was preserved and is annually carried in procession through the streets of Viterbo. Pope Innocent IV immediately after her death ordered an inquiry into the virtues of St Rose, but her canonisation was not achieved until 1457.

If any authentic or early materials for the history of this Saint ever existed, they have perished, and legend plays a large part in what is now presented as her Life. The Bollandists in the eighteenth century collected what they could, but were ill-satisfied with the result. See the *Acta Sanctorum*, September, vol. ii. They have, however, preserved substantial extracts from the later process of canonisation. The best known biographies in Italian are those of Andreucci (1750) and Mencarini (1828), and in more recent years that of L. de Kerval in French (1896), which has been translated into German and Flemish. A short English Life was included in the Oratorian series (1852), and we have also a notice in Léon, *Auréole Séraphique* (Eng. Trans.), vol. iii, pp. 98–109. An article in *The Month* (September, 1899) gives an account of the Festa of the Saint at Viterbo and of the famous " Macchina " which is carried in the procession on that occasion.

BD. CATHERINE OF RACCONIGI, Virg.

A.D. 1547

Racconigi is a small place in Piedmont, and there in 1486 a poor working man called de'Matteis and his wife, made still poorer by the civil strife between the Duke of Savoy and the Marquis of Saluzzo, became the parents of a girl, who was baptised Catherine. She was born in a tumble-down shed, a fact that was symbolic of the whole of the material side of her life throughout which she had to endure indigence, ill-health, and misunderstanding; but spiritually she was enriched with some of the more extraordinary favours which God extends to man. It is told of her that already at five years old she believed herself to have been espoused to the child Jesus by His all-holy Mother, and that He gave her as her special patrons and protectors St Jerome, St Catherine of Siena, and St Peter Martyr. When she was nine and one day broke down in tears of tiredness over her work and the wretched state of her home, she was again visited and comforted by the holy Child. On the feast of St Stephen in the year 1500 she was praying to that saint, and reminding him that as a deacon the Apostles had especially entrusted the care of women to him, when he appeared to her and spoke encouraging words, promising that the Holy Spirit would come upon her in a special way. Then it seemed that three rays of light flashed upon

52

her, and a voice exclaimed : " I am come to take up my dwelling in you, and to cleanse, enlighten, kindle, and animate your soul." After she had made a vow of virginity the mystical espousals were repeated and the mark of a ring appeared upon her finger, and she suffered the pains of a crown of thorns and of the other *stigmata* of our Lord's passion, without, however, their becoming visible to the eye. In these and other things reported of Blessed Catherine there is a very marked resemblance to what we are told of St Catherine of Siena, and the words of her breviary lessons are often quoted, that " between Racconigi and Siena there is only the difference of canonisation." But this is not meant to be taken too literally. It was not until she was twenty-eight years old that she imitated her patron in becoming a secular tertiary of the Friars Preachers, continuing to live in the world and work hard for her family, and then she was said to have been girt by angels with a girdle of chastity, after the example of St Thomas Aquinas. Blessed Catherine often implored God that the mouth of Hell might be for ever shut, and when she learned that this was impossible she offered herself as a victim for others and by her penances and austerities lightened the time of many souls in Purgatory. Many miracles are related of her, as that she was carried with great speed from place to place to bring spiritual help and that she received the holy Eucharist otherwise than by the hand of a priest. Catherine was profoundly distressed by the evils brought upon her land by warfare, and offered herself to bear them also. A long illness would seem to have been an acceptance of this, and she died at Carmagnola in her sixty-second year, deserted by her friends and without the ministrations of a priest. Five months later her body was translated to Garezzo, amid miracles which gave rise to a *cultus* that has never since ceased. It was confirmed by Pope Pius VII in 1810.

It is regrettable that more satisfactory evidence is not available concerning the life of this interesting mystic. Our primary source of information seems to be the account furnished by John Francis Pico della Mirandola, and the Dominican, Peter Martyr Morelli. They knew her intimately, but it is evident that they accepted unquestioningly what she told them about herself, for example, that in some cause of charity she had travelled invisibly to a place 100 miles distant, returning within four hours of the time of starting. The best notice of Bd. Catherine is probably that of M. C. de Ganay, *Les Bienheureuses Dominicaines* (1913), pp. 475–502, but *cf. Miscellanea di Storia ecclesiastica e di Theologia*, vol. ii (1904), pp. 185–191. For a fuller bibliography see Taurisano, *Catalogus hagiographicus O.P.* An English translation of the Life by S. Razzi was published in the Oratorian series in 1852.

SEPTEMBER 5

ST LAURENCE JUSTINIAN, Patriarch of Grado, Conf.

A.D. 1455

ST LAURENCE was born at Venice in 1381. His father,
Bernard Giustiniani, was of illustrious rank among the
nobility of the commonwealth and the extraction of his
mother, a Querini, was not less noble. She was early left a widow
with a number of young children, and she thought it her duty to
sanctify her soul by the means which her state afforded and resolutely rejected all thoughts of marrying again. She looked upon
herself as called to a penitential and retired life and devoted herself
altogether to the upbringing of her children, to works of charity,
and the exercise of virtue. In Laurence she discovered even from
the cradle an uncommon docility and generosity of soul ; and,
fearing some spark of pride and ambition, she chid him sometimes
for aiming at things above his age. He humbly answered that it
was his only desire by the divine grace to become a saint. Realising
that he was made by God only to serve Him and to live eternally
with Him, he kept this end always in view and governed all his
thoughts and actions so as to refer them to God and eternity. When
he was nineteen he was called by God to consecrate himself in a
special manner to His service. He seemed one day to see in a vision
the Eternal Wisdom in the guise of a shining maiden, and to hear
from her the words : " Why do you seek rest for your mind in
exterior things, sometimes in this object and sometimes in that ?
What you desire is to be found only with me : it is in my hands.
Seek it in me who am the wisdom of God. By taking me for your
companion and your lot you shall be possessed of its boundless
treasure." That instant he found his soul so pierced with divine
grace that he felt himself warmed with new ardour to give himself
up entirely to the search of the holy knowledge and love of God, and
a religious state appeared to him that which God pointed out as the
path in which he might attain to the end which he proposed to
himself. Before he made up his mind he prayed earnestly, and
then addressed himself for advice to his uncle, a holy and learned
priest called Marino Querini, who was a secular canon of St George's

chapter, established in a little isle called Alga, a mile from the city of Venice. Don Querini advised him first to make trial of his strength by inuring himself to the habitual practice of austerities. Laurence readily obeyed and in the night left his soft bed to lie on knotty sticks on the floor. During this deliberation he one day represented to himself on one side honours, riches, and worldly pleasures, and on the other the hardships of poverty, fasting, and self-denial. Then he said to himself, " Have you the courage, O my soul, to despise these delights and to undertake a life of uninterrupted penance and mortification ? " After standing some time in consideration, he looked up at a crucifix and said : " Thou, O Lord, art my hope. In this tree are comfort and strength." The strength of his resolution to walk in the narrow path of the cross showed itself in the severity with which he treated his body and the continual application of his mind to the exercises of religion. His mother and other friends, fearing lest his mortifications should damage his health, tried to divert him from that course, and proposed a marriage to him. He replied by retiring to the chapter of St George in Alga, and was admitted to the community.

By the change of his state he found no new austerities which he had not before practised ; his superiors even judged it necessary to mitigate the rigours which he used, for he surpassed in his watchings and fasts all his religious brethren. He went about the streets begging alms with a wallet on his back, and when it was pointed out to him one day that by appearing with his wallet in a public place, he would expose himself to ridicule, he answered : " Let us go boldly in quest of scorn. We have done nothing if we have renounced the world only in words. Let us triumph over it with our sacks and crosses." St Laurence frequently came to beg at the house where he was born, but only stood in the street before the door, crying out : "An alms for God's sake." His mother always filled his wallet, but he never took more than two loaves, and, wishing peace to those who had done him charity, departed as if he had been some stranger. When the storehouse in which were kept the provisions of the community for a year was burnt down, St Laurence, hearing a certain brother lament the loss, said cheerfully : " Why have we vowed poverty ? God has granted us this blessing that we may feel it." When he first renounced the world he often felt a violent inclination to justify or excuse himself upon being unjustly reprehended ; in order to repress it he used to bite his tongue, and so at length obtained a perfect mastery over himself. Whilst he was superior he was one day accused in chapter of having done something against the rule. Laurence could have easily given a satisfactory account of his conduct; but he rose instantly from his seat and, walking into the middle of the chapter-room, fell on his knees and begged pardon of the fathers. The accuser was moved to withdraw his charge and to accuse himself. St Laurence so much dreaded the danger of worldly dissipation that from the day on which he first entered the monastery to that of his death he never set foot in his father's house, except to assist his mother and brothers on their deathbeds. A certain nobleman who had been his intimate friend, returning from the East and hearing of the state he had embraced, determined to try to change his purpose. With this idea he went to St George's with a band of musicians and, on account of his rank, got admittance; but the issue of the interview proved quite contrary to his expectation. Upon the first sight of his old friend he was struck by his modesty, gravity, and composure, and stood for some time silent. However, at length he spoke and endeavoured to shake the resolution of the young religious. Laurence let him finish, and then he spoke in so persuasive a manner on death and the vanity of the world that the nobleman was disarmed and himself resolved upon the spot to embrace the rule which he came to violate.

St Laurence was promoted to the priesthood in 1406, and the fruit of his spirit of prayer and penitence was a wonderful experimental knowledge of spiritual things and of the paths of interior virtue, and great light and prudence in the direction of souls. The tears which he shed whilst he offered the sacrifice of the Mass strongly affected all the assistants and awakened their faith; and he often experienced raptures at prayer, especially in saying Mass one Christmas night. Soon after his ordination he was made prior of St George's, and later was chosen general of his congregation, which he governed with singular prudence. He reformed its discipline in such a manner as to be afterward regarded as its founder, and drew up the constitutions whereby the secular canons became canons regular. He would receive very few novices and these he thoroughly tried, saying that a state of such perfection and obligations is only for the few and that its essential spirit and fervour are scarce to be maintained among large numbers. It is not therefore to be wondered at that he was so attentive and rigorous in examining and trying the vocation of postulants. The most sincere humility was the first thing in which he grounded his religious disciples. Nor was this teaching confined to his canons. He never ceased to preach to the magistrates and senators in time of war and public calamity that to obtain the divine mercy and the remedy of the evils which they suffered they ought in the first place to persuade themselves that they were nothing, for without this disposition of heart they could never deserve the divine assistance.

In 1433 Pope Eugenius IV appointed St Laurence to the bishopric of Castello, a diocese which included part of Venice. He tried hard to avoid this dignity and responsibility, and when he could no longer oppose the repeated orders of the Pope he took possession of his cathedral-church so privately that his own friends knew nothing of the matter till the ceremony was over. As a religious so as a prelate he was admirable for his sincere piety towards God and the greatness of his charity to the poor. He remitted nothing of the austerities which he had practised in the cloister, and from his prayer drew a light, courage, and vigour which directed and animated him in his whole conduct; he pacified violent public dissensions in the state and governed a great diocese in most difficult times with as much ease as if it had been a single well-regulated convent. In the ordering of his household he consulted only piety and humility; and when others told him that he owed some degree of state to his own birth, to the dignity of his church, and to the republic, his answer was that virtue ought to be the only ornament of the episcopal character and that all the poor of the diocese composed the bishop's family. His household consisted only of five persons; he had no plate, making use only of earthenware; he lay on a straw bed covered with a coarse quilt, and wore no fine clothes. He won everyone's heart and effected the most difficult reformations which he introduced both among the laity and clergy. The flock loved and respected so holy and tender a pastor too much not to receive his ordinances with docility and deference. When any private persons opposed his religious reforms he overcame them by meekness and patience. A certain man who was exasperated at a decree the bishop had published against stage entertainments called him a "scrupulous old monk," and tried to stir up the rabble against him. Another time he was reproached in the public streets as a hypocrite. The saint heard these complaints without changing his countenance or altering his pace. He was no less unmoved amidst commendations and applause; and indeed, all his actions demonstrated a constant peace and serenity of mind which no words can express. Under his rule the face of his whole diocese was changed. He founded fifteen religious houses and a number of churches, and reformed others, especially with regard to the devout manner of performing the divine offices and the administration of the sacraments. His cathedral was a model to all Christendom. The number of canons that served it being too small, St Laurence founded several new canonries in it and in other churches; and he increased the number of parishes in the city of Venice from twenty to thirty. Crowds every day resorted to the bishop's palace for advice, comfort, or alms ; his gate and purse were always open to the poor. He gave alms more willingly in bread and clothes than in money, which might be ill spent ; when he gave cash it was always in small sums. He employed married women to find out and relieve the bashful poor or persons of family in decayed circumstances, and in the distribution of his charities he had no regard to flesh and blood. When a poor man came to him, recommended by his brother Leonard, he said to him : " Go to him who sent you, and tell him from me that he is able to relieve you himself." Laurence had a great contempt for finance. He committed the care of his temporals to a steward, and used to say that it is an unworthy thing for a pastor of souls to spend much of his precious time in casting up farthings.

The popes of his time held St Laurence in great veneration. Eugenius IV meeting him once at Bologna, saluted him with the words : " Welcome, ornament of bishops ! " His successor, Nicholas V, equally esteemed him and in 1451 recognised his worth in no uncertain fashion. In that year died Dominic Michelli, Patriarch of Grado,* whereupon the Pope suppressed the see of Castello and transferred that of Grado to Venice, retaining its old title. He named St Laurence as the new patriarch. The senate of the republic, always jealous of its prerogatives and liberty, made difficulties lest his authority should in any cases trespass upon their jurisdiction. Whilst this was being debated in the senate-house, St Laurence asked an audience of the assembly, before which he declared his sincere and earnest desire rather to resign a charge for which he was unfit and which he had borne against his will eighteen years, than to feel his burden increased by this additional dignity. His bearing so strongly affected the whole senate that the Doge himself asked him not to entertain such a thought or to raise any obstacle to the Pope's decree, and he was supported by the whole house. St Laurence therefore accepted the new office and dignity, and for the few years during which he survived to administer it he continually increased the reputation for goodness and charity which he had earned as bishop of Castello. A hermit of Corfu assured a

* There is only one true patriarch in the Latin Church, the Pope himself, who is Patriarch of the West. The title of patriarch borne by the former metropolitans of Grado and Aquileia was due to a sixth-century schism of the metropolitans of Illyricum. It was not till 1751 that the patriarchs of Grado at Venice were named patriarchs of Venice, but St Laurence Giustiniani is usually referred to as first patriarch of Venice. This and the other " minor patriarchs " of the West are actually only archbishops with precedence and other honours.

Venetian nobleman, as if by a divine revelation, that Venice had been preserved from the dangers which threatened it by the prayers of the Patriarch. His nephew, Bernard Giustiniani, who wrote his uncle's life, narrates certain miracles and prophecies of his which he himself witnessed.

St Laurence left some valuable ascetical writings; he was seventy-four years old when he wrote his last work, entitled *The Degrees of Perfection*, and he had just finished it when he was seized with a sharp fever. His servants prepared a bed for him, at which the true imitator of Christ was troubled and said : " Are you making up a feather-bed for me ? No ; that shall not be. My Lord was stretched on a hard and painful tree. Do not you remember that St Martin said in his agony that a Christian ought to die on sackcloth and ashes ? " Nor could he be contented till he was laid on his straw. He forebade his friends to weep for him and cried out in joy : " Behold the Bridegroom ; let us go forth and meet Him," adding, with his eyes lifted up to Heaven : " Good Jesus, behold I come." But when someone said to him that he might go joyfully to his crown, he was disturbed and replied : " The crown is for valiant soldiers, not for cowards such as I." He had no temporal goods to dispose of and made his will only to exhort in it all men to virtue and to order that his body should be buried without pomp, as a simple religious would be, in his convent of St George ; but this clause was set aside by the senate after his death. During the two days that he lived after receiving Extreme Unction many of the city came in turns according to their different rank to receive his blessing. He insisted on having the beggars admitted, and gave to each class a short instruction. Seeing one Marcello, a young nobleman and his favourite disciple, weep most bitterly, he comforted him and assured him that, " I go before, but you will shortly follow. Next Easter we shall meet again." Marcello in fact fell sick at the beginning of Lent, and was buried in Easter-week. St Laurence died on January 8, 1455, but his feast is kept on this date whereon he received episcopal consecration. He was canonised by Pope Alexander VIII in 1690, and his body rests in St Mark's basilica.

With St Laurence Justinian we must first labour strenuously in sanctifying our own souls before we can hope to preach to others with much fruit. Only he who has learned them by experience and whose heart is penetrated with them can inspire in others love of Christian virtue and instruct them in the practical truths of religion. The pastoral obligation is of great extent : it is not confined to those who are charged with the ministry of the word and of the sacraments ; it regards not only pastors of souls ; every king is, in some measure, a pastor to his whole kingdom; and every parent and master to those that are under their care. And he who is not in a qualified sense an apostle or pastor to all that are under his charge will be accountable to God for any harm that may come to their souls on account of his neglect.

There is a Latin Life by his nephew, Bernard Giustiniani, which is reprinted in the *Acta Sanctorum*, January, vol. i, under January 8. Some other materials may be found in D. Rosa, *De B. Laurentii Justiniani vita, sanctitate et miraculis, testimoniorum centuria* (Venice, 1614). There are also several Italian Lives, *e.g.* that of Maffei (1819), Regazzi (1856), and Cucito (1895). See also the *Dictionnaire de Théologie catholique*, vol. ix, cc. 10–11, and Eubel, *Hierarchia catholica Medii Ævi*, vol. ii, pp. 130 and 290.

ST URBAN AND HIS COMPANIONS, MARTS.

A.D. 370

The Roman Martyrology to-day mentions SS. Urban, Theodore, Menedemus, and their seventy-seven companions of ecclesiastical rank put to death at Constantinople. Urban was a leading priest of that city who was put at the head of a clerical deputation sent to Nicomedia to appeal to the Emperor for protection of the orthodox against the persecution and violence of Arian heretics. But Valens was himself an Arian and had no intention of acceding to the request. He put Urban off with temporising words, and shipped the deputation back to Constantinople with secret instructions to the prefect Modestus that they were to be disposed of on the way. Accordingly, when they were some distance from land the sailors set fire to the ship, themselves escaping in the boats which they had ready. The priests who thus perished are venerated as martyrs for the faith in both East and West.

Our knowledge of these martyrs is derived entirely from the Church History of Socrates, book iv, ch. 18. The Constantinople Synaxaries (Ed. Delehaye, cc. 21–22) commemorated them on September 6. But there is also mention of them on May 18, and on that day the martyrdom is discussed in the *Acta Sanctorum*.

ST BERTINUS, ABBOT AND CONF.

c. A.D. 709

This illustrious saint and model of monastic perfection was nobly born in the territory of Constance in Switzerland early in the seventh century. Excited by the example of his kinsman, St Omer (Audomarus), who embraced the monastic state in the great abbey of Luxeuil in Burgundy, he and two companions, SS. Mommolinus and Bertrand, consecrated themselves to God in the same house. Bertinus was then very young, but he distinguished himself in the fervent exercise of virtue among five hundred religious brethren under the direction of the holy abbot Walbertus, who governed that monastery with great distinction after the death of St Eustachius, the immediate successor of St Columbanus, who had established in this abbey an excellent seminary of sacred science which soon furnished many countries with learned and zealous prelates. St Omer, St Mommolinus, and St Bertinus did honour to this school by the progress which they made in their studies, for they all became very learned in ecclesiastical discipline and in the holy Scriptures. St Omer was in 637 sent as a missionary and bishop to Thérouanne, the centre of the half-heathen Morini in Artois, and the Abbot of Luxeuil, understanding how much he stood in need of assistants endowed with the spirit of apostles, sent to him soon after St Bertinus and his two friends.

The country of the Morini had already received the seed of divine faith but only superficially and imperfectly, and had then for almost a whole century been an abandoned field. Great were the fatigues, persecutions, and sufferings of these holy men in rooting out vice and idolatry and in civilising a people who were at that time in a great measure barbarians, but they were tireless in words and works and they reaped by the divine blessing a most abundant harvest. The three missionaries built their first small monastery on a hill on the banks of the river Aa, where is now the village of Saint-Mommolin ; this was afterwards known as the " Old Monastery." The place being very narrow, confined by the river and marshy ground, it soon grew too small for the numbers that came to take the religious habit. Whereupon a convert named Ardwald gave St Omer some land about four miles away upon which another missionary centre might be established. This ground, which was a part of the estate of Sithiu, St Omer bestowed on the missionaries, with instructions that they were to colonise it and start another monastery in accordance with the will of the donor. St Mommolinus as senior was the first abbot of the Old Monastery and probably afterwards of Sithiu. But upon the death of St Giles, Bishop of Noyon, he was chosen to fill that see about the year 659, and taking Bertrand, appointed him abbot of St Quentin's. St Bertinus, who is said to have been chosen head of the original settlement by St Omer and refused because he was the youngest of the three, was left abbot of Sithiu. Under his government the reputation of this monastery (first dedicated in honour of St Peter, but after called St Bertinus) seemed to equal even that of Luxeuil. Rigorous abstinence and fasting was one of the first articles of the discipline established in this house ; the subsistence of one hundred and fifty monks who were here assembled consisted chiefly of root vegetables, herbs, bread and water. They were taught to sanctify by prayer all their exterior employments and the singing of the divine praises was never interrupted in their choir either day or night, the monks succeeding each other in different choirs. The most exacting labour never excused any from this duty, or from any part of their nocturnal watchings. The number of the monks increasing, St Bertinus obtained of St Omer a church which the bishop had built on a hill at a little distance from the monastery, where he established a second abbey. When the bishopric was erected at St Omer, this church, dedicated to God under the patronage of our Lady, was made the cathedral. But during its early days this claustral activity went hand in hand with the evangelising and taming of the Morini and their country, and was a civilising agency characteristic of the monks of the West (it is likely that during the lifetime of Bertinus they still followed the rule of Columbanus, though he is numbered among the Benedictine saints). The country itself was sufficiently bad and discouraging. Even to-day it is depressing in its low-lying wetness : twelve hundred years ago it was undrained and waterlogged. The monks went from Vieux Moutier to take over Sithiu in a boat, and it is not for nothing that a boat is the emblem of St Bertinus in art. The amphibious population was wild and dull of understanding. St Bertinus and his companions brought to them the knowledge of the gospel, the light of learning, and the enterprise and energy which drains land and builds solid houses.

But if he had setbacks and plenty of discouragement to face among these rough people and places, St Bertinus had the comfort of seeing his monastery flourish with illustrious examples of penance and holiness, like to those which had formerly edified the world in the deserts of Egypt. Many renounced the world to pass their life under his direction in the exercise of contemplation, and it is said that in this and succeeding ages his abbey gave to the Church twenty-two known saints. Whatever donations were made to the monastery were only received by Bertinus as the patrimony of the poor, to whose relief he faithfully applied the greatest part of the revenue, very little sufficing for the maintenance of the monks. A certain lord called Heremar, having given him his estate of Wormhoult, the saint erected on it another monastery, dedicated under the patronage of St Martin; and the Breton St Winnoc was appointed by him the first superior of this cell.　Finding himself sinking under the weight of old age, Bertinus resigned in the year 700, in favour of a disciple whose name was Rigobert, that he might close his life in the humble state of obedience and dependence.　From that time he shut himself up in a little hermitage dedicated to the Blessed Virgin, near the cemetery of his monks, where he passed the nights and days in almost perpetual prayer, observing all the exercises of regular discipline with the fidelity and humility of the most fervent novice.　Having a particular devotion to St Martin, he got Rigobert to erect a chapel under the invocation of that saint in the most honourable part of the church.　He died when over a hundred years old, on September 5, 709, and was buried in the chapel of St Martin which Rigobert had built, though it was not completely finished till after his death.　His relics were enshrined in a new tomb in the abbey-church in 1237 and are now in the church of St Denis at Saint-Omer, having been saved from destruction by a wealthy lady at the time of the Revolution.

In the fifth volume of the *Monumenta Germaniæ, Scriptores rerum Merovingicarum* W. Levison has discussed very fully the relative importance and date of the Lives of St Bertinus.　The oldest (early ninth century) is unquestionably that which forms one whole with two other Lives, the one of St Omer (Audomarus), and the other of St Winnoc.　The various sources which have a bearing on the holy abbot's history and *cultus* are catalogued in the *Bibliotheca hagiographica Latina*, nn. 763 and 1290–1298.　The more important texts were already printed in the *Acta Sanctorum*, September, vol. ii, with a full introduction.　See also Van der Essen in *Analectes pour servir à l'hist. ecclés. de Belgique*, xxxii (1905), pp. 6–23.　The representation of St Bertinus in art is dealt with by Künstle, *Ikonographie*, vol. ii, pp. 134–5.

ST ALTO, ABBOT AND CONFESSOR.

c. A.D 760

This saint was a monk, probably an Irishman, who found his way into Germany, and about the year 743 established himself as a hermit in a wood near Augsburg.　The fame of his holiness and missionary labours reached King Pepin, who made him a grant of land where he was living, and on which he founded a monastery at the place now known as Altomünster, in Bavaria.　Its church was dedicated by St Boniface about the year 750.　The abbey followed the Irish mode of life, and St Boniface wanted entirely to interdict the approach of women to its precincts and church in accordance with the strict Celtic custom. To this St Alto would not agree, though he included the well blessed by Boniface within the monks' enclosure. After Alto's time the monastery fell on evil days, but was restored in 1000 as a Benedictine house, and still exists as an abbey of Bridgettine nuns. Nothing further is known of St Alto but in the midst of a barbarous nation, at that time overrun with ignorance, vice, and superstition, his humility and devotion infused into many the perfect spirit of holy religion, and his single life was a sensible demonstration of the power of divine grace in raising vessels of weakness and corruption to the most sublime state of sanctity. He is honoured at Munich on February 9, which seems to have been the day of his death, but the British calendars commemorate him on September 5.

The Life of St Alto, written by Abbot Othlonus in the middle of the eleventh century, is printed in the *Acta Sanctorum* under February 9, but the text has been re-edited in Pertz, *Mon. Germaniæ*, SS., vol. xv, pp. 843–846. See also M. Huber in *Wissenschaft. Festgabe zum Jubilæum des hl. Korbinian* (1924), pp. 14–44 ; and Gougaud, *Gaelic Pioneers of Christianity*, p. 21.

BD. GENTILIS, MART.

A.D. 1340

Was born at the end of the thirteenth century at Matelica, in the Marches, of the noble family of the Finaguerra. He joined the Friars Minor, and after profession and ordination was sent to the convent of Mount Alvernia, where he twice served as guardian. The associations of this place had a strong effect on Gentilis and bred in him a great love of silence and solitude ; but at the same time they fired him with St Francis's own ambition to evangelise the East and Islam. He was eventually sent to Egypt, where he found he could do nothing because not only did he not know Arabic but all his efforts to learn it were without fruit. He was about to return home in despair, but in consequence of a dream or vision persevered and at length overcame his difficulties. He fell in with a Venetian ambassador to the court of Persia, Mark Comaro, who asked the friar to accompany him across Arabia ; while on the journey he tended Comaro in a dangerous illness, and prophesied that he would live to be doge of the Republic. Together they visited the shrine of St Catherine of Alexandria in the desert of Sinai, a great resort of Christian pilgrims in spite of its inaccessible situation. One day Bd. Gentilis disappeared mysteriously for a week, and on his return it was said that he had been miraculously transported to Italy and back to assist at the death-bed of his father in accordance with a promise he had made him.   Arrived in Persia, he preached throughout that country northward as far as Trebizond, and is said to have baptised more than ten thousand converts.   He was put to death for the Faith at Toringa, but the circumstances of his martyrdom are not known.   His body was brought back to Europe by some Venetians and is buried in the church of the *Frari*, at Venice.   The *cultus* of Bd. Gentilis was approved by Pope St Pius V.

Besides Wadding's *Annales, sub anno* 1340 ; consult Mazara, *Leggendario Francescano*, ii, 1, pp. 409–411, and Marcellino de Civezza, *Missions franciscaines*, vol. iii, p. 650.   A short account is also given in Léon, *Auréole Séraphique* (Eng. Trans.), vol. iii, pp. 109–112.

SEPTEMBER 6

SS. DONATIANUS AND OTHERS AND ST LAETUS,
BISHOPS AND MARTYRS

c. A.D. 484

IN the year 484 the Arian king of the Vandals, Huneric, called a conference at Carthage between the Catholic and the Arian bishops, of which the upshot was that all the Catholic churches of Africa were to be closed and the goods and possessions of the clergy to be taken from them and given to the Arian clergy; the bishops, in particular, who had assembled at the royal command were turned out of the city. Outside of the gates Huneric met a party of them, who appealed against his injustice and cruelty. " Ride them down ! " he said to his mounted followers, and that was all the answer he vouchsafed. Shortly after the bishops were called on to take an oath that on Huneric's death they would support his son Hilderic. Most of them, fearing that he also would turn out to be an Arian and a persecutor, refused, and were sentenced to banishment. Among them were SS. Donatianus, Praesidius, Mansuetus, Germanus, and Fusculus, all bishops in the province of Byzacene. They were cruelly beaten, and then driven into the desert, and died of hunger, thirst, and exposure. St Laetus, Bishop of Leptis Minor, whom the Roman Martyrology calls " a zealous and very learned man," had made himself particularly obnoxious to Huneric by his opposition to Arianism. He therefore was thrown into a filthy dungeon, from which he only emerged to be burnt alive, one of the first martyrs of the persecution. The feast of these martyrs, with St Laetus in chief, is kept by the Canons Regular of the Lateran.

See the *Acta Sanctorum*, September, vol. ii, where we are referred to the *Historia Persecutionis Provinciae Africanae* by Victor of Vita, but it is difficult to identify the particular names set down in the martyrology.

ST ELEUTHERIUS, ABBOT AND CONF.
END OF THE SIXTH CENTURY

" The holy man, old father Eleutherius," is spoken of several times in the *Dialogues* of St Gregory, wherein are chronicled certain miracles reported of him by his monks. He was abbot of the monastery of St Mark, near Spoleto, and once when lodging at a convent of nuns he was asked to take over the care of a boy who was nightly troubled by an evil spirit. St Eleutherius did so, and for long nothing untoward happened to the boy, so that the abbot said : " The Devil was having a game with those sisters ; but now that he has to deal with the servants of God he daren't come near the child." As if in rebuke of a speech that certainly savoured of boasting, the boy was at once afflicted by his former trouble. Eleutherius was conscience-stricken, and said to the brethren that stood by : " None of us shall eat food to-day until this boy is dispossessed." All fell to prayer, and did not cease until the child was cured.

One Holy Saturday St Gregory was ill and could not fast, whereat, he tells us, he was considerably disturbed. " When I found on this sacred vigil, when not only adults but even children fast, that I could not refrain from eating, I was more grieved thereby than troubled by my illness." So he asked Eleutherius to pray for him that he might join the people in their penance, and soon by virtue of that prayer Gregory found himself enabled to abstain from food. St Eleutherius lived for many years in St Gregory's monastery at Rome, and died there. His body was afterwards translated to Spoleto. His raising of a dead man to life is mentioned in the Roman Martyrology.

The immediate contrition of St Eleutherius for his fault of the tongue which gave expression to vanity puts us in mind of the urgent words of St Cyprian addressed to all sinners : " Let every one of you make humble and solemn confession of his sins whilst he is yet in the world, whilst his confession can be admitted, whilst his satisfaction and the pardon given him by the priest are available with God." This is not to be obtained without lamentation and sorrow and without renouncing idle pleasures ; if we mourn for a friend that was dead, how much more ought we to do it for their souls ? " You have lost your soul," says he ; " you are dead to all spiritual purposes ; you survive this loss ; and will you not lament and mourn ? Will you not hide yourself for a time from company and diversions ? They are fresh aggravations of your guilt. Penance is left as the only remedy. They who would represent this as needless

67

make the case incurable and hopeless. Whilst persons rashly trust to salvation against the terms of the gospel, there is no hope of it upon any reasonable grounds. Let us then mourn and weep in proportion to the greatness of our sin ; as the wound is large and deep, let our care of it be according ; let not the severity of our penance fall short of the heinousness of our guilt. . . . God can pardon His humble supplicants, His sincere penitents, such as bring forth fruits meet for repentance. He can make available whatever either the martyrs shall ask or the bishop and ministers of His Church shall do on their behalf. Thus the soldier of Christ will rally his broken forces, fight with the more ardour and courage and, being inspired with greater constancy and firmness from an humble remembrance and sense of his sin, he will draw upon himself the divine assistance, and contribute as much to the joy and triumph of the Church, as he had done to her dejection and grief."

We know practically nothing more about St Eleutherius than St Gregory tells us in his Dialogues, notably in book 3, ch. 33 ; but the story is discussed by the Bollandists in the *Acta Sanctorum,* September, vol. ii.

ST CHAINOALDUS, Bp. of Laon, Conf.

A.D. 633

This saint, commonly called Cagnoald or Cagnou in France, is of interest chiefly on account of his association with St Columbanus, who stayed at the house of his father, Agnericus, Count of Meaux, and made a deep impression on Chainoaldus and on his brother and sister, Faro and Burgondofara, all of whom followed him in holiness. He became a monk at Luxeuil, and when St Columbanus was banished by Queen Brunehild followed his master in all his wanderings and helped him in his preaching and ministry. The strife going on at the time between Theodebertus II of Austrasia and his brother Theodericus gave Columbanus an occasion to read a lesson in charity to his disciple. He dreamed one day that he saw the two brothers fighting together, and when he awoke told Chainoaldus sadly of what he had seen. "Pray then, father, that Theodebertus may beat our enemy Theodericus," observed Chainoaldus, whose father was at the Austrasian court. "Not at all," replied Columbanus. "Such prayer would not be pleasing to God, for He tells us to pray for our enemies." Chainoaldus helped in the foundation of the abbey of Bobbio, and after the death of St Columbanus returned to Luxeuil, where St Eustace was then abbot. Eustace soon after had occasion to visit the home of St Chainoaldus, when he cured St Burgundofara of a sickness and obtained her father's permission that she should become a nun. She was therefore clothed by her brother St Faro, Bishop of Meaux, and proceeded to the establishment of the abbey of Faremoutier. In this she had the help of St Chainoaldus, and as the monastery was a double one he was superior of the monks. He became bishop of Laon, was present at the Council of Reims of the year 630, and signed the charter of the abbey of Solignac, which was founded by St Eligius while he was still a layman. St Chainoaldus died by a stroke of apoplexy on August 23, 633 ; his feast is kept on this date at Meaux and Soissons.

Though there is no proper Life of this saint, his activities and *cultus* are discussed at some length in the *Acta Sanctorum*, September, vol. ii. See also Duchesne, *Fastes Épiscopaux*, vol. iii, p. 139.

BD. BERTRAND OF GARRIGA, Conf.

A.D 1230

At the end of the twelfth and the beginning of the thirteenth centuries the south of France was ravaged by heresy and civil war. Albigensianism, supported by the nobles and appealing to the people by offering a life of virtuous austerity to the few and of licence to the many, had almost complete control ; the Catholics, rendered impotent by indifference and ill living, took up arms against the heretics, and the challenge was accepted. Bd. Bertrand was born at Garrigues in the Comtat Venaissin and brought up in the midst of these disturbances. Garrigues was on the estate of the Cistercian nuns of Bosquet, and from them he had his first lessons, was taught the true Faith, and learned the dangers of the heresy that flourished all around them. In the year 1200 the Albigensian Raymund VI of Toulouse marched through Languedoc, harrying the orthodox monasteries, especially those of the Cistercians, who were the official missionaries against the heretics, and the Bosquet nuns fled before him. It is said that the empty convent was saved from destruction by the prompt action of a bee-master, who overturned his rows of hives in the faces of the soldiers. Bertrand himself became a priest and joined himself as a preacher to the Cistercian mission, working in the Midi against the heretics. In 1208 the Cistercian legate, Peter de Castelnau, was murdered, the crusade of Simon de Montfort was let loose, and soon after this time probably Bd. Bertrand first met St Dominic, who was trying to remedy by prayer and preaching some of the harm that his friend Simon was doing by the sword. In 1215 he was one of the group of six preachers gathered round Dominic from which sprang the great order of Friars Preachers ; by the following year they had increased to sixteen, " all in fact and in name excellent preachers," when they met at Prouille to choose a rule and plan the life of their new society. After a year of community life at the priory of St Romanus in Toulouse, the founder made his famous bold stroke of dispersing his religious, and Bd. Bertrand was sent to Paris with Friar Matthew of France and five others. There they made a foundation near the university. But Bd. Bertrand did not stay long in Paris. He was called by St Dominic to Rome and sent thence with Friar John of Navarre to establish the order in Bologna, at the church of Santa Maria della Mascarella. Though Bd. Reginald of Orleans was the friend who influenced him most, early Dominican writers speak of Bd. Bertrand as a beloved companion of St Dominic, the dearest associate in his work, the sharer of his journeys, his prayers, and his holiness. In 1219 he accompanied him on the only visit St Dominic made to Paris ; they went from Toulouse by way of the sanctuary of Rocamadour, and the journey has been surrounded with wonders, such as that they understood German without having learnt it and were not wetted by heavy rain.

At the second general chapter held at Bologna in 1221 the Dominican order was divided into eight provinces, and Bertrand, who had been governing the house at Toulouse, was appointed prior provincial of Provence. The remaining nine years of his life were spent in energetic preaching throughout the south of France, where he greatly extended the activities of his order and founded the great priory of Marseilles. There is a story told that on one occasion a Friar Benedict questioned Bd. Bertrand because he so rarely celebrated a requiem Mass. " We are certain of the salvation of the holy souls," was the reply, " but of the end of ourselves and other sinners we are not certain." " Well, but," persisted Friar Benedict, " suppose there are two beggars, one strong and well, the other disabled. Which would you be the more sorry for ? " " The one who can do least for himself." " Very well then. Such certainly are the dead. They have neither mouths wherewith to confess nor hands wherewith to work, but living sinners have both and can take care of themselves." Bertrand was not at all convinced by this argument, and the fact that he afterwards celebrated Mass more frequently for the dead was attributed to his having had enlightenment in the form of a nightmare of a departed soul, which much distressed him. Bd. Bertrand died where he had passed his earliest years, at the Abbey of Bosquet, in 1230, and when his body was translated twenty-three years later to Orange it was found to be incorrupt. " By his watchings, his fasts, and his other penances," wrote Friar Bernard Guidonis, the inquisitor and historian, " he succeeded in making himself so like his beloved Father that one might have said of him as he passed by : Of a truth the disciple is like the master ; there goes the very image of the blessed Dominic."

A very full account of Bd. Bertrand is given by the Bollandists in the *Acta Sanctorum*, October, vol. xiii, pp. 136–145 and 919–921. Though there was no separate early biography which they could utilise, they at first drew largely from the *Vitæ Fratrum* of Gerard de Fracheto and other Dominican chronicles, but in a supplement to their first account they have added many details from documents submitted to the Congregation of Rites in the process for the *confirmatio cultus* which was accorded in 1881. See also a series of papers by J. P. Isnard in the *Bulletin de la Société archéol. de Drôme*, 1870 to 1872 ; and Procter, *Dominican Saints*, pp. 253–256. A fuller bibliography is provided by Taurisano, *Catalogus hagiographicus O.P.*, p. 9.

SEPTEMBER 7

ST REGINA or REINE, Virg. and Mart.
Third Century (?)

OF St Regina, mentioned in the Roman Martyrology as having been martyred in the territory of Autun, the true history is not known. French legends represent her as the daughter of Clemens, a pagan citizen of Alise, in Burgundy. Her mother died at the child's birth, and Regina was handed over to the care of a Christian woman, who brought her up in the Faith. When Clemens discovered this, he refused to receive his daughter, and she went back to live with her nurse, earning her bread as a shepherdess. She attracted the desire of the prefect Olybrius who, when her good birth was told to him, wanted to marry her. Regina refused him, nor would she listen to the persuasions of her father who, now that his daughter had attracted a distinguished suitor, was willing to own her. She was therefore locked up in a dungeon, and when her spirit remained unbroken Olybrius vented his rage by having her cruelly tortured. That night she was consoled in her prison by a vision of the cross and a voice telling her that her release was at hand. The next day Olybrius ordered her to be tortured again and then that she should be beheaded ; the appearance of a shining dove hovering over her converted many of the onlookers. In the year 864 the relics of St Regina were translated to the abbey of Flavigny ; a part of them are still venerated at Alise-Sainte-Reine where she suffered.

No trust can be placed in what purports to be the *Passio* of St Regina (printed in the *Acta Sanctorum*, September, vol. iii) ; but the *cultus* is certainly early, as is vouched for by the fact of the inclusion of her name in the " Hieronymianum." The foundations of a basilica dedicated in her honour at Alise have been discovered in comparatively recent times ; see *e.g.* J. Toutain in *Bulletin archéologique du Comité des Travaux historiques*, 1914, pp. 365-387. The legend has been set out at length, with pictorial illustrations by Fr. Grignard, *La Vie de Ste Reine d'Alise*, Dijon, 1881 ; and by Quillot, *Ste Reine d'Alise*, Citeaux, 1881.

ST GRIMONIA, Virg. and Mart.
Fourth Century (?)

A French legend relates that St Grimonia was the daughter of a pagan Irish chief, and that when she was twelve years old she was converted to Christianity and made a vow of perpetual virginity. Her father, in defiance of or not understanding such a vow, wished her to marry, and when she refused shut her up. Grimonia escaped and fled to France (the legend says she was delivered by angels, and while on shipboard calmed a storm by her prayers), where she became a solitary in the forest of Thiérache in Picardy. Here the contemplation of the beauty of created things would often bring her to the state of ecstasy. After a prolonged search the messengers of her father traced her to her retreat, where they put before her the alternatives of return and a forced marriage or death. Grimonia remained firm and so she was beheaded on April 20 in an unknown year. A chapel was built over her grave which became famous for miracles, and around it grew up a town, called from its origin La Chapelle. On September 7, 1231, her relics, together with those of St Proba (Preuve), another Irishwoman who is supposed to have suffered with Grimonia, were enshrined at Lesquielles and in 1540 translated to the abbey of canons regular at Henin-Liétard, near Douai. The facts about St Grimonia are hard to come by : she may have been a solitary from Ireland who lost her life in defending her chastity.

What little is known concerning this saint and her *cultus* may be read in the *Acta Sanctorum*, September, vol. iii.

ST JOHN OF NICOMEDIA, Mart.
A.D. 303

When the edict of the Emperor Diocletian against the Christians was published in Nicomedia a certain Christian, " a man of secular dignity," at once tore it down and was punished by death. The name of this man is not known, but his memory is venerated in the Western Church under the name of " John." The Roman Martyrology says that " when he saw the cruel decrees against the Christians displayed in the forum he was fired with zeal for the faith and pulled them down and tore them up with his own hands. When this was told to the Emperors, Diocletian and Maximian, who were

residing in the city, they ordered that all kinds of sufferings should
be inflicted on him. This most noble man endured them with such
readiness both of demeanour and spirit that they seemed not at all
to disturb him." He was burnt alive, on February 24, 303, according to Lactantius. The unknown man whom we call John has
sometimes been erroneously identified with St George the Martyr,
protector of England. The Greeks call him Eleutherius, and seem
to have confused him with the St Eleutherius, martyr, of August 4,
who was *vir ex ordine senatorio.*

Eusebius in his *Ecclesiastical History* (book viii, ch. 3), and also Lactantius, almost certainly make reference to the fate of this martyr, though
they do not actually name him. The passages are quoted and commented on
in the *Acta Sanctorum*, September, vol. iii. We find the name John given,
and the commemoration assigned to this day, in the so-called " Parvum
Romanum." See Quentin, *Martyrologes historiques*, p. 439.

ST ANASTASIUS THE FULLER, Mart.

A.D. 304

The Roman Martyrology refers to-day to the passion " of the
holy Anastasius the martyr at Aquileia," though the martyr indicated did not suffer on this date nor at Aquileia. It would appear
that vij Idus Septembris has been copied for vij Kalendas Septembris, *i.e.* August 26, the day given in earlier martyrologies and on
which his feast is still kept at Spalato. Anastasius was born at
Aquileia of a good family, but remembering the word of the Apostle
to the Thessalonians, " that you do your own business and work
with your own hands," he became a fuller and practised his trade
at Salona in Dalmatia. During the persecution of Diocletian he
would not conceal his faith, but boldly painted up a cross on his
door, wherefore he was arrested and brought before the governor.
He stood firm, and was therefore thrown into the sea with a stone
tied round his neck. A matron of the city, Asclepia, promised their
liberty to any of her slaves who should recover the body, and they
eventually came upon it in the hands of some negroes who had found
it in the water. They threatened the negroes that if they did not
give it up they would be charged with having murdered the man,
and so brought the body back in triumph to their mistress. She
buried it honourably in her garden, which later became a Christian
cemetery with a great basilica. When Salona was destroyed by the
Avars in the seventh century the relics of St Anastasius were translated, and have been claimed both by Rome and by Spalato ; those

transferred under Pope John IV were buried in the chapel of St Venantius in the Lateran basilica.   The St Anastasius, martyr at Salona, named in the Roman Martyrology on August 21 is an invention of hagiographers, though attempts have been made to identify him with St Anastasius the Fuller.

See what has been said in the August volume of this series, p. 259, and *cf.* the *Analecta Bollandiana*, vols. xvi (1897), pp. 488–500 and xxiii (1904), p. 14.

ST SOZON, Mart.

A.D. 304

This was a young shepherd of Cilicia ; he was originally called Tarasius and took the name of Sozon at baptism.   One day while sleeping under a tree our Lord appeared to him, told him to lay aside his weapons, and to follow Him to death.   Sozon awoke and at once made his way to the nearest town, Pompeiopolis, where he found a pagan festival was being celebrated.   He went straight into the temple of the god and with a mighty blow of his crook knocked down the golden image and broke off its hand.   This hand he took and broke into further small pieces, which he distributed as alms among the poor.   Several innocent persons were arrested for this, whereupon Sozon marched into court and gave himself up as the true culprit.   He was offered pardon and freedom if he would worship the god whose statue he had mutilated, but Sozon mocked at the idea of worshipping a god that could be broken by a sheep-crook.   Nails were then driven, points upward, through the soles of his sandals and he was made thus to walk around the arena.   As Sozon passed before the magistrate he pointed at his blood-stained feet and said : " I have finer red shoes than you."   " You are a brave fellow," said the magistrate.   " Play a tune on your pipe and I will let you go."   But Sozon refused, saying that he had often piped to his sheep but would now make music only to God.   So he was sentenced to be burned, and when night had come the Christians of the place collected his charred bones and gave them honourable burial.

Two Greek texts preserve the alleged " Acts " of this martyr.   One has been edited in the *Acta Sanctorum*, September, vol. iii ; the other in vol. cxv of the Greek Patrology of Migne.   *Cf.* Delehaye, *Origines*, p. 266.

ST CLODOALDUS, OR CLOUD, CONF.

c. A.D. 560

On the death of Clovis, King of the Franks, in the year 511 his kingdom was divided between his four sons, of whom the second, Clodomir, inherited Orléans. Thirteen years later he was killed fighting against his cousin, Gondomar, King of Burgundy (he had first murdered St Sigismund of Burgundy, whom the Roman Martyrology calls a martyr), leaving three sons to share his dominions. The youngest of these sons of Clodomir was St Clodoaldus, a name more familiar to English people under its French form of Cloud from the town of Saint-Cloud near Versailles. The three boys were brought up by their grandmother St Clotildis, widow of Clovis, who lavished much care and affection on them in her home at Paris, while their kingdom of Orléans was administered by the King of Paris, their uncle Childebert. When Cloud was eight years old, Childebert entered into a plot with his brother, Clotaire of Soissons, to get rid of these youths and partition their kingdom. A rumour was spread that Childebert was about to give an account of his stewardship and hand over Orléans to its rightful sovereigns, and on the strength of this they were removed from the custody of their grandmother. According to French tradition Arcadius, a familiar of Childebert, was sent to Clotildis asking her to choose whether the three boys should be put to death or forcibly tonsured and shut up in monasteries. Arcadius so twisted the reply of the distracted queen that she was made to appear to choose their death, whereupon Clotaire seized the eldest boy, Theodoaldus, and stabbed him through the lungs. The second, Gunther, fled in terror to uncle Childebert, whose heart was so softened by fear and sickened at the brutal killing that he tried to protect him. But Clotaire did not approve of such faintheartedness, dragged Gunther from Childebert's arms and killed him too. Cloud either was spared or was rescued or escaped, and was taken for safety into Provence. St Clotildis buried the bodies of Theodoaldus and Gunther with great solemnity in what is now the church of St Geneviève, and, broken-hearted at their loss, took refuge from the barbarity of her sons at Tours.

Childebert and Clotaire shared the fruits of their crime and Cloud made no attempt to recover his kingdom when he came of age. He had seen quite enough of the politics of the world, and voluntarily hid himself in a hermit's cell. After some time he put himself under the discipline of St Severinus, a recluse who lived near Paris, from whose hands he received the monastic habit. Under this experienced master the fervent novice made great progress in Christian perfection, and at the request of the people he was ordained priest by Eusebius, Bishop of Paris, about 551 and served that church in the sacred ministry.   He afterwards went to Novigentum (Nogent on the Seine), and built a monastery, dependent on the church of Paris, where is now Saint-Cloud.   His uncles approved and encouraged these unthreatening activities of their nephew, and in this monastery he assembled many men who fled out of the world for fear of losing their souls in it.   St Cloud was regarded by them as their leader, and he animated them to virtue both by word and example, and all his means he bestowed on churches or distributed among the poor.   St Cloud was indefatigable in instructing the people of the neighbouring country, and ended his days at Nogent about the year 560, when he was only thirty-six years old.   By a pun on his name St Cloud is venerated in France as the patron of nail-makers.

Pico della Mirandola, that ornament of his age and country, who after his conversion from the love of success and pleasure had lived as a truly Christian philosopher, expresses himself thus on the happiness of retirement and contempt of the world : " Many think it a man's greatest happiness in this life to enjoy dignity and power and to live amid the riches and splendour of a court.   Of these you know I have had a share ; and I can assure you I could never find in my soul true satisfaction in anything but retreat and contemplation.   I am persuaded that the Cæsars, if they could speak from their sepulchres, would declare Pico more happy in his solitude than they were in the government of the world ; and if the dead could return, they would choose the pangs of a second death rather than risk their salvation again in public offices."

There is a Life which has been critically edited by B. Krusch in *Monumenta Germaniæ, Scriptores rer. Meroving.*, vol. ii, pp. 350–357, as also at an earlier date by Mabillon and the Bollandists. But as the Life is pronounced to be not older than the close of the ninth century, the data provided by St Gregory of Tours and reproduced in the *Acta Sanctorum* are more trustworthy. A modern, but uncritical, booklet is that of J. Legrand, *Saint Cloud, prince, moine, prêtre,* 1922.

SS. ALCMUND AND TILBERT, Bps. of Hexham, Confs.

A.D. 781 AND 789

No details are known of the lives of these holy bishops, respectively the seventh and eighth occupants of the see of Hexham.

St Alcmund succeeded to St Frithebert in the year 767, and at his death was buried beside St Acca in the cemetery outside the cathedral-church. During the Danish raids all trace and memory of his grave were lost, but about the year 1032 it is said that the saint appeared in a vision to a man of Hexham, pointed out the place where his body lay, and asked him to tell the sacristan of the church of Durham to have it translated to a more honourable resting-place within the cathedral. This was accordingly done. Tradition says that during the translation the Durham monk, Alured, secretly abstracted one of Alcmund's bones to take back to his own church ; but the coffin became so weighty that it was found impossible to move it—until Alured restored the stolen relic. Alban Butler includes St Tilbert with St Alcmund on this day, but the chronicler Simeon of Durham records the date of his death as October 2. In the year 1154 the relics of all the six saints among the twelve early bishops of Hexham, which had then ceased to exist as a bishopric owing to the disorders of the times, were collected into one shrine ; they were finally and completely scattered by the Scots when they raided Hexham and pillaged the canons' church in 1296.

For historical details consult the volumes of the younger James Raine, *The Priory of Hexham* (Surtees Society) 1864–5. Here, as in the *Acta Sanctorum*, September, vol. iii, extracts are given from Simeon of Durham and Aelred. See also Stanton, *English Menology*, p. 438.

BB. JOHN DUCKETT AND RALPH CORBY, MARTS.

A.D. 1644

The north country family of Duckett had already given one martyr to the Church in the person of Blessed James Duckett, a layman who had been hanged at Tyburn in 1602 for publishing Catholic books. He had a son who became prior of the English Carthusians at Nieuport in Flanders. Whether the James Duckett who fathered Blessed John was another son is not certain ; but Blessed John was related to Blessed James in some way. He was born at Underwinter in the parish of Sedbergh in the west riding of Yorkshire in the year 1613, presumably was brought up a Catholic, went to the English College at Douay, and was made priest there in 1639. He then studied for three years in the College of Arras at Paris, where the long periods he passed in prayer were commented on and he was rumoured to have gifts of contemplation of a high order. When he was at length sent to the English mission he passed

78

two months of preparatory retreat with the Carthusians at Nieuport, under the direction of Father Duckett, whom Bishop Challoner refers to as his kinsman but does not specify to have been his uncle. When he had ministered in the county palatine of Durham for about twelve months he was arrested while on his way to baptise two children, on July 2, 1644, the day on which the battle of Marston Moor was fought, together with two laymen.   Mr. Duckett was examined before a parliamentary committee of sequestrators at Sunderland, and refused to admit that he was a priest, demanding to see their proofs.   The holy oils and *Rituale* found on him were pretty clear evidence, but the examiners wanted a personal admission, so they put him in irons and threatened to torture him with lighted matches between his fingers.   When he heard that the two laymen were being questioned and that inquiries were to be made among his friends and associates, he decided he must save them from the possibility of their implicating themselves, and therefore confessed his priesthood.   Thereupon he was sent up to London, together with a Jesuit, Father Corby, who had been seized when about to say Mass at Hamsterley, near Newcastle.

Ralph Corby (*vere* Corbington) came of a Durham family, but was born in Dublin in 1598.   When Ralph was five his parents returned to England, and after years of persecution every member of the family entered religion.   The father, Gerard Corbington, became a temporal coadjutor with the Jesuits and reconciled to the Church his own father when he was a hundred years old.   The mother, Isabel Richardson, died a Benedictine at Ghent, and two surviving daughters joined the same order at Brussels, while Ralph's elder and younger brothers also were Jesuits.   He himself was educated at St Omer, Seville, and Valladolid, joined the Society of Jesus at Watten in Flanders, and came on the mission in 1632. " His missionary labours were employed among the poorer sort of Catholics in the bishopric of Durham, where he travelled much, winter and summer, day and night, and generally on foot, to instruct, comfort, and administer the sacraments to a persecuted people, scattered here and there in the villages of that country, and this for the space of twelve years, suffering very much all the while from a bad state of health, and meeting with very indifferent accommodations both as to lodging and diet from his country hosts, whose hearts nevertheless he had gained in such manner by his virtue and charity, that they loved him as their father and reverenced him as an apostle " (Challoner).

On their arrival in London the two confessors were committed to Newgate to await the September sessions.   There was no doubt what the upshot would be, and the English Jesuits abroad were making feverish efforts in concert with the imperial *chargé d'affaires* in London to get Father Corby exchanged for a Scots colonel who was held prisoner in Germany by the Emperor. When it seemed as if this would be successful, Father Corby offered the reprieve to Mr. Duckett. To which he replied : " This thing is being procured and arranged by your friends. Be you therefore pleased to accept it." Corby disclaimed it—Mr. Duckett was younger and better qualified for service on the mission than himself. And thus it was " handed to and fro between them, neither being willing to accept of it, till an expedient was proposed to save them both ; but it succeeded not, for the Parliament, it seems, was resolved they both should suffer." At the trial they both pleaded guilty to being priests, but Father Corby claimed that as he was born in Ireland he did not come within the statute. This plea was overruled (quite properly) and sentence of death was pronounced. The day before the execution they were visited by many Catholics both English and foreign. The Duchess of Guise posted from Dover on purpose to spend the night in watching and prayer with the martyrs. Mr. Duckett excused himself from hearing her confession, doubtless an effect of that humility which others noted in him, for his plea that he had already forgotten his French is hardly convincing. Father Corby supplied the office and administered the holy Eucharist, both to her and to the French envoy, who came with many others to assist at these last Masses in their Newgate lodging. While he was celebrating, Father Corby " appeared to be as it were in an agony of sadness and fear," but the trial passed, and at ten o'clock in the morning of September 7, 1644, they both set out on the journey to Tyburn, " with their crowns shaved, in their cassocks, and with a smiling look." Mr. Duckett spoke little but to give his blessing to the many who asked it and to say to the Protestant minister that would address him : " Sir, I come not hither to be taught my faith but to die for the profession of it." Blessed Ralph made a short speech, they most-lovingly embraced one another, and the cart was drawn away : nor would the sheriff allow them to be cut down and disembowelled before they were both dead. He took extraordinary precautions to prevent any relics of the martyrs escaping the flames, nevertheless a hand of Blessed John and some pieces of their cassocks were saved ; and in the archives of the diocese of Westminster there is treasured a letter written by Blessed John on the eve of his passion to Dr. Richard Smith, titular Bishop of Chalcedon and vicar apostolic of England, who was then living in Paris. " I fear not death," he writes, " nor I contemn not life. If life were my lot, I would endure it patiently ; but if death, I shall receive it joyfully, for that Christ is my life and death is my gain." These martyrs were among those beatified by Pope Pius XI in the centenary year of Catholic emancipation in England, 1929.

See Challoner, *Memoirs of Missionary Priests* (Ed. Pollen), pp. 457–466 ; Foley, *Records of the English Province S.J.*, vol. iii, pp. 68–96 ; Stanton's *Menology*, pp. 438–440 ; and the pamphlet of Dom Bede Camm, *A North-Country Martyr.*

SEPTEMBER 8

THE BIRTHDAY OF THE BLESSED VIRGIN MARY

THE birth of the Blessed Virgin Mary announced joy and the near approach of salvation to the lost world, and so this festival is celebrated by the Church with praise and thanksgiving. It was a mystery of sanctity, distinguished by unique privileges. Mary was brought forth into the world unlike other children of Adam : not deprived of sanctifying grace and prone to sin, but pure, holy, beautiful, and glorious, adorned with all the most precious graces becoming her who was chosen to be the Mother of God. She appeared, indeed, in the weak state of our mortality ; but in the eyes of Heaven she already transcended the highest seraph in purity, brightness, and grace ; " I am black but beautiful, O ye daughters of Jerusalem." The Spouse says to her even more emphatically than to other souls sanctified by His grace : " As the lily among thorns, so is my love among the daughters. . . . Thou art all fair, O my love, and there is not a spot in thee." Man was no sooner fallen in Paradise through the woman seduced by the infernal spirit but God promised another woman whose seed should crush that spirit's head. " I will put enmities," said He to the Serpent, " between thee and the woman, and thy seed and her seed : she shall crush thy head, and thou shalt lie in wait for her heel." At the birth of the Virgin Mary was the accomplishment of this prediction begun.

" Let the life and virginity of Mary," says St Ambrose, " be set before you as in a looking-glass, in which is seen the pattern of chastity and virtue. The first spur to imitation is the nobility of the master. What more noble than the Mother of God ! She was a maiden in body and mind, whose candour was incapable of deceit or disguise ; humble in heart, grave in words, wise in her resolutions. She spoke seldom and little ; read assiduously, and put her confidence not in inconstant riches but in the prayers of the poor. Being always employed with energy, she would have no other witness of her heart but God alone, to whom she referred herself and all things she did or possessed. She injured no one, was beneficent to all, honoured her superiors, envied not equals, shunned vainglory, followed reason, ardently loved virtue. Her looks were sweet, her discourse demure, her behaviour modest. Her actions had nothing unbecoming, her bearing nothing of levity, her voice nothing of overbearing assurance. Outwardly all was so well regulated that in her body was seen a picture of her mind, a model of all virtue." Yet this sanctity of Mary, the admiration of the highest heavenly spirits, consisted chiefly in ordinary actions and in the purity of heart and the fervour with which she performed them.

From her therefore we learn that our spiritual perfection is to be sought in our own state and depends very much upon the manner in which we perform our ordinary actions. True virtue loves to do all things in silence and with as little show and noise as may be ; to avoid whatever would recommend it to the eyes of men, desiring to have no other witness than Him who is its rewarder and whose glory alone it seeks. A virtue which wants a trumpet to proclaim it, or which affects only public, singular, or extraordinary actions, is to be suspected of subtle pride, vanity, and self-love.

To study these lessons in the life of Mary, to praise God for the graces which He has conferred upon her and the blessings which through her He has bestowed on the world, and to recommend our necessities to so powerful an advocate, we celebrate festivals in her honour. This of her birthday has been kept in the Church with solemnity since at least the sixth century, though it was not known at Rome till the seventh, and was not general in the West till the tenth. The birthplace of our Lady is unknown. An ancient tradition favours Nazareth and this was accepted in the West, but a parallel tradition named Jerusalem and specifically the neighbourhood of the Pool of Bethesda, where a crypt under the Crusaders' church of St Anne is now venerated as the spot where the Mother of God was herself born.

We know for certain that Pope Sergius (A.D. 687–701) ordered that four separate feasts of our Blessed Lady should be kept in Rome—to wit, the Annunciation, the Assumption, the Nativity, and the " Hypapante " (*i.e.* the Purification). But there is much probability that in certain other parts of the West, the Nativity was commemorated earlier. It is clearly entered in the Calendar of St Willibrord (*c.* 704), and the mention in the Auxerre *Hieronymianum* (*c.* 600) and in the *Félire* of Oengus is suggestive of a higher antiquity. What strongly supports this view is the fact that a feast of the Nativity of St John the Baptist was known in the time of St Augustine, probably as early as A.D. 401. See Dom G. Morin in the *Revue Bénédictine*, v (1888), pp. 257–264 ; vii (1890), pp. 260–270 ; xix (1912), pp. 469–470. It was inevitable that when people realised that the Decollation of the Baptist and his Nativity were honoured by two separate celebrations, the idea would suggest itself that the birth of the Mother of God ought to be similarly commemorated. Hence to the feast of the Assumption, or " Falling Asleep," was added that of the Nativity. A feast of the Conception of St John the

Baptist can also be traced as far back as A.D. 600 in the *Hieronymianum*, and it is probable that this in time gave rise in like manner to a commemoration of the Conception of the Blessed Virgin, which seems to meet us first in the *Félire* of Oengus. See also Kellner, *Heortology* (Eng. Trans.), pp. 230–231 ; Duchesne, *Christian Worship* (Eng. Trans.), pp. 269–272 ; and the *Calendar of St Willibrord* (Henry Bradshaw Society), p. 39.

<hr>

SS. ADRIAN AND NATALIA, MARTYRS

c. A.D. 304

The *acta* of St Adrian in the amplified and written-up form in which we have them relate that he was as a pagan officer at the imperial court at Nicomedia. He was present at the scourging and ill-treatment of twenty-three Christians whom the Emperor Maximian had ordered to be brought before him, and at the sight of their constancy in suffering Adrian was moved to come forward and say : " Count me in with these men, for I also am a Christian." He was at once arrested and imprisoned, and word was brought to his young wife Natalia, who was herself a Christian and to whom he had been married for only thirteen months. She hurried to the prison and kissed the chains which bound her husband and the other confessors, saying to him : " You are blessed, Adrian, for you have found the riches which your father and mother did not leave to you, and which the wealthy themselves have need of in the day when neither father nor mother nor children nor friends nor earthly goods are of any avail." She recommended him to the care and instruction of his fellows, and then Adrian sent her home, promising to let her know how things went with him. And when he knew that the time of his passion was at hand, Adrian bribed his gaoler to let him go and take leave of his wife. When someone told her that he was approaching the house, Natalia jumped to the conclusion that he had saved himself by apostasy and shut the door in his face, reproaching him for his treachery to Christ. But he explained what had happened and that the other prisoners were hostages for his return, and then they embraced and kissed and Natalia returned with him to the prison. She stayed there a week, waiting on the confessors and dressing their wounds, till Adrian was brought before the Emperor and refused to sacrifice. Then he was violently scourged and carried back to prison. Meanwhile other women had come to help look after the sufferers, and when the Emperor heard it he forbade that they should be allowed. Whereupon Natalia cropped her hair, put on male clothes, and bribed her

way into the gaol like any other man ; and she asked Adrian that
when he was in the glory of Heaven he should pray for her that she
might live sinless in the world and soon follow him out of it. The
martyrs were sentenced to have their limbs broken, and Natalia
asked that her husband might suffer first and so be spared the trial
of seeing the agony of the others. When he was dragged to the
block she herself disposed his legs and arms thereon, and knelt by
while the bones were crushed with blows ; his feet and hands were
cut off, and so he died. Natalia hid one of the severed hands in her
clothes, and when the bodies of the martyrs were heaped up on a
pyre to be consumed with fire she had to be restrained from jumping
in among them.

A sudden storm of rain putting the fire out, the Christians of
Nicomedia were able to gather together many relics of St Adrian
and his companions, which were taken to Argyropolis, on the
Bosphorus near Byzantium, and there buried. Some months after
St Natalia decided to follow them, for she was being persecuted by
an imperial official at Nicomedia who wanted to marry her. So she
went aboard ship, taking her precious relic, the hand of Adrian, and
arrived at Byzantium after a voyage during which, says the legend,
the Devil appeared in a phantom ship during a storm and directed
them out of their course, so that they were like to be lost had not a
vision of St Adrian also appeared and directed them aright. Soon
after arriving at Argyropolis St Natalia died in peace and was buried
with the martyrs, among whom she is reckoned. The Roman
Martyrology gives March 4 as the day of the death of St Adrian and
December 1 of St Natalia, to-day being the anniversary of the
translation of their relics from Constantinople to Rome at the end
of the sixth century. St Adrian was one of the great popular martyrs
of the past, a patron of soldiers and butchers and invoked against
plagues.

This is an entirely different Adrian from the martyr at Cæsarea honoured
on March 5 (see vol. iii of this series, p. 57). But there is another Adrian,
martyr at *Nicomedia*, mentioned on March 4, and the Roman Martyrology
takes for granted his identity with the saint here spoken of. Tillemont, it is
true, was of this opinion ; but the Bollandists, who print the so-called " Acts "
both in Latin and Greek in their third volume for September, strongly urge
that the two Nicomedian Adrians are different. Both martyrs are alleged to
have suffered at Nicomedia, and their remains are said to have been taken to
Argyropolis ; but Adrian, the husband of Natalia, is stated to have been
put to death under Diocletian, the other under Licinius, and the rest of their
stories is entirely different. Père S. Salaville has discussed the matter very
patiently in the *Dict. d'Histoire ecclésiastique*, vol. i, cc. 608–611. All that we
can be sure of is that there was an early and very considerable *cultus* of an
Adrian, Martyr of Nicomedia, both in East and West.

SS. EUSEBIUS, NESTABUS, ZENO, AND NESTOR,
MARTYRS

A.D. 362

In the reign of Julian the Apostate, Eusebius, Nestabus, and Zeno, three Christian brothers who had been concerned in the destruction of a heathen temple at Gaza, were seized by the pagans in their house where they had concealed themselves ; they were carried to prison, and inhumanly scourged. Afterwards the mob assembled in the amphitheatre and began loudly to demand the punishment of the sacrilegious criminals, as they called the confessors. The assembly soon became a tumult, and the people worked themselves into such a ferment that they ran in a fury to the prison, which they forced open and, taking out the three brothers, began to drag them about, bruising them against the pavement, and striking them with clubs, stones, or anything that came to hand. The very women, quitting their work, ran the points of their spindles into them, and the cooks took the kettles off the fire, poured the scalding water upon them, and pierced them with their spits. After the martyrs were thus mangled and their skulls so broken that the ground was smeared with their brains, they were dragged out of the city to the place where dead beasts were thrown. Here the people lighted a fire, burned the bodies, and mingled the bones that remained with those of the camels and asses, that it might not be easy for the Christians to distinguish them. But a certain woman came by night and was able to pick out some of their remains, which she conveyed to another Zeno, a relative of the martyrs who had fled to Majuma. He was chased out of that place and returned secretly to Gaza where he kept the relics carefully until, in the reign of Theodosius, he was made a bishop ; he then built a church outside the walls and buried them therein. With these three brothers there was taken a young man named Nestor, who suffered imprisonment and scourging as they had done. But as the rioters were dragging him through the street, some persons took compassion on him on account of his personal beauty and drew him out of the gate. He died of his wounds within three days in the house of Zeno, who afterwards buried his body with the others.

The people of Gaza had taken the law into their own hands in respect of these martyrs, and were in fear of the Emperor's displeasure thereat. But Julian took no steps to punish them, saying, as is alleged : " What right have I to arrest these citizens merely for

revenging themselves on a few Galileans who had injured them and
their gods ? "

The whole of this story is based upon the Church historian, Sozomen (Bk.
v, ch. 9). The relevant text with a commentary is given in the *Acta Sanctorum*,
September, vol. iii.

ST DISIBOD, Bp. AND CONF.

c. A.D. 700

Is said to have been an Irishman and a bishop in his own country,
some say at Dublin. He was a zealous preacher and apostle, and he
taught many souls to walk in the narrow way of Christian perfection
by his exhortations and example. Sermons that are tinged with
vanity, too careful eloquence, or a worldly spirit, lose their force ;
but the sincere humility and religious spirit of St Disibod gave to his
words an energy which opened the hearts of those who heard him
and irradiated their souls with the light of the Gospel. But this was
not true of all who listened to him, and the example of his charity
and meekness failed to soften many ; he laboured hard to reform
also these members of his flock, but without success, and about the
middle of the seventh century he left Ireland in discouragement to be
a missionary in Germany, being obliged thereto by the persecution of
an unrighteous chieftain. With three companions, Sallustius, Clement,
and Giswald, he eventually founded a monastery on a hill in the valley
of the Nahe, near Bingen, which became known from its founder as
Disibodenberg or Disenberg (*Mons Disibodi*), and from thence
ministered and worked wonders among the surrounding inhabitants.

During the twelfth century this monastery was rebuilt by Benedictine monks from the abbey of Hirschau, and in an adjoining
building was a community of nuns presided over by St Hildegard.
After she had removed to the Rupertsberg, the Abbot of Mount
St Disibod asked her to write a Life of the holy founder of his
monastery, and this she did in 1170. The contents of this Life of
St Disibod were, like nearly everything St Hildegard wrote, attributed to revelation in her visions ; but most of the so-called
biography is taken up with moral and Scriptural disquisitions, and
the few alleged facts about St Disibod are simply the traditions then
current in his monastery and of very little worth. There is, in fact,
practically nothing known certainly about him.

See the *Acta Sanctorum*, September, vol. iii, where St Hildegard's
mystical dissertation is reproduced. Falk has devoted an article to St
Disibod in *Der Katholik* of Mainz, 1880, i, pp. 541–547. Wattenbach
declares that down to the eleventh century nothing was known of St Disibod
but his name. He is mentioned by Gougaud in his *Gaelic Pioneers*, p. 20.

ST SERGIUS I, POPE AND CONF.

A.D. 701

While Pope Conon was lying on his death-bed in September of the year 687 his archdeacon, Pascal, sent off to the imperial exarch at Ravenna offering him a bribe to try and secure the archdeacon's election to the papacy. John Platyn, the exarch, was compliant and managed by his influence to bring about the election of Pascal by a faction in Rome on Conon's death. But at the same time another party elected Theodore, archpriest of the Lateran. Neither side would yield in the resulting rivalry, whereupon a majority of the people chose a priest called Sergius, drove the disputants from the Lateran, and installed their candidate. Theodore at once submitted but Pascal, encouraged by the sudden arrival of the exarch in Rome, stood out. Platyn, however, did not see his way to support his own nominee, and gave his approval to the consecration of Sergius—but not until he had received from him the sum of money which had been offered by the disappointed Pascal. Here was no question of simony: Sergius had been freely elected, and he paid the money only under strong protest. The man who became pope in such distressing circumstances was a Syrian, son of an Antiochene merchant, who had been brought up in Palermo and ordained by Pope St Leo II.

In the year following his elevation there arrived in Rome Caedwalla, King of Wessex, who after reigning for two years had " quitted his crown for the sake of our Lord and His everlasting kingdom." He was a convert of St Wilfrid, and wished to be baptised by the successor of St Peter. During the liturgy of Holy Saturday in 689 he was baptised by the Pope, taking at his suggestion the name of Peter, and ten days later, while still in his white garments, he was taken ill and died, thus fulfilling his hope that " he should lay down the flesh as soon as baptised and at once pass to the endless joys of Heaven." Sergius had him buried in St Peter's and a long epitaph, quoted by St Bede, inscribed over the tomb of the first English prince who came on pilgrimage to Rome. St Sergius wrote letters to the "kings of the Angles" and their bishops when he approved St Brithwald as the successor of St Theodore in the primacy of Britain, and was a supporter of St Wilfrid of York in his difficulties.

The early years of his pontificate were disturbed by troubles arising out of the Council *in Trullo* (*Concilium Quinisextum*), which had been convened by the Emperor Justinian II at Constantinople to supplement the acts of the fifth and sixth oecumenical councils by drawing up some canons of discipline. Over two hundred bishops, all Easterns except one, attended this synod and passed 102 canons, many of which were inspired not simply by a legitimate regard for their own customs but by a deliberate opposition to those of the Western Church. This was seen, for example, particularly in their aggrandisement of the see of Constantinople and their affirmation of the lawfulness of married men being ordained deacons and priests ; any who should seek to separate clerics from their wives, or clerics who should so separate, on account of ordination, were to be excommunicated. The mischief of this gathering was that it professed to legislate, not for the East alone, but for the whole Church (to this day the dissident Orthodox regard it as an integral part of the fifth and sixth general councils). Its acts were signed by the Emperor and the four Eastern patriarchs, and were then sent to Rome to be signed by the Pope also, that they might have force in the West. St Sergius refused to sign. Thereupon Justinian sent the commandant of his bodyguard, Zacharias, to fetch the recalcitrant pontiff to Constantinople. Sergius appealed to the exarch, and the people of Rome, reinforced by soldiers from Ravenna and the Pentapolis, gathered in force. Zacharias was in a position as dangerous as it was false, and he fled to Sergius imploring his protection and that the city gates might be shut. But already the Lateran was surrounded and the outer gates broken down under the impression that Sergius was already carried off ; Zacharias, demented with terror, hid himself in the Pope's own bed. St Sergius (one cannot help thinking with some feeling of quiet amusement) went out to pacify the people, but they refused to disband until the gallant soldier from Constantinople had been removed from the city. Nor has any Roman Pontiff ever done more about the canons of *Quinisextum* than tacitly to approve them for the Eastern Church.

At about the same time St Willibrord, who had begun his mission in Friesland, came to Rome for the blessing of the Pope and " many other things which so great a work required." St Sergius gave him all that he wanted, and when Pepin sent Willibrord there again in 695 to be made a bishop he consecrated him in St Caecilia's, with jurisdiction over the Frisians, and changed his name to Clement. In 698 Sergius was able to bring to an end the schism of Aquileia and its suffragans, which had arisen from the controversy of the Three Chapters and subsisted from the middle of the previous century. The archbishop was allowed to keep the title of patriarch, and all books containing the errors of the schismatics were burned. Pope Sergius received a deputation of monks from St Ceolfrid, to whom he granted confirmation of the privileges of their abbey of

Wearmouth and Jarrow, and in 701 the Pope wrote to Ceolfrid asking him to send " that religious servant of God, Bede, a priest of your monastery " to Rome, as he was in need of the advice of learned men. Sergius promised that Bede should be returned as soon as the business was done, but it is practically certain he did not go, for St Bede himself tells us that he never left his monastery. A little before St Aldhelm of Sherborne had stayed with St Sergius at the Lateran and been granted a charter of privileges for the abbey of Malmesbury, which with Frome Selwood was made immediately subject to the Holy See.

Pope St Sergius was a musician, and when he came to Rome as a young man he was handed over to the prior of the *schola cantorum* to be trained in both singing and theology. He is said later to have recast the melodies of the Antiphonary under the influence of his own Eastern musical tastes. He prescribed litanies and processions for the four chief feasts of our Lady, but his chief liturgical enactment was that " the *Agnus Dei* should be sung by clergy and people at the breaking of the Lord's body " at Mass. It is possible that this was ordered in view of canon 82 of the Council *in Trullo*, which forbade the representation of our Lord under the symbol of a lamb. The private character of this Pope can be judged only by his public acts and the tradition of the Church, wherein he appears, in the words of Bd. Alcuin, a holy and most worthy successor of St Peter, second to none in piety. He died on September 8, 701, and was buried in St Peter's.

On the 25th of this month is kept the feast of ST SERGIUS, founder of the Troitza monastery some way from Moscow, and the reformer of Russian monasticism in the fourteenth century. He is greatly venerated in that country, and Joseph Assemani and others state that he was in communion with the Holy See.

An entry " Sergii Papæ Romæ " under September 7 in the first hand of the Calendar of St Willibrord serves as a *terminus a quo* from which to date that document. It also proves that the *cultus* must have begun immediately after the pope's death. The *Liber Pontificalis*, with Duchesne's notes, and the letters calendared in Jaffé are of primary importance as sources. But Sergius belongs to ecclesiastical history. See, however, the *Acta Sanctorum*, September, vol. iii ; Grisar, *Geschichte Roms und der Päpste ;* and especially Mgr Mann, *Lives of the Popes*, vol. i, part 2, pp. 77–104.

ST CORBINIAN, BP. OF FREISING, CONF.

A.D. 725

This early apostle of Bavaria was born at Châtres, near Melun, in France. He was a posthumous child and was baptised Waldegisus

after his father, but his mother afterwards changed his name to
Corbinian, after herself. He lived as a recluse for fourteen years in
a cell which he built in his youth near a chapel in the same place. The
fame of his sanctity, which was increased by the occurrence of
several miracles and the prudence of the advice which he gave in
spiritual matters to those who consulted him, made his name famous
over the country, and he admitted several persons to form themselves
into a religious community under his discipline. The distraction
which this gave him made him think of seeking some new solitude in
which he might live in obscurity, and his devotion to St Peter determined him to go to Rome and there choose a cell near the church
of the Prince of the Apostles. The Pope becoming acquainted with
his abilities told him he ought not to live alone whilst many nations,
ripe for harvest, were perishing for want of strenuous labourers and,
ordaining him bishop, gave him a commission to preach the gospel.
Corbinian was not expecting such an order, but he had learned
obedience, and, lest he should resist the voice of God, he returned
to his own country and by his preaching produced great fruit among
the people. Seven years later he again set out for Rome, intending
to ask to be released from his office. He came first to Ratisbon where
he made a number of converts, and Duke Theodo tried to persuade
him to stop there. The like happened with Duke Grimoald at
Freising, but St Corbinian pressed on his way. While crossing the
Brenner occurred the legendary incident which gave the saint his
emblem of a bear. A bear attacked and killed Corbinian's pack-
horse, so he ordered his servant to put the leading-rein and pack on
to the bear. Which was done, and they proceeded, and with the
tamed bear arrived at Rome. But not before a certain lord at Trent
had stolen the saint's best horse and another at Pavia stolen his
second best. Retribution soon overtook both these thieves, for the
one died and the other lost forty-two of his own horses from
elephantiasis ! Pope St Gregory II refused to recognise St Corbinian's desire for a more retired life, and sent him back to preach in
Bavaria, where he put himself under the protection of Duke
Grimoald. After having much increased the number of the
Christians, he fixed his episcopal see at Freising, in Upper Bavaria.
Though indefatigable in his apostolic duties he was careful not to
lay on himself more business than he could bear, lest he should
forget what he owed to God direct. He always performed the divine
office with great care, and reserved every day set hours for meditation,
in order to improve the spiritual vigour of his soul and to examine
his conscience before God, constantly making resolutions of more
vigilance in all his actions.

He soon discovered that his patron Grimoald, though a Christian, had defied the discipline of the Church by marrying his brother's widow, Biltrudis, without dispensation. St Corbinian refused to have anything to do with the duke until they separated, and at the end of forty days Grimoald signified his willingness and gave the bishop an estate at Meran for a peace offering. But the lady Biltrudis was not at all satisfied and pursued Corbinian with persecution in the hope that he would allow her to be reinstated. At length she even conspired to have him murdered. Word of this plot came to Erembert, Corbinian's brother (who succeeded him and was probably really the first diocesan bishop of Freising). The saint took refuge at Meran, and wrote thence to Grimoald informing him that Biltrudis ought to be executed for her crime. This the duke refused to do, for he had returned to his former relations with her, but he promised the bishop he would be responsible for his safety if he would return to Freising. However, St Corbinian remained in semi-exile until Grimoald was killed in battle shortly after and all danger from Biltrudis was past, when he continued his missionary work throughout Bavaria. Corbinian was buried at a monastery he had founded at Obermais, at Meran, but his body was brought back to Freising in 769 by Aribo, his second successor and biographer. Aribo says that St Corbinian was a man easily aroused to anger, and a story in illustration is told concerning a woman of Freising who was reported to deal in black magic. Meeting her one day in the street carrying some meat he asked what she was about, and was told that she was going to try and cure a sick man by her art. Corbinian jumped off his horse, gave the woman a sound thrashing with his own hands, and gave the meat away to the poor.

Of Corbinian we have an excellent medieval Life by Arbeo or Aribo, who lived in the same century and was one of his successors in the See of Freising. This biography was afterwards interpolated with legendary incidents, the episode of the bear, for example, being one of the additions. After editing the genuine text in the fourth and sixth volumes of the *Monumenta Germaniæ, Scriptores rerum Meroving.*, Bruno Krusch has produced a very handy edition (1920) *in usum scholarum*. See also the *Acta Sanctorum*, September, vol. iii. In the *Beiträge zur Geschichte*, etc., *des Erzbistums München und Freisingen*, vol. vii (1901), pp. 1–16, M. Fastlinger has proved that Corbinian died, not, as previously supposed in 730, but on 8 Sept., 725, a conclusion now accepted by Bruno Krusch.

SEPTEMBER 9

SS. GORGONIUS, DOROTHEUS, AND PETER,
MARTYRS

A.D. 304

DOROTHEUS and Gorgonius were freedmen in the palace of Diocletian at Nicomedia, who, when they saw another servant, Peter, tortured for his faith, protested to the Emperor and were on that account themselves tortured and then strangled. The bodies of St Dorotheus and his companions were cast into the sea by an order of Diocletian, lest the Christians should worship them as gods, as Eusebius mentions ; which mistake of the heathen could only arise from the veneration which Christians paid to the relics of martyrs. The late *acta* of these martyrs give an entirely imaginary account of the torments to which they were subjected. The body of St Gorgonius was recovered and taken to Rome, where it was buried first on the Via Lavicana and then in St Peter's, and in the eighth century was obtained by St Chrodegang of Metz for his abbey at Gorze. To-day celebrates the translation to Rome, the martyrdom having taken place on March 11.

The martyrs show by example that a true Christian is invincible in virtue and fortitude, for, as St Gregory Nazianzen says, he looks upon misfortunes and crosses as the seeds of heroic virtues. Therefore he exults in adversity and torments do not discompose the serenity of his countenance ; much less do they change the steadfastness of his heart. Nothing is able to pull him down ; every thing yields to the magnanimity and wisdom of his faith. If he is stripped of the goods and conveniences of life, he has wings to raise him to Heaven. He flies to the bosom of God, who abundantly makes amends for all and is all things to him. He is in the world but not of the world. In the midst of passions and sufferings, he is as invincible as if he were impassible ; he lets himself be vanquished in everything except in courage. Where he submits he triumphs, by humility, patience, and constancy, even over death itself. Do we show forth this character, even under the light trials we meet with ?

Alban Butler is unquestionably mistaken here in identifying the Gorgonius of Nicomedia with the Gorgonius who was buried " inter duas

93

lauros " on the Via Lavicana. The two martyrs were distinct, as Delehaye, Quentin and J. P. Kirsch are all agreed ; and Dorotheus was associated
not with the Roman Gorgonius, but with the Gorgonius of Nicomedia,
of whose sufferings an account has been left by Eusebius in his *Eccles. Hist.*,
Bk. viii, chs. 5 and 6. The martyrologist, Ado, was the author of the confusion, as Quentin, *Martyrologes historiques*, 613–615, has fully demonstrated.
See also the paper of Kirsch in *Ehrengabe Deutscher Wissenschaft für J. G. von
Sachsen* (1920), pp. 58–84 ; and especially Delehaye's commentary on the
Hieronymianum in *Acta Sanctorum*, November, vol. ii, part 2, pp. 497–498.

ST ISAAC, or SAHAK, THE GREAT, Conf.,
Katholikos of the Armenians

c. A.D. 440

At the end of the fourth century the state of matrimony was still
not a bar to the episcopate in the Armenian Church, and St Isaac,
sometimes called " of Armenia," or " the Parthian," was the
son of the katholikos St Nerses I, also known as " the Great "
(though he was probably a widower when ordained). There were
indeed families in which the episcopate was hereditary, and Isaac
himself was the great-great-great-grandson of the great bishop
St Gregory the Illuminator ; to abolish this abuse and do away with
married bishops was to be part of Isaac's work. He was left father-
less when young, Nerses being poisoned by the shameless King Pap,
and he thereafter studied at Constantinople, where he married.
After the death of his wife he became a monk and devoted himself to
learning, making a particular study of languages. When Isaac was
called to rule the Armenian Church, about the year 390, both it and
the nation were in a very critical state. The Emperor Theodosius I
had recently ceded the greater part of Armenia to Persia, and the
two divisions of the kingdom were nominally ruled by princes
subject to their Byzantine and Persian masters. Some fifteen years
previously the successor of St Nerses I had repudiated the dependence of his church on Caesarea, of which St Basil was at that time
the metropolitan, and the Armenians were in consequence regarded
as being more or less in schism. Though St Isaac found a small
pro-Caesarean party he disregarded it and got himself recognised
at Constantinople as primate of the Armenian Church, which would
appear to be an appeal to the imperial power as against the rights of
his true patriarch at Antioch. This bold move may have been
partly due to Persian pressure, but it ushered in a period of solid
ecclesiastical progress which was joined with the beginning of the
golden age of Armenian letters. His father Nerses had begun the

reform of his church by bringing it more into line with Byzantine custom and law, and Isaac completed this work, being greatly helped in imposing his reforms by the position he occupied in Armenia. Soon after his appointment King Khosrov sent him to Seleucia-Ctesiphon as his representative to acknowledge the suzerainty of Persia over Armenia, but in fact four-fifths of the kingdom was for some years ruled practically by St Isaac himself. Byzantine canon law was strictly enforced, which meant the end of married bishops, and Isaac was in fact the last of the house of St Gregory the Illuminator to rule over the church which is sometimes called after him " Gregorian." Monasticism began to flourish, schools and hospitals were established, and churches destroyed by the Persians rebuilt. Isaac had to contend on the one hand with the influence of Persian paganism and on the other with those Christians who resented the enforcement of ecclesiastical discipline.

When Theodosius II came to the throne of Constantinople in the year 408 he adopted the policy of promoting Greek influence throughout Armenia by encouraging the diffusion of Christianity, and he gave invaluable support to the undertakings of St Isaac who, faced with Greek ambitions in the small Byzantine part of his territory and the absolute forbiddance of Greek language and culture in all the rest of it, made this disparity a unity by taking elements from both Byzantine and Syrian sources and giving them an Armenian dress. For this purpose it was necessary to invent an Armenian alphabet, which was done on a Greek basis by St Mesrob. The first literary work undertaken was a translation of the Bible, which was made partly by Isaac himself. Finding it impossible to get a good Greek manuscript, on account of the destruction by the apostate Merujan of such in order to lessen Byzantine influence, he began his undertaking from a Syriac version. Later he obtained a Septuagint and a New Testament from Constantinople, and in the meantime he had sent students to study there, at Edessa, Alexandria, and elsewhere, principally to perfect themselves in Greek in order to help in the work of translation. The Armenian version of the Old Testament is one of the most valuable for biblical scholars, and several of the translations of other books made under the direction of St Isaac are of the first importance because the originals are now lost ; by the time of his death the Armenians already had the works of the principal Greek and Syrian doctors in their own tongue, and the beginnings of a native literature had been made. He also contributed greatly to the formation of the national Liturgy from that of Caesarea, now represented by the Byzantine St Basil.

In the year 428 the Persians drove out the Armenian tributary prince, Ardashes IV, and Isaac, whose leaning towards Christian Byzantium was notorious, was driven into retirement in the western corner of the country. There is a story that the Emperor Theodosius told his general Anatolius to build the city of Theodosiopolis (Karin, Erzerum) to shelter the fugitive bishop, but that city has a much older origin and had already been renamed in honour of the Emperor thirteen years before. After some years he was invited to return to his see, but did not at once do so, appointing a vicar in his stead. Upon his death Isaac resumed the direct government, but he was now very old and could not for that reason attend the Council of Ephesus, whose acts he accepted in 435. He held some of his synods at Etshmiadzin, but seems to have retained the first Armenian ecclesiastical centre at Ashtishat as his see, in which place he died at the age of 110 years. He was, as has been said, the last katholikos of the family of St Gregory and appropriately he consolidated and gave shape and voice to the work which the Illuminator began, whence St Isaac also is often called by the Armenians the " Illuminator of Learning."

The transliteration of Armenian names varies greatly in France, Germany and England. Thus we find Sahak or Sahaq ; Pap or Bab ; Ardashes, Ardaches or Artachir ; Ashtishat, Aschdichad, or Achedichad. The principal sources are Moses of Khorene, Lazarus of Pharp and other chronicles which may be consulted in Langlois, *Collection des historiens de l'Arménie.* Among modern books Sahak is frequently referred to both in Fr. Tournebize, *Histoire politique et religieuse de l'Arménie* (1901) and in S. Weber, *Die Katholische Kirche in Armenien* (Freiburg, 1903). See also F. C. Conybeare, " The Armenian Canons of St Sahak," in the *American Journal of Theology,* 1898, pp. 828–848.

ST KIERAN, OR CIARAN, ABBOT OF CLONMACNOIS, CONF.

A.D. 556 (?)

Kieran of Clonmacnois, sometimes called "the Younger" to distinguish him from St Kieran of Ossory, was born in the year 515 in Roscommon or Westmeath. His father Beoit was a cartwright, but he is also called a carpenter, like the ostensible father of our Lord. Kieran was said to have died at the age of thirty-three (though he was probably older) and other parallels to the life of Christ can be found in his legends. It has been suggested that these were unconscious inventions on the part of simple people impressed by the holiness of Kieran's character. His mother was named Darerca and belonged to the tribe of the Glasraige, granddaughter of a bard called Glas, and both families may have been of pre-Celtic blood. Owing to oppression by his chieftain, Beoit fled from Antrim into Connacht, and there Kieran was born, one of seven children. He was baptised by the deacon St Justus, who had been ordained by St Patrick. Several fabulous incidents are told of his boyhood, as that he revivified a dead hound, changed water into honey, and played a practical joke on his mother. She was dyeing and turned him out of the house, " for it was thought unbecoming that males should be in the house when garments were being dyed."* Kieran was annoyed, and " May there be a dun stripe on them," he exclaimed. The clothes came out of the blue dye with a dun stripe accordingly, and they were put in again. This time they came out white. But at the third dyeing Kieran had recovered his temper, and the dye was so blue that not only the clothes but also dogs, cats, and trees that it came into contact with were turned blue. Kieran had some teaching from the deacon Uis at Fuerty, and when he was about fifteen he asked his parents to give him a cow for his support, that he might go to the school of St Finian at Clonard. Darerca refused, so he blessed one of the cows and she followed him for the rest of his life, the Dun Cow of Kieran. At Clonard he was one of those twelve holy ones afterwards known as the Twelve Apostles of Ireland (see St Finian, December 12), and at this time was the greatest among them, for whereas the others had to grind their own corn every day, angels would come and grind it for Kieran. St Finian esteemed him above the rest, so that all the others except Columcille were jealous of him, and when the daughter of the King of Cualu was sent to learn to read, her instruction was confided to St Kieran. So indifferent was he to her person that it was said of him that he saw nothing but her feet.

When the time came for St Kieran to leave Clonard, Finian wanted to give up his place to him, but the young disciple refused. " Leave not your monastery for any save God only," he said, " seeing He has favoured you above us all." Then he departed and made his way to the Arans, where St Enda still ruled on Inishmore. Here he lived for seven years, and became so skilful at threshing and winnowing that not a grain of corn could be seen in the chaff-heaps. Then one day Enda and Kieran saw a vision of a great tree growing beside a river in the middle of Ireland, whose branches overhung the sea, laden with fruit which the birds pecked. And Enda said : " That tree is yourself, for you are great before God and man and

---

* Ingenious explanations and suggestions have been made about this statement. But need it be anything more than the gloss of a monastic writer who did not realise that hardworked housewives don't want boys messing around when they are busy ?

Ireland shall be full of your honour. It shall be protected under your shadow and many shall be satisfied with the grace of your fasting and your prayer. Go, therefore, at the word of God to the shore of the stream and found a church there." Then Kieran arose and left Aran and came to Scattery Island, where he visited St Senan who gave him a new cloak, a kindness which Kieran afterwards repaid by floating another cloak down the Shannon to Senan. Afterwards he proceeded on his journey towards the middle of Ireland and came to a place called Isel where he stayed in a monastery for a time, but had to leave because the monks complained that his excessive generosity left them nothing. He followed a stag, which led him to Lough Ree, above Athlone, where he went across to Inis Aingin (Hare Island) and lived in the monastery there. His holiness and the number of his disciples excited the envy of a priest, called Daniel and said to be a Briton, who tried to get him expelled, but Kieran won him over by the gift of a golden cup, as a token of his good will. At last, having named an abbot in his place at Inis Aingin, he set out on his journey again, having eight companions. He was urged to settle at a beautiful place called Ard Manntain, but he refused, saying, " If we live here we shall have much of the riches of the world, and few souls will go from us to Heaven." But when they came to the grassy ridge of Ard Tiprat, on the west bank of the Shannon in Offaly, Kieran said : " We will stay here, for there shall be many souls going to Heaven from this place, and God and man shall visit it for ever." To Diarmaid MacCerrbeill was promised the high-kingship of Ireland, and together with St Kieran he planted on his land the first post of the monastery that was to be famous as Clonmacnois. One account says that as they were about to plant the post a wizard, who feared for his authority, said : " This is not a good hour for beginning, for the sign of the hour is contrary to the beginnings of building." To which St Kieran made reply : " Wizard, I fix this post into the ground against your sign. I care nothing for the art of wizards, but do all my works in the name of my Lord, Jesus Christ." The rest of the records of Kieran are anecdotes concerning his virtues and the miracles to which they gave rise ; one of them, about that " boy of great wit but mischievous and wanton," Crichidh of Cluain, has already been told in the life of St Kieran of Ossory (March 5). There is extant a " law " or monastic rule attributed to St Kieran the Younger which consists of moral and ascetical precepts of a very severe kind ; it is probably not of his authorship but accurately represents the spirit that obtained in his and other early Irish monasteries, a spirit of austerity that has characterised Gaelic religion down to our own day. According to his Lives St Kieran lived to govern his monastery only seven months. When the time of his death was near he asked to be carried out to the Little Hill. Then he looked up at the heavens and said : " Awful is this road upward."—" Not for you is it awful," replied his monks. " Indeed, I do not know," said he, " that I have transgressed any of the commandments of God, yet even David the son of Jesse and Paul the Apostle dreaded this way." They made to take away a stone from under him for his greater comfort, but he stopped them. " Put it under my shoulders," he said. " ' He that shall persevere unto the end, he shall be saved.' "—" Then angels filled the space between Heaven and earth to receive his soul."

The account of the death of St Kieran is one of the few almost certainly authentic stories in his *vitae*, but is immediately followed by the statement that he came to life for the space of time from one canonical hour to another to converse with St Kevin of Glendalough. Clonmacnois remained his living monument for many centuries, the chief school of Ireland and the burial place of princes. During the evil days of the ninth and ten centuries its monks must often have called to mind the question put by their predecessors to their dying founder who had prophesied persecution. " What shall we do in that time ? Is it by your relics we shall stay, or go elsewhere ? " and his reply : " Arise and leave my bones as the bones of a deer are left in the sun. For it is better for you to live with me in Heaven than to stay here with my relics." Under the form *Queranus* the name of St Kieran figures in the Roman Martyrology, and his feast is kept throughout Ireland.

Four short Lives of St Kieran have been preserved to us, three in Latin and one in Irish. The first Latin Life has been critically edited by C. Plummer in his *Vitæ Sanctorum Hiberniæ* with occasional illustrations from the others ; the Irish Life was made accessible by Whitley Stokes in his *Lives of Saints from the Book of Lismore*. But translations of all these with much other matter may be found in the admirable little volume of Professor R. A. Stewart Macalister, *Saint Ciaran* (S.P.C.K., 1921). See also the *Acta Sanctorum*, September, vol. iii ; J. Ryan, *Irish Monasticism ;* J. F. Kenney, *The Sources for the Early History of Ireland*, vol. i ; and Gougaud, *Christianity in Celtic Lands* (1932).

ST AUDOMARUS, or OMER, Bp. of Thérouanne, Conf.

c. A.D. 670

The name of St Audomarus is more familiar to English readers in its French form of Omer, on account of the famous penal-times

Jesuit college in the then episcopal city of Saint-Omer; a college which afterwards came into the hands of the secular clergy, over which Alban Butler presided for a time, and at which he died. St Omer was the only son of Friulphus and Domitilla, persons of noble extraction and plentiful fortune. The place of his birth was not far from Coutances. The thoughts of his parents were wholly taken up in him, and his education was their chief care. Though they applied him to profane study their principal aim was to train him up in virtue and religion. He made the most happy progress, and his father upon the death of his wife sold his estate, distributed the price among the poor, and accompanied his son to the monastery of Luxeuil. St Eustachius, who had succeeded St Columbanus, the founder, in the government of that house, received them kindly, and they made their religious profession together. The humility, obedience, devotion, and purity of manners which shone forth in Omer distinguished him among his brethren even in that house of saints. His proficiency in sacred learning was very remarkable, and his reputation spread over the whole kingdom. After some twenty years from his becoming a monk, Thérouanne, the capital of the Morini in Belgic Gaul, stood in need of a zealous pastor, and that country which contained what is now called the Pas-de-Calais and Flanders was overrun with vice and error, so that King Dagobert was looking about his dominions for a person in every way well qualified to establish the faith and practice of the gospel in that district. The abbey of Luxeuil was at that time the most flourishing school of learning and piety in all France, and a fruitful seminary of holy prelates. In it St Omer was pointed out as a person most capable for this arduous employment, and proposed as such to the King by St Acharius, Bishop of Noyon and Tournai. The choice was approved by the prince, and also by the bishops and nobility of the whole kingdom, and St Omer, who had been happy and content in his retreat, was suddenly called on to leave the pleasure of his solitude. Upon receiving the message, with a command to obey without demur, he cried out : " How great is the difference between the secure harbour in which I now enjoy calm, and that tempestuous ocean into which I am pushed, against my will and destitute of experience." The King, without listening to the objections which his humility made against the choice, presented him to the bishops, by whom he was obliged to receive the episcopal character towards the close of the year 637.

The first undertaking of his pastoral care was to re-establish the faith in its purity among the few Christians he found, whose reformation was a task no less difficult than the conversion of idolaters. Yet such was the success of his labours that he left his diocese almost equal to those that were most flourishing in France. His sermons were full of a divine fire which could scarcely be resisted, but his exemplary life preached still more powerfully ; for it was not easy for men to reject a religion which they saw produced so many good works and animated men with so divine a temper and such a spirit of devotion towards God, and of meekness, courage, and beneficence towards all men, whether friends or enemies. It encouraged others to spend themselves freely in redeeming captives, feeding the poor, comforting the sick, reconciling enemies, and serving everyone without any other view than that of their eternal salvation and the glory of God. This was the character of the holy bishop and his fellow-labourers who were employed under his direction. The chief among these were St Mommolinus, St Bertrand, and St Bertinus, monks whom St Omer invited to his assistance from Luxeuil, and whose association with him has been related in the life of the third-named on the 5th of this month. St Omer founded with them the monastery of Sithiu, which became one of the greatest seminaries of sacred learning in France, and was possessed of a very large library in the eleventh and twelfth centuries, at which time schools were established in all the priories dependent on it. The Lives of St Omer recount a number of not very convincing miracles performed by him. In his old age he was blind some years before his death, but that infliction made no abatement in his pastoral concern for his flock. The third and least reliable of his Lives says that when St Aubertus, Bishop of Arras and Cambrai, translated the relics of St Vedastus from the cathedral to the monastery which he had built in his honour, St Omer was present and recovered his sight for a short time on that occasion. St Omer died between the years 667 and 670, on September 9, the day on which his feast is celebrated. His body was buried by St Bertinus at our Lady's church, which became the cathedral of the diocese of Saint-Omer (now absorbed in Arras).

The least unsatisfactory Life of St Omer is that already referred to above in the bibliographical note to St Bertinus, on September 5. The edition of that text by W. Levison, there spoken of, is accompanied by a discussion of the relations between the different Lives printed in the *Acta Sanctorum*, September, vol. iii. It seems clear that St Omer came from the neighbourhood of Coutances—not Constance, as stated by Butler, who was misled by the later biographers. He probably died after 670. See Duchesne, *Fastes Épiscopaux*, vol. iii, p. 133.

ST BETTELIN, OR BECCELIN, HERMIT
EIGHTH CENTURY

In the history of Croyland which bears the name of the eleventh-century abbot Ingulphus, though compiled long after his time, we are told that the great hermit St Guthlac had four disciples, who led penitential lives in separate cells not far from their director in the midst of the fens of Lincolnshire. These were Cissa, Egbert, Tatwin, and Bettelin. The last-named, after he had overcome a temptation which once came to him while shaving St Guthlac to cut his throat and succeed to his authority, became of all others the most dear to his master. When St Guthlac was near death he counselled Bettelin with such wisdom that "he never before or after heard the like," and in his last moments sent him into Northamptonshire with a last loving message to his sister, St Pega. St Bettelin and his companions lived on at Croyland under Kenulphus, first abbot of the monastery founded there by King Ethelbald of Mercia, and there died and were buried. Their bodies were burnt, with those of the monks and the church, when the abbey was destroyed by the Danes in the year 866.

St Bettelin (or another) was honoured as patron of the town of Stafford, which boasted his relics—some may have been taken there from Croyland before the Danes came. But the story of his life as told by the chronicler Capgrave is, as Alban Butler says, " of no authority." It is, in fact, popular fiction, according to which Betellin was a son of the Prince of Stafford who went on a visit to Ireland. There he fell in love with a princess, who ran away with him to England. While making their way through a forest the princess was overtaken by the pains of childbirth, and Betellin hurried away to try and find a midwife. While he was gone the girl was found by a pack of hungry wolves, and Betellin returned only to find them tearing her to pieces. The loss of his bride and baby in so terrible a fashion drove Bettelin to offer himself entirely to God in a solitary life, and he became an anchorite near Stafford. On the death of his father he was induced to leave his cell to help in driving off a usurping invader, which he did by the assistance of an angel sent from Heaven to oppose the demon who led the opposing forces. Then Bettelin returned to his cell and lived there for the rest of his days.

Very little seems to be known of St Bettelin or Berthelm. In the *Acta Sanctorum* an account is printed from a MS. source which is in substance identical with that preserved by Capgrave in the *Nova Legenda Angliæ*. See also Stanton's *Menology*, pp. 389 and 666.

ST WULFHILDA, Virg. and Abbess

c. A.D. 980

She belonged to a noble English family and founded the monastery of Horton in Dorsetshire, of which she became the first abbess. When King Edgar restored the abbey of Barking, which had been devastated by the Danes, as a house for nuns only, St Wulfhilda was put in charge, and under her rule it attained some of the glory it had formerly enjoyed under its first abbesses. When Edgar died his queen, Elfrida, drove her out, but she was reinstated by Ethelred and died in peace shortly after. She was buried at Barking, and her tomb was graced with miracles, so that thirty years later her body was translated to a shrine. It was then found to be incorrupt. St Wulfhilda has often been confused and identified with the following saint.

The sources for this confused story are mainly John of Tynemouth, Capgrave, Goscelin and William of Malmesbury, *Gesta Pontificum.* See the *Acta Sanctorum,* September, vol. iii, and Stanton's *Menology,* pp. 442–443.

ST WILFRIDA, or WULFRITHA, Abbess

c. A.D. 988

A natural desire to divert attention from the scandals associated with the name of King Edgar and Wilfrida gave rise to the following legend. The King's first wife, Ethelfleda, being dead, he fell in love with the young Wilfrida and wanted to make her his queen ; she, however, was determined to consecrate herself to God in the abbey of Wilton. Her kinswoman, Wenfleda, undertook to try and bring about Edgar's wish, and, on the pretence that she was dying and needed her, sent for Wilfrida, who came to the court. On her arrival she was made to sit between her aunt and the King at table, and Edgar announced his forthcoming marriage. Her bedroom door was guarded during the night, but she got out of the window and made her way back towards Wilton. When her flight was discovered Edgar set off in pursuit and caught her up at the door of the abbey-church. He seized her hand—but it parted at the wrist and Wilfrida fled into the church without it. This marvel persuaded Edgar that the lady was not for him, and so left her.

In fact things did not happen at all like this, though the exact circumstances are somewhat uncertain and complicated by chronological difficulties. What is certain and the matter of chief importance is that Edgar and Wilfrida were the parents of St Edith of Wilton, and it is generally said that he carried Wilfrida off, or induced her to leave, while she was a nun at Wilton. It is known that for such a crime the King was visited by St Dunstan with a penance extending over seven years. But William of Malmesbury states that the mother of St Edith was not a nun : she had only taken refuge in the convent from her unwelcome suitor, or perhaps was being educated there. Nor is it certain whether or no King Edgar had yet married his second wife, Elfrida, at the time of this happening. If he had not, and was desirous of marrying Wilfrida, still he did not do so, for after Edith's birth her mother retired with the baby to Wilton, and was there professed by St Ethelwold, Bishop of Winchester. " Urged on by that love for Christ which is as strong as death, the venerable Wilfrida withdrew herself from the kingdom and bride-chamber of this world and went into a monastery. . . . Instead of purple and fine gold she wore a black tunic and instead of a royal crown a dark veil. And having so taken upon herself the religious habit she made such progress in the paths of perfection that she was looked on as a teacher of holiness and made abbess." Her daughter also elected to take the veil at Wilton at a very early age, but Wilfrida survived her by at least three years, for she was still alive when St Dunstan enshrined St Edith's body on November 3, 987. Whatever may have been unhallowed in the association of St Wilfrida with King Edgar, she by penitence and mortification made ample amends, while the memory of Edgar himself was revered as that of a saint by our forefathers.

The Bollandists accord no separate treatment to St Wulfrida, but she is mentioned by William of Malmesbury and Florence of Worcester. See also Stanton's *Menology*, p. 450.

BD. SERAPHINA SFORZA, Matron and Abbess

A.D. 1478

Was born at Urbino about the year 1432, the daughter of Guy Antony of Montefeltro, Count of that city, by his second wife, Catherine Colonna. In baptism she received the name of Sueva. Her parents died while she was a child, she was sent to Rome to be brought up in the household of her uncle, Prince Colonna, and at the age of about fourteen she was joined in marriage to Alexander Sforza, Lord of Pesaro and Grand Constable of Sicily. This man was a widower, with two children, whom Sueva greatly loved, and for some years she lived very happily with her husband. Then he was called away to take up arms on behalf of his brother, the Duke of Milan, leaving his estate to the care of Sueva, and his absence was prolonged. On his return, none the better man for so long a period of campaigning and absence from home, Alexander began an intrigue with a woman called Pacifica, the wife of a local physician. Sueva used all the means at her disposal to win her husband back, but with so little success that he added physical cruelty and insult to unfaithfulness. He even tried to poison her, and thenceforward the unhappy woman gave up active efforts towards reconciliation, and confined herself to prayer and quietness. This served only to irritate Alexander, and he at last drove her from the house with violence, telling her to take herself off to some convent.

Sueva was received as a guest by the Poor Clares of the convent of Corpus Christi, where she lived the life of the nuns. Her cause was taken up by her Colonna relatives, and Alexander Sforza retorted on them that his wife had been guilty of adultery and that, moreover, she would admit it if they sent a representative with him to the convent. He warned Sueva of the intended inquisition and threatened to burn down the convent if she denied her guilt. He then waited on her with his witnesses and taxed her with unfaithfulness at a specific place and time. Sueva stood mute : she would not falsely admit so shameful a charge but feared to protest her innocence lest her husband's anger should be visited on the nuns who sheltered her. Alexander hoped that Sueva's relatives would interpret her silence as an admission of guilt ; perhaps they did : but it is more likely that they were not taken in by so transparent a ruse and decided that Sueva was well rid of so villainous a husband. Certainly the nuns were not deceived, for, her husband having behaved so scandalously, they urged Sueva to join them. For a time she was unwilling, doubting her vocation, but eventually was clothed and took the name of Seraphina, in honour of St Francis. This was exactly what Alexander wanted her to do, and, feeling himself free, he went from bad to worse ; Pacifica was flaunted about Pesaro as though she were his lawful wife and even, it is said, had the insolence to visit the convent wearing Sueva's jewels. Sister Seraphina was an exemplary nun and she did not forget her obligations to her husband. She never ceased to pray and offer her penances for his conversion, and before his death in 1473 her desire was fulfilled : he gave up his mistress, humbled himself before his wife, and entered on a new life of penance and charity. Two years after Blessed Seraphina was made abbess of Corpus Christi. With the help of her stepson

Constant, who had always taken her part, she rebuilt the convent, and redoubled her efforts for the spiritual edification of its nuns, giving all her thoughts and prayers to their welfare until she died on our Lady's birthday in the year 1478. The *cultus* of Blessed Seraphina was confirmed by Pope Benedict XIV in 1754.

There is an anonymous Life printed with prolegomena in the *Acta Sanctorum*, September, vol. iii. See, however, B. Feliciangeli, *Sulla monacazione di Sueva Montefeltro Sforza, Ricerche* (Pistoia, 1903), a brochure which makes public certain new documents. From them it would appear, that Sueva at the time of her leaving the world was not so entirely an innocent victim as has been assumed. The problem is discussed by Père Van Ortroy in the *Analecta Bollandiana*, vol. xxiv (1905), pp. 311–313. This evidence was unknown to such earlier biographers as Mgr Alegiani, or to Léon, *Auréole Séraphique* (Eng. Trans.), vol. iii, pp. 114–120. Sueva entered the convent in 1457 at the age of twenty-five, and whatever she may have had to repent of, she had more than twenty years in which to grow holy in the practice of a most austere religious rule.

ST PETER CLAVER, Conf.,
Apostle of the Negroes

A.D. 1654

If to England belongs the honour of having begun the work of abolishing the slave-trade in 1815, it was she also who, in the person of such national heroes as Sir John Hawkins, played a great part in establishing that trade between Africa and the New World in the sixteenth century. And of the heroes who in the intervening period devoted their lives to the interests of the victims of this nefarious exploitation, the most were Catholics from countries which had not received the enlightenment of the Reformers. Among them none was greater than St Peter Claver, a native of that Spain whose history in his time is represented for most Englishmen by the buccaneering of an unscrupulous imperialism and the fantastic cruelty of an ecclesiastical inquisition. He was born at Verdu, in Catalonia, in 1581, the son of a farmer, and as he showed fine qualities of mind and spirit was destined for the Church and sent to study at the University of Barcelona. Here he graduated with distinction and, after receiving minor orders, determined to offer himself to the Society of Jesus. He was received into the novitiate at Tarragona at the age of twenty, and, after studying the humanities for a year at Gerona, was sent for his philosophy to the college of Montesion at Palma, in Majorca. Here he met St Alphonsus Rodriguez, who at that time was porter in the college, though with a reputation far

above his humble office, and this meeting was to set the direction of
Peter Claver's life. He studied the science of the saints at the feet
of the lay-brother, and Alphonsus conceived a corresponding regard
for the capabilities of the young scholastic, and saw in him a man
fit for a new, arduous and neglected work for the good of souls.
He fired him with the idea of going to the help of the many who were
without spiritual ministrations in the colonies of the New World.
" I cannot tell you my grief," St Alphonsus would exclaim, " at
seeing God unknown in the greater part of the world, because there
are so few who go to make Him known. What tears are called for
at the sight of so many wandering in the wilderness because there
is none to guide them, who are lost not through their own fault but
because no effort is made to save them. There are plenty of useless
workmen where there is no harvest, and where the harvest is great
the labourers are few. How many idle priests in Europe might
save souls in America ! Cannot charity cross the seas that have
already been charted by greed ? Does the love of Christ stir men
to seek souls less than love of the world stirs them to seek riches ?
If you love the glory of God's house, go to the Indies and save these
perishing people. Do not wait to be sent under obedience ; be a
volunteer ! "

In after years St Peter Claver said that St Alphonsus had actually
foretold to him that he would go and the very place wherein he would
work. Moved by the fervour of these exhortations Peter Claver
approached his provincial, offering himself for the West Indies, and
was told that his vocation would be decided in due course by his
superiors. He was sent back to Barcelona for his theology and after
two years was, at his further request, chosen to represent the province
of Aragon, on the mission of Spanish Jesuits being sent to New
Granada. Father Gaspar Parrigas, who was a fellow-student of
Peter at this time, testified after his death : " All that I can say of
him is that I knew him to be holy and a perfect religious. He was
modest, courteous, and obliging to all ; he never complained of
anybody and was always speaking of God and spiritual things. I
do not hesitate to say that I never knew him to break a single rule.
He tried always to follow the example of Brother Alphonsus
Rodriguez, who had given him some books written by himself. He
had the same spirit of prayer, of union with God, of penance. I am
not surprised that after having been so holy in life he should perform
miracles after his death." Peter Claver left Spain for ever in
April 1610, and after a wearisome voyage landed with his companions at Cartagena, in what is now called the Republic of
Colombia. Thence he went to the Jesuit house of Santa Fé to

complete his theological studies, and was employed as well as sacristan, porter, infirmarian, and cook, and was sent for his tertianship to the new house of the Society at Tunja. He returned to Cartagena in 1615 and was there ordained priest ; he was the first Jesuit to say his first Mass in that place.

By this time the slave-trade had been established in the Americas for nearly a hundred years, and the port of Cartagena was one of its principal centres, being conveniently situated as a clearing-house. The trade had recently been given a considerable *impetus*, for the local natives were not physically fitted to work in the gold and silver mines, and there was a big demand for Negroes from Angola and the Congo. These were bought in West Africa for four crowns a head, or bartered for goods, and sold in America for two hundred crowns. The conditions under which they were conveyed across the Atlantic were so foul and inhuman as to be beyond belief, and it was reckoned that there would be a loss in each cargo by death during the six or seven weeks' voyage of fifty per cent ; but in spite of this an average of ten thousand living slaves was landed in Cartagena every year. In spite of the condemnation of this great crime by Pope Paul III and by many lesser authorities, this "supreme villainy," as slave-trading was designated by Pius IX, continued to flourish ; all that most of the owners did in response to the voice of the Church was to have their slaves baptised. They received no religious instruction or ministration, no alleviation of their physical condition, so that the sacrament of Baptism became to them a very sign and symbol of their oppression and wretchedness. The clergy were practically powerless ; all they could do was to protest and to devote themselves to the utmost to individual ministration, corporal and material, among the tens of thousands of suffering human beings. They had no charitable funds at their disposal, no plaudits from humanitarian audiences ; they were hampered and discouraged by the owners and often rebuffed by the Negroes themselves.

At the time of Father Claver's ordination the leader in this work was Father Alfonso de Sandoval, a great Jesuit missionary who spent forty years in the service of the slaves, and after a year under him Peter Claver declared himself "the slave of the Negroes for ever." Although by nature shy and without self-confidence, he threw himself into the work, and pursued it not with unreliable enthusiasm but with method and organisation. He enlisted bands of assistants, whether by money, goods, or services, and as soon as a slave-ship entered the port he went to wait on its living freight. The slaves were at once disembarked and shut up in the yards where

crowds came to watch them, "idle gazers," wrote Father de
Sandoval, "drawn thither by curiosity and careful not to come too
close." Hundreds of men who had been for several weeks shut up
like cattle in the ship's hold were now, well, ill, or dying, all herded
together in a confined space in a climate that was unwholesome from
damp heat. So horrible was the scene and revolting the conditions
that a friend who came with Father Claver once could never face it
again, and of Father de Sandoval himself it was written in one of the
"relations" of his province that, "when he heard a vessel of Negroes
was come into port he was at once covered with a cold sweat and
death-like pallor at the recollection of the indescribable fatigue and
unspeakable work on the previous like occasions. The experience
and practice of years never accustomed him to it." Into these yards
or sheds St Peter Claver plunged, with medicines and food, bread,
brandy, lemons, tobacco, to distribute among the Negroes, some of
whom were too frightened, others too ill, to accept them. "We
must speak to them with our hands, before we try to speak to them
with our lips," Claver would say. When he came upon any who
were dying he baptised them or gave them the last Sacraments, and
then sought out all babies born on the voyage that he might baptise
them. During the time that the Negroes spent in the sheds, penned
so closely that they had to sleep almost upon one another and freely
handed on their diseases, St Peter Claver cared for the bodies of the
sick and the souls of all. Unlike many, even among the clergy, he
did not consider that ignorance of their languages absolved him
from the obligation of instructing them in the truths of religion and
Christian morals and in bringing to their degraded spirits the
consolation of the words of Christ. He had a band of seven interpreters, one of whom spoke four Negro dialects, and with their help
he taught the slaves and prepared them for baptism, not only in
groups but individually; for they were too backward and stupid
and the language difficulty too great for him to make himself understood otherwise. He made use of pictures, showing our Lord
suffering on the cross for them and popes, princes, and other great
ones of the "white men" standing by and rejoicing at the baptism
of a Negro; above all did he try to instil in them some degree of
self-respect, to give them at least some idea that as redeemed human
beings they had dignity and worth, even if as slaves they were outcast
and despised. Not otherwise could he hope to arouse in them a
shame and contrition for their vices more perfect than that evoked
by the picture of Hell which he held up as a warning. He showed
them that they were loved even more than they were abused, and
that that divine love must not be outraged by evil ways, by cruelty

and lust. Each one had to be taken apart and drilled, time and again, even in so simple a matter as making the sign of the cross or in learning the prayer of love and contrition that each had to know : " Jesus Christ, Son of God, thou shalt be my Father and my Mother and all my good. I love Thee much. I am sorry for having sinned against Thee. O my Lord, I love Thee much, much, much." How difficult was his task in teaching is shown by the fact that at baptism each batch of ten catechumens was given the same name—to help them to remember it. It is estimated that in forty years St Peter Claver thus instructed and baptised over 300,000 slaves. When there was time and opportunity he took the same trouble to teach them how properly to use the sacrament of Penance, and in one year is said to have heard the confessions of more than five thousand. He never tired of persuading them from the occasions of sin or of urging the owners to care for the souls of the slaves ; he became so great a moral force in Cartagena that a story is told of a Negro frightening off a harlot who was pestering him in the street by saying : " Look ! Here comes Father Claver."

When the slaves were at length allotted and sent off to the mines and plantations, St Peter could only appeal to them for the last time with renewed earnestness, for he would be able to keep in touch with only a very few of them. He had a steady confidence that God would care for them and, not his least difference from the social reformers of a later age, he did not regard the most brutal of the slave-owners as despicable barbarians, beyond the mercy or might of God. They also had souls to be saved, no less than the Negroes, and to the masters St Peter appealed for physical and spiritual justice, for their own sakes no less than for that of their slaves. To the cynical mind the trust of the saint in the goodness of human nature must seem *naïf*, and no doubt could he have known he would have been far more often disappointed than not. But the conclusion cannot be avoided that only the worst of the Spanish masters can be compared for iniquity with, say, the English slave-owners of Jamaica in the seventeenth-eighteenth centuries, whose physical cruelty was no less than fiendish and moral indifference diabolical. The laws of Spain at least provided for the Christian marriage of slaves, forbade their separation from their families, and defended them from unjust seizure after liberation. St Peter Claver did all he could to provide for the observance of these laws, and every spring after Easter would make a tour of those plantations nearer Cartagena in order to see how his Negroes were getting on. He was not always well received. The masters complained that he wasted the slaves' time with his preaching, praying, and hymn-singing ;

their wives complained that after the Negroes had been to Mass it was impossible to enter the church ; and when they misbehaved Father Claver was blamed. " What sort of a man must I be, that I cannot do a little good without causing so much confusion ? " he asked himself. But he was not deterred, not even when the ecclesiastical authorities lent too willing an ear to the complaints of his critics.

Many of the stories both of the heroism and of the miraculous powers of St Peter Claver concern his nursing of sick and diseased Negroes, in circumstances often that no one else, black or white, could face, but he found time to care for other sufferers besides slaves. There were two hospitals in Cartagena, one for general cases, served by the Brothers of St. John-of-God ; this was St Sebastian's ; and another, of St Lazarus, for lepers and those suffering from the complaint called " St Antony's Fire." Both these he visited every week, waiting on the patients in their material needs and bringing hardened sinners to penitence. He also exercised an apostolate among the Protestant traders, sailors, and others whom he found therein, and brought about the conversion of an Anglican dignitary, represented to be an Archdeacon of London, whom he met when visiting prisoners-of-war on a ship in the harbour. Temporal considerations stood in the way of his making his submission, but he was taken ill and removed to St Sebastian's, where before he died he was received into the Church by Father Claver. A number of other Englishmen followed his example, and very prudently, at the suggestion of their instructor, elected to enter the service of the King of Spain rather than be repatriated to the England of the penal laws. St Peter Claver was less successful in his efforts to make converts among the Mohammedans who came to Cartagena, who, as his biographer remarks, " are well known to be of all people in the world the most obstinate in their errors," but he brought a number of Moors and Turks to the Faith, though one held out for thirty years before succumbing, and even then a vision of our Lady was required to convince him. Father Claver was also in particular request to minister to condemned criminals, and it is said that not one was executed at Cartagena during his lifetime without his being present to console him ; under his influence the most hardened and defiant would spend their last hours in prayer and penance. But many more, uncondemned by man, would seek him out in the tribunal of penance, where he often had to spend fifteen hours at a stretch, reproving, advising, encouraging, absolving. His country missions in the spring, during which he refused as much as possible the hospitality of the planters and owners and lodged in the quarters of the slaves, were succeeded in the autumn by a mission among the traders and seamen, who landed at Cartagena in great numbers at that season and further increased the vice and disorder of the port. Sometimes St Peter Claver would spend almost the whole day in the great square of the city, where the four principal streets met, preaching to all who would stop to listen. He became the apostle of Cartagena as well as of the Negroes, and in so huge a work was aided by God with those gifts that particularly pertain to apostles, of miracles, of prophecy, and of reading hearts. Few saints carried out their active work in more repulsive circumstances than did he, but these mortifications of the flesh were not enough ; he continuously used penitential instruments of the most severe description, and would pray alone in his cell with a crown of thorns pressed to his head and a heavy cross weighing down his shoulders. He avoided the most innocent gratification of his senses, lest such should divert him from his path of self-imposed martyrdom ; never would he extend to himself the indulgence and kindness he had for others. Once when commended for his apostolic zeal, he replied : " It ought to be so, but there is nothing but self-indulgence in it ; it is the result of my enthusiastic and impetuous temperament. If it were not for this work, I should be a nuisance to myself and to everybody else." And he put down his apparent indifference to handling loathsome diseases to lack of sensibility : " If being a saint consists in having no taste and having a strong stomach, I admit that I may be one."

In the year 1650 St Peter Claver went to preach the jubilee among the Negroes along the coast, but sickness attacked his emaciated and weakened body, and he was recalled to the residence at Cartagena. But here a virulent epidemic had begun to show itself, and one of the first to be attacked among the Jesuits was the debilitated missionary, so that his death seemed at hand. After receiving the last sacraments he recovered, but he was a broken man. For the rest of his life pain hardly left him, and a trembling in his limbs made it impossible for him to say Mass. He perforce became almost entirely inactive, but would sometimes hear confessions, especially of his dear friend Doña Isabella de Urbina, who had always generously supported his work with her money. Occasionally he would be carried to a hospital, a dying prisoner, or other sick person, and once when a cargo arrived of slaves from a tribe which had not been seen in Cartagena for thirty years his old strength returned ; he was taken around till he found an interpreter who spoke their tongue, then baptised all the children, and gave brief instructions to the adults. Otherwise he remained in his cell, not

only inactive but even forgotten and neglected; the numbers in the
house were much reduced, and those who remained were fully
occupied in coping with the confusion and duties imposed by the
spreading plague, but even so their indifference to the saint is
surprising. Doña Isabella and her sister remained faithful to him,
doubtless his old helper, Brother Nicholas Gonzalez, visited him
when he could. For the rest, St Peter Claver was left in the hands
of a young Negro, who was impatient and rough with the old man,
and sometimes left him nearly helpless for days on end without any
attention whatsoever. Once the authorities woke up to his existence,
when a complaint was laid that Father Claver was in the habit of
re-baptising Negroes. This, of course, he had never done, except
conditionally in cases of doubt, but he was nevertheless forbidden to
baptise in future. " It behoves me," he once wrote, " always to
imitate the example of the ass. When he is evilly spoken of, he is
dumb. When he is starved, he is dumb. When he is overloaded,
he is dumb. When he is despised and neglected, he is still dumb.
He never complains in any circumstances, for he is only an ass. So
also must God's servant be : ' Ut jumentum factus sum apud te.' "
    In the summer of 1654 Father Diego de Fariña arrived in
Cartagena from Spain with a commission from the King to convert
the Negroes. St Peter Claver was overjoyed and dragged himself
from his bed to greet his successor. He shortly afterwards heard
the confession of Doña Isabella, and told her it was for the last time,
and on September 6, after hearing Mass and receiving Holy Communion, he said to Nicholas Gonzalez : " I am going to die." That
same evening he was taken very ill and became comatose. The
rumour of his approaching end spread round the city, everyone
suddenly remembered the saint again, and numbers came to kiss his
hands before it was too late ; his cell was stripped of everything
that could be carried off as a relic. St Peter Claver never fully
recovered consciousness, and died two days later on the birthday of
our Lady, September 8, 1654. The civil authorities who had looked
askance at his solicitude for mere Negro slaves, and the clergy, who
had called his zeal indiscreet and his energy wasted, now vied with
one another to honour his memory. The city magistrates ordered
that he should be buried at the public expense, Doña Isabella de
Urbina supplied the coffin, the Duke of Estrada the lights, the city
churches the hangings ; high Masses of requiem were sung by all
the religious orders, a Mercedarian preached the panegyric, and the
vicar general of the diocese officiated at the funeral. The Negroes
and natives arranged for a Mass of their own, to which the Spanish
authorities were invited ; the church was ablaze with lights, a

special choir sang, and an oration was delivered by the treasurer of the church of Popayan, than whom " no other preacher was more diffuse on the virtues, holiness, heroism, and stupendous miracles of Father Claver." St Peter Claver was never again forgotten and his fame spread throughout the world. He was beatified by Pope Pius IX in 1850, and canonised at the same time as his friend St Alphonsus Rodriguez in 1888. In 1896 he was declared by Pope Leo XIII patron of all missionary enterprises among Negroes, in whatever part of the world.

It would seem that no quite adequate Life of St Peter Claver has yet seen the light, though the depositions obtained in the various " processes " conducted in view of his beatification afford a good deal of material. Perhaps the most reliable summary is that set out in chapter 8 of the 5th volume of Astrain, *Historia de la Compañía de Jesús en la Asistencia de España*, pp. 479-495. The best accessible biography is probably that of J. M. Solá, *Vida de San Pedro Claver* (Barcelona, 1888), which is based on the early Life by J. M. Fernandez. There are a number of other Lives, mostly of small compass, amongst which may be mentioned that of Jean Charruan, *L'Esclave des Nègres* (Paris, 1914) ; J. R. Slattery, *St Peter Claver, Apostle of the Negroes* (Philadelphia, 1893) ; Höver (in German, Dülmen, 1905) ; G. Ledos (Paris, 1923) and M. D. Petre, *Æthiopum Servus* (in English, London, 1896).

SEPTEMBER 10

ST NICHOLAS OF TOLENTINO, Conf.

A.D. 1305

THIS saint received his surname from the town which was his residence for the most considerable part of his life, and in which he died. He was a native of Sant' Angelo, a town near Fermo in the March of Ancona, and was born in the year 1245. His father, Campagnone, was a member of the house of Guarutti, and lived many years in happiness with his wife, Amata de Giudiani but when both had reached middle age they were still childless. Nicholas was the fruit of their prayers and a devout pilgrimage to the shrine of St Nicholas of Bari, in which his mother especially had earnestly begged of God a son who should faithfully serve Him. At his baptism he received the name of his patron. In his childhood he spent hours together at his prayers with wonderful application of his mind to God, and he heard the divine word with the utmost eagerness, so that the people of the place used to say : " If God spares that child he will be a saint." When he was only seven he began to impose penances and mortifications on himself, and would go to a little cave near the town and pray there in imitation of the hermits who then lived among the Apennines. People now go to pray there in honour of St Nicholas of Tolentino. He loved the poor, and would often bring home beggars from the streets to be helped by his parents. He was a sharp child, and they neglected nothing that was in their power to improve his ability and happy dispositions. In his studies he had the tuition of a local priest, and his progress was rapid. His talents and promise attracted the notice of the Bishop of Fermo, and while still a boy he received minor orders and was presented to a canonry in the collegiate church of St Saviour at Sant' Angelo. His duties were principally to take part in the daily singing of the Divine Office ; this was in accordance with his inclination, as by it he was always employed in the divine service. He became known as " the angel of the choir," and there were not wanting those who were willing to use their influence for his promotion within the ranks of the secular clergy. Nicholas, however, aspired to a state which would allow him to consecrate his whole time and thoughts directly to God, and it happened that he one day went into the Augustinian church and heard a friar preaching on the text : " Love not the world nor the things which are in the world. . . . The world passeth away, and the concupiscence thereof." This sermon finally determined him absolutely to quit the world and to embrace the order of that preacher. This he did so soon as his age would allow, and he was accepted by the Augustinian friars at Sant' Angelo. He went through his novitiate under the direction of the preacher himself, Father Reginald, and made his profession before he had completed his eighteenth year.

After completing his philosophical studies, Friar Nicholas was sent to San Ginesio for his theology, where he was taught by Father Rupert di Gilberti, who had given up a marquisate to become an Augustinian. Here the promise of his novitiate was fulfilled, and he was entrusted with the daily distribution of food to the poor at the monastery gate. He made so free with the resources of the house that the procurator complained and reported him to the prior. It was while discharging this labour of love that his first miracle was recorded of St Nicholas, when he put his hand on the head of a diseased child, saying : " The good God will heal you," and the boy was there and then cured. After three years at San Ginesio he was sent to Macerata to finish his studies, and in 1271 was ordained priest at Cingoli by Bd. Benvenuto Scotivoli, Bishop of Osimo. During his first Mass he was rapt in ecstasy, and always he appeared like a seraph at the altar, so wonderfully did the divine fire which burned in his breast manifest itself in his countenance. Devout persons strove every day to assist at his Mass as at a sacrifice offered by the hands of a saint. In the secret communications which passed between his soul and God in contemplation, especially after he had been employed at the altar or in the confessional, he seemed already to enjoy a kind of anticipation of the delights of Heaven. His zeal for the salvation of souls produced wonderful fruit, and his sermons were always followed by remarkable conversions. His exhortations, whether in the confessional or in giving catechism, were such as reached the heart and left lasting impressions on those that heard him. Already while at Cingoli he became famous among the people, particularly on account of his healing of a blind woman from Urbisaglia, with the same words which he had used to the child at Macerata. But he did not stay there long, for during four years he was continually moving from one to another of the friaries and missions of his order in the dioceses of Osimo and Fermo. For a short time he was novice-master at San Elpidio, where there was a large community which included two friars who are venerated as

beati among the Augustinians to-day, Angelo of Furci and Angelo
Conti. While visiting a relative who was abbot of a monastery near
Fermo, Nicholas was tempted by an invitation to make a long stay
in the monastery, which was comfortable and well off compared with
the hard poverty of the friaries to which he was accustomed. But
while praying in the church he seemed to hear a voice directing him :
" To Tolentino, to Tolentino. Persevere there." Shortly after to
Tolentino he was sent, and stopped there for the remaining thirty
years of his life.

This town had suffered much in the strife of Guelf and Ghibelline,
and civil discord had had its usual effects of wild fanaticism, schism,
and reckless wickedness. A campaign of street-preaching was
necessary, and to this new work St Nicholas was put. He was an
immediate success. " He spoke of the things of Heaven," says
St Antoninus. " Sweetly he preached the divine word, and the
words that came from his lips fell like burning flame. When his
superiors ordered him to take up the public ministry of the gospel,
he did not try to display his knowledge or show off his ability, but
simply to glorify God. Amongst his audience could be seen the
tears and heard the sighs of people detesting their sins and repenting
of their past lives." His preaching aroused opposition among those
who were unmoved by it, and a certain man of notoriously evil life
did all he could to shout down the friar and break up his audiences.
Nicholas refused to be intimidated, and his perseverance began to
make an impression on his persecutor. One day when the man had
been trying to drown his voice and scatter the people by fencing
with his friends in the street, he sheathed his sword and stood by to
listen. Afterwards he came and apologised to St Nicholas, admitted
that his heart had been touched, and began to reform his ways.
This conversion made a strong impression, and soon Nicholas had
to be spending nearly whole days in hearing confessions. He went
about the slums of Tolentino, comforting the dying, waiting on
(and sometimes miraculously curing) the sick and bed-ridden,
watching over the children, appealing to the criminals, composing
quarrels and estrangements : one woman gave evidence in the cause
of his canonisation that he had entirely won over and reformed her
husband who for long had treated her with shameful cruelty.
Another witness, Bernard Apillaterra, gave evidence of three
miracles performed by the saint in his family. " Say nothing of
this," was his usual comment after these happenings (and they were
numerous), " give thanks to God, not to me. I am only a pot of
clay, a poor sinner." Jordan of Saxony (not the Dominican *beatus*,
but an Austin friar) in his Life of St Nicholas, written about 1380,

relates a happening which has the distinction of being referred to by the Bollandists as the most extraordinary miracle which they find attributed to the saint. A man was waylaid by his enemies at a lonely spot on Mont' Ortona, near Padua, and, disregarding his entreaties in the name of God and St Nicholas for mercy or at least a priest to shrive him, they killed him and threw his body into a lake. A week later his body was recovered by one wearing the habit of an Austin friar, who led him back alive and well to his family. He asked for a priest, received the last sacraments, and then, declaring that he had been brought back to make a good end in response to his desperate appeal to St Nicholas, he again died. His flesh at once shrivelled up and dropped off, leaving only his bare bones for Christian burial. On a wall at Montecchio there is still an inscription recording his restoration of a child supposed to have been drowned : " Near by this Montana gate St Nicholas of Tolentino recalled a dead child to life. Hail, thou guardian of the Catholic Church." Many of the marvels attributed to the intercession of St Nicholas are in connection with the bread blessed on his feast by the friars of his order, with a special benediction authorised by Pope Eugenius IV. In his later years when he was ill and weak from work and austerities his superiors wished him to take meat and other strengthening food, and St Nicholas was troubled between the obligation of obedience and his desire not to give in to his body. One night it appeared to him that our Lady was present, with St Augustine, and that she told him to ask for a small piece of bread, to dip it in water and eat it, and he would recover. So it fell out, and Nicholas in grateful memory would afterwards bless pieces of bread and give them to the sick, thus originating the Augustinians' custom.*

The final illness of St Nicholas lasted nearly a year, and in the last months he got up from bed only once, to absolve a penitent who he knew intended to conceal a grevious sin from any priest but himself. His last days were one long appeal to our Lady to aid him at the end, which came quietly on September 10, 1305. His last words to the community gathered round his bed were : " My dearest brethren, my conscience does not reproach me with anything—but I am not justified by that." A commission was appointed which at once began to collect evidence for his heroic virtues and miracles,

* The spirit in which the Church desires her children to make use of such things is illustrated by the prayer to be said by those who use St Nicholas's bread : " Grant, we beseech Thee, Almighty God, that Thy Church, which is made illustrious by the glory of the marvels and miracles of Blessed Nicholas, Thy confessor, may by his merits and intercession enjoy perpetual peace and unity, through Christ our Lord. Amen."

but the transfer of the papacy to Avignon intervened and canonisation was not achieved till the reign of Eugenius IV, in 1446. About the year 1345 a German lay-brother severed the arms from the saint's body and made an unsuccessful attempt to decamp with the relics to a monastery in his own country. To prevent further attempts of this sort the friars of Tolentino hid the body, but the secret of the place was forgotten or lost and from that day to this it has never been found. The two arms, however, remain, and it is recorded that on twenty-six occasions these arms have been known to bleed. Unlike the famous case of St Januarius (September 19) these bleedings do not occur at more or less fixed times, but have usually taken place just before some calamity has overtaken the Church or Christendom, and have so come to be looked on as miraculous warnings, *e.g.* in 1452, before the fall of Constantinople ; in 1510, before the revolt of Luther (himself an Augustinian friar). The last time this happened was in 1830, at the beginning of that unrest in Italy under Austrian domination which led to union under the house of Savoy and the spoliation of the Holy See in 1870. Pope Benedict XIV in his treatise on canonisation refers to the prophetic nature of these occurrences.

The saints, however much they subdued their passions and strengthened themselves in virtue, always watched with vigilance over all their words and actions and every emotion of their hearts, knowing this life to be a state of perpetual warfare and danger. To prevent attacks from the Enemy it is the duty of a Christian to be always ready, and in time of peace to expect his return ; this disposition will help to keep him at a distance, and neglect of it will certainly invite him to take advantage of our indifference. By frequent self-examination, self-denial, a state of humble fear and penitence, and by watchfulness against all occasions of danger we must continually be armed and ready to repulse him: if we leave the ways of our soul open or unguarded, and trust him within the gates, he enters smoothly—and brings death.

There is a Life of St Nicholas by a contemporary, Peter de Monte Rubiano, who was a religious of his own Order. This is accessible in the *Acta Sanctorum*, September, vol. iii. Of the later Lives none seem to have treated this work and the other materials there provided in a very critical spirit. The most copious biography is that of Philip Giorgi, *Vita del taumaturgo S Niccola da Tolentino* (1856–1859, in 3 vols.). The others are for the most part of a popular character ; notably, for example, that by A. Tonna Barthet (Brussels, 1896) ; and that by " H.P.," *St Nicolas de Tolentin* (Paris, 1899). At Tolentino itself, in view of the centenary kept in 1905, a sort of periodical was brought out, beginning in 1899, under the title of *Sesto Centenario di San Nicola da Tolentino*. This includes copies of certain documents preserved in the archives of the city, but it is mainly interesting for the information it provides concerning the later *cultus* of the Saint. It must be remembered that the accounts of miracles, etc., belong for the most part to a very uncritical age. Several little booklets, notably one by N. G. Cappi (1725), were published in Italy concerning the alleged bleeding of St Nicholas's severed arms. A short English biography by E. A. Foran was issued in 1920.

ST NEMESIANUS AND MANY COMPANIONS, MARTYRS

A.D. 257

In the first year of the eighth general persecution, raised by Valerian in the year 257, St Cyprian, Bishop of Carthage, was banished by the proconsul of Africa to Curubis. At the same time the president of Numidia proceeded with severity against the Christians, tortured many, and afterwards put several to barbarous deaths and sent others to work in the mines, or rather quarries of marble. Out of this holy company some were taken at intervals to be tormented afresh or inhumanly butchered, whilst others continued their lingering martyrdom in hunger, nakedness, and filth, exhausted with hard labour, persecuted with daily blows, hardships, and insults. St Cyprian wrote from the place of his banishment to comfort and encourage these gallant sufferers for their faith.

Those to whom his noble letter was addressed thanked St Cyprian for it through their leader, Nemesianus, Bishop of Tubunae. It had, they said, eased the pain of their blows and sufferings, and made them indifferent to the stench and filth of their prison. They tell him that by gloriously confessing his faith in the proconsul's court, and going before them into banishment, he had sounded the charge and animated all the soldiers of God for the conflict. They conclude by begging his prayers, and say : " Let us assist one another by our prayers, that God and Christ and the whole choir of angels may send us help when we shall most want it." This glorious company of saints is commemorated on this day in the Roman Martyrology, nine of them being mentioned by name : Nemesianus, Felix, Lucius, another Felix, Litteus, Polyanus, Victor, Jader, and Dativus. These were all bishops, but there also suffered, as St Cyprian tells us, lower clergy and lay-people of all ages and states of life. Some were deliberately put to death, a few survived, but the most part died of exposure, hardship, ill-treatment, or sickness brought on by their captivity.

The mention of SS Nemesianus, Felix and Companions in the Roman Martyrology on this date seems to be due to a confusion. There was a martyr, Nemesius, who suffered with companions at Alexandria, and he, as the *Hieronymianum* bears witness, belongs to this day, being probably identical with a martyr who in the Syriac *breviarium* appears as " Menmais," also on September 10. Dom Quentin has shown that Florus, the martyrologist, has identified this group of martyrs of Alexandria with those to whom St Cyprian's letter is addressed (see the *Martyrologes Historiques*, p. 289). We have no evidence beyond Cyprian's letter that the bishops to whom it was addressed were honoured subsequently as martyrs. The Carthaginian calendar names a Nemesianus on December 23, but this may be a boy martyr of whom St Augustine speaks. The text of St Cyprian, with comments, is quoted in the *Acta Sanctorum*, September, vol. iii.

SS. MENODORA, METRODORA, AND NYMPHODORA, VIRGINS AND MARTYRS

c. A.D. 304

The " acts " of these martyrs are known only in the tenth-century version of Simeon Metaphrastes, wherein they are represented as having been three orphan sisters who lived a life of solitude and good works in Bithynia, " near the Pythian baths." During the persecution under Diocletian and Maximian they were reported to Fronto, governor of the province, who had them brought before him. The beauty and modest carriage of the three girls touched his heart, and when they made a profession of Christianity he offered to be their protector if they would submit themselves to his gods. They gently refused his offer, asking instead that as they had lived so might they die, all together. When he was unable to make them change their minds, Fronto had Menodora beaten in barbarous fashion before the two others to shake their constancy, but even the sight of her mangled and dead body putrefying in the fierce sun did not move them. " We are three branches of the same good tree," said Metrodora, " nor will we disgrace the root from which we are sprung by doing as you wish." Then she was tortured with fire after she had been beaten, and was at last beheaded. But Nymphodora, the youngest, died under the blows of the scourges.

The Greek " Passio," so called, is printed in Migne, P.G., vol. cxv ; a Latin translation in the *Acta Sanctorum*, September, vol. iii.

ST PULCHERIA, EMPRESS IN CONSTANTINOPLE, VIRG.

A.D. 453

In this princess virtue shone forth on the imperial throne in an unusual manner, and showed itself equally invincible in the trials of adversity and those (which are usually more dangerous) of flattering prosperity. The Empress Pulcheria was granddaughter to Theodosius the Great and daughter to Arcadius, Emperor of the East, who died in the year 408. She was born in 399, and had three sisters, Flacilla, who was the eldest but died soon, and Arcadia and Marina, who were younger than Pulcheria. Arcadius left a son, Theodosius II, eight years old, and appointed for his minister and tutor Anthimus, one of the wisest men in the empire, who was a constant friend of St John Chrysostom. St Pulcheria was only five years old when she lost her mother, and nine when she lost her father ; but her prudence and piety matured at an early age, and she added to virtue intelligence, personal beauty, and administrative ability. Theodosius was mild, humane, and devout, incapable in public affairs, and not sufficiently strong for his exalted position ; he was more interested in writing and painting than in the art of government, and was nicknamed " the Calligrapher." In the year 414 Pulcheria, though only fifteen years of age, was declared, in the name of her young brother, *Augusta* and partner with him in the imperial dignity, and charged with the care of his instruction. Her wisdom, capacity, and quickness, in which she exceeded any of her age, supplied her want of experience. To cultivate her brother's mind and give him an education suitable to his rank she placed about him the most learned and virtuous masters, and made it her first concern to instil into him sentiments of religion and piety, for all other qualifications are useless and often dangerous when not guided by these principles. She taught him to pray with devotion, to love the places of divine worship, and to have a great zeal for the Catholic Church and its holy doctrine. Whatever was valuable in that prince was, under God, owing to Pulcheria, and if she did not make him greater, all agree that nothing was wanting on her side. She also took care of the education of her two surviving sisters who, to the end of their lives, endeavoured to tread in her steps. Both from a motive of personal virtue, and also because she realised that the good of the State would be enhanced by the absence of suitors for the hands of the young Emperor's sisters, Pulcheria at the same time made a public vow of virginity, and induced her sisters to do the same. They had a share in all her activities except those that regarded the State ; they ate together, were united in all acts of devotion and charity, and time not devoted to exercises of piety and to useful studies they employed in working at the arts proper to their sex. Pulcheria only absented herself when she was obliged to attend business of state, finding a solitude in the palace itself. The austerities which she practised were such as seemed rather to suit a

recluse than one who lived in a court. Men were denied entrance to
her and her sisters' apartments to avoid the least suspicion or
shadow of danger ; and she never associated with men except in
public places. The imperial palace under her direction was as
regular as a monastery. Upon all emergencies she consulted Heaven
by devout prayer, and then listened to the advice of able counsellors
before she took any resolution in matters of weight. The imperial
council was, through her discernment, composed of the wisest, most
virtuous, and most experienced persons in the empire ; yet in
deliberation all of them readily acknowledged the superiority of her
judgement and penetration. Her resolutions were the result of
mature consideration, and she took care that all orders should be
executed with precision and despatch, but always in the name of her
brother, to whom she gave the honour and reputation of all she did.
She was herself well skilled in Greek and Latin, in history and
literature ; and was, as everyone must be who is endowed with
greatness of soul and a just idea of the dignity of the human mind, the
patroness of the sciences and of both the useful and fine arts. Far
from making religion subservient to policy, all her views and projects
were regulated by that consideration, and thus the happiness of her
government was complete. She prevented by her prudence all
revolts which ambition, jealousy, or envy might stir up to disturb the
tranquillity of the Church or State ; she cemented a firm peace with
neighbouring powers and abolished the remains of idolatry in several
places. Never did virtue reign in the Eastern Empire with greater
lustre, never was the state more happy or more flourishing or its
name more respected, even among the barbarians, than whilst the
reins of the government were in the hands of Pulcheria. Both the
supineness of Theodosius and the thoroughness of his sister are
illustrated by the story that on one occasion, in order to test him,
Pulcheria drew up and presented to him a decree containing a
sentence of death against herself. He signed it without reading it.

Theodosius was twenty years old when it was thought proper for
him to marry, and by the advice of Pulcheria he pitched upon
Athenais, the daughter of an Athenian philosopher, who had given
her an excellent education but no dowry. She came to court to
try and get redress, and by her beauty, genius, and uncommon
accomplishments gained the admiration of everyone, so that
St Pulcheria judged her most worthy to be the Emperor's consort.
She was first baptised, for she had been brought up an idolater, and
her name Athenais being derived from Athene or Minerva she
changed it into that of Eudocia. Theodosius married her in 421,
and two years after he declared her *Augusta*. This marriage made no

alteration in the state, the chief administration being still entrusted to Pulcheria, till the eunuch Chrysaphius, a great favourite with the Emperor, prepossessed Eudocia against her, because of the great sway her sister-in-law had in the government. In 431 Nestorius was condemned in the Council of Ephesus, which had been summoned by Theodosius, who with his wife was inclined towards Nestorianism. St Cyril of Alexandria had written on behalf of orthodoxy both to Pulcheria and Eudocia, and Pulcheria had used all her influence on behalf of St Cyril. She prevailed on her brother to accept the condemnation of Nestorius, and was grossly slandered by his partisans in consequence, and still further estranged from Eudocia, who continued with Chrysaphius her intrigues against her benefactress. The Emperor (whose misfortune was indolence and weakness of understanding), after having been long deaf to their insinuations, at length was so far worked upon as to give in to all that they said against her. Upon their suggestion he sent an order to St Flavian, Bishop of Constantinople, to make her a deaconness of his church. The prelate waited on the Emperor, and urged cogent reasons against the proposal. Finding Theodosius resolutely bent on the thing, he went home and sent a private message to Pulcheria, telling her to take care to be out of the way. The princess understood by this hint the contrivance of her enemies, and retired to a country seat in the plains of Hebdomon, with a resolution of spending the remainder of her days in silence and retirement. But the fall of Eudocia was also at hand. She was accused, unjustly, of infidelity with an officer of the court, and was banished; she passed the remainder of her life at Jerusalem, and there made a most holy end. St Pulcheria in the meantime looked upon her retreat as a favour of Heaven and consecrated all her time to God in prayer and good works. She made no complaints of her brother's ingratitude, of the empress who owed everything to her, or of their unjust ministers. Her desire was both to forget the world and to be forgotten by it, esteeming herself happy in having no other business on her hands than that of conversing with God, and meditating on divine truths. Nothing could have drawn her from this solitude but the dangers which threatened the Church and State and compassion for her brother, whose credulity was such as to make him lose both his wife and his sister. Soon after the exile of Eudocia she returned to the court, where Theodosius, under the pressure of Chrysaphius and with a fine disregard for theological consistency seeing that he had formerly inclined to Nestorius, was now supporting the heresiarch Eutyches. In 449 Pope St Leo the Great appealed both to St Pulcheria and the Emperor to reject Monophysism. The answer of Theodosius was to approve the acts of the "Robber Synod" of Ephesus, and to drive St Flavian from the see of Constantinople. Pulcheria was firmly orthodox, but her influence with her brother had been weakened. The Pope wrote again, and the Archdeacon of Rome, Hilarus, and the Western Emperor, Valentinian III, with Eudocia his wife and Galla Placidia his mother—and amid all these appeals Theodosius suddenly died, killed by a fall from his horse while hunting.

St Pulcheria, now fifty-one years old, at once became, or remained, mistress of the Eastern Empire. To strengthen her authority she chose a partner in the throne, an excellent general, a wise statesman, zealous for the Catholic faith, virtuous, and charitable to the poor. His name was Marcian ; he was a native of Thrace, and a widower. Pulcheria, judging it would be of advantage to the state and enhance Marcian's credit and authority, proposed to marry him, on condition she should be at liberty to keep her vow of virginity. Marcian agreed to the proposal, and these two governed together like two friends who had in all things the same views and sentiments, which centred in the advancement of religion and the public weal. Marcian was the first Christian prince to have a religious ceremony of coronation, and the first act of his reign was the trial and execution of Chrysaphius. The two sovereigns received favourably and with great joy four legates sent by St Leo the Great to Constantinople, and their zeal for the Catholic faith earned the highest commendations of that Pope and of the general Council of Chalcedon which, under their protection, condemned the Monophysite heresy in 451. They did their utmost to have the decrees of this synod executed over all the East, but failed lamentably in Egypt and Syria, where Monophysism is professed by many to this day. St Pulcheria wrote herself two letters, one to certain monks, another to an abbess of nuns in Palestine, to convince them that the Council of Chalcedon did not revive Nestorianism, but condemned that error together with the opposite heresy of Eutyches. Twice already, in 414 and 423, Pulcheria had been responsible for remissions of arrears of unpaid taxes, covering a period of sixty years, and she and her husband inaugurated a policy of low taxation and as little warfare as possible. The admirable spirit in which they undertook their duties was expressed by Marcian in his *dictum* : "It is our business to provide for the care of the human race." But the excellent partnership lasted only three years, for in July 453, the Empress St Pulcheria died.

This great Empress built many churches, and among them three in honour of the all-holy Mother of God, namely, that of Blakhernae, that of Khalkopratia, and that of the Hodegetria, that were among the most famous Marian churches of Christendom. In the last she placed a famous picture of the Blessed Virgin, which the Empress Eudocia had sent from Jerusalem as the work of St Luke the Evangelist. She and Theodosius were the first rulers of Constantinople who were Greek rather than Latin ; she encouraged the establishment of a university there, with an emphasis on Greek literature and the recognition of Greek as an official language, which her brother carried out ; and she gauged the needs of rulers and people for fixed principles of law which were met by the Code of Theodosius. If we consider her actions and heroic virtues we shall see that the great commendations which St Proclus, in his panegyric on her, St Leo, and the Council of Chalcedon, bestowed on this Empress were, so far from being compliments or mere eloquence, thoroughly well deserved. Writing to her in April 451, to thank her for all she had done for the Church and its orthodox champions, Pope Leo said that the truth had triumphed over both Nestorianism and Monophysism largely through her own efforts ; and the Fathers of Chalcedon called her " Guardian of the Faith, peacemaker, religious, orthodox, and a second St Helen." She is named on this day in the Roman Martyrology, having been inserted by Cardinal Baronius, and her feast is kept in many places in the East.

Pulcheria played a prominent part in the ecclesiastical history of her time, but she has no separate biography. See the *Acta Sanctorum*, September, vol. iii, and also vol. iv, pp. 778–782 ; Hefele-Leclercq, *Conciles*, vol. ii, pp. 375–377, etc., and *Dict. of Christ. Biog.*, vol. iv, pp. 520–521.

ST HILARUS, POPE AND CONFESSOR

A.D. 468

On August 8 in the year 449 the heretical Dioscorus, Patriarch of Alexandria, opened in the church of the Mother of God at Ephesus the council which is known to history by the ominous name of the Robber Synod. Protected by troops of violent soldiers, the heresiarch Eutyches was declared innocent by the rebel bishops and those who maintained orthodoxy were abused and physically maltreated, St Flavian of Constantinople so that he died. The legates of the Pope were powerless : they made their protest and withdrew, barely escaping with their lives. One of these legates was Hilarus, a Sardinian by birth. His letter to the Empress St Pulcheria is extant, in which he apologises for not personally delivering to her the Pope's letter after the synod, explaining that owing to the violence and intrigues of Dioscorus he could not get to Constantinople and was only just able to escape to Rome. As a votive offering for his preservation at this time he afterwards built the chapel of St John the Apostle in the baptistery of St John Lateran. Over the door may still be seen the inscription he put up there : *Liberatori suo beato Iohanni evangelistæ Hilarus episcopus famulus Christi :* " Hilarus, the bishop and servant of Christ, to his liberator, the blessed John the Evangelist." On the death of St Leo the Great in 461, the Archdeacon Hilarus was elected to the pontifical throne. His chief work as pope was to strengthen ecclesiastical discipline in Gaul and Spain, both by curbing the excesses of individual bishops and by maintaining their rights. Several episcopal disputes were brought to him to be settled from these countries, in the course of which he forbade bishops to nominate their successors or to leave their dioceses without the written permission of the metropolitan. At a synod held in Rome in 465, the first of which the original records have come down to us, the canon that no bishop might be transferred from one see to another was reiterated. St Hilarus is said also to have sent a letter to the East confirming the oecumenical councils of Nicæa, Ephesus, and Chalcedon, and the " dogmatic tome " of St Leo, and on one occasion he publicly rebuked the Emperor Anthemius in St Peter's for allowing one of his favourites to encourage and abet the teaching of heretical doctrines. In addition to that of St John the Evangelist, St Hilarus built chapels of St John the Baptist and of the Holy Cross in the Lateran baptistery ; the last named was for use as a *consignatorium,* that is, the place where the newly baptised is anointed with holy Chrism and clothed in the white garment. Among his other benefactions to the city were a library and two public baths. Pope St Hilarus died on February 28, 468, and was buried at St Laurence-outside-the-Walls. His feast was formerly observed on this day, but the latest edition of the Roman Martyrology names him on the day of his death.

Beside the notice in the *Liber Pontificalis* (Duchesne, vol. i, 242–248) and the letters, which may be consulted in Thiel and in Jaffé, the Bollandists reproduce most of the relevant materials in the *Acta Sanctorum,* September, vol. iii. See also Hefele-Leclercq, *Conciles,* vol. ii ; Grisar, *Geschichte Roms und der Päpste,* pp. 323, and *passim, Dict. Christ. Biog.,* iii, 72–74.

ST FINNIAN OF MOVILLE, Bp. AND CONF.

c. A.D. 575

Ulster is a name which now has unhappy associations for many Catholics, but its history is no less glorious than that of any other part of Ireland, and one of its greatest sons was this Finnian. He was a son of Corpre, of royal race, born in the neighbourhood of Strangford Lough, and presumably his parents were Christians, for he was sent when young to be educated by St Colman at Dromore and St Mochae on Mahee Island. From thence he went across the sea to Whitern in Strathclyde, and stayed at the monastery founded by St Ninian, called *Candida Casa*. There is a story told that here he attracted the love of a Pictish princess, probably Drustic, the daughter of Drust, who for a time was made ill by his indifference. When she realised that Finnian really meant to be a monk, the young woman quickly recovered and transferred her affections to another youth, and Finnian acted as a go-between between them. Whether by accident, treachery, or as a practical joke, he brought about a meeting between Drustic and a third young man, and a scandal was raised which made it desirable for Finnian to leave Whitern. Very likely this was just gossip or misunderstanding, for Finnian went from Whitern to Rome, a very natural decision for one who had been brought up by St Colman and in the community of St Ninian, both of whom had been to Rome. He spent seven years in the City, where he was ordained priest, and then returned to Ulster, bringing with him, among other treasures, a copy of St Jerome's text of the New Testament and the Pentateuch. On his way he is said to have preached in various places, including Anglesey, and to have there founded the church of Llanfinnan. He established a monastery at Moville (Maghbile) in County Down, and another at Dromin in Louth ; Moville was and continued to be one of the great schools of Ireland, and so late as the eleventh century produced the chronicler Marianus Scotus (Maelbrigte), who went to Cologne and Fulda. But its chief influence was through St Columcille, who was a disciple of St Finnian. The incident of the dispute between the saints concerning the copy made by Columcille of the psalter brought by Finnian from Rome is referred to under St Columba on June 9. King Diarmaid adjudged that surreptitious copy to belong to St Finnian, and the alleged remains of it were formerly carried in their casket before them into battle by the O'Donnells of Mayo, in which family it is still an heirloom. By them it has been put on permanent loan in the museum of the Royal Irish Academy at Dublin.

A miracle related of St Finnian concerns his sister, who was moved to such imprudent mortifications by his preaching that she died as a result. This not unnaturally led to very strong feeling against the saint, who vindicated himself by raising the dead woman to life by the power of his prayer. The life of his community was regulated in accordance with a code of penitential canons he had brought from Rome, but Finnian found that their proper observance was considerably hampered by the long distance from the monastery of the mill in which many worked. He therefore built another mill nearer at hand, and, as there was no stream to work it, prayed beside a stream on a nearby hill which altered its course so as to make a convenient mill-race. Such a miracle is easily " rationalised," but is of interest because of its resemblance to the story told in the *Diologues* of St Gregory of the diverting of the course of the river Serchio by St Frigidian (Frediano) of Lucca. This saint has often been identified with St Finnian of Moville—and still is in Ireland and in the breviary of the Canons Regular of the Lateran—but it is impossible to reconcile what is known of the lives of either of them : St Frigidian lived for over twenty-eight years in Lucca and died there, whereas Finnian died in Ireland, where he had passed most of his life. His death took place between the years 572 and 579, according to a Scottish tradition at Kilwinning, near Cunningham. The Breviary of Aberdeen says that he founded a monastery and set up a cross of St Brigid at Holywood in Dumfries, and he is supposed to have changed the course of a river in Scotland as well, namely, the Garnoch. In Ireland the feast of St Finnian of Moville is not observed separately from that of St Frigidian on March 20 (*vere* 18th). He is the principal patron of Ulster.

For any connected Life of Finnian we have to turn to such unreliable sources as Capgrave and the Aberdeen Breviary. But there are many passages which refer to him in such books as Gougaud, *Christianity in Celtic Lands*, and J. Ryan, *Irish Monasticism*. All admit the confusion between the legends which attach to this Finnian and those belonging to other holy men who bear this and similar names. In the *Félire* of Oengus under this day, September 10, we read : " A kingpost of red gold with purity, over the swelling sea he came with law, a sage for whom Ireland is sad, Findbarr of Mag Bili." This seems to endorse the idea of foreign travel and the bringing of some important text from beyond the seas. Most probably it is this Finnian who was credited with the authorship of the Penitential, the *Pœnitentiale Vinniani*. See Esposito, *Latin Learning*, vol. i, pp. 236–240. Under the name " Wynnin " in Forbes, *Kalendars of Scottish Saints*, there is (p.465) an interesting note by Dr. Reeves, who also identifies Finnian of Moville with St Frigidianus of Lucca. See the March volume of this series, vol. iii, pp. 310–312.

ST SALVIUS, or SAUVE, Bp. of Albi, Conf.

A.D. 584

St Salvius belonged to a family which gave several saints to the Church during the sixth–eighth centuries. He was at first a lawyer and magistrate of the province, but his love for retirement and the desire of being freed from the distractions which impede a constant union with God induced him to become a monk, and his brethren afterwards chose him for their abbot. He chiefly confined himself to a cell at a distance from the rest, and here, being seized by a violent fever, he grew so ill that he was dead in the opinion of all about him. Indeed the saint himself was always persuaded that he really died, and was restored to life by a miracle ; he that as it will, he was in the year 574 taken from his retreat and placed in the see of Albi. He lived as austerely as ever, and constantly refused the presents that were made him : if anything were forced upon him, he on the spot distributed the whole among the poor. The patrician Mommolus, general of King Gontramnus, having taken a great number of prisoners at Albi, the saint followed him and ransomed them all. The king of Soissons, Chilperic, fancied himself as a theologian and was responsible for an unorthodox treatise ; it was even rumoured that he wanted to impose the Sabellian heresy upon his people. St Salvius, together with his friend St Gregory of Tours, succeeded in bringing the monarch back to orthodoxy. In the year 580 St Salvius was present at the synod of French bishops which Chilperic convened at Braine, and four years later an epidemic made great havoc among his flock. It was in vain his friends advised him to be careful of his health ; animated, unwearied, undaunted, he went everywhere he thought his presence necessary. He visited the sick, comforted them, and exhorted them to prepare for eternity by such good works as their condition admitted. When he knew that his own hour was near, he ordered his coffin to be made, changed his clothes, and prepared himself to appear before God, to whom he was called on September 10, 584, on which date he is named in the Roman Martyrology.

Nearly all we know of St Salvius is contained in the *Historia Francorum* of Gregory of Tours. See also the Bollandists, September, vol. iii, and Duchesne, *Fastes Épiscopaux*, vol. ii, p. 43.

ST THEODARDUS, Bp. of Maestricht, Mart.

c. A.D. 670

Was a disciple of St Remaclus, whom he helped in the establishment of the monasteries of Malmédy and Stavelot and succeeded when he retired from the government of the diocese of Maestricht. St Theodardus was an energetic bishop and a man of cheerful and sympathetic disposition, but little of interest is known of his life except his manner of leaving it. Some unscrupulous nobles having taken possession of lands which rightly belonged to his church, he made up his mind about the year 669 to go personally to Childeric II of Austrasia to ask that justice might be done. While passing through the forest of Bienwald near Speyer he was set upon by robbers and killed. His biographer informs us that St Theodardus made a long speech to his murderers, to which they replied with a quotation from Horace ! As his death was occasioned by a journey undertaken in defence of the rights of the Church he was venerated as a martyr, and his successor, St Lambert, translated his body to the church of Liége. The Roman Martyrology speaks of St Theodardus as a martyr " who lay down his life for his sheep and after his death was resplendent with significant miracles."

There is an anonymous Life of this saint written in the eighth century, and another, of later date perhaps, by Heriger, Abbot of Lobbes. The former is printed in the *Acta Sanctorum*, September, vol. iii. See also G. Kurth, *Etude critique sur St Lambert* (1876), pp. 67 *seq.*, and Duchesne, *Fastes Épiscopaux*, iii, p. 191.

ST AUBERTUS, Bp. of Avranches, Conf.

Eighth Century

Nothing definite is known of this saint except that he was the founder of the church of Mont-Saint-Michel early in the eighth century. Tradition says that an apparition of St Michael the Archangel told St Aubertus to build a church on the Rocher de la Tombe on the sea-board of his diocese, which the bishop undertook to do. The undertaking was beset with great and unexpected difficulties, and it was not until he had received two more visions of the Archangel and a divine rebuke for his want of energy that St Aubertus was able to carry it through. The church was dedicated in 709, in honour of St Michael for those in peril on the sea, and it was entrusted to a chapter of canons. These became relaxed and in later ages were replaced by Benedictines. The year of the death of St Aubertus is not known. He was buried at Mont-Saint-Michel and three hundred years after his relics were found and enshrined. On October 16, the anniversary of the dedication of the church, a feast of St Michael *in Monte Tumba* is kept in France.

Some slight materials for the history of this Saint are provided by the Bollandists in the *Acta Sanctorum* on June 18, vol. iii. See also Motet in *Mém. Soc. archéolog. d'Avranches*, 1847, pp. 28 *seq.* ; and C. Claireux, *Les reliques de S. Aubert* (1909).

BB. APOLLINARIS FRANCO AND HIS COMPANIONS, MARTS.

A.D. 1622

In 1867, the same year in which persecution began again in Urakami, though not to blood, Pope Pius IX solemnly beatified 205 of the martyrs of Japan, of whom the Franciscan Martyrology to-day refers to eighteen members of its first order and twenty-two tertiaries. Owing to various causes—among them it seems we must sadly recognise national jealousies and even religious rivalries between the missionaries of various orders—the *shogun* Ieyasu Tokugawa in 1614 decreed that Christianity should be abolished, and these Franciscan *beati* all suffered between the years 1617 and 1632. The persecution gradually increased in intensity until in 1622 took place the " great martyrdom," in which Blessed Apollinaris Franco was one of the principal victims. He was a Castilian of Aguilar del Campo, who after taking his doctor's degree at Salamanca became a Friar Minor of the Observance in the province of St James. In 1600 he went on the Philippine mission and thence to Japan, where after the persecution began he was named commissary general in charge of the mission. While he was at Nagasaki in 1617 he heard that there was not a single priest left in the province of Omura, where Christians were numerous, and he went thither without disguise to minister to them. He was thrown into a filthy prison, where he was left for five years. Blessed Apollinaris never ceased to comfort his flock by messages and letters, and ministered to those who were able to make their way into the gaol. A number of other Christians were confined with him, and a fellow-religious, BLESSED RICHARD-OF-ST-ANNE, wrote to the guardian of his friary at Nivelles : " I have been for nearly a year in this wretched prison, where are with me nine religious of our order, eight Dominicans, and six Jesuits. The others are native Christians who have helped us in our ministry. Some have been here for five years. Our food is a little rice and water. The road to martyrdom has been paved for us by more than three hundred martyrs, all Japanese, on whom all kinds of tortures were inflicted. As for us survivors, we also are all doomed to death. We religious and those who have helped us are to be burnt at a slow fire ; the others will be beheaded. . . . If my mother is still alive, I beg you to be so kind as to tell her of God's mercy to me in allowing me to suffer and die for Him. I have no time left to write to her myself." Early in September 1622, twenty of the prisoners were removed to Nagasaki. On the 12th Blessed Apollinaris and the seven remaining with him at Omura were there burnt to death, including BB. FRANCIS-OF-ST-BONAVENTURE and PAUL-OF-ST-CLARE, whom he had clothed with the Franciscan habit while in captivity. Two days previously those who had been removed to Nagasaki had there met the same death. Prominent among the Franciscans were Blessed Richard, mentioned above, and BLESSED LUCY DE FREITAS. The last-named was a Japanese of high birth, widow of a Portuguese merchant who had died many years before. She became a Franciscan tertiary and devoted the rest of her life to the cause of the poor and the encouragement and help of persecuted Christians. She was afflicted with this cruel death when she was over eighty years old, because it was in her house that Blessed Richard had been captured.

The first in time of the friars commemorated to-day, BLESSED PETER-OF-THE-ASSUMPTION, was also the first martyr of the second great Japanese persecution. When he first came to the country from Spain he distinguished himself by the extraordinary facility with which he learned the language. After ten years of fruitful missionary work he was beheaded with Blessed John Machado, S.J., at Nagasaki on May 22, 1617. BLESSED LOUIS SOTELO, burnt at Simabura on August 25, 1624, was a remarkable man and a very able missionary, who went to Japan in 1603. After he had preached there for ten years, making a large number of conversions and breaking entirely fresh ground, he was sent with Hasekura Rokuyemon and a large suite on an embassy to Pope Paul V and the King of Spain by Date Masamune, the prince of Sendai, who was a catechumen, or pretended to be. They travelled *via* Mexico, where on Holy Saturday 1614, seventy-eight members of the embassy were baptised (they all afterwards apostatised). Blessed Louis accompanied the ambassador throughout his peregrinations in Spain and Italy, an office which required much tact and earned some obloquy for the Franciscan, for behind the embassy lay considerations of both ecclesiastical and secular politics (the last named *vis-à-vis* the Dutch in the Far East). Blessed Louis landed in Japan again in 1622, at the height of the persecution of Ieyasu, which was intensified by the fact that Date had sent an embassy to Europe, and was at once imprisoned. Two years later he gained his crown. Of BLESSED ANTONY-OF-ST-BONAVENTURE the commissary general in Japan wrote : " He was a tireless worker and gained very many souls for God. He worked night and day, hearing confessions, baptising, catechising, raising those who had fallen through fear in the persecution. Within a short time he thus reconciled more than two thousand, and many of them persevered unto martyrdom. In these difficult days when Christianity was everywhere reviled and suppressed he baptised more than a thousand pagans. For the ten years of his ministry nothing could check his zeal." Blessed Antony was burned at Nagasaki on September 8, 1628, after being in prison for many months. Among the secular tertiaries included in these *beati* are some who are claimed equally by the Friars Minor and by the Friars Preachers, such as BB. JOHN TOMAKI and his four sons, all under sixteen ; BB. LOUIS NIFAKI and his sons aged five and two ; and BLESSED LOUISA, an aged woman who was burnt with her husband and daughter. The object of the persecutors who perpetrated these crimes was to destroy Christianity, not Christians. And therefore, as in some other persecutions, every effort was made by the infliction of physical and moral suffering to induce apostasy ; the ingenious tortures which were sometimes inflicted with this object are sickening to read of, and justly deserve the epithet diabolical. Many broke down under them. Many more, priests, religious, men and women, boys and girls in their 'teens, even small children, were faithful to the terrible and glorious end.

Much has been written concerning the Japanese martyrs both collectively and individually. It must suffice here to mention the works of Léon Pagès, *Histoire de la Religion chrét. au Japon*, 2 vols., 1901 ; Marcellinus de Civezza, *Histoire universelle des Missions franç.*, ii (Paris, 1890), pp. 343 *seq.* and 381 *seq. ;* L. C. Profillet, *Le Martyrologe de l'Église du Japon* (Paris, 1895), vol. i, pp. 175 *seq. ;* H. Leclercq, *Les Martyrs*, vol. ix. See also Léon, *Auréole Séraphique* (Eng. Trans.), pp. 124–178.

BB. CHARLES SPINOLA AND HIS COMPANIONS, MARTS.

A.D. 1622

Among the confessors who in September 1622 were taken from prison at Omura to Nagasaki, as mentioned above, were Blessed Charles Spinola and Blessed Sebastian Kimura of the Society of Jesus. Blessed Charles was an Italian by birth who, after a first abortive attempt to reach Japan, landed there in the first years of the seventeenth century and laboured as a missionary for eighteen years. At this time the Jesuits (and after them the Lazarists) in the Far East made a special study and practice of astronomy, which recommended them to the favour of the Chinese and Japanese. Blessed Charles was a keen mathematician and astronomer, and in 1612 wrote a technical account of a lunar eclipse as seen from Nagasaki. When he was arrested six years later there was imprisoned with him at Omura BLESSED SEBASTIAN KIMURA, the first Japanese to be ordained priest and a grandson of the first Japanese baptised by St Francis Xavier. When on September 10, 1622, these two Jesuits and their companions reached the place of execution, on a hill outside Nagasaki, they had to wait an hour for the arrival of another body of confessors, from Nagasaki itself. It was a moving moment when in the presence of a huge crowd of Christians and pagans, these two groups of dedicated ones met and gravely greeted one another. Among the new-comers was BLESSED ISABELLA FER-NANDEZ, a Spanish widow who was condemned for sheltering Blessed Charles and whose son he had baptised. " Where is my little Ignatius ? " he asked. " Here he is," replied the mother, picking up the four-year-old child from amongst the crowd. " I brought him with me to die for Christ before he is old enough to sin against Him." And the boy knelt down for Father Spinola to bless him. He watched his mother's head struck off without flinching, and with his own hands loosed his collar to bare his neck to the sword.

The priests and some of the others were reserved for a more terrible death. They were tied to stakes and large fires lit around them at a distance of some twenty-five feet ; when the heat was seen to gain too quickly on its victims, the fires were damped down. Some died within a few hours, suffocated by the atmosphere, and of these were Blessed Charles and Blessed Sebastian ; others lingered on in the fiercest agony until well into the night or even till the next morning. Two young Japanese wavered and begged for mercy : but they did not ask for life at the price of apostasy, only for an easier and quicker death. It was denied them, and they died with the others.

Five days later there suffered by fire at Firando BLESSED CAMILLUS COSTANZO, an Italian Jesuit from Calabria. He was a missionary in Japan for nine years till he was exiled in 1611. From Macao he wrote several treatises in Japanese defending Christianity from pagan attacks, and in 1621 got back into the country disguised as a soldier. He was captured in the following year. The Society of Jesus keeps his feast on September 25, and joins in it BLESSED AUGUSTINE OTA and BLESSED CASPAR COTENDA, Japanese catechists, BLESSED FRANCIS TAQUEA, aged twelve, and BLESSED PETER KIKIEMON, aged seven, all of whom were slain from hatred of the faith within a few days of one another.

In such ways was consummated the " great martyrdom " of 1622. An English skipper, Richard Cocks, testified to having seen about this time fifty-five persons martyred together at Miako. " Among them little children five or six years old burned in their mother's arms, crying out, ' Jesus, receive our souls ! ' Many more are in prison who look hourly when they shall die, for very few turn pagans." And it was in the face of such happenings that certain English and Dutch sailors, having seized a Japanese vessel off Formosa and found missionaries aboard, handed them over to the authorities at Nagasaki to save themselves from a charge of piracy.

More than one of the books mentioned in connexion with the preceding group of martyrs, notably those of Pagès, Profillet and Leclercq, also supply information concerning Bd. Charles Spinola. See further E. Séguin, *Vie du C. Charles Spinola* (Tournai, 1868) ; *Analecta Bollandiana*, vol. vi (1887), pp. 53–72 ; Boero, *Relazione della gloriosa Morte di* 205 *martiri*, etc. There is also a short sketch in English by D. Donnelly.

BD. AMBROSE BARLOW, MART.

A.D. 1641

In the year 1611 Benedictine monks of the reviving English congregation moved into the monastery which the beneficence of Abbot Philip de Caverel had provided for them at Douay, and three years later there offered himself to them as a novice a young cleric who had already been imprisoned in London for his faith. This was Edward Barlow, son of Sir Alexander Barlow of Barlow, near Manchester. He was born, the fourth of fourteen children, in 1585, and, coming under Protestant influence in his youth, he ceased to practise his religion for a time ; but he was brought back to it by Lady Margaret Davenport, a neighbour, and in due course followed his elder brother to the English College at Douay. He went for philosophy to Valladolid, returned to Douay, then came to England for a year during which he was imprisoned. On his release he came back again to Douay, but not to the English College. Instead he went to St Gregory's, where his brother, Dom Rudesind, was now prior, and was clothed with the Benedictine habit, taking the name of Ambrose. He did most of his novitiate in a temporary monastery at Saint-Malo, but was professed at and for St Gregory's, was ordained priest in 1617, and sent on the English mission to work in his native Lancashire.

Father Ambrose's principal headquarters was at Morleys Hall in the parish of Leigh, " where," wrote Mr. Knaresborough at the beginning of the next century, " his memory is held in great esteem to this day by the Catholics of that county, for his great zeal in the conversion of souls and the exemplary piety of his life and conversation." His stipend at this mission-centre was £8 a year, of which three-quarters went in board and lodging, though his duties called him away for three months in the year. A penitent of his wrote of him : " Although God had put into his hands (as I think) enough wherewithal to have played the housekeeper, he chose rather to subject himself, and become a sojourner with a poor man and his wife, to avoid thereby (as I did conceive) distracting solicitude and dangerous dominion, and to expose sensuality to be curbed with the simple provision of poor folks. . . . Notwithstanding his infirmities, I never knew him to tamper with the physicians, surely he was to himself Dr. Diet, Dr. Quiet, and the only Dr. Merriman that ever I knew."* In over twenty years in England he never once omitted to celebrate Mass daily and sometimes several times in a day, as was allowed in the circumstances. He was so " mild, witty, and cheerful in his conversation, that of all men that ever I knew he seemed to me the most lively to represent the spirit of Sir Thomas More. . . . Neither did I ever see him moved at all upon occasions of wrongs, slanders, or threats which was frequently raised against him : but as one insensible of wrong, or free from choler, he entertained them with a jest, and passed over them with a smile and a nod." The writer gives a vivid description of Father Ambrose saying Mass of Christmas at Morleys, in a venerable vestment " that came out on great days " at a poor, clean altar, whereon great candles he had himself helped to make. And afterwards they sang carols round a " fair coal fire." Bishop Challoner from other sources gives a similar account of the work, emphasising his piety, humility, and temperance at table and in company. " He always abstained from wine, and being asked why he did so, he alleged the saying of the wise man : ' Wine and women make the wise apostatise.' "

In 1628, according to Challoner, Father Ambrose ministered the last sacraments in prison to Blessed Edmund Arrowsmith, who after his martyrdom appeared in sleep to Father Ambrose (who knew not he was dead) and said to him : " I have suffered and now you will be to suffer. Say little, for they will endeavour to take hold of your words." And so the monk laboured on for thirteen years in daily expectation of his hour. Four times he was in prison and four times released, till in March 1641 the House of Commons bullied King Charles I into ordering that all priests should leave the realm or incur the penalties of traitors. Six weeks later the Protestant vicar of Leigh, a Mr. Gatley, celebrated Easter by leading his congregation, armed with weapons of offence, to Morleys Hall, where they seized Blessed Ambrose Barlow while he was preaching to his flock after

---

* He consulted a doctor once, and was told to " Go into your own country and for your physic drink in the morning a mess of new milk and eat a roasted apple at night."

Mass. They carried him off to a justice of the peace, who committed him to Lancaster Castle. After four months' imprisonment he was brought for trial before Sir Robert Heath, and at once acknowledged he was a priest. When asked why then had he not obeyed the order to leave the kingdom, he replied that the decree specified "Jesuits and seminary priests," whereas he was neither, but a Benedictine monk; moreover, he had been too ill to travel far at the time. To the judge's question as to his opinion of the penal laws, he replied that he held them to be unjust and barbarous, and those who condemned the innocent were in danger from the divine judgement. Sir Robert Heath was surprised at his boldness, but said he would be set free if he undertook "not to seduce the people any more."—"I am no seducer but a reducer of the people to the true and ancient religion. . . . I am in the resolution to continue until death to render this good office to these strayed souls." On September 8 he was condemned in the usual form. Five days before a general chapter of the English Benedictine Congregation in session at Douay had accepted the resignation by Father Rudesind Barlow of the titular cathedral-priorship of Coventry, and elected his brother, Father Ambrose, in his place. On that day week, a Friday, Blessed Ambrose Barlow, monk of the order of St Benedict and prior of Coventry, was drawn on a hurdle from Lancaster Castle to his place of execution, where, after pacing three times round the gallows saying the psalm *Miserere*, he was hanged, disembowelled, and quartered.

The mortuary notice of Blessed Ambrose sent round to his Benedictine brethren contained the request that instead of requiem Masses and prayers for the dead they should say Masses of the Holy Trinity, *Te Deum*, and other prayers of thanksgiving. At Wardley Hall, which must have been familiar to the martyr and is now the residence of the Bishop of Salford, is preserved a skull said to be his, and his left hand is at Stanbrook Abbey in Worcestershire.

See Challoner, *Memoirs of Missionary Priests* (Ed. Pollen), pp. 392–400 ; Stanton, *Menology*, pp. 444–445 ; and especially B. Camm, *Nine Martyr Monks* (1931), pp. 258–292.

SEPTEMBER 11

SS. PROTUS AND HYACINTH, MARTS.

c. A.D. 257

THESE martyrs under Valerian, by tradition brothers and slaves in the service of St Basilla, are mentioned in the Liberian Kalendar of the middle of the fourth century. They were buried in the cemetery of St Basilla or St Hermes on the Old Salarian Way, and here in the year 1845 Father Joseph Marchi, S.J., found the burial-place of St Hyacinth undisturbed. It was a niche closed with a slab bearing the inscription D P III IDUS SEPTEBR/YACINTHUS/MARTYR : Hyacinthus the Martyr, buried September 11. Within it were the remains of the martyred, ashes and pieces of charred bone wrapped in costly material. He had evidently met his death by fire. These precious relics were translated to the church of the Urban College of Propaganda in 1849 (there had already in previous centuries been translations of " relics of St Hyacinth "). Near by was found part of a later inscription, bearing the words SEPULCRUM PROTI M : The tomb of Protus, M[artyr], but no other trace of him. The relics of St Protus (and of St Hyacinth) are supposed to have been removed into the city by Pope St Leo IV in the middle of the ninth century, and parts thereof have been translated several times since.

The simple certitude of the passion, burial, and finding of St Hyacinth is in marked contrast with their " acts ", which are contained in those of St Eugenia (December 25) and are entirely fictitious. The story is that Eugenia, the Christian daughter of Philip, prefect of Egypt, fled from her father's house with Protus and Hyacinth, her two slaves (alternatively " gentlemen of noble lineage " and " teachers of the holy law "). Eugenia becomes a monk (!), and after various adventures converts her family and many others. Among them, the Roman lady Basilla is brought to the Faith by the efforts of Protus and Hyacinth, whom Eugenia has given to her as servants. Basilla refuses any longer to live with her pagan husband, and she, Protus, and Hyacinth are all beheaded together. These happenings are placed variously under Pope St Soter and the Emperor Commodus, Pope St Cornelius I, and the Emperor

Gallienus; they are a romance woven round the names of martyrs who suffered in the persecution of the last-named and Valerian.

No words can be found adequately to praise the heroic virtue and invincible fortitude of the martyrs. They stood out against the fury of those tyrants whose arms had subdued the most distant nations, to whose yoke almost the whole known world was subject, and whose power both kings and people feared. They, standing alone, without any preparation, appeared undaunted in the presence of those proud conquerors, who seemed to think that the very earth ought to bend under their feet. Armed with divine grace, the martyrs were a match for all the powers of the world and Hell; they fought with wild beasts, fire, and sword; with intrepidity and cheerfulness they braved the most cruel torments, and by patience and constancy baffled their enemies and triumphed over men and devils. And yet we, having before our eyes the examples of so many holy saints, are we yet so weak as to shrink under temptations and to lose patience under the most ordinary trials.

In Père Delehaye's commentary on the *Hieronymianum* will be found a succinct but very complete statement of the facts, with exact references. See the *Acta Sanctorum*, November, vol. ii, part 2, pp. 501–502. See also Delehaye, *Origines du Culte des Martyrs*, pp. 311–312. The so-called "Passio" of Eugenia, Protus and Hyacinthus was printed by Rosweyd in his *Vitæ Patrum*, pp. 340–349.

ST PAPHNUTIUS, Bp. and Conf.

c. A.D. 356

The holy confessor Paphnutius was an Egyptian who, after having spent several years in the desert under the direction of the great St Antony, was made bishop in the Upper Thebaid. He was one of those confessors who under the Emperor Maximinus lost their right eye, were hamstrung in one leg, and were afterwards sent to work in the mines. Peace being restored to the Church, Paphnutius returned to his flock, bearing all the rest of his life the glorious marks of his sufferings for the name of his crucified Master. He was one of the most zealous in defending the Catholic faith against the Arian heresy and for his eminent sanctity, and as one who had confessed the faith before persecutors and under torments was an outstanding figure of the first general council of the Church, held at Nicaea in the year 325. Constantine the Great during the celebration of that synod sometimes conferred privately with him in his palace, and never dismissed him without saluting respectfully the scars he had received for the Faith. St Paphnutius, a man who had

observed the strictest continence all his life, distinguished himself
at the council by his opposition to clerical celibacy. The Fathers in
the third canon strictly forbad all clergy to entertain in their houses
any woman, except a mother, aunt, sister, or such as could leave no
room for suspicion, and many of the bishops were for making a
general law forbidding all bishops, priests, deacons, and subdeacons
to live with wives whom they had married before their ordination.
Whereupon Paphnutius rose up in the assembly and opposed the
motion, saying that it was enough to conform to the ancient tradition of the Church, which forbade the clergy marrying after their
ordination. For the married the use of wedlock is chastity, he
reminded the Fathers, and implored them not to lay the yoke of
separation on clerics and their wives. St Paphnutius carried the
council with him, and to this day it is the law of the Eastern churches,
whether Catholic or dissident, that married men may receive all
holy orders below the episcopate, and continue to live freely with
their wives. St Paphnutius remained always in a close union with
St Athanasius and the other Catholic prelates. He and forty-seven
other Egyptian bishops accompanied their holy patriarch to the
Council of Tyre in 335, where they found the greater part of the
members who composed that assembly to be professed Arians.
Paphnutius, seeing Maximus, Bishop of Jerusalem, among them and
full of concern to find an orthodox prelate who had suffered in the
late persecution in such bad company, took him by the hand, led him
out, and told him that he could not bear that anyone who bore the
same marks as himself in defence of the Faith should be led away
and imposed upon by persons who were resolved to condemn the
most strenuous asserter of its fundamental article. Maximus was
overcome by the saint's appeal and let himself be led to a seat among
the supporters of St Athanasius, whom he never afterwards deserted.
But the Arian party triumphed in the council and Athanasius was
unjustly banished to Trier.

St Paphnutius is sometimes called " the Great " to distinguish
him from other saints of the same name. Cardinal Baronius added
his name to the Roman Martyrology, which on the 24th of this
month mentions the passion of another ST PAPHNUTIUS in Egypt,
about the year 303. " He was living alone in the desert, when he
heard that many Christians were kept in chains, and, stirred by the
spirit of God, he gave himself up of his own will to the prefect and
openly confessed the religion of Christ. He was first bound with
iron chains and tortured on the rack for a long time, and then was
sent with many others to Diocletian, by whose orders he was nailed
to a palm tree and the others slain with the sword." The spurious

Greek *acta* say that these martyrs numbered 547, of whom many wavered but were confirmed in the faith by Paphnutius.

There is no early Life of St Paphnutius, but in the *Acta Sanctorum*, September, vol. iii, a number of passages, notably from the historians Socrates and Theodoret, have been brought together. See also the *Dict. of Christ. Biog.*, vol. iv, p. 185. The authenticity of the pronouncement attributed to Paphnutius on the celibacy question has been often discussed. Consult on this the *Dictionnaire de Théol. cath.*, vol. ii, c. 2078.

ST THEODORA, PENITENT

FIFTH CENTURY

The Roman Martyrology speaks to-day of the death at Alexandria of St Theodora, " who, having transgressed through carelessness, was repentent therefor and persevered in the religious habit, unknown and with marvellous abstinence and patience, until her death." These restrained words are very different in tone from the legends of St Theodora. They relate that she was the wife of Gregory, prefect of Egypt, and that, having fallen into grave sin, she fled away from her home to expiate it in a monastery of the Thebaid. Disguised as a man she lived for many years among the monks a life of extraordinary austerity. Once when she went into Alexandria in charge of some camels she was recognised by her husband, but she insisted on returning to the desert where she lived for the rest of her life. There was a St Theodora who was known to the Fathers of the Desert, and whose wise sayings are repeated in their Lives, but the above story, decked out with other fictitious particulars, is nothing but a romance, belonging to that class which Père Delehaye traces to the tale of St Pelagia of Antioch (October 8). For example, like St Reparata, St Marina, and others who lived as men among monks, St Theodora was accused of being guilty of seduction and was vindicated only after her death. St Susanna, named in the Roman Martyrology on the 20th of this month, is also reputed to have been a " monk " but was discovered and dismissed. She afterwards suffered a cruel martyrdom at Eleutheropolis under Julian the Apostate.

On September 17 the Roman Martyrology makes mention of another ST THEODORA, a matron of Rome who zealously ministered to the holy martyrs during the persecution under Diocletian.

The Greek text of the fictitious story of Theodora has been printed by K. Wessely in *Fünfzehnter Jahresbericht des KK. Staatsgymnasiums in Hernals* (Wien, 1889). See also the *Acta Sanctorum*, September, vol. iii ; and Delehaye, *Les Légendes hagiographiques*, p. 189 and *passim*.

ST PATIENS, ABP. OF LYONS, CONF.

c. A.D. 491

God was pleased to raise up this holy prelate for the comfort and support of his servants in Gaul under the calamities with which that country was afflicted during a great part of the fifth century. He was a man of rank and wealth, noted for his munificence towards the needy, and about the year 456 the suffrages of the clergy and citizens promoted him to the metropolitan see of Lyons. An incursion of the Goths into Burgundy in 473–74 brought on a serious famine, during which St Patiens fed thousands at his own expense ; St Sidonius Apollinaris gives a nominal roll of the citizens whom he succoured, but the archbishop diffused the effects of his boundless charity over all the provinces of Gaul. Providence wonderfully multiplied his revenues to furnish him with abundant supplies to build a number of stately churches, to repair and embellish old ones, and to feed the poor wherever they might be in Gaul, as St Sidonius assures us. That illustrious prelate and friend of St Patiens calls him a " holy, active, ascetic, and merciful man," and declares that he knew not which to admire and praise more in him, his zeal for God's honour or his charity for the poor. By his pastoral solicitude and sermons many heretics were converted to the Faith, and the Catholic Church every day enlarged its pale. A great field was open to the holy prelate for the exercise of his zeal in this respect, for the Burgundians, who were at that time masters of the city of Lyons, were infected with the heresy of the Arians, and some of his fellow-bishops were not free from it. St Patiens found the secret first to gain their hearts, and afterwards to open their understanding, convince them of the truth, and draw them out of their errors. Nevertheless at a synod held at Arles in 475 he himself had the misfortune in good faith to sign a Semipelagian letter drawn up by St Faustus of Riez against the Predestinarian presbyter Lucidus. When the diocese of Chalon-sur-Saône was thrown into confusion and disagreement by the death of its bishop, St Patiens was invited by the great St Euphronius of Autun to help him in its pacification and the removal of the scandal. At the order of St Patiens, Constantius, a priest among his clergy, wrote the Life of St Germanus of Auxerre, which he dedicated to his bishop and to Censurius of Auxerre. All pastoral virtues shone in an eminent degree in this apostolic bishop Patiens ; like another Ambrose he knew how to join severity with compassion and activity with prudence and discretion. He seems to have died about the year

491, and his name is honoured on this September 11 in the Roman Martyrology.

There is no ancient Life of St Patiens of Lyons, but the Bollandists have collected from Sidonius Apollinaris, Gregory of Tours and others, a sufficient account of his activities. See also S. L. Tatu, *St Patient évêque de Lyon* (Lyon, 1878), and Duchesne, *Fastes Épiscopaux*, vol. ii, p. 163.

ST DEINIOL, or DANIEL, Bp. and Conf.

c. A.D. 584

St Dunawd, son of Pabo Post Prydain who came into north Wales from Ayrshire, had three sons, one of them being St Deiniol, known as "the Elder" or "the Carpenter." Deiniol had been married before he was a monk, and he was the father of St Deiniol the Younger, also called Deiniolen. St Deiniol went into Arfon and established the monastery of Bangor Fawr on the Menai Straits, which is supposed to have been patronised and endowed by Maelgwn, Prince of Gwynedd, and became the nucleus of the medieval diocese of Bangor. Deiniol was probably also the founder of the monastery of Bangor Iscoed on the Dee, and is alleged to have been consecrated bishop by St Dyfrig or St Teilo or St David himself, of whom the last-named is the most likely; he is said to have sent Deiniol into Gaul to fetch a bishop to help combat a recrudescence of Pelagianism. The same crisis is put forward to account for a synod at Llanddewi Brefi about the year 560, though the decrees of the synod are concerned with penitential discipline and not at all with Pelagianism. Rhygyfarch in his *vita* of St David says that David refused to attend this assembly, whereupon Deiniol and Dyfrig were sent to fetch him and succeeded in persuading him to come ; David's eloquence swept all before him and he superseded St Dyfrig as "primate" of Wales. A number of miracles are related of St Deiniol, not always free from that element of haughty pride and revenge which is a characteristic of so many Celtic hagiological stories. When he died he was buried at Ynys Ynlli, now commonly called Bardsey, and his son succeeded him as abbot of Bangor. St Deiniol is named on various dates, September 11 being the day on which his feast is now kept in the diocese of Menevia.

Very little can be stated with any certainty about this saint, but Baring-Gould and Fisher, *Lives of the British Saints*, vol. ii, profess to give an account of him ; and something may be gleaned from A. W. Wade-Evans, *Life of St David* (1923). See also Stanton's *Menology*, pp. 445–446.

ST PETER OF CHAVANON, Conf.

A.D. 1080

The Canons Regular of the Lateran to-day keep the memory of this saint, who adorned their order in the eleventh century. He was born in the year 1003 at Langeac in Haute-Loire, and was given a good education in the course of which he discovered his vocation to the priesthood. After his ordination he was appointed archpriest of his birthplace, where he faithfully fulfilled his duties and secretly led a very austere life. He for long desired to leave pastoral work and submit himself to a rule in community, and eventually found an occasion to do so when he was persecuted by the attentions of a woman who was attracted towards him. He was given permission to leave the town, and the Bishop of Clermont gave him some land at Pébrac in Auvergne. Here St Peter founded and built a monastery for canons regular under the Rule of St Augustine, and himself governed it as the first provost. The success of his undertaking caused several bishops to call him in to help them to bring rule and order into the collegiate chapters of their cathedrals. St Peter de Chavanon died on September 9, 1080, and was buried at Pébrac, of which house the holy M. Olier was made abbot *in commendam* at the age of eighteen, in 1626.

There is a Life by Stephen, a canon of Pébrac, who was almost a contemporary. It is printed in the *Acta Sanctorum*, September, vol. iii, with an ample commentary.

BD. LOUIS IV, Landgrave of Thuringia, Conf.

A.D. 1227

If we were bound to take all the writings of hagiographers at the foot of the letter we should be faced with the conclusion that most women saints who were married were hindered (or helped) on the path of sanctity by the ill will or general shortcomings of their husbands ; the unworthy husband of the holy wife is almost common form, and as such it is to be distrusted. No one has tried to find such unhappy tension between Elizabeth of Hungary and Louis of Thuringia, for the good reason that it so obviously did not exist (though even here there is a book by a well-known clerical writer in which the author has been betrayed by careless adhesion to common form into applying it to these two) ; veneration for Louis was as spontaneous among his people as it was for his wife : it is true that the *cultus* has not been officially confirmed (it has not been put forward), but it is nevertheless worthy of respect.

Louis was the eldest son of the Landgrave Hermann I and was born in 1200. When he was eleven years old a betrothal was arranged for him with Elizabeth, daughter of King Andrew II of Hungary, who was then four. Later the child was taken to the Thuringian court, the two grew up together, and in 1221, when Louis succeeded his father, the marriage was ratified. In its origin this alliance was purely one of political expedience, but it proved to be none the worse for that ; they had a son and two daughters, of whom the younger is known as Blessed Gertrude of Altenburg. In 1225 there came into Germany as synodal visitor the Dominican Conrad of Marburg, who was to have so great influence over St Elizabeth ; Louis admired and trusted him, made him his almoner, and appointed him to name clerics to all benefices of which the Landgrave held the patronage. Louis in every way encouraged the charity and devotion of his wife. Once he found a leper, who had come to the castle for relief, laid in their bed ; for a moment he was tempted to anger but then he saw, as it were, not the leper but the crucified Son of God lying there, and he made no complaint but instead paid for the building of a lazar-house on the slope of the Wartburg. St Elizabeth told him they could serve God better if, instead of a castle and a county they had land enough for one plough and a couple of hundred sheep. Her husband laughed. " We should hardly be poor," he said, " with so much land and so many sheep. And there would be plenty of folk to say we were far too well off."

The Landgrave was a good ruler as well as a good man. In 1225 some Thuringian merchants were robbed and beaten over the Polish border. Louis demanded reparation ; none was forthcoming. So at the head of his troops he rode into Poland and by force extorted satisfaction from the citizens of Lubitz. The same thing happened at Würtzburg ; he marched into the prince-bishopric to recover the stock of which a trader had been robbed. He was a good soldier and a good leader ; when in 1226 Bologna and the cities of Lombardy were in revolt, the Emperor sent for Louis of Thuringia to help bring them to order, and he assisted with his counsel at the Diet of Cremona. He was away for a winter, a hard winter, and a spring ; when he returned, Elizabeth " a thousand times and more," says friar Berthold, " kissed him with her heart and with her mouth," and when he inquired how his people had fared in the terrible frost, " I gave to God what was His, and God has kept for us what was ours," she replied. " Let her do good and give to God whatever she will, so long as she leaves me Wartburg and Neuenburg," was

Louis's answer to a complaining treasurer. In the following year he volunteered to follow the Emperor Frederick II on the sixth crusade (the story of Elizabeth finding the cross in his purse is well known) ; he made his brother Henry regent, and turned all his energies to enlisting crusaders. To rouse men's hearts he had a Passion play presented in the streets of Eisenach, and visited the monasteries of his dominion, asking for prayers. The Central German forces concentrated at Schmalkalden, and Louis was in command ; here on the birthday of St John he parted from Elizabeth, and set out towards the Holy Sepulchre. In August he met the Emperor at Troja, and in September the army embarked ; three days later the fleet put into Otranto, and Louis took to his bed. He had a malarial fever and was dying ; he received the last sacraments, and it seemed to him that the cabin wherein he lay was full of doves. " I must fly away with those white doves," he said, and died. When the news was brought to his wife, " The world is dead to me," she cried, " and all that was pleasant in it." The young Landgrave was buried in the Benedictine abbey of Reinhardsbrunn, and there he is popularly called " St Ludwig " to this day.

There is a German fourteenth-century translation of a still earlier Latin Life of the Landgrave. This Latin biography, written by Bertoldus, who was Louis' chaplain and a monk of Reinhardsbrunn, seems not to have been separately preserved to us, though some contend that it is practically incorporated in the *Annales Reinhardsbrunnenses* which were edited by Wegele in 1854. There is an excellent article on Louis by C. Wenck in the *Allgemeine deutsche Biographie*, vol. xix, pp. 589–597, and a biography in German by G. Simon (Frankfurt a. M., 1854). See also Michael, *Geschichte des deutschen Volkes seit dem* 13 *Jahrh.*, vol. i, p. 221, and ii, pp. 207 *seq.* Further, the many Lives of St Elizabeth of Hungary all contain some notice of her husband.

BD. JOHN-GABRIEL PERBOYRE, Mart.

A.D. 1840

Though John-Gabriel Perboyre was the first Christian in China to be beatified (in 1889) he was very far from being the first martyr in that country. Ever since the re-establishment of the missions there in the beginning of the seventeenth century there have been only relatively short periods during which Christians were free from the danger of persecution. At the end of the eighteenth century fierce persecution was carried on by the Emperor Kia-K'ing, and was continued sporadically till after the death of Father Perboyre in 1840, thousands of Christians gladly giving up their lives. Perboyre was born at Puech, Cahors, in 1802, and when he was fifteen he was fired by a sermon with the ambition to be a missionary to the heathen. After his preliminary studies in the *petit seminaire* at Montaubon, of which his uncle was rector, he joined the Congregation of the Mission (Lazarists, Vincentians), and was ordained in 1825. At first his desire to carry the gospel to foreign parts had to give way before the requirements of religious obedience. His theological course had been a brilliant one, and so after his ordination he was appointed professor of dogmatic theology in the seminary of Saint-Flour, and two years later rector of the *petit seminaire* in the same place. His own personal goodness was very apparent in these employments, and in 1832 he was sent to Paris to be assistant-director of the general novitiate of his congregation. At intervals since the taking of his vows twelve years before he had asked to be sent to China, from whence reports of the sufferings and heroic deaths of the local Christians continued to come in, but it was not till 1835 that the permission was given.

In that year he arrived at Macao with two companions, and at once was set to learn Chinese, for which he showed such aptitude that at the end of four months he was appointed to the mission of Honan. On the eve of setting out he wrote to his religious brethren in Paris : " If you could see me now in my Chinese ' get-up ' you would see a very curious sight : my head shaved, a long pig-tail and moustaches, stammering my new language, eating with chopsticks. They tell me that I don't make a bad Chinaman. That is the only way to begin making oneself all things to all men : may we be able thus to win all to Jesus Christ ! " The Lazarists had been given charge of the Pekin mission in place of the Jesuits some fifty years before, and they had elaborated a system of rescuing abandoned children, who are so numerous in China, and bringing them up in the Faith. In this work Father Perboyre was especially active, and he devoted much of his time to instructing these children in Christian doctrine and practice, illustrating his lessons by apt stories to which his very colloquial Chinese gave an added flavour. After two years at Honan he was moved to Hupeh, and here in September 1839 there was a sudden and unexplained renewal of persecution.

The missionaries went into hiding, but a neophyte betrayed Father Perboyre (with a horrid fitness, for thirty *taels*—about £9), and he was dragged in chains from functionary to functionary, each of whom questioned him and sent him on to someone else. Finally he came into the hands of the governor and mandarins of Wuch'ang-Fu. These required him to betray the hiding-places of his *confrères*, particularly of Mgr. Rameaux, vicar-apostolic of Kiang-Si, to trample on the cross, and to perform an act of worship of an idol. The sufferings endured by Father Perboyne were incredible, in the literal sense of the word. Twenty times he was dragged before his judges to be bullied into compliance, and more than twenty times he was tortured because he refused. The ingenuity of the Chinese in inflicting physical pain is notorious, and Father Perboyre underwent torments beside which those invented by hagiographers for some of the martyrs of the Ten Persecutions are crude and clumsy. He was branded on the face with four characters, which stood for "teacher of a false religion," and a Chinese priest who bribed his way into his prison described him as a mass of open wounds, his very bones in places exposed. On September 11, 1840, almost a year after his capture, Blessed John-Gabriel, with bare feet and only a pair of drawers under the red robe of the condemned, was strangled with five common criminals at Wuch'ang-Fu. He was buried beside another Lazarist martyr, Francis-Regis Clet, who was also to be beatified. In China the feast of Blessed John-Gabriel is kept on November 7, the nearest convenient date to that of his beatification in 1889.

The murder of Blessed John-Gabriel Perboyre was the occasion of the British Government insisting on a clause in the Treaty of Nanking in 1842 which provided that any foreign missionary who was arrested should not be dealt with by the Chinese authorities but handed over to the nearest consul of his nation.

See the anonymous volume which appeared in 1853 under the title of *Le Disciple de Jésus ;* also the biography by Father Huonder, *Der selige Johann Gabriel Perboyre, Ein Martyrbild aus dem* 19 *Jahrh.* More or less lengthy accounts will also be found in Kempf, *Holiness of the Church in the XIX Century* (Eng. Trans.), pp. 300–303 ; in Leclercq, *Les Martyrs,* vol. x, and in the various works of A. Launay, dealing with the Chinese missions.

SEPTEMBER 12

THE HOLY NAME OF MARY

THE object of this feast is our blessed Lady bearing the name of Mary, and it was instituted that on it the faithful might in a special manner recommend to God, through the intercession of His all-holy Mother, the needs of the Church, and thank Him for His almighty protection and numberless mercies, especially those we receive on account of the graces and mediation of the Blessed Virgin. The feast was first observed at Cuenca in Spain in 1513 ; it spread in that country, and in 1671 was granted to all its dioceses and to the kingdom of Naples. Twelve years later Pope Innocent XI extended it to the whole Western Church, as an act of thanksgiving for the raising of the siege of Vienna and the defeat of the Turks by John Sobieski, King of Poland ; it was at that time assigned to the Sunday within the octave of our Lady's birthday, but is now kept on the date of Sobieski's triumph.

Our name Mary is derived from Maria and Mariam, later forms of Miryam, which was our Lady's name in Hebrew, but the most learned scholars have been unable certainly to decide what was the derivation and meaning of that name. " Mistress," " the rebellious one," " the fat (that is, in the East, the beautiful) one " have been suggested, or it may be of Egyptian origin and mean " the perfect one " ; a good case has been made for the last two and they are the most in accord with Christian sentiment. But that sentiment has sometimes to give way before hard fact, and it is certain that the name of Mary has nothing to do with " bitterness," " the sea," or " a star."

If we would avert divine anger, justly provoked by our sins, we must join to our prayers the tears of a sincere sorrow and strive after a complete conversion of life. The first grace we must always beg of God is that He will bring us to a state of contrition and penitence. Only thus can our prayers for His mercies and our thanksgiving for His benefits be acceptable in His eyes ; by no other means can we deserve His blessing or hope to be recommended before His throne by the intercession of our Lady. For to the invocation of the Son we should frequently join invocation of the

Mother, that through her loving-kindness we may the more surely and abundantly obtain what we ask, which we should always ask in complete and humble submission to the divine will; thus joining the holy name of Mary to the holy name of Jesus we may approach the throne of grace with affection, confidence, and detachment from self.

The various stages in the adoption of the feast of the Holy Name of Mary are set out in Holweck, *Calendarium Liturgicum Festorum Dei et Dei Matris Mariæ* (1925), p. 317, and *cf.* Kellner, *Heortology* (Eng. Trans.), p. 264. This special commemoration is probably somewhat older than 1513, though definite evidence does not seem to be forthcoming. All we can say is that the great devotion to the holy name of Jesus, which we identify in part with the preaching of St Bernardine of Siena (†1444) will naturally have prepared the way for a similar commemoration of the holy name of Mary. One curious point with regard to this name which deserves to be noticed is that while in the case of the other Marys who appear in the New Testament we find in the Greek Text simply the form Μαρία, the best manuscripts almost uniformly spell the name of our Blessed Lady as Μαριάμ. This seems to mark at least a sense of her dignity. For her alone the Old Testament form of the name is preferred.

ST AILBHE, or ALBEUS, Bp. and Conf.

c. A.D. 527 OR 541

A commemoration of St Ailbhe is made throughout Ireland on this day, and in the diocese of Emly his feast is kept as that of its patron and first bishop, but the recorded Life of the saint is a confusion of valueless legends and contradictory traditions. One concerns his birth of a serving-girl by a chieftain, who ordered that the baby should be exposed to perish. A she-wolf found him and suckled him along with her own cubs, till a hunter found the child in the wolf's lair and took him away. Years later Ailbhe was present at a run, when an aged she-wolf, hard-pressed by hounds, deliberately ran to him for protection. The bishop recognised his foster-mother, gave her sanctuary, and every day thereafter fed her and her family at his own table. When Ailbhe was a boy in the north of Ireland, he was one day considering the wonders of the natural world, and said aloud : " I pray that I may know the Creator of all things, and I will believe in Him who made the heavens and the earth. For I perceive that these things did not come into existence without a maker, and no human work could produce them." He was overheard by a Christian priest, who thereupon instructed and baptised him. Another account says he was brought up and baptised by a British colony in Ireland. He is supposed to have gone to Rome and there studied the Scriptures under a bishop named

Hilarius (Pope Hilarus ?), and to have been himself consecrated bishop in the city. But perhaps he really went to St Hilarius of Arles, since St Patrick himself probably spent three years at Lérins, where this Hilarius was a monk. Anyway, he came back and landed in northern Ireland, where he baptised a chieftain called Fintan and raised to life his three sons, who had been killed in battle.

He then preached up and down the country, and with such commanding authority did this apostolic man deliver the eternal wisdom to a barbarous people, such was the force with which both by words and example he set forth the sanctity of the divine law, and so evident were the miracles with which he confirmed the truths which he preached, that the sacred doctrine made its way to the hearts of many of his hearers ; he not only brought over a multitude to the faith of Christ but infused into many the spirit of perfection, for he had a wonderful art of making men not only Christians but saints. Though zeal for God's honour and charity for the souls of others kept him in the world, he was always careful to nourish in his own soul the love of heavenly things by habitual recollection, and to live always in intimate acquaintance with himself and in the habitual practice of interior virtues. In his old age it was his desire to commit to others the care of his flock, that he might be allowed to prepare himself for death in solitude. For this purpose he begged that he might be suffered to retire to Thule, the remotest country toward the northern pole that was known to the ancients (which seems to have been Shetland or, according to some, Iceland or some part of Greenland), but the king guarded the ports to prevent his flight. Another legend tells us that from this same king, Aengus of Munster, St Ailbhe begged the isles of Aran for St Enda. Aengus did not know he had such islands in his dominions until they were shown to him in a vision or dream ; whereupon he handed them over, and at Killeaney on Inishmore was founded a monastery which was so famous for holiness that the island was called " Aran of the saints." It does not detract from the sanctity of Killeaney to point out that among Celtic peoples " saint " was often used synonymously with " monk " or " recluse " ; on Ynys Ynlli (Bardsey) were buried 20,000 " saints."

After his return from Rome St Ailbhe is said to have met St Patrick at Cashel, and after a certain feeling of constraint between the two missionaries, to have settled at Emly and worked in concert with him. It is often said on the poor authority of Ailbhe's *acta* that he preached in Ireland before St Patrick, but according to the latter's biographer Tirechan, Patrick ordained Ailbhe priest, and he was in all probability a young disciple. But the picturesque legends and astounding miracles of St Ailbhe, and the speculations to which they have given rise, add nothing of much value to the eulogy of St Cuimin of Connor : " Ailbhe loved hospitality. The devotion was not untruthful. Never entered a body of clay one that was better as to food and raiment."

The Life in the *Codex Salmanticensis* was edited in that collection by the Bollandists in 1888, pp. 235–260. A somewhat different version has been printed by C. Plummer in his *Vitæ Sanctorum Hiberniæ*, vol. i, pp. 46–64 ; and note also what is said in the preface to the same work, pp. xxviii–xxxi. What is of more importance than the extravagant incidents of this mythical Life, St Ailbhe [the name, by the way, is spent Ailbe by such experts as J. Ryan, J. O'Neill, C. Plummer, W. Stokes and Dom Gougaud] is the reputed author of a monastic rule. It was edited by J. O'Neill in *Ériu*, vol. iii, 1907. See also James Kenney, *The Sources for the early History of Ireland*, vol. i.

ST EANSWIDA, Virg. and Abbess

c. A.D. 640

St Ethelbert, the first Christian king among the English, was succeeded in the kingdom of Kent by his son Eadbald, who, though he was at first impious and idolatrous, became afterwards a zealous Christian. His daughter Eanswida added lustre to her birth by the sanctity of her life. The truths of our holy religion sank so deep in her heart that from childhood her whole delight was in prayer and the love of God. She despised the world, and rejected all proposals to engage herself in marriage, fearing the duties of that state, though good and just in themselves, would interrupt the way of life she had imposed upon herself. In particular, she had to oppose her father's wish that she should marry a pagan prince from Northumbria. " I will marry him," she said, " when by prayer to his gods he has made this log of wood a foot longer." In the year 630 she obtained her father's consent and founded a monastery of nuns upon the sea-coast, hard by Folkestone in Kent. Here she sacrificed herself to her heavenly spouse night and day in penance and prayer, till she was called to rest on the last day of August about the year 640, the date on which she is named in some kalendars. Her convent was destroyed by the Danes but was refounded for Benedictine monks in 1095. The sea afterwards swallowed up part of this priory and it was removed into Folkestone, and the saint's relics were deposited in that church which had been built by her father, King Eadbald, in honour of St Peter ; the successor of this church is now known as SS. Mary and Eanswida's. September 12 is probably the day of the translation of her relics about the year 1140. Many legends about the miraculous powers of St Eanswida were current in England in the Middle Ages, some of which are preserved by the chronicler Capgrave.

St Eanswida (or Eanswitha) seems to have been unknown to Bede, but her connexion with Folkestone is alluded to in an Anglo-Saxon document printed by Cockayne (*Leechdoms*, iii, p. 422). The mention of her name in certain calendars and martyrologies suggests that there was some *cultus*. See Stanton, *Menology*, pp. 429 and 432. The statements made by John of Tynemouth and Capgrave can inspire little confidence.

ST GUY, or GUIDO, CONF.

c. A.D. 1012

Although the accounts of this saint derive from late and not very reliable sources, and have been touched up and filled out with edifying but very doubtfully authentic miracles, it is clear that he belongs to that category of simple, hidden souls who, whether as wanderers or workmen, are familiar to us from St Alexis and St John Calybites through St Isidore of Madrid and St Walstan of Costessey down to St Benedict-Joseph Labre and Matt Talbot in our own time. As such he finds a place in the Roman Martyrology.

St Guy, commonly called the Poor Man of Anderlecht, was born in the country near Brussels, of poor parents, but both virtuous and consequently content and happy. They were not able to give their son a school education nor did they let that perturb them, but instead they were diligent in instructing him early in the rudiments of the Christian doctrine and in the practices of our holy religion, often repeating to him the lesson which old Tobias gave his son, " We shall have many good things if we fear God." The curse which Christ pronounces against riches regards the inordinate pleasure that is sought in them and all they stand for. St Augustine says that God ranks among the reprobate, not only those who shall have received their comfort on earth, but also those who shall have grieved to be deprived of it. This was what Guy dreaded. In order to preserve himself from it he never ceased to beg of God the grace to love the state of poverty in which divine providence had placed him, and to bear all its hardships with joy and in a spirit of penance, without which all the tribulations of this world are of no advantage for Heaven. The charity which Guy had for his neighbour was no less active. He divided his pittance with the poor, and often fed them whilst he fasted himself.

When he grew up St Guy wandered about for a time, until one day he came to the church of our Lady at Laeken, near Brussels, whose priest was struck with the piety and willingness of the man, and retained him in the service of his church as sacristan. Guy rejoiced to have an opportunity of being employed in the most humble offices of religion and accepted the offer with pleasure. The cleanliness and good order that appeared in everything under his direction struck all that came to that church ; for, out of a true spirit of religion, the servant of God looked upon nothing as insignificant which belonged to the service of God or to the decency of His house. His silence and recollection in the church seemed to say to others : " This is the house of the Lord : approach His sanctuary with fear."

Guy, like other simple folk before and since, was induced by a merchant of Brussels to invest his small savings in a commercial venture, but with the unusual motive of having more at his disposal wherewith to relieve the poor. The merchant offered to put him in a way of thus making more provision for them by admitting him into partnership with himself. It was not easy for him to throw off the importunities of the merchant : the bait was specious and he was taken by it. But the ship carrying their goods was lost in going out of the harbour, and Guy, whose place in the church of Laeken had upon his leaving been given to another, was left destitute. He saw his mistake in following his own ideas and in forsaking secure and humble employment to embark, though with a good intention, on the affairs of the world, in which by prosperity his character would perhaps have been impaired and material ambitions have taken root in his heart. For though this trade was good in itself yet he conceived that God had justly punished his rashness, for riches and prosperity do not always refresh and increase the tender plant of virtue; they much more frequently wash away the earth from its roots like a flood and leave it buried in rubbish. This St Guy clearly saw, and he blamed himself for the false step he had taken. In reparation for his folly and to avoid the popular attention he had begun to attract, he made a pilgrimage on foot first to Rome and then on to Jerusalem, and visited all the most celebrated shrines in that part of the Christian world. When he had returned as far as Rome he met Windulf, dean of the church of Anderlecht (a town about two miles from Brussels) who with some others was ready to set out for the Holy Land. Guy was prevailed upon by them to be their guide, seeing that he was their countryman and known to them by name, and he again made the long journey to Jerusalem. But just as they were going to set sail from Palestine to return to Europe, the dean and his friends were taken sick and died of plague. Guy attended them in their sickness, took care of their funerals, and after seven years' absence again reached Belgium, where he made his way to Anderlecht. Here he reported to the chapter what had happened to their dean and delivered his ring to them. But he himself was dying from exhaustion and illness brought on by the fatigue of his journeys and other hardships, and shortly after he was received into the hospital of Anderlecht he yielded up his soul to God. He was buried in the cemetery of the canons who, after miracles had taken place at his grave, translated his body into a shrine.

The Cistercians on the 23rd of this month commemorate BLESSED GUY OF DURNES, a personal disciple of St Bernard, who was first abbot of Notre Dame de Cherlieu in the diocese of Besançon. He helped in the work of editing the Cistercian liturgical chant.

St Guy, who is known to the Flemings as St Wye, is honoured in a relatively long biography, printed in the *Acta Sanctorum*, September, vol. iv. A good deal of folklore is associated with his *cultus*. See E. H. van Heurck, *Les Drapelets de pèlerinage en Belgique*; F. Mortier in *Folklore brabançon*, vol. x (1930), pp. 46–55; and also a popular account of the Saint by Gooris and Bossaerts, Brussels, 1893.

BD. MARY VICTORIA FORNARI-STRATA,
WIDOW AND ABBESS

A.D. 1617

Blessed Mary Victoria was born at Genoa of the noble Fornari family in the year 1562. She was well brought up and her youthful goodness made so strong an impression that the sudden recovery of her brother from a very serious illness was attributed to her prayers. At the age of seventeen there was some talk of her becoming a nun, but she deferred to the wishes of her father and married Angelo Strata. They lived together very happily for nine years, Angelo joining gladly in his wife's religious observances and helping her in her charitable works, and defending her from the adverse criticism of those who wished to see her take more part in social pleasures. They had six children, four boys and two girls. When Angelo died in 1589 Mary was for long inconsolable, both for her own sake and for the sake of the children, whom she felt she was incapable of properly looking after alone. A certain rich nobleman of the city wanted her to marry him and perhaps she thought she ought to for her children's sake. But her uncertainty was put an end to by a happening of which she wrote down an account by the direction of her Jesuit confessor, Father Bernardino Zannoni. Our Lady appeared in vision and said to her : " My child Victoria, be brave and confident, for it is my wish to take both the mother and the children under my protection ; I will care for your household. Live quietly and without worrying. All I ask is that you will trust yourself to me and henceforth devote yourself to the love of God above all things." Blessed Mary Victoria now saw clearly what she must do and ceased to be disquieted. She made a vow of chastity and lived in retirement, giving her whole time to God, her children, and the poor. She allowed no superfluity or luxury in her home, and set herself a standard of severe mortification ; when, for example, the Church directed a fast she would always observe it on bread and water.

After her children were all gone into religion or otherwise provided for, Mary Victoria put before the Archbishop of Genoa a project she had formed for a new order of nuns, who were to be devoted in a special way to our Lady. For a time the archbishop withheld his approval, for Blessed Mary Victoria had so reduced her means by her charities that there was lack of sufficient funds to support such a foundation. But when one of her friends, Vincenza Lomellini, offered to bear the expense of providing a building, the archbishop's consent also was forthcoming. Father Zannoni drew up the constitutions, added to the Rule of St Augustine, which were approved by the reigning pope, Clement VIII. In the year 1604 Blessed Mary Victoria and ten others were clothed, and professed in the following year. Their object was to honour in their lives and worship our Lady in the mystery of her Annunciation and hidden life at Nazareth ; each nun added Maria Annunziata to her baptismal name and the rule of enclosure of their convent was particularly strict. By the enthusiasm and zeal of Blessed Mary Victoria a second house was founded in 1612, and soon after the order spread to France and other countries. It underwent a crisis just after Pope Paul V had confirmed their constitutions in 1613, when an attempt was made behind the back of the foundress to affiliate the nuns to another order, on the pretence that they were not strong enough to exist on their own. Blessed Mary Victoria learned what was happening and, as always, appealed for the help of our Lady, by whose intercession the danger was overcome. Blessed Mary Victoria continued to govern her foundation, encouraging her sisters in their penitential life and setting them an example of complete humility and love, till her death at the age of fifty-five. This took place on December 15, 1617, but to-day is her feast in the order that she founded. These nuns are distinguished from those of the Annunciation (*Annonciades*)

founded by St Joan of Valois by the epithet " Celestial " or " Blue,"
with reference to the colour of their mantles.

On the occasion of the beatification of Maria Victoria in 1828, an Italian
Life was printed with the title *Vita della b. Maria Vittoria Fornari Strata,
fondatrice dell' Ordine della Santissima Annunziata detto " Le Turchine,"*
in other words, called by Italians " the Blue Nuns." This Life is anonymous,
but was issued by the official representatives of the Order. See also a French
account published in 1902 by a Redemptorist, Father F. Dumortier, *La
bienheureuse Marie Victoire Fornari Strata, Fondatrice des Annonciades
célestes* (1902).

SEPTEMBER 13

ST MAURILIUS, Bp. of Angers, Conf.

c. A.D. 430

THIS Maurilius was a native of Milan who came into Touraine and became a disciple of St Martin, by whom he was ordained. He was a vigorous missionary, who knew how to make the most of an opportunity. When a pagan temple was struck by lightning he showed it to the people as an indication of God's anger, and at once set to work to build a church in its place. He was made bishop of Angers and governed that see in virtue and prudence for thirty years. Later writers have embroidered his life with a number of quite false tales, particularly one of a dying boy to whom he did not go to minister till it was too late. Overcome with remorse he deserted his see and made his way to the Breton coast. There, having written with his finger on a rock the words, " I, Maurilius of Angers, passed this way," he took ship for Britain. In the Channel he accidentally dropped the key of his cathedral overboard into the sea. The people of Angers were stricken with grief at the loss of their bishop, and eventually traced him to Brittany, where the inscription on the rock was found. Some of them then passed over into Britain to seek him there, and on the way a fish jumped into the boat ; in its belly was found the key of the cathedral of their city. St Maurilius was presently found working as a gardener on a nobleman's estate and they besought him to return. " I cannot come back to Angers," he said, " without the key of my church." But when he was shown that they had the key he gladly went with them, and when they had safely arrived he went to the grave of the boy who by his fault had died unconfirmed and called him by his name. The boy rose from the grave and was therefore given the name of Renatus (René), and lived to succeed St Maurilius as bishop of Angers. He is venerated as a saint both there and as bishop of Sorrento in Italy. The fable of an object recovered from the belly of a fish is found in the legends of St Ambrose of Cahors, St Kentigern, St Maglorius, and others, as well as in several non-Christian sources, particularly the story of the ring of Polycrates. There is a tradition at Angers that St Maurilius introduced the feast of the Birthday of our Lady into that diocese, in consequence of a man having a vision of singing angels on the night of September 8 ; but it deserves no more credence than the other stories told about this holy bishop.

On the 3rd of this month is celebrated the feast of another ST MAURILIUS, a bishop of Cahors who died in the year 580. He is said to have known the whole Bible by heart.

Deliberate fraud has been associated with what at one time passed current as the Life of St Maurilius. A certain deacon, named Archanaldus (in A.D. 905), rewrote an earlier account of the saint, and pretended that it had originally been compiled by Venantius Fortunatus and had afterwards been corrected by Gregory of Tours. The deception was exposed by Launoy in a dissertation (1649), and the whole matter will be found discussed in the *Acta Sanctorum*, September, vol. iv. The genuine Life by Magnobodus, written *c.* 620, has also in part been edited by Bruno Krusch when writing of Venantius in *Monumenta Germaniæ, Auctores Antiquissimi*, vol. iv, part 2, pp. 84–101. See also the *Analecta Bollandiana*, vol. xviii (1899), pp. 417–421, and Duchesne, *Fastes Épiscopaux*, ii, p. 357.

ST EULOGIUS, PATRIARCH OF ALEXANDRIA, CONF.

A.D. 607

St Eulogius was a Syrian by birth and while young became a monk, and at length abbot of his monastery of the Mother of God. Owing to the necessities of the Church he was drawn out of his solitude and made a priest of Antioch by the patriarch, St Anastasius I. Eulogius whilst he lived at Antioch made the acquaintance of St Eutychius, Patriarch of Constantinople, and joined his forces with that holy prelate against the heretics. Amongst the evils with which the Church was then afflicted, the disorder and confusion into which the Monophysites had thrown the church of Alexandria called for strong measures, and an able and zealous pastor endued with prudence and vigour to apply them. Upon the death of the patriarch John, in 579, St Eulogius was raised to that patriarchal dignity at the earnest desire of the Emperor Tiberius II, who wished to see peace restored to the Church. Two or three years later Eulogius was obliged to make a journey to Constantinople on the affairs of his church, and there he met St Gregory the Great, who was at that time the papal representative (*apocrisiarius*) at the Byzantine court. Between the two a friendship soon sprang up, and there are extant a number of letters which in after years Gregory addressed to Eulogius. In one of these letters St Gregory, now pope, refers to the success of the monk Augustine among the pagan Angli, " living in an angle of

the world," stating that on the preceding Christmas Eve ten thousand
of them had been baptised ; he goes on to use this as an encouragement for Eulogius in his efforts against the Monophysites and other
heretics. A passage in another letter almost seems to imply that
St Eulogius had something to do with originating St Augustine's
mission to England. St Gregory, who had already had to rebuke
the Patriarch of Constantinople, John IV the Faster, for assuming
the pompous title of " Oecumenical Patriarch " and had thenceforward in protest signed himself " Servant of the Servants of God,"
likewise reproved St Eulogius for addressing him as " Oecumenical
Pope." " I do not wish to be exalted in words but in virtue," he
wrote. " Away with these words which puff up pride and offend
charity." Elsewhere he praises Eulogius for his defence of the primacy
of the see of Rome. Of the numerous writings of St Eulogius,
chiefly against heresies, only a sermon and a few fragments remain.
A treatise which he wrote in refutation of the Agnostae, who denied
the omniscience of our Lord, was submitted to St Gregory before
its publication, and he approved it with the words : " I have nothing
in your writings but what is admirable." St Eulogius did not long
survive his friend, dying at Alexandria in the year 607.

We admire the great actions and the glorious triumph of the
saints, yet it is not so much in these that their sanctity consisted as
in the habitual heroic disposition of their souls. There is no one who
does not sometimes do good actions ; but he can never be called
virtuous who does well only when he is in the mood, by fits and
starts, not by steady habits. It is an *habitual* meekness of spirit,
humility, patience, purity, piety, and charity which our divine
Master recommends to us. We must take pains to plant the seeds of
virtue in our souls and must watch and labour continually to improve
and strengthen them, that they may be converted into nature and
be the principle by which all the affections of our souls and all the
actions of our lives are governed. If these pure heroic sentiments
perfectly possess and fill our hearts the whole tenour of our conduct,
whether in private or in public life, will be an uniform train of
virtuous actions, which will derive their perfection from the degree
of fervour and disinterestedness from which they spring, a degree
which, according to the essential property of virtue, is always
improving and always improvable.

Besides the *Acta Sanctorum*, September, vol. iv, an account of Eulogius
will be found in Bardenhewer's *Patrology* (Eng. Trans.), pp. 575–576, and
in the *Dict. of Christ. Biog.*, vol. ii pp. 283 *seq.* His works are printed in
Migne, P.G., vol. lxxxvi. See also the *Theologische Quartalschrift*, vol.
lxxviii, pp. 353–401.

ST AMATUS, or AMÉ, Abbot of Remiremont, Conf.

c. A.D. 630

The first in time of the two saints of this name commemorated to-day was born of a noble Gallo-Roman family at Grenoble. While still a child he was taken to the abbey of St Maurice at Agaunum where he passed over thirty years of his life, first as a schoolboy, then as a religious in the community, and finally as a hermit in a cell on the cliff behind the monastery. There he lived alone, supporting himself by the cultivation of a small patch of land, helped therein, it was said in after ages, by divine intervention. Continually enlarging the capacity of his soul by purifying his desires and increasing his affections more and more, he received new accessions of grace and virtue and thereby made perpetual approach towards the Fountain of all perfection. He considered that a uniform religious life is not an idle dull round of the same exercises, but a daily advancing in fervour and purity of heart, by which all the regular practices of devotion and penance become as it were every day new. Thus persevering and improving in every grace and virtue, he in the year 614 attracted the attention of St Eustace, when he visited Agaunum on his way back from a visit to Italy. He induced Amatus to return with him to Luxeuil and become a monk in that monastery.

The most important achievement of St Amatus was the conversion of Romaricus, a nobleman of Merovingian blood and of influence at the court of Clotaire II, who had a castle at Habendum, on the Moselle. This conversion was begun when one day St Amatus was dining at the table of Romaricus, who asked the question of another certain ruler : " What shall I do to possess everlasting life ? " Amatus pointed out a silver dish as representing the possessions to which his questioner was enslaved, and added the words of our Lord : " Sell all whatever thou hast and give to the poor, and thou shalt have treasure in Heaven. And come, follow Me." Romaricus (who was canonised by Pope St Leo IX) took these words to heart and was given the grace to interpret them literally : he manumitted his serfs, gave most of his goods, except Habendum, to the poor and the Church, and became a monk at Luxeuil. This monastery was soon undergoing a time of trial and internal schism on account of a disobedient monk, Agrestius, who, against the abbot, St Eustace, and the majority of the community, wished to substitute for their rule of St Columbanus (supplemented from that of St Benedict) the rule of St Benedict pure and simple. It is likely that this dispute was the occasion of the foundation about the year 620 by St Romericus of a double monastery under the Benedictine rule, St Amatus being appointed its first abbot. This monastery was on his estate at Habendum, and was afterwards called after the founder Remiremont (*Romarici Mons*). As in so many disputes, the controversy at Luxeuil was a complex affair, not all right was on the side of authority, and there was plenty of room for men of good will to be mistaken and to disagree among themselves. Amatus and Romaricus were not the only good men who were definitely on the side of Agrestius against St Eustace. Even after a synod at Mâcon, convoked by Clotaire II in 626 to deal with the trouble, had pronounced in favour of the Rule of St Columbanus, they continued to support Agrestius. But that unhappy man came to a bad end : he was murdered (it is said by a wronged husband) and after his death peace was gradually restored. St Amatus died about the year 630, in love and charity with St Eustace and the monks of Luxeuil. During his last years he reverted to the solitary life of his earlier ones, living in a cell apart, cultivating his garden and looking after their bees for the nuns, and coming to choir only on Sundays and great feasts. His friend and convert Romaricus took over the direction of the two communities.

The Latin Life, which was formerly accepted (*e.g.* in the *Acta Sanctorum* September, vol. iv) as written by a monk of Remiremont who was practically a contemporary of the saint, has been re-edited by Bruno Krusch in the *Monumenta Germaniæ, Scrip. rerum Meroving.*, iv, pp. 215–221. Krusch arrives at the conclusion that the document is quite untrustworthy and fabricated in the ninth century. The matter is not altogether clear, though the Life must in any case have been written as much as fifty years after the death of St Amatus. As against Krusch see Besson in the *Zeitschrift für Schweitzerische Kirchengeschichte*, vol. i (1907), pp. 20–51, and *cf.* the *Analecta Bollandiana*, xxvi, pp. 342–343.

ST AMATUS, Bp. of Sion in Valais, Conf.

A.D. 690

St Amatus, called in French Amé, was born of a wealthy family but had the happiness to learn the spirit of Jesus Christ rather than that of the world from the example and instruction of his parents. He for some time deliberated with himself what course of life to adopt wherein every desire of his soul and every action of his life might be a step advancing towards that happiness for which he was created by God. The result of his deliberation and prayer was that, with the consent and advice of those to whom prudence or duty obliged him to listen, he became a priest, and was chosen bishop of

Sion in the Valais about the year 669. He had governed his diocese almost five years when the Devil, jealous of the victories which the holy bishop daily gained over his empire, stirred up against him certain wicked men who could not bear in others that virtue which they had not courage to practise themselves. Theodericus III, son of Clovis II, king, first of Austrasia, afterwards of all the Franks, was for several years abandoned to vice and evil counsellors, and was the first of those who, governing by the mayors of the palace, are called by some historians the " Idle Kings." Ebroin, mayor of his palace, was one of the wickedest tyrants that ever had any share in the administration of the French kingdom ; the murder of St Leodegarius and the persecution and banishment of many other holy bishops and saints for which he was responsible are instances of his injustice, cruelty, and irreligion. The enemies of St Amatus, whether Ebroin himself or others, made a false accusation against him to the King ; its nature is not known. Theodericus, without examination or so much as allowing the holy man a hearing, banished him to St Fursey's monastery at Péronne, where St Ultan, the abbot, treated him with all respect and veneration. The exile rejoiced to find the tranquillity of retirement, in which he enjoyed calm and the means of living to God alone, conversing always in Heaven and giving free scope to his rigorous penitential austerities. The flagrant injustice that was done did not draw from him the least complaint, though no synod had been assembled to hear him, no sentence of deposition issued, no crime laid to his charge in a juridical manner. The only thing that troubled him was to see a wolf intruded by the King into his see, not to feed but to devour his flock.

After the death of St Ultan, St Amatus was given into the care of St. Maurontus at his newly founded abbey at Breuil in Flanders. On his way thither the bishop, while vesting himself in the church at Cambrai, emulated St Goar and other saints by hanging his cloak not on a beam but on a sun-beam. But it was the holiness of St Amatus and the injustice of his position, rather than this imaginary incident, that caused St Maurontus to kneel at his feet and apologise for being his guardian. At Breuil St Amatus both by words and example excited the monks to fervour and humility. He himself lived in a cell near the church, and occupied his soul with so much ardour in heavenly contemplation as scarcely to seem to be any longer an inhabitant of the earth. Thus he lived some years with these monks, and only left them to become an intercessor with Christ in His glory for them, about the year 690. When they came to prepare his body for burial there was found a chain of sharp spikes wound around it. King Theodericus before his death severely condemned himself for having unjustly persecuted St Amatus, and in satisfaction made several donations to the abbey of Breuil, where he visited the saint's tomb, which was famed as a place of miracles. In the year 870 the relics were translated to a church in Douai, which came to be known by the saint's name.

The Roman Martyrology implies that St Amatus was bishop of Sens, as indeed he is generally called; Mgr. Duchesne, however, has shown that his name was interpolated in the episcopal lists of that see during the tenth century. Nevertheless his attribution to Sion in Valais is not without its difficulties.

There are two Latin Lives of the Saint, the one printed in the *Acta Sanctorum*, September, vol. iv, the other in the Catalogue of the Hagiographical MSS. of Brussels, pp. 44–55. The Bollandists formerly described him as Bishop of Sens, and this view has been supported in modern times by H. Bouvier, *Histoire de l'Église de Sens*, vol. i (1906), pp. 457–460 On the other side see Besson, *Monasterium Agaunense* (1913), p. 171. *Cf.* also Duchesne, *Fastes Épiscopaux*, ii, p. 239.

SEPTEMBER 14

THE EXALTATION OF THE CROSS
(HOLY CROSS DAY)
A.D. 629

ON this day the Western Church celebrates, as we learn from the Roman Martyrology and the lessons at Matins, the veneration of the holy Cross at Jerusalem after the Emperor Heraclius had recovered it from the hands of the Persians. After a war of ten years against the Empire in the East the forces of the Persian king Chosroes II in 614 stormed and captured Jerusalem, with the aid of a large contingent of Jews eager to re-occupy their holy city. Thousands of Christians were put to the sword in the sack which followed, many more were carried off into slavery, and over three hundred churches, monasteries, and other religious buildings were burned or thrown down. Among them were the *Anastasis*, or church of the Resurrection (Holy Sepulchre), and the *Martyrion* basilica adjoining the hill of Calvary. From these were taken away their vessels and other material valuables and many precious relics, including a substantial piece of the true Cross, in a jewelled reliquary, which had been preserved at the scene of the Crucifixion after the finding of the Cross about the year 326, as related herein on May 3. The Persians continued their triumphant way and in the following years overran Egypt and Proconsular Africa. The Emperor Heraclius vainly tried to negotiate a peace, and then gathered his forces for a counter-offensive. At Easter 622, he began driving the invaders from Asia Minor and Armenia; he followed up his successes, obtained a crushing victory near Mosul in 627, and entered on his final campaign. Chosroes fled, and was deposed and barbariously murdered by his son Siroes, who made a treaty with Heraclius; the Emperor recognised him as king of Persia, and he in return released all the Roman prisoners, among the rest, Zachary, Patriarch of Jerusalem, restored the provinces which the Christians had lost and, among other spoils, the relic of the true Cross, which had been carried into Persia fourteen years before.

The Emperor brought this precious relic with him to Constantinople, where he made his entry with a most splendid triumph. In the beginning of the spring of the following year, 629, he embarked to carry the cross again to Jerusalem, and to return thanks to God in that holy place for his victories. He determined to carry it upon his own shoulders into the city, with the utmost pomp ; but stopped suddenly at the entrance to the Holy Places and found he was not able to go forward. The patriarch Zachary, who walked by his side, suggested to him that his imperial splendour was hardly in agreement with the humble appearance of Christ when He bore His cross through the streets of that city. " You," said he, " walk in your royal robes ; He was meanly clad. You have on your head a rich diadem ; He was crowned with a wreath of thorns. You go with your shoes on ; he walked barefoot." Thereupon the Emperor laid aside his purple and his crown, put on simple clothes, went along barefoot with the procession, and devoutly replaced the Cross where it stood before. It was still in the silver case in which it had been carried away, and the patriarch and clergy finding the seals whole, opened the case with the key, venerated it and showed it to the people. The original writers always speak of this portion of the Cross in the plural number, calling it the pieces of the wood of the true Cross. This solemnity was performed with the most devout thanksgiving, and honoured with miraculous cures of several sick persons. The ceremony of exposing this sacred relic, the memorial of the suffering of our divine Redeemer, to the veneration of the faithful on this and other days was very solemn, and is often mentioned both before and after the recovery of this part of the Cross from the infidels. With what ceremony and respect the like was done with the part of the Cross that was kept at Constantinople, and with what devotion the Emperor, his court, the clergy, and all ranks among the people assisted at this religious act is described at length by the Emperor Constantine Porphyrogenitus himself in the tenth century. The triumph of Heraclius was short-lived. In 632 the Mohammedan Arabs invaded Syria ; two years later they took Damascus, and in 635 the Emperor abandoned Syria and took the Jerusalem relic with him to Constantinople.

In the Eastern Church the feast of the World-wide Exaltation of the Holy and Life-giving Cross is one of the greatest of the year, and principally commemorates the Finding of the Cross and (on the previous day) the dedication of Constantine's churches at the Holy Sepulchre and Calvary. The pilgrim Ætheria in the fourth century tells us that these dedications were fixed for the same day as that on which the Cross was found, and in early times, especially in the East, the feasts of the Cross were connected more with Constantine's vision of the *Labarum*, the Finding, the dedications, and a vision accorded to St Cyril of Jerusalem in 351, than with the recovery by Heraclius. It would appear certain that September 14 was the original date of the commemoration of the Finding even at Rome, but that after the seventh century the Exaltation under Heraclius took its place and the Finding was fixed for May 3 ; thus the apparent actual dates of the events concerned have become exchanged in liturgical observance.

The spirit of the cross, or of Christ crucified, is the spirit of humility, meekness, charity, patience, and all other virtues, which He preaches to us by that cross. So long as self-love, pride, sensuality, or impatience find any place in us we are so far strangers to this spirit of Christ and enemies to His cross. We justly glory in this holy instrument of our salvation, in this adorable and sweet mystery of love, in this most tender and precious memorial of our infinitely loving God and Saviour and of the price by which He has redeemed us and made us His own. But can we look on a crucifix or form the cross on our foreheads without being covered with shame to see ourselves so little filled with it and its happy fruits and so filled with the contrary spirit of the world ? Let us most earnestly implore our loving Saviour, by His holy cross and by His infinite love and mercy, to subdue our obstinacy, to extinguish in us whatever opposes His reign, perfectly to form His spirit in our hearts, and entirely to subject all our powers and affections to Himself. He promised that when He should be exalted on His cross He would draw all things to Himself. Can our hearts resist so wonderful a mystery of love ? Let us beg that He fulfil His gracious word to us and that His spirit of humility, meekness, and pure love may at length triumph. Then we shall begin to taste the most sweet manna that is found hidden in the cross, that is, in the devout remembrance and contemplation of that mystery and in the participation or imitation of it by patient suffering. Then shall we understand the glory, the happiness, and unspeakable joys and treasures that are its portion.

Duchesne (*Christian Worship* (Eng. Trans.), p. 274) states that this Holy Cross day in September was a festival of Palestinian origin " on the anniversary of the dedication of the basilicas erected by Constantine on the sites of Calvary and the Holy Sepulchre," and he adds : " This dedication festival was celebrated in 335 by the bishops attending the Council of Tyre who had pronounced upon Athanasius the sentence of deposition. There was associated with it also the commemoration of the discovery of the true cross." In the same work (pp. 522 and 570) will be found the text and translation of Ætheria's description of the celebration. See also Bludau, *Die Pilgerreise der Ætheria* (Paderborn, 1927), pp. 185–190. The earliest mention in the West of the feast of the " Exaltation of the Holy Cross," under this name, appears to occur in the notice of Pope Sergius (687–701) in the *Liber Pontificalis* (Ed. Duchesne, i, pp. 374–378). See also Kellner, *Heortology* (Eng. Trans.), pp. 333–341 ; *Dict. d'Archéologie chrét.*, vol. iii, cc. 3131–3139 ; and Holweck, *Calendarium Festorum Dei et Dei Matris*, pp. 319 and 323. *Cf.* what is said in the fifth volume of this series under May 3.

ST MATERNUS, Bp. of Cologne, Conf.

c. A.D. 325

Maternus was the first bishop of Cologne of whom there is any certain knowledge : he is heard of in connection with the Donatist controversy. The schismatic bishops in Africa presented to the Emperor Constantine a petition against the Catholic bishop, Cæcilian, asking that the case might be judged by bishops from Gaul, who had no practical interest in the matters at issue. This disregard of jurisdiction could not be allowed, but Pope St Melchiades sent for three Gallic bishops to assist at the trial in Rome : these were Reticius of Autun, Marinus of Arles, and St Maternus of Cologne. The trial took place in the Lateran palace in the year 313 ; Cæcilian was unanimously vindicated. The Donatists angrily demanded a fresh trial and, as they were a formidable party, the Emperor directed that a council be held to deal with the matter. This took place in the following year, at Arles, and St Maternus was again one of the bishops present. It is probable that at one time he was bishop at Trier, where he seems to have died and where his principal relics are preserved, and the foundation of several churches in that part of Germany is attributed to him.

But the legends of Cologne and Trier, accepted in their liturgical books and referred to by the Roman Martyrology, make of St Maternus a very different figure. Many ancient sees have naturally sought to find for themselves an apostolic or sub-apostolic origin, and among those that have associated themselves with St Peter are Cologne and Trier—the first named claims two bishops called Maternus, in the first and the fourth centuries. He was, asserts the apocryphal story, the resurrected son of the widow of Naim, who was sent by St Peter himself with St Eucharius and St Valerius to evangelise the Gauls. When they got so far as Ehl, in Alsace, Maternus died, and his companions returned to Rome, where St Peter gave them his staff, with instructions to lay it upon the dead man. This was done, and St Maternus underwent another resurrection, and lived to bring the gospel to " the peoples of

Tongres, Cologne, and Trier and other neighbouring parts."
Almost exactly the same tale is related of other apostolic missionaries
to Gaul, and it is of course quite worthless. That there were
Christian missionaries in Alsace before the end of the first century
is not impossible, but there is no reason for supposing that this
St Maternus is other than the bishop who attended the Synod of
Arles in 314.

The extravagant legend summarised above seems to have been fabricated
towards the close of the ninth century by one Eberhard, a monk of St
Matthias at Trier. It is discussed at some length in the *Acta Sanctorum* for
September, vol. iv. The text is printed in January, vol. ii (January 29).
See also *Dict. Chrét. Biog.*, vol. iii, p. 862 ; Hauck, *Kirchengeschichte Deutschlands*, i, pp. 46–47 ; W. Neuss, *Die Anfänge des Christentums im Rheinlande*
(1923), pp. 13–20, and Duchesne, *Fastes Épiscopaux*, iii, 34 and 178.

ST NOTBURGA, Virg.

A.D. 1313

Some fourteen years before the death of St Zita at Lucca there
was born at Rattenberg in Tirol a girl who was to become as well
known as a patron of domestic servants in her own neighbourhood
as is St Zita in a more extended area. This girl, Notburga by name,
was the daughter of a small peasant, and at the age of eighteen
entered the service of Count Henry of Rattenberg and was employed
in the kitchen. There was a good deal of food left over from the
tables of this feudal establishment, and Notburga used to take it to
one of the side doors of the castle and give it away to the poor people
who daily waited there. Not content with this, she would even
stint her own meals to increase the portion of the poor. When
Count Henry's mother died, his wife, the Countess Ottilia, looked
less favourably on the charity of the kitchen-maid, and gave orders
that the broken food was to go into the pig-buckets as heretofore,
and fed to the swine. For a time Notburga did as she was told, and
gave to the poor only what she could save from her own portions
of food and drink, but she soon began secretly to continue her old
practice, till one day her master caught her at it and she was dismissed. The Countess Ottilia died shortly after, and the victims
of her parsimony, with that whimsical realism with which the poor
watch the antics of the rich, said that her ghost haunted the pigsties
of Rattenberg castle, and that the Count had had to have the place
exorcised.

Notburga now hired herself to a farmer at Eben, and a legendary incident during her time with him is familiar to all good Tirolese children. One Saturday afternoon in harvest-time Notburga was reaping, when at last the church bell rang for Vespers, indicating that Sunday was begun. Notburga stopped work and was preparing to go to church, when her employer came along and told her to go on working. She refused : Sunday begins with Saturday Vespers, and good Christians do not reap on Sundays in fine weather. The farmer argued ; the weather might change. " Very well," replied St Notburga, " let this decide it." Picking up the sickle, she threw it into the air—and there it remained suspended, looking like the first quarter of the harvest moon against the evening sky.

Count Henry in the meantime had been suffering considerably in the strife between the Count of Tirol and the Duke of Bavaria, and St Notburga's biographer, who wrote in the seventeenth century and had a lively and credulous imagination, says that Henry attributed all his misfortunes to the meanness of his late wife and the consequent dismissal of Notburga. So, when he married a second time and somebody was required to manage the household, she was installed as housekeeper and lived a happy and holy life at Rattenberg for the rest of her days. Before she died she particularly recommended her beloved poor to her master, and asked him to lay her body on a farm-wagon and bury it wherever the oxen should finally rest. This was done, and after a journey of which the usual miraculous accompaniments are recorded, the oxen brought the burden to a halt before the door of the church of St Rupert at Eben. Here accordingly St Notburga was buried, and in 1718 her relics were enshrined above the high altar. In 1862 Pope Pius IX confirmed her local *cultus* as patroness of poor peasants and hired servants.

Although we are dependent almost entirely upon the Life originally published in German in 1646 by H. Guarinoni, still there seem, as we learn from Rader's *Bavaria Sancta* and other sources, to have been materials of earlier date. In the *Acta Sanctorum*, September, vol. iv, Guarinoni's narrative is translated into Latin, and accompanied with a full prolegomena and a number of curious engravings of the *cultus* of St Notburga. She was supposed to be particularly interested in multiple births, twins, triplets, etc. See especially E. A. Stückelberg, *S. Notburga vidua, die Patronin der Mehrgeburten* in *Archives Suisses des Traditions populaires*, vol. xii, 1908, pp. 191–200. *Cf.* Dunbar in *Dictionary of Saintly Women*, vol. ii, pp. 111–112 ; and for her treatment in art Künstle, *Ikonographie*, vol. ii.

BD. LOUIS-GABRIEL TAURIN DUFRESSE, Titular Bishop of Tabraca, Mart.

A.D. 1815

Mgr. Taurin Dufresse, one of the seventy-seven martyrs in China beatified by Pope Leo XIII in the year 1900, was a victim of the persecution under the Emperor Kia K'ing and one of the most effective missionaries ever sent out by the Paris Society of Foreign Missions. He went to China as a priest at the age of twenty-six, and worked for seven years in the province of Sze-ch'wan, till in 1785 he was denounced by name and went into hiding. He successfully eluded capture for several months, but being afraid that the search for him would lead to the finding of some of his *confrères* he gave himself up and was imprisoned at Pekin. He was released with other prisoners and deported from Canton to Manila, where he remained for four years till he accompanied the vicar apostolic, Mgr. de Saint-Martin, back to Sze-ch'wan. In 1800 M. Dufresse was consecrated as his auxiliary, and in the following year succeeded to the vicariate. For a time persecution was lessened and Mgr. Dufresse administered his district with great vigour. Forty thousand pagans had been converted and the mission required a complete organization, which was taken in hand by a synod held in 1803. In 1811 a decree was issued ordering a search for foreign preachers. Only seven were found at Pekin, three of whom were officials in charge of the observatory (European skill in astronomy and mathematics provided a lever at the imperial court of which missionaries took full advantage). But the inquisition was extended to the provinces and persecution began again in Sze-ch'wan worse than ever. On May 28, 1815, Mgr. Dufresse was betrayed and taken to Ch'in-Tu, the capital of the province.

It is satisfactory to be able to record that the venerable bishop, now sixty-four years old, was treated without barbarity and indeed with consideration by the local mandarins. His books were returned to him and he was allowed to speak freely in court, a permission that he availed himself of with such effect that many of his auditors were deeply moved by his passionate plea for Christianity. The several interrogations to which he was submitted were conducted without bullying and the bishop's replies were courteously listened to : his known character and works were such that his judges were somewhat prejudiced in his favour. On September 14 he was brought before the governor, who sentenced him to death by beheading. According to the law this sentence required the imperial confirmation before it could be carried out, but the governor disregarded this and ordered the execution on the spot, in order, as he hoped, to terrify and weaken the other captive Christians, who were sent for to be present. But the bearing and words of Blessed Louis-Gabriel had the contrary effect, and as he gave them his last blessing they affirmed aloud that they too would die for Jesus Christ, as in fact many of them did. The head of the martyr was put on a pole and with his trunk was publicly displayed for a week as a warning, guarded day and night by Christians, who when they were allowed gave them decent burial.

See A. Launay, *La Salle des Martyrs du Séminaire des Missions ;* Leclercq, *Les Martyrs,* vol. x ; Kempf, *Holiness of the Church in the Nineteenth Century* (Eng. Trans.), pp. 304–305.

SEPTEMBER 15

THE SEVEN SORROWS OF OUR LADY

TWICE during the year the whole Latin Church commemorates the sorrows of the Blessed Virgin Mary, on the Friday in Passion week and again on this September 15. The first is the older feast, and it was instituted at Cologne in the fifteenth century in reparation for the blasphemies of the Hussites and to implore the help of God against those heretics. It was then called the Commemoration of the Distress and Sorrow of the Blessed Virgin Mary, and had in view specifically our Lady's suffering during the passion of her divine Son. When the feast was extended to the whole Western Church by Pope Benedict XIII under the title of the Seven Sorrows, the original reference of the Mass and Office to the Crucifixion was retained, and the feast is still called the Compassion of our Lady in some calendars, *e.g.* those of the Benedictines and Dominicans, as it was in many places before the eighteenth century.

In the Middle Ages there was a popular devotion to the Five Joys of Mary, and this was soon complemented by another in honour of five of her sorrows at the Passion. During the fifteenth century these were increased to seven, and extended back from Calvary to embrace her whole life. The Servite friars, who from their beginning had a particular devotion to the sufferings of Mary at the foot of the Cross, were in 1688 granted a feast for the third Sunday in September on which these Seven Sorrows should be commemorated, and this feast also was extended to the Western Church, by Pope Pius VII in 1814. For long there were several different ways of enumerating these mysteries, but since the composition of the liturgical Office they have been fixed by the responsories at Matins as : (i) The prophecy of holy Simeon. "There was a man named Simeon, and this man was just and devout ; and he said unto Mary : Thine own soul also a sword shall pierce." (ii) The flight into Egypt. "Arise, and take the Child and His mother and fly into Egypt ; and be there until I shall tell thee." (iii) The three days' disappearance of the boy Jesus. "Son, why hast thou done so to us ? Behold, thy father and I have sought thee, sorrowing."

(iv) The painful progress to Calvary. "And bearing His own cross He went forth. And there followed Him a great multitude of people, and of women who bewailed and lamented Him." (v) The crucifixion. "And when they were come to the place which is called Calvary, they crucified Him there. Now there stood by the cross of Jesus His mother." (vi) The taking down from the cross. "Joseph of Arimathæa begged the body of Jesus. And taking it down from the cross His mother received it into her arms." (vii) The entombment. "What a sadness of heart was thine, O Mother of sorrows, when Joseph wrapped Him in fine linen and laid Him in a sepulchre."

Pope Pius VII gave to-day's feast to the world in order to recall to mind the sufferings which the Church and her earthly head had undergone at the hands of Napoleon I, and in thanksgiving for the ever-watchful care of the Mother of God, by whose intercession these tyrannies were at an end. Those events are now long ago, but the Church of Christ on earth is always suffering and Mary ever pleads. As the feast of her sorrows in Passiontide shows the part which she took in the sacrifice of Jesus, so this second feast speaks of her compassion for the Church : the Spouse of Christ who is crucified in her turn and whose devotion to Mary's sorrows ever grows with her own sufferings. Moreover, the liturgy appointed for this feast emphasises the close union which exists between our Lord and our Lady in the work of our redemption, and the foremost place she occupies in the economy of salvation. She stood at the foot of the very cross whereon her Son gave Himself for the world ; she was a willing co-operator in His sacrifice, a willing victim of the sword that pierced her heart also. She received His last sigh, and the compassion of her maternal heart at that moment merited to obtain for her a martyr's palm without the martyr's death. Our Lady is the queen of martyrs, because her martyrdom had its principle in that love which, after the love of Jesus, has no equal. She has devoted herself to the saving of the human race far better than Judith to the saving of Israel, whence in the epistle at Mass the Church applies to her the words of Ozias : " Blessed art thou, O daughter, by the Lord the most high God, above all women upon the earth. Blessed be the Lord who made Heaven and earth because He hath so magnified thy name this day that thy praise shall not depart out of the mouth of men, who shall be mindful of the power of the Lord for ever."

Much has been written about the gradual evolution of this consecrated number of our Lady's sorrows or " dolours," but the subject has by no means been exhausted. One of the most valuable contributions to the history is an article in the *Analecta Bollandiana* (vol. xii, 1893, pp. 333–352), under the title " *La Vierge aux Sept Glaives,*" written in reply to a foolish attempt of the folklorist, H. Gaidoz, to connect the devotion with a Chaldean cylinder at the British Museum. It bears a representation of Assyrian goddess Istar, and around this is a sort of trophy of arms, which can be resolved into seven separate weapons. The coincidence is by no means striking in itself, and there is not a shadow of evidence to suggest any link between Assyria and this very late Western devotion. We know for certain that in the Middle Ages, as stated above, a recognition of five joys and then of seven preceded any specified numbering of our Lady's sorrows. Moreover, before a settled convention was arrived at we hear occasionally of nine joys, fifteen sorrows, or twenty-seven sorrows, etc. On all this consult S. Beissel, *Geschichte der Verehrung Marias in Deutschland,* vol. i (1909), pp. 404–413, and, on the liturgical commemoration, vol. ii, of the same work (1910), pp. 364–367. Further information as to the local observance of the feast in the past is afforded by Holweck, *Calendarium,* etc. ; see the Index to that work.

ST NICOMEDES, Mart.

Date unknown

Nicomedes was a martyr of the Roman Church who was buried in a catacomb on the Via Nomentana, just outside the Porta Pia. A church dedicated in his honour was one of the *tituli* of the City, and he is mentioned in several of the early martyrologies. The Roman Martyrology says that, " on saying to those who tried to make him sacrifice, ' I do not sacrifice except to the almighty God who reigns in Heaven,' he was for a long time beaten with leaded whips and under this torture passed to the Lord." But this is derived from an account of him in the worthless *acta* of SS. Nereus and Achilleus, wherein he is represented as a priest who buried the body of St Felicula (first century), was arrested and put to death, and his body thrown into the Tiber whence it was recovered by the deacon Justus. Another recension of his passion makes him suffer in the third-fourth century, under the Emperor Maximian. His body was translated to the church of Santa Prassede by Pope St Pascal I in 817 ; his catacomb, undoubtedly very ancient, was discovered in 1864.

It is curious that the name of Nicomedes does not occur in the Roman list, " Depositio Martyrum," of 354. But the Itineraries, as well as the Sacramentaries, authenticate his early *cultus* in Rome. The evidence has been set out in Père Delehaye's notes to the *Hieronymianum,* see the *Acta Sanctorum,* November, vol. ii, part 2, p. 510.

ST NICETAS THE GOTH, Mart.

c. A.D. 378

Saints Sabas and Nicetas are the two most renowned martyrs among the Goths. The former is honoured on April 12, the latter, whom the Greeks place in the class of the "great martyrs," is commemorated on this day. He was a Goth, born near the banks of the Danube, and converted to the faith in his youth by Ulfilas, who was bishop of the Scythians and Goths, a great missionary among those people, and translator of the Bible into the Gothic tongue. Unfortunately he was also an Arian. By him Nicetas was ordained priest, and if he adopted his master's errors he did so in ignorance of their falsity and heinousness. When Valens ascended the imperial throne in the East, in the year 364, the nation of the Goths was divided into two kingdoms. Athanaric, king of the Eastern Goths who bordered upon the Roman Empire toward Thrace, being a savage prince and a declared enemy to the Christian religion raised a furious persecution against the Christians; this was occasioned by the ill-treatment by the Roman authorities of a number of Goths who had taken refuge in Moldavia from the Huns. By his order an idol was carried in a chariot through all the towns and villages where it was suspected that any Christians lived, and all who refused to adore it were put to death. The usual method of the persecutors was to burn the Christians with their children in their houses or in the churches where they were assembled together; sometimes they were stabbed at the foot of the altar. In the numerous army of martyrs which glorified God amongst that barbarous people on this occasion, St Nicetas sealed his faith and obedience with his blood, and triumphing over sin passed to eternal glory by the death of fire. His relics were taken to Mopsuestia in Cilicia and there enshrined, whence it came about that this Visigothic martyr is venerated throughout the Byzantine and Syrian churches. He is named in the Roman Martyrology on this date, which is the anniversary of the translation of his relics.

On September 12 the feast is observed at Venice of another St Nicetas, a martyr under Diocletian. He was alleged to be a son of the Emperor Maximian, but his story is purely fictitious.

The Greek text of the "Passion" of S. Nicetas, as presented by the Metaphrast, was printed with a commentary in the *Acta Sanctorum*, September, vol. v. But in the *Analecta Bollandiana*, vol. xxxi (1912), pp. 209–215, the earlier original of this account has been critically edited, with a commentary which occupies pp. 281–287 of the same volume. The year of the martyrdom, as computed by the writer of the Passion, is A.D. 375, upon which see the remarks of M. D. Serruys in the same volume of the *Analecta Bollandiana*, pp. 292–294.

ST JOHN THE DWARF, ANCHORITE

FIFTH CENTURY

St John, surnamed *Kolobos*, that is " the Little " or " the Dwarf," was famous among the eminent saints that inhabited the deserts of Egypt. He retired with an elder brother into the vast wilderness of Skete and, putting himself under the direction of a holy old hermit, he set himself with his whole heart and strength to labour in subduing himself and in putting on the divine spirit of Christ. The old hermit, St Poemen, who was his director, for his first lesson bade him plant in the ground a dry walking-stick which he held in his hand, and water it every day till it should bring forth fruit. John did so with great simplicity, though the river was at a considerable distance. It is related that when he had continued his task, without speaking one word about it, into the third year the stick, which had taken root, pushed forth leaves and buds and produced fruit. The old hermit, gathering the fruit, carried it to the church, and giving it to some of the brethren, said : " Take, and eat the fruit of obedience." Posthumian, who was in Egypt in 402, assured St Sulpicius Severus that he was shown this tree, which grew in the yard of the monastery and which he saw covered with shoots and green leaves. St John used to say that, as a man who sees a wild beast or a serpent coming towards him climbs up a tree to be out of their reach, so a person who perceives any evil thoughts coming upon him in order to guard himself against the danger must ascend to God by earnest prayer. While yet a novice in the monastic state he said one day to his elder brother : " I wish to live without distraction or earthly concerns, like the angels, that I may be able to serve and praise God without interruption." Saying this, and leaving his cloak behind him, he went into a more remote part of the wilderness. After being absent a week he returned, and knocked at the door of his brother's cell. Being asked who was there, he said : " Your brother John." " How can that be ? " replied the other, " for my brother John has become an angel, and lives no more among men."

By continual watchfulness over himself he acquired so perfect a habit of meekness, humility, and patience that nothing was able to disturb him. When one said to him : "You have a heart full of venom," he gently answered : "That is true, and much more so than you think." He taught the necessity of overcoming ourselves, if we desire truly to serve God, by the following tale. A certain young man asked a celebrated philosopher to permit him to attend his lectures. "Go first," said the philosopher, "to the marble quarries, and carry stones to the river with the condemned criminals for three years." He did so, and came back at the end of that time. The philosopher bid him go again, and pass three years in receiving all sorts of injuries and insults, and make no answer but give money to those who should most bitterly revile him. He did this too, and upon his return the experienced tutor told him he might now go to Athens and be initiated in the schools of the philosophers. At the gate of that city sat an old man who amused himself by making rude remarks about those who came that way. The young novice never was angry but laughed to hear himself so outrageously abused, and, being asked the reason, said : "I have given money these three years to all who have treated me as you do. Shall I not laugh, now it costs me nothing ?" Quickly the old man replied : "Welcome to the schools of philosophy ! You are worthy of a seat in them."

St John believed that the perfection of a monk consists in his keeping always to his cell, watching constantly over himself, and having God continually present to his mind. He never discoursed on worldly affairs and never spoke of "news," the ordinary amusement of the superficial. He was so intent on the things of God that he became very absent-minded. At his work he sometimes platted into one basket the material which should have made two, and often went wrong through forgetting what he was doing. One day when a carrier knocked at his door to carry away his materials and tools to another place, St John thrice forgot what he went to fetch in returning from his door, till he repeated to himself : "The camel, my tools. The camel, my tools. The camel, my tools." The same happened to him when someone came to fetch the baskets he had made, and as often as he came back from his door he sat down again to his work, till at last he called the brother to come in, and take them himself. How St John tested the good dispositions of St Arsenius has already been related in the account of that saint on July 19. His own humility was the more remarkable because of his natural quick temper and good opinion of himself. But he knew his faults and he knew what provoked them, and therefore he avoided the ways of men and their discussions and so cultivated the things of peace that his words held the attention of all. It is said that a certain brother coming one day to speak to him only for two or three minutes, being in haste, so ardent and sweet was their conversation on spiritual things that they continued it the whole night till morning. Perceiving it was day, they went out of the saint's cell, the one to return home, the other to go with him for a few steps, but their talk again turned to God and His kingdom and it lasted till midday. Then St John took him again into his cell to eat a little ; after which they really parted. A certain charitable young woman, named Paesia, fell gradually into a disorderly life. The monks of Skete entreated St John to try to reclaim her and he went to her house, but was refused entrance. Persisting a long time and repeating that she should have no reason to repent that she had spoken to him, he at last got admittance, and sitting down by her he said with his accustomed sweetness : " What reason can you have to complain of Jesus that you should thus abandon Him ? " At these words she was struck silent, and seeing the saint in tears she said to him : " Why do you weep ? " St John replied : " How can I not weep whilst I see Satan in possession of your heart ? " She was moved by his gentleness and concern for her, and grace entered into her heart and she asked him : " Father, is the path of penitence still open to me ? " " It is," he replied. " Then lead me into it." He rose up and she followed him without saying another word, and without giving any orders about her household or servants. As they slept in the desert, their heads pillowed only on mounds of cold sand, St John dreamed he saw the soul of Paesia ascending into Heaven and heard a voice telling him that her penitence was as perfect before God as it was short before man. And in the morning he found Paesia dead.

When the Berbers passed through the desert of Skete St John and his monks fled to Mount Kolzim near the Red Sea, and there, in the place hallowed by St Antony, he died. When he drew near his end, his disciples entreated him to leave them by way of legacy some final lesson of Christian perfection. He sighed, and that he might out of humility shun the air of a teacher alleging his own doctrine and practice, he said : " I never followed my own will ; nor did I ever teach another what I had not first practised myself."

The most reliable source of information seems to be the *Apophthegmata* (see Bousset, *Apophthegmata, Studien zur Geschichte des ältesten mönchtums*, 1923) ; but consult also the *Acta Sanctorum*, October, vol. viii, pp. 39–48. The panegyric of Zachary, Bishop of Khoïs, published in Coptic by Amélineau (*Annales du Musée Guimet*, vol. xxv, 1894), and translated by Nau, from the Syriac, in the *Revue de l'Orient chrétien*, vols. vii to ix, is not very trustworthy.

ST AICHARDUS, or ACHARD, Abbot and Conf.
c. A.D. 687

Anschar, the father of this saint, an officer in the court and armies of King Clotaire II, and Hermina his mother, were distinguished for their birth among the nobility of Poitou. Hermina's particular characteristic was a tender devotion and piety, and this she desired above all things to see her son inherit and in that perfection in which it is possessed by the saints. There flourished at Poitiers at that time the monastery of St Hilary in the suburbs of the city, whither Aichardus was taken to school when he was ten years old. He was put in charge of a monk called Ansfridus, who asked his father what he should be taught. " About God and farming," interrupted the boy promptly. Here he had his education till his father thought it was time for him to come home and be introduced to the life of court and camp. Hermina trembled at the thought of the danger of forgetting God to which she feared he would be exposed, and earnestly desired that their ambition for their son should have no other view than that he should become a saint, and that, whatever choice was made, this end alone should be considered in it. This led to considerable disagreement between Anschar and his wife, and to end it Aichardus himself was called in to give his opinion. This he expressed to his father with so much earnestness and in so dutiful and respectful a manner that he gained his consent upon the spot ; seeing his son chose God alone, he should be at liberty to consecrate himself to the divine service in whatever manner he desired. Aichardus went without further delay to the abbey of St Jouin at Ansion in Poitou, near the borders of that province, a house then renowned for the severity of its discipline and the sanctity of its monks.

St Aichardus had been at Ansion for thirty-nine years when the priory of St Benedict at Quinçay, near Poitiers, was founded by St Philibert who, on account of the tyranny of Ebroin, mayor of the palace to Theodericus III, had been obliged to leave his monastery of Jumièges, which he had founded in what is now called Normandy. This holy abbot peopled Quinçay with a colony of fifteen monks from Jumièges, as he had done a little before another monastery which he founded (Hermoutier), and made Aichardus their superior. Under his rule the new house prospered and soon augmented its numbers. When St Philibert finally retired from Jumièges, which he looked upon as the principal among the religious foundations he had established, he resigned that abbacy to

St Aichardus, whose nomination was accepted by the community in consequence of a vision granted to one of their number. This was not the only occasion in the career of Aichardus that, according to tradition, a vision was vouchsafed at a particularly useful moment. There were then at Jumièges nine hundred monks, among whom he promoted monastic perfection, and sacred studies for those whom he judged best qualified for them. He at first exhorted his brethren only by his example, and this manner of exhorting proved most effectual for some of them. But others were not so easily led, until their abbot had a dream warning them of their approaching death and judgement, and this had a great effect in heightening their monastic observance. His own assiduity in prayer, modesty, austerity of penance, and scrupulous observance of the rule made everyone extremely desirous to hear him preach whom they saw do so well. He satisfied their desire by giving them admirable lessons on all the duties of Christian perfection, especially self-denial and entire disengagement of the heart from the world. His instructions were delivered in so moving a manner that every word made a deep impression on the hearts of all that heard him.

There is a story told in a late Life of St Aichardus to illustrate the saint's scrupulous respect for the customs of his house and for the due observance of the Lord's Day. It was the custom in his community for every monk to shave his crown on Saturday. St Aichardus having once been hindered on the Saturday, began to shave himself very early on Sunday morning, before the divine office, but was touched with remorse when he saw a devil picking up every hair which he had cut off at so undue a time, to produce against him at the divine tribunal! He at once stopped, and passed the day with his head half shaved, and in that condition accused himself in chapter with many tears. Though exaggerating in this instance, he was of those who truly consider the infinite sanctity of God and the great purity of affections and fidelity in all duties which we owe to Him, and watch like Job with holy fear over all they do, being well assured that no failures will escape the vigilance of their accusers or the all-seeing eye and rigorous justice of their Judge. St Aichardus was forewarned of the death of St Philibert very shortly before his own, and when his time came he was laid on ashes and covered with sackcloth, and said to the monks : " My dear children, never forget the last advice and, as it were, the testament, of your most loving father. I implore you in the name of our divine Saviour always to love one another, and never to suffer the least coldness toward any brother to be for a moment in your breasts, or anything by which perfect charity, which is the mark of the elect, may suffer any harm in your souls. You have borne the yoke of penance and are grown old in the exercise of religious duties in vain, if you do not sincerely love one another. Without this, martyrdom itself cannot make you acceptable to God. Fraternal charity is the soul of a religious house." Having spoken these words, lifting up his hands and eyes towards Heaven, he happily surrendered his soul into the hands of his Creator on September 15, about the year of our Lord 687.

The Cistercian menology on this same day commemorates a BLESSED AICHARDUS who received the habit at Clairvaux about the year 1124. He was evidently a man whose virtues and abilities were equally above the average, for he was master of novices at Clairvaux and was used by St Bernard in the work of his foundations. He is sometimes confused with his contemporary, Aichardus of Saint-Victor, Bishop of Avranches, who is called " Aichardus the Blessed." He died about 1170.

A full account is given in the *Acta Sanctorum,* September, vol. v, but little trust can be placed in the published Lives of the saint.

ST CATHERINE OF GENOA, Widow

A.D. 1510

The Fieschi were a great Guelf family of Liguria, with a long and distinguished history. In 1234 it gave to the Church the vigorous Pope Innocent IV, and in 1276 his nephew, who ruled for a few months as Hadrian V. By the middle of the fifteenth century it had reached the height of its power and splendour in Liguria, Piedmont, and Lombardy ; one member was a cardinal, and another, James, descended from the brother of Innocent IV, was viceroy of Naples for King René of Anjou. This James Fieschi was married to a Genoese lady, Francesca di Negro, and to them was born at Genoa in the year 1447 the fifth and last of their children, Caterinetta, now always called Catherine. Her biographers give particulars of her promising childhood which may be well dismissed as common-form panegyric, but from the age of thirteen she was undoubtedly strongly attracted to the religious life. Her sister Limbania was already a canoness regular and the chaplain of her convent was Catherine's confessor, so she asked him if she also could take the habit. In consultation with the nuns he put her off on account of her youth, and about the same time Catherine's father died. Then, at the age of sixteen, she was married. It is alleged of many saints, both male and female, that, though wishing to enter a monastery, they married in obedience to the will of those in authority over them, and of many of them these circumstances are only doubtfully true. But about St Catherine of Genoa there is no question. The star of the Ghibelline family of the Adorni was in decline, and by an alliance with the powerful Fieschi they hoped to restore the fortunes of their house. The Fieschi were willing enough, and Catherine was the victim. Her bridegroom was Julian Adorno, a young man with too poor a character to bring any good out of his marriage as a marriage. Catherine was beautiful in person (as may be seen from her portraits), of great intelligence and sensibility, and deeply religious ; of an intense temperament, without humour or wit. Julian was of very different fibre, incapable of appreciating his wife, and to that extent to be commiserated ; but if he failed to win more than her dutiful submission and obedience it was either because he did not try, or because he set about it in the wrong way. He was, on his own admission, unfaithful to her ; for the rest, he was pleasure-loving to an inordinate degree, undisciplined, hot-tempered, and spendthrift. He was hardly ever at home, and for the first five years of her married life Catherine lived in solitude and moped amid vain regrets. Then for another five she tried what consolations could be found in the gaieties and recreations of her world, and was little less sad and desperate than before.

She had, however, never lost trust in God, or at least so much of it as was implied in the continued practice of her religion, and on the eve of the feast of St Benedict in 1473 she was praying in a church dedicated in his honour near the sea-shore outside Genoa. And she asked that saint : " St Benedict, pray to God that He make me stay three months sick in bed." Two days later she was kneeling for a blessing before the chaplain at her sister's convent when she was suddenly overcome by a great love of God and realisation of her own unworthiness. She repeated over and over interiorily, " No more world ! No more sins ! " and she felt that " had she had in her possession a thousand worlds, she would have cast them all away." She was able to do nothing but mumble an excuse and retire, and within the next day or two she had a vision of our Lord carrying His cross which caused her to cry out : " O Love, if it be necessary I am ready to confess my sins in public ! " Then she made a general confession of her whole life with such sorrow " as to pierce her soul." On the feast of the Annunciation she received Holy Communion, the first time with fervour for ten years, and shortly after became a daily communicant, so remaining for the rest of her life—a most rare thing in those days, so that she used to say she envied priests, who could receive our Lord's body and blood

daily without exciting comment. At about this time his luxury and
extravagance had brought Julian to the verge of ruin, and his wife's
prayers, added to his misfortunes, brought about a reformation in his
life. They moved from their *palazzo* into a small house, much
more humble and in a poorer quarter than was necessary ; agreed
to live together in continence ; and devoted themselves to the care
of the sick in the Hospital of Pammatone. Associated with them
was a cousin of Catherine, Tommasina Fieschi, who after her widowhood became first a canoness and then a Dominican nun. This
went on for six years without change, except in the development of
St Catherine's spiritual life, till in 1479 the couple went to live in
the hospital itself, of which eleven years later she was appointed
matron. She proved as capable an administrator as she was a devoted
nurse, especially during the plague of 1493, when four-fifths of those
who remained in the city died. Catherine caught the distemper off
a dying woman whom she had impulsively kissed, and herself nearly
died. During the visitation she first met the lawyer and great
philanthropist Hector Vernazza, who was soon to become her ardent
disciple (and also the father of the Venerable Battista Vernazza)
and to whom is due the preservation of many precious details of her
life and conversation. In 1496 Catherine's health broke down and
she had to resign the control of the hospital, though still living
within the building, and in the following year her husband died
after a painful illness. " Messer Giuliano is gone," she said to a
friend, " and as you know well he was of a rather wayward nature,
so that I suffered much interiorly. But my tender Love assured me
of his salvation before he had yet passed from this life." Julian
provided in his will for his illegitimate daughter Thobia, and her
unnamed mother, and St Catherine made herself responsible for
seeing that Thobia should never be in want or uncared for.

For over twenty years St Catherine had lived without any spiritual
direction whatsoever, and going only rarely to confession. Indeed,
it is possible that, having no serious matter on her conscience, she
did not always make even an annual confession, and she had, without
fussiness, found no priest who understood her spiritual state with a
view to direction. But about 1499 a secular priest, Don Cattaneo
Marabotto, was made rector of the hospital, and " they understood
each other, even by just looking each other in the face without
speaking." To him she said : " Father, I do not know where I am,
either in soul or body. I should like to confess, but I am not con-
scious of any sin." And Don Marabotto lays bare her state in a
sentence : " And as for the sins which she did mention, she was
not allowed to see them as so many sins thought or said or done by

herself. She was like a small boy who has committed some slight offence in ignorance, and who, if someone tells him, 'You have done wrong,' starts and blushes, yet not because he has now an experimental knowledge of evil." We are also told in her Life " that Catherine did not take care to gain plenary indulgences. Not that she did not hold them in great reverence and devotion and consider them of very great value, but she wished that the selfish part of her should be rather chastised and punished as it deserved. . . ." In pursuance of the same heroic idea she but rarely asked others, whether on earth or in Heaven, to pray for her; the invocation of St Benedict mentioned above is a very notable exception and the only one recorded as regards the saints. It is also noteworthy that throughout her widowhood St Catherine remained a lay-woman. Her husband on his conversion joined the third order of St Francis (and to become a tertiary of any order was in those days a far more serious matter than it is now), but she did not do even that. These peculiarities are mentioned neither for commendation nor reprobation; those to whom they appear shocking may be reminded that those who examined the cause of her beatification were perfectly well aware of them: the Universal Church does not demand of her children a uniformity of practice compatible neither with human variousness nor the freedom of the Holy Spirit to act on souls as He wills. From the year 1473 on St Catherine without intermission led a most intense spiritual life combined with unwearying activity on behalf of the sick and sad, not only in the Pammatone Hospital but throughout Genoa. She is one more example of the Christian universality which those who do not understand call contradictions: complete " other-worldliness " and efficient " practicality "; concern for the soul and care for the body; physical austerity which is modified or dropped at the word of authority, whether ecclesiastical, medical, or social; a living in the closest union with God and an " all-thereness " as regards this world and warm affection for individuals in it. The life of St Catherine has been taken as the text of one of the most searching works on the mystical element in religion—and she kept the hospital accounts without ever being a farthing out and was so concerned for the right disposition of property that she made four wills with several codicils.

Catherine suffered from ill health for some years and had to give up not only her extraordinary fasts, but even to a certain extent those of the Church, and at length in 1507 her health gave way completely. She rapidly got worse, and for the last months of her life suffered great agony; among the physicians who attended her was John-Baptist Boerio, who had been the principal doctor of King

Henry VII of England, and he with the others was unable to diagnose her complaint. They eventually decided " it must be a supernatural and divine thing," for she lacked all pathological symptoms which they could recognise. On September 13, 1510, she was in a high fever and delirium, and at dawn of the 15th "this blessed soul gently breathed her last in great peace and tranquillity, and flew to her tender and much-desired Love." She was beatified by Pope Clement XII in 1737, and Benedict XIV added her name to the Roman Martyrology, with the title of saint. St Catherine left two written works, a treatise on Purgatory and a Dialogue of the soul and the body, which the Holy Office declared were alone enough to prove her sanctity. They are among the more important documents of mysticism, but Alban Butler says of them very truly that " these treatises are not writ for the common."

Apart from a short notice by Giustiniano, Bishop of Nibio, in his *Annali di Genova* (1537), the earliest biographical account of St Catherine seems to be preserved in MSS. varying considerably in their Italian text and belonging to the years 1547–1548. From these in the main was compiled the first book concerning her which was printed in any detail. It is commonly known as the *Vita e Dottrina*, and was issued in 1551. This work, which has been often reprinted, is our principal source of information concerning the saint, and it contains also a collection of her sayings and meditations. The many problems connected with its text have been discussed in great detail by Baron Friedrich von Hügel in his important work, *The Mystical Element of Religion*, 2 vols., 1908 ; see especially vol. i, pp. 371–466. His conclusions are beyond doubt justified in the main, but there is room for some difference of opinion as to details, as noted, *e.g.* in *The Month*, June, 1923, pp. 538–543. See also the *Acta Sanctorum*, September, vol. v. The numerous modern Lives of S. Catherine of Genoa, *e.g.* by Fliche, de Bussière and others are based on the *Vita e Dottrina*.

SEPTEMBER 16

ST CORNELIUS, Pope and Mart.

A.D. 253

THE holy Pope Fabian having been crowned with martyr-dom on January 20 in the year 250, the see of Rome remained vacant about thirteen months, the clergy and people not being able all that while, through the violence of the persecution, to assemble for the election of a bishop. St Cyprian says that the persecutor Decius would more easily have suffered a competitor in his empire than a bishop in Rome. At length, however, the Emperor had two rivals to cope with, and during his absence Cornelius was chosen to fill the apostolic chair, in 251. St Cyprian testifies that he was a person of an unblemished character, remarkable for his fortitude ; and that he was not advanced to the episcopal dignity suddenly, but had gone through all the orders of the clergy and served the Lord in the functions of each distinct order, as the canons require. At the time of St Fabian's death he was a priest in the Roman church, and had a chief share in the direction of affairs during the vacancy of the Holy See. His election was made by a due assembly of almost all the clergy of Rome ; a great number also of the laity, who were present, consented to and demanded his ordina-tion. The concurring suffrages of sixteen bishops (two of whom were Africans), who were then in Rome, confirmed the same, and the elect received the episcopal consecration. Suddenly and with-out any warning, one Novatian procured his own consecration and proclaimed himself bishop of Rome in opposition to St Cornelius. Both bishops at once wrote to all the local churches and the Church was torn by schism ; it only lasted intensely for a short time, for soon the churches of Africa followed St Cyprian, and those of the East St Dionysius of Alexandria, in their adhesion to St Cornelius. But it was important, for the progress of the dispute showed clearly how all Christians recognised the necessity of being in communion with the true bishop of Rome. Before the end of the year St Cornelius had convened a synod of sixty bishops and Novatian was excommunicated. But what had begun as a schism continued as a heresy, and the tenets called Novatianism persisted for several centuries. They arose from differences as to the treatment of those who lapsed from the faith under stress of persecution. Of such there were several classes ; principally the *sacrificati*, who actually sacrificed to the false gods or ceremoniously ate the sacrificial meats ; the *thurificati*, who had offered incense to idols ; and the *libellatici*, who gave a written declaration that they were not Christians and were ready to sacrifice or else purchased with money of the imperial officers certificates of safety as if they had offered sacrifice (by which they were guilty of the same scandal). All the lapsed, upon giving marks of sincere repentance, were admitted by the Church to a severe canonical penance, which was shorter and milder for the *libellatici* than for apostates ; when it was finished (or abridged by an indulgence given by the bishop) they were received to communion. If any penitent during the course of his penance was in danger of death, the benefit of absolution and communion was granted him. This discipline was confirmed by several councils at Rome, in Africa, and other places, and against it Novatian set himself, claiming that the lapsed ought never to be again admitted to communion, or to receive absolution, not even after having performed any course of penance or in the hour of their death. Yet he did not bid them despair, but left them to the divine mercy, exhorting them to pray privately to God, hoping that He would be moved to show them compassion at the last day. Novatian soon added heresy to this rigorous discipline, maintaining that the Church had not received from Christ power to absolve sinners from the crime of apostasy, however penitent they might be. His followers afterwards taught the same of murder, adultery, and fornication, and condemned second marriages. Novatian was a learned and eloquent man, in talent the superior of St Cornelius, but he had fundamental defects of ambition and pride. His very consecration he obtained by a trick, beguiling three bishops from a corner of Italy to come to Rome and ordain him bishop. He was the first anti-pope, author not only of a schism but also of a heresy, and was eventually acknowledged bishop only by heretics.

St Cyprian praises the zeal and piety with which St Cornelius behaved in his pastoral charge, and the courage and steadfastness with which he adhered to his duty in most perilous times. " Should not he be ranked among the most illustrious martyrs and confessors, he says, " who waited so long in the expectation of tormentors and savage executioners to be sent by the enraged tyrant to mangle his body, to behead, or to burn, or to crucify ; or, with some new invention of malice and cruelty, to tear and torture the bowels of this intrepid champion for opposing the dreadful edicts and, through the mighty power of his faith, despising the torments wherewith he was threatened ? Though the goodness of God has hitherto protected His bishop, yet Cornelius gave sufficient evidence of his love and fidelity by being ready to suffer all he could suffer, and by conquering the tyrant [Decius] first by zeal who was soon after conquered in battle." After the death of Decius his persecution was renewed with violence by Gallus, and Pope Cornelius was the first person that was apprehended at Rome. Having made a glorious confession of his faith, he was sent into banishment to Centumcellæ (Civita Vecchia). St Cyprian wrote him a congratulatory letter upon the news of his happiness in suffering for Christ, and even more upon the glory of his church, for not a single Roman Christian apostatised : " With one heart and one voice the whole Roman church confessed. Then was seen, most dear brother, that faith which the blessed Apostle praised in you,* for even then he foresaw in spirit your glorious fortitude and firm strength." He also clearly foretells the approaching conflicts of them both and says that God had warned him of his own, and that he therefore earnestly exhorted his people to prepare for it. He adds : " Whoever of us shall be first favoured with removal hence, let our charity persevere in never-ceasing prayers unto the Father for our brethren and sisters." St Cornelius was the first to be called, in June of the same year, 253. St Cyprian often refers to him as a martyr, but, though later accounts say he was beheaded, he was probably not put directly to death but died of hardships at Centumcellæ. His body was taken to Rome and buried, not in the papal crypt proper but in the near-by crypt of Lucina, which was probably the burying-place of the *gens Cornelia.*

The great supporter of Pope St Cornelius, both as Supreme Pontiff and as defender of the Church against Novatian's rigorism, was Cyprian of Carthage, and their close association has ever since been recognised. St Cyprian's feast was kept at the tomb of Cornelius in the fourth century and his image painted on the wall of the crypt in the sixth ; they are named together in the canon of the Mass and in the Roman Martyrology on September 14, the date of Cyprian's martyrdom ; and two days later their joint feast is kept by the whole Western Church. These two holy bishops now reign with the saints because in this life they truly sought to follow their example. "We have solemnly renounced the world," wrote St Cyprian himself, " and therefore whilst we continue in it should behave like strangers and pilgrims. We should welcome that happy day [of our death] which is to fix us every one in our

* *See* Romans i 8

proper habitation, to rescue us from the troubles and snares of this world, and remove us to the kingdom of Heaven. Who amongst us, if he had been long a sojourner in a foreign land, would not desire to return to his native country ? What person, when he had begun to sail thither, would not wish for a fair wind to carry him swiftly to his desired home that he might the sooner embrace his friends and relations ? We must account Paradise our own country. There friends and parents and brethren and children without number wait for us, and long to greet our happy arrival. They are in secure possession of their own felicity and are solicitous for ours. How great will be our common joy at our meeting together in those blessed abodes ! How unutterable must be the pleasures of that kingdom, which have no lessening or interruption and where endlessness is added to the highest bliss ! There we shall meet with the glorious choir of the apostles, with the goodly company of the prophets, with an innumerable multitude of martyrs ; there we shall be blessed with the sight of those triumphant virgins who have subdued the inordinate lusts of the flesh ; and there we shall behold the rewards of those who, by feeding the hungry and succouring the afflicted, have with their earthly treasure purchased to themselves a treasure in Heaven."

The story of St Cornelius forms an important episode in ecclesiastical history, and from Eusebius downwards it has engaged the attention of all writers who deal with the Christian Church in the early centuries. Besides the *Acta Sanctorum*, September, vol. iv, and the works of Grisar, Duchesne, J. P. Kirsch, etc., see especially A. d'Alès, *Novatien* (Paris, 1925) and J. Chapman, *Studies on the early Papacy* (London, 1928), pp. 28 *seq.* As for the " martyrdom," the place of interment, and the inscription and fresco of St Cornelius in the catacombs, see Wilpert, *La cripta dei Papi e la cappella di santa Cecilia* (1910); Franchi de' Cavalieri, *Note agiografiche*, vol. vi, pp. 181–210, and Delehaye in the *Analecta Bollandiana*, vol. xxix (1910), pp. 185–186, Dom Leclercq in the *Dictionnaire d'Archéologie* (vol. iii, cc. 2968–2985) reproduces several illustrations from de Rossi and Wilpert. The so-called " Passion " of St Cornelius (the various redactions of which are catalogued in the *Bibliotheca Hagiographica Latina*, nn. 1958–1966) is an historically worthless document.

ST CYPRIAN, Bp. of Carthage, Mart.

A.D. 258

St Cyprian played an important part in the history of the Western Church and the development of Christian thought in the third century, particularly in Africa where his influence was preponderant. As a bishop he left his mark on the local church, of which he was the soul and the pattern ; as a writer and orator he dominated the literature of his time ; everywhere his voice was heard and his influence felt. He was the great man of his generation in the African church and his figure stands out boldly in the history of his time ; the numerous synods of his episcopate were summoned and presided over by him, and his ideas and policies ordinarily prevailed, though he was scrupulous to constrain no one and to respect the rights of his brother-bishops. By his personal prestige, even more than by that of his see, he became recognised as in fact the primate of the African church, and he is daily named in the canon of the Mass. He was called officially Caecilius Cyprianus, popularly known as Thascius, and was born about the year 210, probably at Carthage ; certainly he was, according to St Jerome, a native of Proconsular Africa. Very little is known of his pre-Christian life ; he was a public orator, teacher of rhetoric, and pleader in the courts, and engaged to the full in the pagan life of Carthage, both public and social. After his conversion he wrote of this time to his friend Donatus : " I wandered like an eagle in the darkness of the night, thrown hither and thither on the boisterous sea of this world, a stranger to the light and the truth. I then thought that what I was told of a second birth, and the means of salvation by it propounded by the divine goodness, hard and impracticable. . . . But as soon as the life-giving waters of baptism had washed my soul, my heart received the light of the heavenly truth, the Spirit of God descended upon me, and I was become a new creature ; soon all my difficulties were surprisingly cleared, my doubts were resolved, and all my former darkness was dispelled. Things appeared easy which before I looked upon as difficult and discouraging : I was convinced that I was able to do and suffer all that which heretofore had seemed impossible. I then saw that the earthly principle, which I derived from my first birth, exposed me to sin and death ; but that the new principle, which I have received from the Spirit of God in His spiritual birth, gave me new ideas and inclinations, and directed all my views to Him." Probably the need of answers to those fundamental questions which only the Catholic Church can answer, and the disgust at self-indulgence which all men of a fine nature who have given way to it sooner or later experience, turned Cyprian's mind seriously to Christianity. God's instrument of his conversion, somewhere about middle age, was an old priest, Caecilian, and Cyprian ever after reverenced him as his father and guardian angel. Caecilian, in turn, had the greatest confidence in his virtue and on his death-bed recommended his wife and children to Cyprian's care and protection. He also became as it were the heir of Caecilian's virtue, and St Pontius, the saint's deacon and biographer, tells how the convert set himself with eagerness to read the holy Scriptures and to learn all those lessons which would be of use to him in his design of serving God. A complete change came over Cyprian's life. Before his baptism he made a vow of perfect chastity, which greatly astonished the Carthaginians and drew even from Pontius the exclamation : " Who ever saw such a miracle ! " He soon sold his whole estate, and gave almost all the money and whatever else he possessed for the support of the poor ; by which he gained two points of principal importance, renouncing all secular ties (than which nothing is more fatal to the true interests of piety and religion) and fulfilling the law of charity which God prefers to all sacrifices. With the study of the holy Scriptures St Cyprian joined that of their best expositors, and in a short time became acquainted with the works of the greatest religious writers. He particularly delighted in the writings of his countryman Tertullian, scarce passed a day without his reading something in them, and when he wanted them he used to say : " Reach hither my master." But though he admired his genius and the variety of his learning he was upon his guard not to imitate any of his faults or errors. Not the least of his sacrifices was the renouncement of all profane literature, and in his own extensive writings there is not a single quotation from any pagan author. In the earlier centuries of Christianity such a policy had a value which it no longer has to-day. He led a retired life and made such progress in virtue that he was ordained priest while still a neophyte, and so great was his moral authority in the city that shortly afterwards he was designated for the bishopric of Carthage. At first he refused and sought to fly, but the people surrounded his house and guarded all the ways that led to it, so that he could not escape. He attempted to get out at a window, but finding it in vain he yielded and was consecrated with the unanimous approbation of the bishops of the province about the year 249. Five priests with some of the people opposed his election, which, however, was validly carried out, "after the divine judgement, the choice of the people, and the consent of the episcopate." Cyprian administered his office with charity, goodness, and courage mixed with vigour and steadiness. His aspect was reverend and gracious beyond what can be expressed, says Pontius, and no one could look him in the face without awe ; his countenance had a mixture in it of cheerfulness and gravity, so that a person who beheld him might doubt whether he should love or respect him most : but this was certain, that he deserved the highest degree both of respect and love.

The Church continued to enjoy peace for about a year after

St Cyprian's promotion to the see of Carthage, till the Emperor Decius began his reign by raising a persecution. Thirty-eight years of quietness and prosperity had had a weakening effect among the Christians, and when the edict reached Carthage there was a stampede to the capitol to register apostasies with the magistrates, amid cries of " Cyprian to the lions ! " from the pagan mob. The bishop was proscribed, and his goods ordered to be forfeited, but Cyprian had already retired to a secret hiding-place, a proceeding which brought upon him much adverse criticism both from Rome and in Africa. He felt put on his defence, and set out justifying reasons for his action in several letters to the clergy. And there is no doubt that he did right to hide in the circumstances : to remain at Carthage meant certain death as he was a bishop and his church would have been left without a head ; moreover, his presence uncaptured in the city would have provoked the persecutors to greater violence, and in the event the havoc which the enemy made there would have been much greater if Providence had not preserved St Cyprian that by his active zeal and authority he might maintain discipline and repair the ruin caused by the persecution. He wrote to his clergy : " We have to watch over the common good and so we must unwillingly resign ourselves to being parted from you for a time. Our presence would increase the hate and fury of the Gentiles ; we, whose business it is to care for the safety of all above all, would be the cause of further violence to peace." And to the clergy of Rome : " Since the beginning, when the first troubles broke out and popular clamour was so often directed against myself, I have for the time being withdrawn, in the interests less of my own safety than of the public tranquillity of our brethren ; for I fear that our presence would have been out of place and the agitation already begun made worse thereby." He supplied the want of his personal presence with his flock by frequent letters, counsel, admonition, exhortation, and prayer to Heaven. He exhorted them also to continual prayer, saying : " What has moved me more particularly to write to you in this manner was an admonition which I received in a vision from Heaven saying to me : ' Ask and you shall receive.' " " Let each of us," he wrote, " pray to God not for himself only but for all the brethren, according to the pattern which our Lord gave us wherein we are taught to pray as a common brotherhood, for all, and not as individuals, for ourselves alone. When the Lord shall see us humble, peaceable, in unity among ourselves, and made better by our present sufferings, he will deliver us from the hands of our persecutors." He assured them that Christians by falling into sloth and relaxation of life during the long peace had deserved this scourge for their trial and amendment ; and that this storm had been revealed by God, before it happened, to a devout person at Carthage in a vision of the enemy under the figure of a *retiarius** watching to destroy the faithful, because they did not stand upon their guard. In the same letter the saint mentions another revelation of God, which he himself had received concerning the end of the persecution and the restoration of peace to the Church. By such letters he warned and encouraged his flock, heartened the confessors in prison, and took care that priests in turns should visit them and offer the Sacrifice of the altar and give them Holy Communion every day in their dungeons.

During the absence of St Cyprian one of the priests who had opposed his episcopal election, named Novatus, went into open schism. He was a man of unsavoury reputation, who was said to have deserted his wife and to have suffered his aged father to perish with hunger without so much as taking care to bury him. The brethren were urgent to have him deposed and excommunicated, and the time of his trial was near at hand, when the persecution began and no assemblies could be held. In order to prevent his condemnation, Novatus separated himself from his bishop, persuading some others to do the same and pretending to ordain one Felicissimus as his deacon. Some among the lapsed, and confessors who were displeased at St Cyprian's discipline towards the former, adhered to them, for Novatus received, without any canonical penance, all apostates who desired to return to the communion of the Church. St Cyprian, finding other remedies only served to make the schismatics more insolent, denounced Novatus and Felicissimus, and at a council of bishops and lower clergy, convened at Carthage when the persecution slackened in 251, he read a treatise on the Unity of the Church. " There is," said he, " one God and one Christ and but one episcopal chair, orginally founded on Peter, by our Lord's authority. There cannot therefore be erected another altar or another priesthood. Whatever any man in his rage or rashness shall appoint, in defiance of the divine institution, must be a spurious, profane, and sacrilegious ordinance " ; as Peter is the earthly foundation of the whole Church, so is its lawful bishop of each diocese. The leaders of the schismatics were excommunicated, and Novatus departed to Rome to help stir up trouble there. After the martyrdom of Pope St Fabian, St Cornelius was elected to the apostolic throne ; a few weeks later a Roman priest, Novatian, was set up as anti-pope and, although he adopted a rigorous attitude

* A gladiator who was armed with a net (*rete*) wherein he tried to entangle his opponent.

towards lapsed Catholics, Novatus nevertheless attached himself to his party. After he had informed himself of all the circumstances, St Cyprian recognised Cornelius as the true pope and was active in his support both in Italy and Africa during the ensuing schism ; with St Dionysius, Bishop of Alexandria, he rallied the bishops of the East to Cornelius, making it clear to them that to adhere to a false bishop of Rome was to be out of communion with the Church. In connection with these disturbances he added to his treatise on Unity one on the question of the Lapsed.

Virtue which has stood the fiercest persecution is often seen to waver at the first ray of prosperity, so dangerous are its flatteries. St Cyprian complains in many parts of his works that the peace which the Church had enjoyed had enervated in some Christians the watchfulness and spirit of their holy profession, and had opened a door to many converts who had not the true spirit of our faith, so that there was much relaxation and, their virtue being put to the test in the persecution raised by Decius, many lacked courage to stand the trial. These, whether apostates who had sacrificed to idols or *libellatici* who, without sacrificing, had purchased for money certificates that they *had* offered sacrifice, were the lapsed (*lapsi*), concerning the treatment of whom so great a controversy raged during and after the Decian persecution : on the side of excessive lenience Novatus went into schism, while Novatian's severity crystallised into the heresy that the Church cannot absolve an apostate at all. At this time those guilty of less heinous sins than apostasy were not admitted to assist at the holy Mysteries before they had gone through a rigorous course of public penance, consisting of four degrees and of several years' continuance. When, during this penitential term, absolution was given in danger of death, if the penitent recovered he was obliged to accomplish the rest of the austerities enjoined him. Relaxations of these penances were granted on certain extraordinary occasions, as on account of the uncommon fervour of a penitent or on occasion of a new persecution being raised in the Church. It was also customary to grant " indulgences " to penitents who received a recommendation from some martyr going to execution, or from some confessor in prison for the faith, containing a request on their behalf, which the bishop and his clergy examined and often ratified.* In St Cyprian's time this custom degenerated in Africa into an abuse, by the number of such *libelli martyrum*, and their often being given in too vague or peremptory terms and without examination or

* The terms of time (30 days, 7 years, etc.) in which indulgences are granted to-day is a survival from the days when the discipline of public penance was still in force in the Church.

discernment, to the prejudice of souls and the relaxation of the discipline of penance. One Lucian at Carthage even obtained from a martyr named Paul a general commission to grant peace, *i.e.* the full communion of the Church, to any penitent who should ask for it. St Cyprian severely condemned these abuses in three letters, to the martyrs and confessors, to the clergy, and to the people. To the first he expresses surprise that they were not better instructed, so that on their recommendations priests had improperly allowed *lapsi* to make their offerings at Mass and to receive the Body of the Lord. The saint's letter to the priests is a much more severe rebuke ; he complains that some of their order (whom he threatens to suspend), forgetting the rule of the gospel as well as the rank which they held in the Church, rashly and hastily admitted penitents to communion upon the recommendation of confessors, " though," says he, " they have not performed their penance, made no humble confession of their sin, nor received the imposition of hands from the bishop and his clergy ; the holy Eucharist is administered to them in defiance of the Scripture, which saith : ' Whosoever shall eat this bread or drink the chalice of the Lord unworthily, shall be guilty of the Body and Blood of the Lord.' " In his letter to his people he recommends them to restrain, by their advice, the imprudence of such confessors, and to keep them within the limits of episcopal authority. He, however, dispenses in case of sickness, or other extreme danger, and allows those with *libelli* from the martyrs to be reconciled, " when they have made humble confession of their sin before any priest or deacon whom they can procure to attend them."* Though it would appear that St Cyprian himself tended to severity he in fact pursued a middle way, and in practice was considerate and lenient. After he had consulted the Roman clergy he insisted that his episcopal rulings must be followed without question until the whole matter could be brought up for discussion by all the African bishops and priests. This was eventually done at the council at Carthage mentioned above, and it was decided that, whereas *libellatici* might be restored after terms of penance varying in length according to the case, *sacrificati* could receive Communion only at death. But in the following year the persecution of Gallus and Volusianus began, and another African council decreed that " all the penitents who professed themselves ready to enter the lists afresh, there to abide the utmost heat of battle and manfully to fight for the name of the Lord and for their own salvation, should receive the peace of the Church."

* A deacon might be deputed to give canonical, but not sacramental, absolution, *i.e.* absolution from censures.

This, said the bishop, was necessary and desirable in order " to make a general rendezvous of Christ's soldiers within His camp for those who are desirous to have arms put into their hands and seem eager for the engagement. So long as we had peaceable times there was reason for a longer continuance of penitents under a state of mortification, to be relaxed only in the case of sickness and danger. Now the living have as much need of Communion as the dying then had, otherwise we should leave naked and defenceless those whom we are exhorting and encouraging to fight our Lord's battle : whereas we should rather support and strengthen them with the Body and Blood of Christ. The object of the Eucharist being to be a defence and security for those who partake of it, we should fortify those whose safety we are concerned for with the armour of our Lord's banquet. How shall they be able to die for Christ it we deny them the Blood of Christ ? How shall we fit them for drinking the cup of martyrdom, if we will not first admit them to the chalice of the Lord ? "

St Cyprian was forewarned by God of the revival of the persecution under Gallus, of which he wrote to Pope Cornelius : " A storm is coming and a furious enemy will soon declare himself against us ; the struggle will not be like the late one [that under Decius], but more sharp and insupportable. This we have had frequently revealed to us from above, and the merciful providence of God often reminds us of it ; through whose assistance and compassion we trust that He, who in times of peace has foretold to His soldiers the approaching battle, will crown them with victory when engaged in it." During this persecution, in 253, St Cornelius made a glorious confession of his faith at Rome and was banished to Centumcellæ. St Cyprian congratulated him by a letter in which he foretells his own approaching martyrdom. After the death of St Cornelius, which happened in the same year, St Cyprian wrote a letter of congratulation to his successor, St Lucius, who was banished at once after his election. Being recalled, he received another letter from Cyprian, rejoicing at his return and referring to God's vindication, by the incidence of persecution, of His true pontiff, presbyters, and people against Novatian and his heretical followers.

Between the years 252 and 254 Carthage was visited by a terrible plague, of the ravages of which St Pontius has left a vivid description. In this time of terror and desolation St Cyprian organised the Christians of the city and spoke to them strongly on the duty of mercy and charity, teaching them that they ought to extend their care not only to their own people, but also to their enemies and persecutors. The faithful readily offered themselves to follow his

directions. Their services were severally distributed : the rich contributed large alms in money ; the poor gave their personal labour
and attendance. Everyone was eager to join in a work wherein they
might so closely imitate Christ their Lord, and in which they had
at their head so great a leader and commander as their bishop. How
much the poor and necessitous were, not only during this pestilence,
but at all times the objects of Cyprian's most tender care appears
from the concern he expressed for them and the orders he frequently
gave about them in his letters during his absence. It was one of
his usual sayings : " Do not let that sleep in your coffers which
may be profitable to the poor. That which a man must of necessity
part with some time or other it is well for him to distribute voluntarily, that God may recompense him in eternity." To comfort and
fortify his flock during the plague, St Cyprian wrote his treatise *de
Mortalitate.*

All orders of men shared the good bishop's attention, but the
clergy above the rest. So careful was he that they should be wholly
taken up in the spiritual duties of their charge that he reckoned it
among the great disorders which had crept into the Church during
the long peace before Decius that some bishops, " neglecting their
high trust, entered upon the management of secular affairs." In the
town of Furni, one Geminius Victor had in his last will appointed
Geminius Faustinus, a priest of that church, his executor. The
sixth apostolic canon and other synodal decrees of the earliest ages
forbade any bishop, priest, or deacon to engage in secular business
under pain of being deposed. The Roman laws made it penal for
anyone to refuse the office of executor or guardian, when offered, so
the synods inflicted a penalty on him who should appoint a bishop,
priest, or deacon either executor or guardian, forbidding any remembrance of him to be made at the Eucharist or any offering to be
made for him after his death. " The reason of which was that the
clergy should not be distracted from their holy ministrations—that
they might attend their altar and their sacrifice without interruption,
and fix all their attention upon religious duties," as St Cyprian says.
He therefore ordered " that the name of the said Victor should not be
mentioned at the altar, and that no oblation should be made for his
repose, nor the customary prayers of the Church be offered up on his
behalf." St Cyprian hoped, by this example of severity, to prevent
any person from calling down to a lower employment the priests and
ministers of God, whose whole time and care should be devoted to
his altar.

About the year 255 began a controversy concerning the validity of
baptism given by heretics. St Cyprian's opinion was quite definite,

that all heretical and schismatical baptisms are invalid, and when he was consulted by eighteen bishops of Numidia on the matter a council over which he presided replied accordingly that such baptism is null and to be reiterated ; this decree was soon after confirmed in a synod of seventy-two bishops held at Carthage, and the decision was communicated to the pope, Stephen I. In what manner St Stephen maintained the tradition of the Church upon this head has been related in the life of that holy pope and martyr (August 2). It was the practice of the Roman Church to recognise as valid the baptism conferred by heretics (other things being equal), and this practice was no mere matter of discipline but represented the doctrinal teaching of the Church at large. The African bishops were threatened with excommunication. This angered Cyprian ; he wrote to one Jubaianus defending himself and setting out his reasons, and to Pompeius very violently. These letters brought some of the wavering bishops of Mauretania and Tripolitana to his side, and at a council in 256 eighty-seven bishops unanimously supported him. The Pope refused to receive their representatives, and St Cyprian appealed to Firmilian, Bishop of Caesarea in Cappadocia, who enthusiastically agreed with the African bishops. The further progress and end of the controversy is not known, but what the behaviour of St Cyprian would have been had he seen it determined by the decision of the Church cannot be doubted, from the principles which he himself lays down. He did not question the superior authority of St Stephen, though in a point which he believed to belong to discipline, not to faith, he thought he should maintain the custom which he found established at Carthage by a predecessor, Agrippinus. Neither was he unmindful of the dignity of the Roman see, which he calls " The chair of Peter, the principal church, the origin of the sacerdotal unity." If he for some time betrayed undue warmth in this controversy this offence was effaced by his perfect charity and glorious martyrdom, as St Augustine declares. During the very height of this dispute about heretical baptism he published a treatise on the Goodness of Patience. In it he takes this virtue not only for the restraint of resentment and revenge, but for the spring of all those virtues which contribute to make a man merciful, gentle, forbearing, and forgiving, and which enable him to endure all sorts of hardships and to oppose all sorts of temptations.

In the month of August 257, was promulgated the first edict of Valerian's persecution, which forbade all assemblies of Christians and required bishops, priests, and deacons to take part in official worship under pain of exile, and on the 30th the Bishop of Carthage was brought before the proconsul.   The source for what followed is the *Acta Proconsularia Sancti Cypriani*, an unique record of the trials and death of a martyr in its authenticity and purity.   The *acta* comprise three distinct documents, namely, a copy of the official *acta proconsularia* for his trial in 257, which resulted in banishment ; the same of the second trial, in 258, at which he was condemned ; a short account of his passion written by the compiler, an eyewitness, who also adds a few words to connect the three parts into one narrative.   It runs as follows :

"When the Emperor Valerian was consul for the fourth time and Gallienus for the third, on August 30 [A.D. 257], Paternus the proconsul said to Cyprian the bishop, in the private audience-chamber : ' The most sacred emperors Valerian and Gallienus have deigned to give me letters in which they have commanded those who do not follow the Roman religion to observe that ceremonial hence-forth.   For this reason I have enquired about you.   What do you answer me ? '

CYPRIAN : I am a Christian and a bishop.   I know no other gods but the one and true God who made Heaven and earth, the sea, and all that is in them.   This God we Christians serve ; to Him we pray day and night, for ourselves and for all men and for the safety of the Emperors themselves.

PATERNUS : Do you persist in this intention ?

CYPRIAN : A good intention which acknowledges God cannot change.

PATERNUS : You will, then, according to the edict of Valerian and Gallienus, go as an exile to the city of Curubis.

CYPRIAN : I go.

PATERNUS : The Emperors have deigned to write to me not only about the bishops but also about the priests.   I wish therefore to know from you who are the priests who live in this town.

CYPRIAN : By your laws you have wisely forbidden any to be informers, so I am not able to betray them by revealing their names. But they can be found in their towns.

PATERNUS : I will to-day seek them out in this place.

CYPRIAN : Our discipline forbids that any should voluntarily give himself up, and this is contrary to your principles ; but you will find them if you look for them.

PATERNUS : I will find them.   The Emperors have also forbidden any assemblies to be held in any place, and also access to the ceme-teries.   If any one then has not observed this salutary precept, he incurs the penalty of death.

CYPRIAN : Do what is ordered you.

" Then Paternus the proconsul ordered the blessed Cyprian to be exiled, and when he had already been some time in his place of exile, Galerius Maximus the proconsul succeeded to Aspasius Paternus the proconsul. The first-named ordered holy Cyprian the bishop to be recalled from exile and brought before him [August 258]. When Cyprian, the holy martyr chosen by God, had returned from the city of Curubis* (where he had been in exile according to the decree of the then proconsul Aspasius Paternus), he remained in his own gardens according to the imperial decree, hoping daily that they would come for him as had been revealed to him in a dream†. And while he was staying there, suddenly on September 13, in the consulship of Tuscus and Bassus, two officers of the proconsul came to him : one was the chief gaoler of the proconsul Galerius Maximus, who had succeeded Aspasius Paternus, and the other was marshal of the guard of the same office. They put him between them in a carriage, and took him to Villa Sexti, whither Galerius Maximus the proconsul had retired to recover his health. This same Galerius Maximus the proconsul ordered the trial of Cyprian to be deferred to another day, and the blessed Cyprian was taken to the house of the chief gaoler of this same Galerius Maximus and remained as a guest with him in the quarter called Saturn, between the temple of Venus and the temple of Public Welfare. Thither all the brethren came together. And when the holy Cyprian learnt this he ordered that the young girls should be protected, since all remained together in that quarter before the gate of the officer's house. The next day, September 14, in the morning, a great crowd came together to Villa Sexti according to the command of Galerius Maximus the proconsul, who ordered Cyprian on that same day to be brought before him in the court called Sauciolum. When he was brought in, Galerius Maximus the proconsul said to Cyprian the bishop : ' You are Thascius Cyprianus ? '

CYPRIAN : I am.

* Curubis was a small town fifty miles from Carthage, on a peninsula of the coast of the Libyan sea, not far from Pentapolis. The place was pleasant and healthy, with good air and, though in desert country, green fields and plenty of fresh water. Cyprian was accompanied by his deacon, St Pontius, and others, and his banishment was attended with that consideration which characterised the official attitude towards him throughout.

† He had been brought back in accordance with a further edict which ordered that bishops, priests, and deacons should be at once put to death (Pope St Sixtus II was one of the first to suffer) and the persecution in other ways aggravated.

MAXIMUS : You have made yourself the father (*papa*) of these sacrilegious men ?

CYPRIAN : Yes.

MAXIMUS : The most sacred Emperors have ordered you to sacrifice.

CYPRIAN : I will not sacrifice.

MAXIMUS : Think about it.

CYPRIAN : Do what is required of you ; there is no room for reflexion in so clear a matter.

"Galerius Maximus, having discussed the matter with his council, gave sentence most reluctantly, as follows : ' You have lived long in sacrilege ; you have gathered round you many accomplices in unlawful associations ; you have made yourself an enemy of the Roman gods and their holy religion : and our most pious and sacred princes, Valerian and Gallienus the *Augusti* and Valerian the most noble *Cæsar*, have not been able to recall you to the practice of their rites. Therefore, since you are found to be the author and ringleader of shameful crimes, you yourself shall be made an example to those whom you have joined with you in your wickedness : your blood shall be the confirmation of the laws.' At these words he read the decree from a tablet : ' Thascius Cyprianus shall be put to death by the sword.' Cyprian the bishop answered, ' Thanks be to God.'

"When this sentence was passed the assembled brethren said : ' Let us be beheaded with him.' For this reason a tumult arose among them, and a great crowd followed him. So Cyprian was led out into the plain of Sextus, and there he took off his cloak and knelt down and bowed himself in prayer to God. And when he had taken off his dalmatic* and given it to his deacons, he stood up in his linen undergarment and waited for the executioner. When he had come, Cyprian ordered his friends to give him twenty-five pieces of gold. Sheets and napkins were laid down before Cyprian by the brethren, and then he bandaged his eyes with his own hand. When he could not himself fasten the ends of the handkerchief Julian the priest and Julian the subdeacon fastened them for him. So suffered blessed Cyprian ; and his body was laid in a place near by to satisfy the curiosity of the pagans. It was carried away thence by night with candles and torches, with prayers and with great triumph, to the grave-yard of Macrobius Candidianus the procurator, which is on the road to Mappala near the reservoirs. A few days later Galerius Maximus the proconsul died."

* A pattern of tunic originating in Dalmatia. At this time it had not yet become a distinctively ecclesiastical garment.

The letters of St Cyprian, a brief notice in the *De Viris Illustribus* of St Jerome, the " Passion " of the Saint, and a biographical sketch ascribed to his deacon Pontius, form the main sources of our information. The " Passion " and the Pontius Life have been much discussed. Harnack in the thirty-ninth volume of *Texte und Untersuchungen* has devoted a paper to *Das Leben Cyprians von Pontius,* and describes it as the earliest Christian biography in existence. Reizenstein, on the other hand, in the Heidelberg *Sitzungsberichte,* Phil.-Hist. Klasse, 1913, takes a less favourable view. For him it is unimportant as a historical source. See upon the whole matter Père Delehaye, *Les Passions des Martyrs et les Genres littéraires* (1921), pp. 82–104. If Delehaye is right, we cannot even describe the so-called " Proconsular Acts " of St Cyprian as " an unique record of the trials and death of a martyr in its authenticity and purity." Trustworthy as the document may be, it is not an exact copy of the official record. The same writer, in the *Analecta Bollandiana,* vol. xxxix (1921), pp. 314–322, has also drawn attention to the curious confusion which has arisen between the story of St Cyprian of Carthage and the fictitious legend of Cyprian of Antioch. The literature which has grown up around the writings of St Cyprian is extensive and highly controversial. In connexion with the well-known work, *St Cyprian,* of Archbishop Benson, consult Abbot J. Chapman's articles on the *De Unitate Ecclesiæ* in the *Revue Bénédictine* for 1902 and 1903. A fuller bibliography is provided in Bardenhewer, in the *Dictionnaire de Théologie,* and in the *Lexikon für Theologie und Kirche,* vol. iii, pp. 99–102. An excellent English translation of the " Passion " will be found in A. J. Mason, *Historic Martyrs,* pp. 151–172.

SS. ABUNDIUS, ABUNDANTIUS, AND THEIR CAMPANIONS, MARTYRS

c. A.D. 303

In the Lateran museum is part of an epitaph of the fourth century, found at Rignano, which the archæologist de Rossi believed to appertain to the martyr Abundius referred to in the Roman Martyrology on this day. "At Rome, on the Flaminian Way, the holy martyrs Abundius the priest and Abundantius the deacon, whom, together with the distinguished man Marcian and his son John who had been raised from the dead by Abundius, the Emperor Diocletian ordered to be slain by the sword at the tenth milestone from the City." The untrustworthy " acts " of these martyrs relate that St Abundius and his deacon were ordered to worship Hercules and refused ; they were then thrown into the Mamertine prison, though thirty other Christians charged with them were at once put to death. A month later they were brought out, tortured, and condemned. While on their way to the place of execution they met the senator Marcian, who was mourning the death of his son. St Abundius asked for the boy's body to be brought, and when this was done he prayed over it and life returned. Marcian and John thereupon both confessed Christ and were baptised on the spot, and were beheaded on the same day and in the same place as Abundius and Abundantius. They were buried in the cemetery of the matron Theodora, near Rignano on the Via Flaminia, and it has been suggested that Abundus and Abundantius were the priest and deacon of the Christians of that place, who brought the bodies back to their own town to be buried. Their relics with those of St Theodora (whom the Roman Martyrology names on September 17) were afterwards translated to Rome, and SS Abundius and Abundantius eventually found a resting-place in the church of the Holy Name of Jesus in 1583. It was at their shrine here that St Aloysius Gonzaga assisted at Mass before entering the Society of Jesus two years later.

The text of the legendary " Acts " has been printed by F. Cardulus (Rome, 1584). A summary, with a discussion of the relics, will be found in the *Acta Sanctorum,* September, vol. v. Of greater interest is an inscription now preserved in the Christian Museum at the Lateran. Its authenticity is accepted by de Rossi, but rejected by Mgr Wilpert. See Delehaye, *Origines du Culte des Martyrs*, p. 366.

ST EUPHEMIA, VIRG. AND MART.

c. A.D. 307

The city of Chalcedon was the scene of her glorious martyrdom ; she suffered in the persecution continued by the successors of Diocletian, about the year 307. Having embraced the holy state of virginity, Euphemia by the black or dark-coloured garments which she wore declared to all her purpose of taking no share in the pleasures and amusements which fill the hearts, set an edge on the passions, and take up the most precious part of the time of those devoted to them. When she refused to attend a pagan festival in honour of the god Ares, she was apprehended by the persecutors and cruelly tortured by the command of an inhuman judge named Priscus. The torments she underwent were represented in the most moving manner in a series of frescoes in the great church at Chalcedon, described by St Asterius in his panegyric of the saint. Whilst one soldier pulled her head back, another with a mallet beat out her teeth and bruised her mouth, so that her beautiful face, her hair, and her clothes were covered with blood. After having suffered many other torments, she was killed by a bear, while the other beasts fawned harmlessly around her feet. The *acta* of St Euphemia are worthless, consisting principally of a catalogue of the tortures which she miraculously overcame; the Roman Martyrology summarises them, " imprisonments, stripes, the wheel, fire, heavy stones, beasts, scourging, sharp nails and burning pans." But there undoubtedly was a martyr at Chalcedon of this name, whose *cultus* was formerly exceedingly popular throughout the Church.

Evagrius, the historian, testifies that emperors, patriarchs, and all ranks of people resorted to Chalcedon to be made partakers of the blessings which God abundantly conferred on men through her patronage, and that manifest miracles were there wrought. A great church was erected there in her honour and in it was held in the year 451 the fourth general council, which condemned the errors of the Monophysites. A legend says that at this council the Catholic Fathers agreed with their opponents that each side should write down its views in a book, lay them down, and ask Almighty God to show by a sign which expressed the truth. This was done and the two books were sealed up in the shrine of St Euphemia. After three days of prayer the shrine was opened : the Monophysite book lay at the feet of the martyr but the Catholic book was held in her right hand. It can be hardly necessary to say that this great council reached its conclusions by no such methods.

There were three other churches of St Euphemia in Constantinople, one of them built by Constantine himself; this was pulled down by Constantine V, the iconoclast, who also threw the saint's coffin into the sea. It was recovered by the Empress Irene, and her relics are now claimed by the Orthodox patriarchal church in Constantinople; but they are also said to have been brought to Rome in the seventh century. This martyr is often referred to in the East as Euphemia the Far-renowned, and she is among the saints named in the canon of the Milanese Mass.

On the third of this month the Roman Martyrology mentions another St Euphemia, virgin and martyr, who suffered with Dorothea, Thecla, and Erasma at Aquileia under Nero and was buried by St Hermagoras ; and on this day is commemorated another virgin-martyr of the same name who was put to death with her sister Innocentia at Vicenza under Diocletian.

Famous as was St Euphemia, it is to be noted that the account given by Butler is based upon the Acts which are quite correctly described above as " worthless." Beyond the fact of her martyrdom we know nothing whatever about her except that her *cultus* from an early date was widespread. Pope Sergius (687–701) restored in Rome the church dedicated to her, which even in his time had fallen into ruin. See the *Acta Sanctorum*, September, vol. v, and especially Delehaye's commentary upon the *Hieronymianum* in November, vol. ii, part 2, of the same collection, p. 511

ST NINIAN, Bp. and Conf.

A.D. 432 (?)

The Church in Scotland to-day keeps the feast of St Ninian (Ninias, Ninnidh, Ringan, etc.), "the first authentic personage that meets us in the succession of Scottish missionaries," of whom the most reliable source of information is a short passage in St Bede's *Ecclesiastical History :* " The southern Picts who dwell on this side of those mountains had, it is reported, long before forsaken the errors of paganism and embraced the truth by the preaching of Ninias, a most reverend bishop and holy man of the British nation, who had been regularly instructed at Rome in the faith and mysteries of the truth. His episcopal see, named after St Martin the Bishop and famous for a church dedicated in his honour (wherein Ninias himself and many other saints rest in the body), is now in the possession of the English nation. The place belongs to the province of the Bernicians and is commonly called the White House, because he there built a church of stone, which was not usual amongst the Britons." St Bede states definitely that St Ninian was a Briton, and there is no good reason for believing that he was ever in Ireland, but Irish writers have identified him with Moinenn of Cluain Conaire in county Kildare, who is spoken of as abbot of Rosnat where St Tighernach studied. More details of the life of St Ninian are given by St Ælred in the twelfth century, who claims to have had the help of " a book of his life and miracles, barbarously written," but Ælred's *vita* contains a lot that is clearly untrustworthy. He states that St Ninian was the son of a converted chieftain of the Cumbrian Britons, and that, while others take so much pains in their education to advance themselves in the world, this noble youth, sensible of the treasure of holy faith which he had received, thought nothing too difficult and no labour too great that he might improve his soul in the knowledge and practice of religion. With this view he renounced the world, cut off covetousness, sensuality, and ambi-tion by renouncing whatever might arouse those passions and, forsaking his friends and country, undertook the long journey to Rome. In that city he spent many years, applying himself with his whole heart to the exercise of Christian virtue and to the study of the sacred sciences. His soul was daily more and more inflamed with a mighty love and zeal for God, whose honour he studied in all things to promote. This motive and a compassion for his native country, which had received the grace of faith more slowly and more imperfectly than the southern provinces of Britain, prevailed on him at length to return home, to impart to his countrymen a share of that blessing in which their happiness consisted and which was the sole end of their being. He set out after being consecrated bishop by Pope St Siricius.

St Ninian travelled by way of Tours, where he made the acquaintance of St Martin, who greatly befriended him. Ninian had already determined to build a church of stone, in the likeness of those he had seen at Rome, and while at Tours borrowed some masons from St Martin for the purpose. When he got back he established his see and built his church at the place now called Whithorn or Whitern, in Wigtownshire, " which place, situated on the shore, while it runs far into the sea on the east, west, and south, is closed in thereby. From the north only can it be approached by land. There he built the first stone church in Britain and, hearing of the death of St Martin while building it, he dedicated it in his honour." That fixes the date of the church as 397. This famous church may have been the first built of stone in Strathclyde, but it was certainly not the first in Britain. It became known as the White House (Whithern); it was the centre of the most ancient ecclesiastical foundation in Scotland, and *Candida Casa* is still the official name of the Catholic diocese of Galloway. The monastery attached was distinguished as the Great Monastery, and from it St Ninian and his monks set out not only to preach to the Britons of the neighbourhood but also to the Picts of the former Roman province of Valentia; they may even have penetrated to the northern Picts beyond the Grampians. The mission received an impetus from Ninian's cure of the blindness and subsequent conversion of a local chieftain. The Britons and Picts received baptism in large numbers and Ninian consecrated bishops to minister to them. St Ælred recounts many miracles by which the saint was reported to confirm his message. Through the foundation of Whitern, St Ninian's effect on Celtic Christianity was considerable for the next two hundred years, but his success among the Picts seems to have been rather short-lived. After his death there was a resurgence of paganism, and Teutonic invaders helped to undo his work; St Patrick in his letter to Coroticus refers to the Picts as apostates. But he had paved the way for St Columba and St Kentigern, and it has been suggested that he had indirect influence on Wales, by the conversion of the family of Cunedda, which probably came from the district of Kyle, in Ayrshire.

The notes in C. Plummer's edition of Bede's *Ecclesiastical History* (vol. ii, pp. 128–130) tell us all that is to be known about St Ninian. See, however, Forbes, *Lives of St Ninian and St Kentigern* (1874); Stanton's *Menology*, pp. 448 and 669; and Gougaud, *Christianity in Celtic Lands* (1932), pp. 26–27 and *passim*.

ST LUDMILA, Mart.

A.D. 921

Ludmila was born about the year 860, the daughter of a Slav prince in the country between the confluence of the Elbe and the Moldau. She married Borivoj, Duke of Bohemia, bringing him as her marriage portion the duchy of Psov, and when her husband was baptised by St Methodius, the apostle of the Slavs, she followed him into the Church. They built the first Christian church in Bohemia, at Levy Hradec to the north of Prague where Borivoj had a castle, and dedicated it in honour of St Clement. The princely neophytes had a very difficult time, for most of the leading families were utterly opposed to the new religion. In accordance with the all-too-common practice of those days Borivoj tried to force Christianity on his people, which led to a rising, and he and Ludmila had to fly to the protection of Swatopluk, the Christian prince of Moravia, until the leader of the rebels was in his turn assassinated. Borivoj died when he was only thirty-five and was succeeded within a few years by his sons Sphytihnev and Ratislav. The latter had married a Slav princess, Drahomira, who was only nominally Christian, and when a son, Wenceslas, was born to them, Ludmila, who lived in retirement at Prague, was entrusted with his upbringing. She was now about fifty years of age, a woman of great virtue and considerable learning, and it was to her unfailing care and interest that Wenceslas in a large measure owed his own sanctity. Ludmila joined with herself in this task a priest, her chaplain Paul, who had been a personal disciple of St Methodius and had baptised Wenceslas ; under his tuition the boy, by the time he was ready to go to the college at Budec, " understood Latin books as if he were a bishop and read Slavonic with ease," while the example of both the priest and his good grandmother had grounded him equally well in virtue. The premature death of Ratislav and the consequent regency of Drahomira removed Wenceslas from Ludmila's immediate charge. The regent was in the hands of the anti-Christian party in Bohemia, and was, moreover, not unnaturally, jealous of the responsibility which had been confided to Ludmila and of the influence she exercised over her grandson. St Ludmila's gentleness and charity had made her greatly beloved among the people, and probably she hoped that, if young Wenceslas could be persuaded to seize the government before his time, they would rally to him, and Christianity in Bohemia, now threatened, be saved. The opposing party saw this possibility clearly, and every effort was made to keep Wenceslas and Ludmila apart. The more desperate characters decided to take no risks ; on September 16, 921, two of them came to the castle of Tetin, near Podjbrad, and there strangled the holy Ludmila. That this crime was instigated by Drahomira is often asserted, but it is not certain, nor is she surely known to have been privy to it. Her body was buried in the church of St Michael at Tetin, till three years later St Wenceslas removed it to St George's at Prague with great honour ; here it still lies and the saint is greatly venerated throughout Czechoslovakia.

What purports to be the " Passio " of St Ludmila exists in more than one form and has been printed in the *Acta Sanctorum*, September, vol. v, and in Pertz, *Monumenta Germaniæ, Script.*, vol. xv, pp. 573–574. An account in much greater detail (which is attributed to one Christianus de Scala, alleged to have been a great grand-nephew of the saint, but which many scholars believe to date only from the thirteenth century) has been edited by the Bollandists in the same 5th volume for September. For a sober and reasoned defence of the authenticity of these materials see J. Pekar, *Die Wenzels—und Ludmila Legenden und die Echtheit Christians* (Prag, 1906). The question has given rise to much controversy, but see the *Analecta Bollandiana*, vol. xxv (1906), pp. 512–513, and vol. xlviii (1930), pp. 218–221. A little book on St Wenceslas (*Svaty Václav*), by Fr. Dvornik, which has been published in several languages (1929), also touches on the Ludmila legend.

ST EDITH OF WILTON, Virg.

A.D. 984

The parentage of Edith of Wilton has been referred to in the account of St Wilfrida on September 9. Soon after she was born, in the year 962, at, according to local tradition, Kemsing in Kent, she was taken by her mother to Wilton Abbey which she never left, so that the words of the Roman Martyrology are literally true : " She was dedicated to God from her earliest years in a monastery and rather knew not this world than forsook it." She never knew the allurements of sin or the enticements of the world, but she feared these unknown things from a distance, for her heart was always open to the love of God and sensitive to what would impair it. As the daughter of a king she had at times to dress in accordance, and this too she knew how to do with detachment and humility, for the bishop of Winchester, St Ethelwold, having on one occasion expressed surprise and regret at her clothes, she answered him : " Believe me, father, a mind may be as modest and God-fearing beneath these fine garments as under the roughest habit. God looks at the heart, not the appearance." The bishop "did not reply, but blushed for pleasure," says the chronicler. Her mother, St Wilfrida, took great care to improve her religious sensibility by constantly showing to her lessons of Christian perfection and setting before her eyes the most illustrious examples of sanctity, and Edith repaid her care with an admirable docility and proficiency. She united the active life of Martha with the contemplation of Mary and, though it was her greatest delight to hear the voice of her heavenly Spouse speak to her heart in silence and retirement, she frequently deprived herself that she might attend and serve Him in His distressed members. She fed the poor, took care of the sick, and dressed their bodies, " preferring the lepers to the king's children." She had a great devotion to the memory of the Passion which she expressed by the constant use of the sign of the cross, as St Dunstan noticed, prophesying that the thumb wherewith she signed her forehead would remain uncorrupt.

When she was less than fifteen years old, her royal father, Edgar, visited Wilton on the occasion of her profession. He had a carpet laid down before the altar on which were put gold and silver ornaments and jewels, while St Wilfrida stood by with a nun's veil, a Psalter, a chalice and paten. " All prayed that God, who knows all things, would show to one still at so wayward an age what life she should choose." Perhaps Edgar was trying to avoid the foregone conclusion. Certainly he shortly after offered Edith the abbacy of three different houses (Winchester, Barking, and another) which she obviously was not old enough to govern other than nominally. But she humbly declined all superiority and chose to remain in her own community, subject to her mother, who was now abbess there. But the nuns insisted on giving her the honorary title of abbess, though she remained as before " serving her sisters in the most menial offices like a very Martha." Soon after King Edgar died and was succeeded by his son, Edward the Martyr. Upon the death of the latter, the nobility who adhered to the martyred king wanted Edith, his half-sister, to quit her monastery and ascend the throne : but she preferred a state of humility and obedience to the prospect of a crown. When after lying at Wareham for three years St Edward's body was taken to the abbey church of Shaftesbury, St Edith and St Wilfrida left their convent to assist at the translation. Edith built the church of St Denis at Wilton, to the dedication of which she invited the Archbishop of Canterbury, St Dunstan. This prelate was observed to weep exceedingly during Mass, the reason of which he afterwards said was because he learned that Edith would shortly be taken out of this world, whilst we, said he, shall still continue sitting here below in darkness and in the shades of death. According to this prediction, forty-three days after this solemnity, she happily reposed in our Lord, on September 16, 984, being but twenty-two years old. St Dunstan, who had assisted her in her last illness, performed the funeral rites when she was buried in the church of St Denis. The same prelate three years later translated the relics to a more worthy shrine, on which occasion several miracles were reported. A pleasing story is told of St Edith appearing after her death at the baptism of a child for whom she had promised to stand godmother, holding the baby in her arms at the font. She also appeared, but rather indignantly, to King Canute, who had had the temerity to doubt some of the marvels attributed to her.

Our main authorities are William of Malmesbury, Simeon of Durham and Capgrave. See Stanton's *Menology*, pp. 449–450 ; and *Dictionary of National Biog.*, vol. xvi, p. 387.

BD. VICTOR III, POPE AND CONF.

A.D. 1087

The young man who was to become pope as Victor III was known in secular life as Dauferius, and he belonged to the Lombard family of the dukes of Benevento. As he was an only son his father was particularly anxious for him to marry, but Dauferius, whose "nobility of soul was greater even than that of his birth," was confident that he was called to serve God as a monk. His father was killed in battle in 1047 and Dauferius, who was about twenty years old, took the opportunity to slip away from his family and take up his residence with a hermit. His relatives found him, tore his religious habit off his back, and forced him to return to his home at Benevento. A sharp watch was kept on him, but after twelve months he managed to escape and entered the monastery of La Cava, at the same time putting himself under the protection of his kinsman, the Duke of Salerno. His family then accepted the fact of his vocation, only stipulating that he should leave La Cava and come to the abbey of St Sophia at Benevento. To this he agreed, and his new abbot gave him the name of Desiderius, because he was well beloved. But for some years the young monk seemed unable to find stability : he was at a monastery on an island in the Adriatic, he studied medicine at Salerno, he was a hermit in the Abruzzi. He had attracted the favourable notice of Pope St Leo IX, and about 1054 he was at the court of Victor II, with his friend Alfanus who was afterwards

archbishop of Salerno. Here he met monks from Monte Cassino,
went on a pilgrimage to that cradle of Benedictine monasticism, and
joined the community. In the year 1057 Pope Stephen X summoned Desiderius to Rome, intending to send him as his legate to
Constantinople. Stephen had been abbot of Monte Cassino and
had retained the office on his elevation to the papacy, but now,
believing himself to be dying, he ordered the election of a successor.
The choice fell on Desiderius, and he had got to Bari on his way to
the East when he learned of the Pope's death and was told to return.
There was a disputed succession to Stephen X, in which Desiderius
supported Pope Nicholas II, who bestowed on him the abbatial
benediction and made him a cardinal before he was permitted to go
and take up his duties at his monastery.

Desiderius was the greatest of the abbots of Monte Cassino
after St Benedict, and under his rule the archcœnobium reached the
height of its glory. He rebuilt first the church and then the whole
range of buildings on a larger and more convenient scale than those
of St Petronax and Abbot Aligernus, who had restored them after
the Lombard and Saracenic spoliations. The basilica in particular
Desiderius made of the greatest beauty ; " by influence and money " he
procured fine materials from Rome and sent for workmen from Lombardy, from Amalfi, from Constantinople itself. Under the combined
Lombard and Byzantine influences new artistic forms emerged which
had far-reaching effect on building, mosaics, painting, and illuminating, the activity of the monks of Monte Cassino themselves doing
much to spread it. The church with its gilded beams, frescoed walls,
marble pavements, and great golden altar from Byzantium was consecrated by Pope Alexander II in 1071 in the presence of a concourse
than which " it would have been easier to number the stars of heaven."
All this magnificence was no empty show or to house " vile bigots,
hypocrites externally devoted." The number of monks at Monte
Cassino rose to two hundred, and Desiderius insisted on the most
strict observance of the rule. Among those whom he attracted
thither was Constantine Africanus, the best known physician of the
early Salerno school and a personal friend of Desiderius ; he spent
the last twenty years of his life at Monte Cassino and died in the
same year as his friend and master. On the side of manual work the
buildings gave continual employment, and the Cassinese *scriptorium*
was famous both for its illuminating and for the books copied therein :
works of Virgil, Cicero, Seneca, Ovid, and Terence as well as the
Bible and the Fathers and the laws of Justinian. As well as abbot
and cardinal, Desiderius was papal vicar for Campania, Apulia,
Calabria, and Capua, and so well was he regarded by the Holy See

that he was authorised himself to appoint prelates for vacant bishoprics and abbeys.

When he was at Bari in 1058 Desiderius had commended himself to the good graces of Robert Guiscard, the Norman duke of Apulia and Calabria, and in consequence was much used by Pope Gregory VII as his intermediary with the Normans in Italy. He was a very different type of man from Gregory, gentle by nature and afterwards much weakened by ill-health, but he had shown himself a determined upholder of the Papacy against the Emperor, and was one of the people named by St Gregory on his death-bed as a suitable successor. Twice during the vacancy Desiderius fled from Rome to Monte Cassino in order to avoid election, but in May 1086 he was elected by acclamation and the papal red cope forced upon his shoulders in the church of Santa Lucia. He was given the name of Victor. Four days later a rising under the Prefect of Rome gave him the excuse again to flee to his monastery, where he laid aside the papal insignia and could not be induced finally to take up the office until Easter of the following year. Rome was by then occupied by the imperial anti-pope, Guibert of Ravenna (" Clement III "). Norman troops drove him out of St Peter's long enough for Victor to be consecrated there, after which he went back again to Monte Cassino. He was again in Rome, for the last time, a few weeks later when the Countess Matilda of Tuscany made a strong effort to dislodge Guibert. The peace-loving Pope, so ill that he rarely said Mass, could not bear to see the apostolic City turned into a battlefield, and left it finally towards the end of the summer. Hugh, Archbishop of Lyons, who, having also been recommended by St Gregory VII, had had some ambition for the papal throne, started a campaign of rebellion and slander against Blessed Victor. A synod over which the Pope presided at Benevento censured Hugh, confirmed the excommunication of Guibert, and strongly repeated the condemnation of lay investiture ; at the same time an Italian fleet that Blessed Victor had induced to go on a punitive expedition to Tunis had forced the Mohammedan emir to release all his Christian slaves and pay a tribute to the Holy See. Immediately after the council and this victory, the last gestures of the short-lived successor of Gregory VII, he was carried back dying to his monastery. Stretched on a couch in the chapter-house he gave final directions to be observed in the house, and with the consent of the community named the prior, Cardinal Oderisius, to succeed him ; then he recommended Otho, Cardinal-Bishop of Ostia, to fill the apostolic see ; and two days later died, September 16, 1087. He had been pope for four months. The *cultus* of Blessed Victor III began some sixty years later ; it was approved by

Benedict XIII in 1727, and confirmed by Leo XIII, who added his name to the Roman Martyrology with a reference to the victory at Tunis.

A detailed account of Bd. Victor occupies considerable space in the *Chronica Monasterii Casinensis*, Bk. iii. The text has been published in Pertz, *Monumenta Germaniæ, Scriptores*, vol. vii, pp. 698–754 ; and also in the *Acta Sanctorum*, September, vol. v. See further Mgr. H. Mann, *Lives of the Popes*, vol. vii, pp. 218–244.

BD. LOUIS ALLEMAND, Abp. of Arles and Cardinal, Conf.

A.D. 1450

The history of this holy prelate is a striking example of how the Church, looking so far as possible at the souls rather than the exterior actions of men, raises to the honours of her altars those whom she judges to have been interiorly holy, whatever and however serious the errors of action or of judgement apparent in their lives : always provided that she finds those errors to have been due to *bona-fide* mistake, inculpable ignorance, or otherwise made in good faith. This particular example, Louis Allemand, was born near the end of the fourteenth century at the castle of Arbent in the diocese of Belley, the son of the Lord of Arbent and Coiselet and his wife, Mary of Châtillon. He read law at the University of Avignon and, having taken his degrees, he received through the influence of his uncle Francis de Conzié, a chamberlain at the papal court, a number of ecclesiastical benefices. Young Louis, while probably not yet a priest, held the precentorship of Narbonne, a commendatory abbacy, five canonries, and other offices. In 1409 he accompanied his uncle to the Synod of Pisa, an assembly which vainly tried to cure the scandalous and terrible rivalry between claimants to the papal throne (the " Great Schism of the West ") by the illegitimate means of " deposing " both Gregory XII and Benedict " XIII " and electing a third " pope." The Cardinal de Thury was made papal legate for France and Provence, and Louis Allemand was his delegate. In 1414 he was present at the gathering of the assembly, summoned by the Emperor Sigismund and John " XXIII," which was to become the Œcumenical Council of Constance, and two years later was vice-chamberlain in charge of the conclave that elected Pope Martin V and put an end to the " great schism."

Louis was attached to the court of the new pope, who named him bishop of Maguelonne and entrusted him with very responsible missions. While Martin was at Florence in 1419–20 he had to re-establish papal authority in the Patrimony of St Peter and bring about some sort of pacification in a district reduced to the depths of misery and penury by famine, pestilence, and strife. The Pope was thus enabled to take possession of his city on September 30, 1420. When, in accordance with the decisions of the Council of Constance, a council was convened at Pavia and had to be transferred to Siena because of an epidemic, Louis was given the task of negotiating with the Sienese for a peaceful reception of the Pope and prelates in that city. In the same year, 1423, he was promoted to the archbishopric of Arles and appointed governor of Romagna, Bologna, and Ravenna. His predecessor in this office, instead of remaining neutral between the ambitions of Florence and Milan, had brought in a Florentine garrison. Louis Allemand restored the balance by secretly favouring Milan, recovered Imola and Forlì for the States of the Church, and successfully ruled Bologna for four years. His services were recognised by making him cardinal-priest of St Cæcilia-in-Trastevere. But soon after a rising of the Canetoli faction drove him from Bologna, he was unable to retake the city, and retired to Rome in political disgrace. An envoy of the Order of Teutonic Knights writes at this time of five cardinals who were well disposed towards his order, but " they dare not speak before the Pope, save what he likes to hear, for he has so crushed the cardinals that they say nothing before him except as he wishes, and they turn red and white when they speak in his hearing." Blessed Louis Allemand was one of these five cardinals. When Martin V died in 1431 he was succeeded by Eugenius IV, who had been Louis's predecessor at Bologna and with whom he was at variance both personally and in policy. Louis had come more and more to identify himself with the party, now waxing very strong, that maintained the supremacy of a General Council over the Pope and practically reduced him to the position of a servant of the council. During the last year of his pontificate Martin V had convened a general council at Basle, and one of the first acts of Eugenius was to issue a bull dissolving it. The few fathers assembled refused to separate and announced their intention of carrying on the council.

Blessed Louis was then in Rome, and, on account of his known sympathies, was forbidden to leave. But he made an adventurous escape, boarded a Genoese ship in the Tiber, and went to his episcopal city of Arles. Doubtless his object was to avoid having to declare himself openly against the Holy See, in the hope that the troubles would blow over. But in 1433 he was at Basle, daily becoming more clearly the leader of the extreme majority who opposed Cardinal Cæsarini, the Pope's representative—for Eugenius had withdrawn his decree of dissolution. The anti-papal activities of the council became so strong that in 1437 the Pope himself was summoned to appear before it to answer charges. He refused, and ordered the council to reassemble at Ferrara ; Cardinal Cæsarini and his other adherents obeyed, leaving an illegal assembly at Basle under the skilful direction of Cardinal Allemand. In 1439 it went to the extreme length of declaring Eugenius deposed as a heretic in consequence of his opposition to the council, and electing Amadeus of Savoy in his stead as Felix " V," the last of the anti-popes. This was the work principally of Cardinal Allemand and only eleven bishops and Louis himself consecrated Amadeus bishop and crowned him. In the following year Eugenius IV pronouced Louis Allemand to be excommunicated and deprived of his cardinalate.

It cannot be questioned that many of the " conciliar party " at the Council of Basle were sincerely animated by zeal for the improvement of the condition of the Church, for the conversion of those in error, and for the restoration of peace and unity. Nor must it be supposed that Blessed Louis was the only great and good man to be grossly mistaken as to the right methods to be employed to attain these ends. For a long time he had the support of the holy and learned Cardinal Nicholas of Cusa, and also of Æneas Sylvius Piccolomini, who, though at that time a layman and certainly not a holy one, afterwards himself became pope, as Pius II. The council, after it had become a rebellious assembly, discussed the doctrine of the Immaculate Conception of our Lady, and with the vigorous encouragement of Blessed Louis declared it to be consonant with Catholic faith and worship, right reason, and holy Scripture. Basle for a time was visited by the plague, and Cardinal Allemand was foremost in organising relief for the victims, encouraging the other bishops to join with him in ministering to the sick and dying. During all this time he disregarded the suspension that had been pronounced against him by Pope Eugenius, and was zealous in the service of the anti-pope Felix. But in 1447 Eugenius died, and Felix declared his willingness to resign in favour of the duly elected Nicholas V. Thereupon Nicholas with a magnificent gesture of peace revoked all suspensions, excommunications, and other penalties incurred by the anti-pope, the recalcitrant council, and their adherents, and Blessed Louis was restored to his cardinalitial dignity. He was profoundly repentant for the part he had taken in involving the Church in schism, and retired to his see of Arles where he spent the remaining year of his life in those exercises of prayer and penance that had always characterised his private life. He was buried in the church of St Trophimus, where his tomb was the scene of many miracles, and the *cultus* that then began was approved by Pope Clement VII in 1527. The feast of Blessed Louis Allemand is observed in several dioceses of southern France.

Some inconsiderable biographical materials will be found, with prolegomena, in the *Acta Sanctorum*, September, vol. v. But see more particularly G. Pérouse, *Le Cardinal Louis Aleman et la fin du grand Schisme* (Paris, 1904); N. Valois, *Le Pape et le Concile* (Paris, 1909); and the various writings of Prof. H. Finke on the period of the schism.

BD. FRANCIS OF CAMPOROSSO, Conf.

A.D. 1866

Camporosso is a small town on the coast of Liguria, and there was living there at the beginning of the last century a family called Croese, who were farmers and olive-cultivators in a small way. To the master and mistress was born in 1804 a son, whom they had baptised John, because he was born on the feast of the Evangelist of that name. John was one of four children and had a simple and religious upbringing. His mother took him with her to daily Mass as soon as he was old enough and he learned Christian doctrine and the three R's at the village school conducted by the parish priest. He made his first communion at twelve years of age, was soon afterwards confirmed, and as a matter of course began to work on his father's farm. When he was about eighteen, however, John met a lay-brother of the Friars Minor Conventual, who gave him the idea of the same vocation. John presented himself at the friary of the Conventuals at Sestri Ponente and was accepted as a tertiary and given the name of Antony. He spent two years in the service of that house, and then, desiring a life of greater austerity, he offered himself to the Friars Minor Capuchin. He was sent to their novitiate at Genoa and in 1825 was clothed as a lay-brother, with the names Francis Mary. In the following year he was professed and set to work in the infirmary, from whence he was taken to be questor, whose office it is to beg food from door to door for the community. This was a new experience for Brother Francis, and he disliked it so much that he thought of asking to be relieved of it. But instead, when the guardian asked him if he would undertake to beg in the city of Genoa itself, he accepted with alacrity. The Genoese were not invariably well disposed towards the religious, and Brother Francis sometimes received stones instead of bread, but he persevered for ten years and became the best-known and most welcome questor in the place. He was a particularly familiar figure in the dockyard, where people would come to ask of him news of their friends and relatives overseas, for he was reputed to be able to give correct information about people in distant lands and whom he had never seen.   Miracles of healing too were attributed to him and, though there were some still who insulted and jeered at him, to the majority he was known as " Padre santo."   It was in vain that he protested that he was a lay-brother and not a priest—" good father " he remained, and he was indeed a father to the poor and afflicted who flocked to him.

During two years Brother Francis suffered from varicose veins, of which he told nobody till his limp betrayed him, and he was found to be in a most shocking state.   By the time he was sixty he was nearly worn out, and his leg had to be operated on, without much effect.   In August 1866 Genoa was devastated by cholera. The Capuchins and other religious of the city were out among the sufferers at once, and Blessed Francis was so moved by all he saw around him that he solemnly offered his own life to God that the epidemic might cease ; and he accurately predicted the circumstances of his approaching death.   On September 15 he was himself smitten by the disease, and two days later, at the time of the evening *Angelus*, he was called to God.   From that time the cholera began to abate.   The tomb of Blessed Francis became famous for miracles, and in 1911 his relics were enshrined in the Capuchin church at Genoa ; eighteen years later he was solemnly beatified by Pope Pius XI.

Apart from the materials available in the process, the decree of Beatification (printed in the *Acta Apostolicæ Sedis*, vol. xxi, 1929, pp. 485–488) includes a biographical sketch of his life. Several other little biographies were issued or republished at the same time. The most considerable is one in Italian by Father Luigi da Porto Maurizio, which originally appeared in 1915. Another, also of some length, is in French, and is written by Père Constant de Pélissanne (1929). Two other Italian Lives, compiled respectively by Father Amadeo de Varazze and M. Pongiglione, were issued in the same year.

SEPTEMBER 17

THE IMPRESSION OF THE STIGMATA UPON
ST FRANCIS

A.D. 1224

IN the month of August of the year 1224 St Francis of Assisi withdrew himself from the world for a while to commune with God on the summit of La Verna, a lonely mountain in the Appenines which had been given for the use of the Friars Minor by Orlando dei Cattani, Lord of Chiusi. He was accompanied by Brother Leo and five or six others, but he chose a hut apart, under a beech tree, and gave instructions that no one was to come near him except Leo when he brought him food or other ministrations. About the feast of the Exaltation of the Holy Cross, Francis, being in prayer on the side of the mountain, raised himself towards God with seraphic ardour and was transported by a tender and affective compassion of charity into Him who out of love was crucified for us. In this state he saw as it were a seraph, with six shining wings blazing with fire, bearing down from the highest part of the heavens towards him with a most rapid flight, and placing himself in the air near the saint. There appeared between his wings the figure of a man crucified, with his hands and feet stretched out, and fastened to the cross. The wings of the seraph were so placed that two he stretched above his head, two others he extended to fly, and with the other two he covered his whole body. At this sight Francis was extremely surprised : a sudden joy, mingled with sorrow, filled his heart. The close presence of his Lord under the figure of a seraph, who fixed on him His eyes in the most gracious and loving manner, gave him great joy, but the sorrowful sight of His crucifixion pierced his soul with a sword of compassion. At the same time he understood by an interior light that, though the state of crucifixion in no way agreed with that of the immortality of the seraph, this wonderful vision was manifested to him that he might understand he was to be transformed into a resemblance with Jesus Christ crucified, not by the martyrdom of the flesh, but in his heart and by the fire of love. Suddenly in a moment of great pain the seraph smote him as it were in body and soul, and Francis had great fear, till the seraph spoke and made plain many things which had hitherto been hidden from him. Then, after a moment which seemed an age, the vision vanished. But the saint's soul remained interiorly burning with a seraphic ardour, and his body appeared exteriorly to have received the image of the crucifix, as if his flesh, like soft wax, had received the marks of a seal impressed upon it. For the scars of nails began to appear in his feet and hands, resembling those he had seen in the vision of the man crucified. His hands and feet seemed bored through in the middle with four wounds, and these holes appeared to be pierced with nails or hard flesh ; the heads were round and black, and were seen in the palms of his hands and in his feet in the upper part of the instep. The points were long, and appeared beyond the skin on the other side, and were turned back as if they had been clinched with a hammer. There was also in his right side a red wound, as if made by the piercing of a lance, and this often shed blood, which stained the clothes of the saint. This wonderful miracle was performed whilst Francis's understanding was filled with the most vivid ideas of Christ crucified, and his love employed in the utmost strength of its will in directing its affections on that object and assimilating them to his Beloved in that suffering state ; so that in the imaginative faculty of his soul he seemed to form a second crucifix, with which impression it acted upon and strongly affected the body. To produce the exterior marks of the wounds in the flesh, which the interior love of his heart was not able to do, the fiery seraph, or rather Christ Himself in that vision, by darting bright piercing rays from His wounds represented in the vision, really formed exteriorly in St Francis those signs which love had interiorly imprinted in his soul.

Whether or no St Francis was the first person to be thus marked with the *stigmata* (Gk., marks) of our crucified Lord his is unquestionably the most famous example, and the best authenticated until we come to recent and contemporary times ; moreover, it is the only occurrence of the sort to be celebrated by a liturgical feast throughout the Western Church. The happening and general nature of the phenomenon are beyond doubt. It is referred to by Brother Leo in the note which he wrote with his own hand on the " seraphic blessing " of St Francis, a document preserved by the Conventual friars at Assisi, and in announcing the death of their patriarch to the friars of France Brother Elias wrote in 1226 : " From the beginning of ages there has not been heard so great a wonder, save only in the Son of God who is Christ our God. For a long while before his death, our father and brother appeared crucified, bearing in his body the five wounds which are verily the Stigmata of the Christ ;

for his hands and feet had as it were piercings made by nails fixed in from above and below, which laid open the scars and had the black appearance of nails ; while his side appeared to have been lanced, and blood often trickled therefrom." In the earliest Life of the saint, written by order of Pope Gregory IX between two and four years after his death, the stigmata are described thus : " His hands and feet seemed pierced in the midst by nails, the heads of the nails appearing in the inner part of the hands and in the upper part of the feet and their points over against them. Now these marks were round on the inner side of the hands and elongated on the outer side, and certain small pieces of flesh were seen like the ends of nails bent and driven back, projecting from the rest of the flesh. So also the marks of nails were imprinted in his feet, and raised above the rest of the flesh. Moreover his right side, as if it had been pierced by a lance, was overlaid with a scar, and often shed forth blood. . . ." *The Book of Miracles*, probably written by the same eyewitness about twenty years later (Thomas of Celano), adds that the crowds who flocked to Assisi " saw in the hands and feet not the fissures of the nails but the nails themselves marvellously wrought by the power of God, indeed implanted in the flesh itself, in such wise that if they were pressed in on either side they straightway, as if they were one piece of sinew, projected on the other." The statement, repeated above by Alban Butler from the *Fioretti*, that the points of the nails were " bent back and clinched on such wise that under the clinching and the bend, which all stood out above the flesh, it would have been easy to put a finger of the hand, as in a ring," can be traced back to before 1274, but the most careful critics are inclined to reject its truth as a literal statement ; nothing of the like kind is reported of any other well-attested cases of stigmata. There is not, of course, any suggestion that the " nails " referred to were other than fleshy or sinewy substances, and that they were even this (rather than part of the appearance and shape of the wounds or raised scars) is hardly warranted by the evidence, and not at all by comparison with the stigmata of others.

The fact of stigmatisation has been confirmed by many modern examples and no satisfactory natural explanation is forthcoming ; the stigmata often bleed periodically, especially on Fridays, and in no recorded case do the wounds suppurate. It would appear then that God singles out certain noble souls to be united more closely with the sufferings of His Son, souls who are willing and in some degree worthy to expiate the sins of others by bearing before the world the form of Jesus crucified, " not portrayed upon tables of stone or wood by the hand of an earthly artist but drawn in their flesh by the finger of the living God." In the large number of reported stigmatisations in the past seven hundred years only some fifty or sixty are at all well attested, and some of these are explainable by fraud or other natural means, so the valid phenomenon remains a rare and remarkable indication by God of some of those who are heroically His servants. With some few exceptions the best-known *stigmatisés* were either friars, nuns, or tertiaries of one or other of the mendicant orders, and nearly all of them women.

Nearly all the many published Lives of St Francis give prominence to the stigmata. The contemporary evidence, notably that of Brother Elias, of the document called the " Blessing " of Brother Leo, and of the *Vita prima* by Thomas de Celano, is quite conclusive as to the existence of these wound marks. Paul Sabatier, Dr. J. Merkt (*Die Wundmale des Franziskus von Assisi*, Leipzig, 1910), and others have propounded a naturalistic explanation, on which see Bihl in *Archivum Franciscanum Historicum*, July, 1910, and Königer in the *Historisches Jahrbuch*, 1910, pp. 787 *seq*. In the collection *Studi Francescani* (1924) a volume was devoted to the seventh centenary of the Stigmatisation. This contains an important article (pp. 140–174) by A. Gemelli, the Franciscan Rector of the University of the Sacred Heart at Milan, on " Le Affirmazione della Scienza intorno alle Stimate di S. Francesco." *Cf.* also V. Facchinetti, *Le Stimmate di S. Francesco* (Quaracchi, 1924), Faloci Pulignani, *Miscellanea Francescana*, vol. xv, pp. 129–137, and *The Month*, July and August, 1919, pp. 39–50 and 144–156.

SS. SOCRATES and STEPHEN, Marts.

c. A.D. 304 (?)

Nothing whatsoever is known of these martyrs and they are only of interest because the Roman Martyrology, following the " Martyrology of Jerome," says that their passion took place in Britain. Dom Serenus Cressy refers to them in his *Church History of Britanny or England* as " two noble British Christians," desciples of " St Amphibalus." They are supposed to have suffered in the persecution of Diocletian, and Monmouth is put forward as the place because, it is said, there are churches dedicated in their honour in that neighbourhood, but these churches have not been identified. The *Britannia* of the martyrologists may have been a mistake for *Abretania*, a province of Mysia, where there was a martyr of the name of Socrates, or it may have been Bithynia.

Père Delehaye has discussed this entry in a paper printed in the *Proceedings of the British Academy*, vol. xvii (1932). He abandons the suggestion made by D. Serruys that " Britannia " has been written by mistake for Abretannia, and suggests that the original reading was probably Bithynia ; pp. 12–13.

ST SATYRUS, Conf.

c. A.D. 392

Satyrus was the elder brother of St Ambrose, born sometime before the year 340, probably at Trier. The sister, St Marcellina, was the eldest. When their father, who was prefect of the *prætorium* of the Gauls, died about 354 the family moved to Rome, where the two boys were well educated under the watchful eyes of their mother and sister. Satyrus undertook a public career, practised as a lawyer,* and became prefect of an unnamed province. When St Ambrose was elected bishop of Milan in 374, Satyrus resigned his post to undertake the administration of the temporal concerns of the see for his brother. He made several voyages to Africa, on the last of which he nearly lost his life through shipwreck, and in consequence took the first opportunity to receive the sacrament of baptism, from a Catholic bishop, having hitherto been only a catechumen. Before jumping overboard from the wrecked vessel he was given a particle of the Blessed Sacrament by one of his fellow-voyagers, which he wrapped in a scarf and fastened about his neck. He died suddenly at Milan, in the arms of his sister and brother, who distributed his estate among the poor in accordance with his wish that they should deal with it as they thought best. The mighty merits of St Satyrus, his integrity and his kindness, were eulogised by St Ambrose in his funeral sermon, in the course of which he asks God mercifully to accept the priestly sacrifices which he offers for his dead brother.

The passages in the writings of St Ambrose, upon which all our knowledge of St Saturus is based, are printed in the *Acta Sanctorum,* September, vol. v.

ST LAMBERT, Bp. of Maestricht, Mart.

c. A.D. 700

St Landebertus, called in later ages Lambert, was a native of Maestricht, and born of a noble and wealthy family between the years 633 and 638. His father caused him to be instructed from childhood in sacred learning, and afterwards sent him to St Theodardus to perfect his education. This holy bishop had such an

* *A propos* of this, the Rev. Sabine Baring-Gould observes in his *Lives of the Saints,* vol. x, " one of the rare instances of a lawyer who has got into the martyrology." Mr. Baring-Gould and the jocular rhyme about St Yves of Tréguier to the contrary notwithstanding, holy men-of-law are not so rare as is commonly supposed.

esteem for his pupil that he spared no trouble in instructing and training him in learning and Christian virtue, and he was a credit to his master : his biographer, who was born soon after Lambert's death, describes him as, " a prudent young man of pleasing looks, courteous and well behaved in his speech and behaviour ; well built, strong, a good fighter, clear headed, affectionate, pure and humble, and fond of reading." When St Theodardus, who was bishop of Maestricht, was murdered by robbers about 668 Lambert was chosen to succeed him, with the consent of King Childeric and the applause of his whole court, where the saint was in great repute. The tyrannical Ebroin, who had been shut up in the monastery of Luxeuil, was reinstated as mayor of the palace when King Childeric was slain by a conspiracy of noblemen in 674, and he at once began to revenge himself on those who had supported Childeric. This revolution affected St Lambert, because he had been heretofore greatly favoured by Childeric. He was expelled from his see, in which was placed one Pharamundus, a canon of Cologne. He retired to the monastery of Stavelot with two of his domestics, and during the seven years that he continued there he obeyed the rule as strictly as the youngest novice could have done. One instance will suffice to show how he devoted his heart to serve God according to the perfection of his temporary state. One night in winter he happened to let fall his shoe in rising from his bed, so that it made a noise. This the abbot heard and, looking upon it as a breach of the silence then to be observed in the community, he ordered him who was responsible for that noise to go and pray before the cross. This was a great cross which stood in the open air, before the church door. Lambert, without making any answer or showing who he was, laid down the upper garment he was going to put on and went out as he was, barefoot and covered only with his shirt ; and in this condition he prayed, kneeling before the cross, three or four hours. Whilst the monks were warming themselves after Matins, the abbot inquired if all were there. Answer was made that he had sent someone to the cross who had not yet come in. The abbot ordered that he should be called, and was surprised to find that the person was the Bishop of Maestricht, who made his appearance quite covered with snow and almost frozen. At the sight of him the abbot fell on his knees and asked pardon. " God forgive you," said Lambert " for thinking you stand in need of pardon. Is it not in cold and nakedness that, according to St Paul, I am to tame my flesh and serve God ? "

In 681 Ebroin was assassinated by a nobleman whose estate he had seized. Pepin of Heristal, grandson of Blessed Pepin of Landen, being made mayor of the palace in his place set himself to repair the evils done by Ebroin, expelled the usurping bishops whom he had intruded into many sees, and, among other exiled prelates, restored St Lambert to the see of Maestricht. The holy pastor, from the exercise of the most heroic virtues to which he had devoted the time of his exile, returned to his flock animated with redoubled fervour, preaching and discharging his other duties with wonderful zeal and fruit. Finding there still remained many pagans in Taxandria, a province about Kempenland and Brabant, he applied himself to convert them to the Faith, softened their barbarous temper by his patience, regenerated them in the water of baptism, and destroyed many superstitious observances. In the course of his missionary journeys he went down the Meuse as far as Tiel in Utrecht. In the neighbourhood of his own see he founded with St Landrada the monastery of Munsterbilsen for nuns.

Pepin of Heristal, after living many years in wedlock with St Plectrudis, entered into adulterous relations with her sister Alpais (of whom was born Charles Martel), and St Lambert expostulated with the guilty couple. Alpais feared what effect this might have on Pepin, and complained to her brother Dodo, who with a party of his followers set upon St Lambert and murdered him as he knelt before the altar in the church of SS. Cosmas and Damian at Liége. That is the generally accepted story of the circumstances of St Lambert's death, but his earliest biographers, writing in the eighth and tenth centuries, tell a quite different tale. According to them, two members of a powerful family, Gall and Reinhold, by their violence and plundering of the possessions of the see of Maestricht had become insupportable and could not be restrained. At this certain relations of St Lambert were so exasperated that, finding themselves driven to the last extremity, they slew the two brothers. Dodo, a kinsman of the men that were slain, an officer under Pepin and related to Alpais, resolved to revenge their death upon the innocent bishop, and to attack him with a considerable body of armed men, at a small village which is now the city of Liége. St Lambert had retired to sleep after Matins, when Dodo with his troop surrounded the house. The bishop would not suffer his two nephews nor any of his domestics to take arms to defend him, reminding his nephews, Peter and Audolec, that they were guilty of murder and must expiate their crime. With Dodo's men hammering at the outer doors he retired to his own room, whence he excluded everybody and bolted the door. Then, prostrating himself on the ground with his hands extended in form of a cross, he prayed with many tears. The troop of his enemies, entering the house, put to the sword all they met;

when the bishop's room was found to be barred, one of them climbed to the roof and cast thence a spear which transfixed and killed him.

Lambert's unjust death, suffered with patience and meekness, joined with the eminent sanctity of his life, caused him to be venerated as a martyr. His body was conveyed in a boat down the Meuse to Maestricht, where it was interred in St Peter's cemetery. Several miracles which ensued excited the people to build a church on the spot where the house stood in which he was slain, and his successor, St Hubert, translated thither his relics in 720. At the same time he removed to the same place the episcopal see of Maestricht, and around the cathedral which enshrined the relics of St Lambert the city of Liége grew up. He is to this day the principal patron of that place.

Fortitude, which appears most heroic and most conspicuous in martyrdom, is a cardinal virtue and the mother of many virtues, as courage, greatness of soul, tranquillity of mind under danger, patience, long-sufferingness, constancy, and perseverance. As the root of a tree bears the trunk, branches, flowers, and fruit, so fortitude sustains and is the strength of the whole system of moral and Christian virtues, which sink at the first shock without it. It therefore is an ingredient of every perfect virtue, by which a man is ready to suffer any hardship, or death, to expose himself to any dangers and to forego all temporal advantage, rather than swerve from the path of justice. By confusing rashness, carelessness, and fury with courage, many form a false idea of fortitude, which may be defined as the habit and gift of the Holy Ghost whereby a man is inclined to face those evils which he most dreads, and to resist the motions of mere recklessness. It moderates in us the two opposite extremes of fear and confidence ; it teaches us reasonably to fear dangers and death, and to avoid them when nothing obliges us to expose ourselves to them : for to be foolhardy and needlessly to precipitate ourselves upon danger is the height of folly and vice, and a mark of a corrupt and abandoned heart. But it is true fortitude to undertake and encounter all dangers when duty or the cause of virtue requires it. This noble and heroic virtue of fortitude is necessary in every Christian, especially in a pastor of souls, that neither worldly views nor fears may ever in the least warp his integrity or blind his judgement.

There are several medieval Lives of St Lambert, and most of them may be found printed in the *Acta Sanctorum*, September, vol. v. The earliest in date, and much the most important, has been critically edited by Bruno Krusch in the *Monumenta Germaniæ, Scriptores rerum Meroving.*, vol. vi, the text being supplemented by notable extracts from the later biographies written by Stephen, Sigebert of Gembloux, and Nicholas. The long-standing controversy regarding the precise cause which brought about the assassination of St Lambert has been very well stated in the *Analecta Bollandiana*, vol. xxxiii (1914), pp. 247–249 ; but see also pp. 219–347 in the second volume of G. Kurth's *Études franques* (1919). This last scholar many years before (in the *Annales de l'Académie archéol. de Belgique*, vol. xxxiii (1876) had set the whole controversy in a new light. *Cf.* further Hauck, *Kirchengesichte Deutschlands*, vol. i, pp. 400–401, and J. Demarteau, *Vie la plus ancienne de S. Lambert*, Liège, 1890.

ST COLUMBA, Virg and Mart.

A.D. 853

This Columba was one of the victims of the persecution of Christians in Spain begun by the Moors in the year 850, when the priest St Perfectus was beheaded on Easter Sunday. According to St Eulogius, who wrote an account in three volumes of those who suffered, called *The Memorial of the Saints*, and then himself gave his life for the Faith, Columba was a native of Cordova. Her brother Martin was an abbot and her sister Elizabeth had, with her husband St Jeremias, founded a double monastery at Tabanos, whither they both retired with their children. Inspired by these examples Columba herself determined to give herself to God in the cloister, but was hindered by her widowed mother, who wished her to marry. The mother tried to prevent her visiting her sister, where she knew Columba got her encouragement to persevere, but her efforts were fruitless and the girl became a nun at Tabanos. In the year 852 the persecution drove the religious away from this place, and the nuns took refuge in a house at Cordova, near the church of St Cyprian. In spite of the fact that in the same year a council at Cordova under the Archbishop of Seville had forbidden Christians to provoke persecution, Columba secretly left this house, presented herself before the Moorish magistrate, and openly and deliberately denied the false prophet Mohammed and his law. She was beheaded for her temerity, and her body thrown into the river Guadalquivir, whence it was recovered and buried in the church of St Eulalia.

The notice of St Columba in the *Acta Sanctorum*, September, vol. v, reproduces all that St Eulogius has recorded concerning her history.

ST HILDEGARD, Virg. and Abbess
A.D 1179

A dean of the women's college at Columbia University, in the United States of America, the country where feminism, if not the influence of women, is stronger than in any other, has written that : " No institution in Europe has ever won for the lady the freedom of development that she enjoyed in the convent in the early days. The modern college for women only feebly reproduces it. . . . Great spiritual rewards and great worldly prizes were alike within [the nun's] grasp. She was treated as an equal by the men of her class, as is witnessed by letters we still have from popes and emperors to abbesses. She had the stimulus of competition with men in executive capacity, in scholarship and in artistic production. . . . " There is no better illustration of Mrs. E. J. Putnam's words than St Hildegard, Abbess of Rupertsberg, who, called in her own day the " Sibyl of the Rhine," was one of the great figures of the twelfth century and one of the most remarkable of all women. She was the first of the great German mystics, a poet and a prophet, a physician and a political moralist, who rebuked popes and princes, bishops and lay-folk, with complete fearlessness and unerring justice. She was born in the year 1098 at Böckelheim, on the Nahe. Her father was a vassal of the Count-palatine of Spanheim, but it is not known to what families her parents belonged, though they were noble by birth, wealthy, and religious. Hildegard was the youngest of ten children and delicate in health, and from very early years was subject to unusual experiences. " When I was three," she writes, " I saw a light so great that my soul feared it, but the shyness of infancy prevented me from saying anything of it. . . . This light was the shadow of the living Light and like an azure sky." From the age of five she knew that she could see visions and hidden things, but mentioned them only to a few religious people who had the like experiences. When she was eight years old her parents confided Hildegard to the care of the Blessed Jutta, sister to Count Meginhard of Spanheim, who was living as a recluse in a cell (cottage) adjoining the church of the abbey founded by St Disibod on the Diessenberg (*Mons Disibodi*) close by her home. The child continued to be sickly, but she continued her education, learning to read and sing Latin and other things appertaining to a nun, as well as those domestic accomplishments which adorned all medieval women, from queens to peasants. By the time Hildegard was old enough to receive the veil of a nun the hermitage of Blessed Jutta had received several recruits so that it had become a community, following the rule of St Benedict. She was clothed when she was fifteen by the Bishop of Bamberg, and continued for another seventeen years to lead an uneventful life ; exteriorly uneventful only, for she grew in the grace of God, her visions continued, and " it became habitual with me to foretell the future in the course of conversations. And when I was completely absorbed in what I saw I used to say many things that seemed strange to those who heard me. This made me blush and cry, and often enough I would have killed myself had that been possible. I was too frightened to tell anyone what I saw, except the noble woman to whom I was entrusted, and she told a little to a monk whom she knew." In 1136 Blessed Jutta died, and the election of Hildegard as prioress in her place was confirmed by Conon, the new abbot of St Disibod's, who insisted that she should accept the charge.

Her revelations and visions pressed more and more upon her. There was a continual interior urging that she should write them down, but she feared what people would say, their mockery, and her own inadequate Latin. But the voice of God seemed to say to her : " I am the living and inaccessible Light, and I enlighten whomsoever I will. According to my pleasure I show forth through any man marvels greater than those of my servants in times past." At last she opened her heart fully to her confessor, the monk Godfrey, and authorised him to refer the matter to his abbot, Conon, who after careful consideration ordered Hildegard to write down some of the things she said God had made known to her. They dealt with such matters as the charity of Christ and the continuance of the Kingdom of God, the holy angels, the Devil and Hell. These writings Conon submitted to the Archbishop of Mainz, who examined them with his theologians and gave a favourable verdict : " These visions come from God." The Abbot then appointed a monk named Volmar to act as secretary to Hildegard, and she at once began the dictation of her principal work, which she called *Scivias*, for *Nosce vias* [*Domini*]. In the year 1141, she tells us, " a shaft of light of dazzling brilliancy came from the opened heavens and pierced my mind and my heart like a flame that warms without burning, as the sun heats by its rays. And suddenly I knew and understood the explanation of the Psalms, the Gospels, and the other Catholic books of the Old and New Testaments, but not the interpretation of the text of the words nor the division of the syllables nor the cases and tenses." This book took ten years to complete, and consists of twenty-six visions dealing with the relations between God and man by the Creation, the Redemption, and the Church, mixed with apocalyptic prophecies, warnings, and praises expressed in symbolical fashion. She reiterated time and again that she saw these things in vision, and they were the inspiration of all her active work. In 1147 the pope, Blessed Eugenius III, came to Trier and the Archbishop of Mainz referred St Hildegard's writings to him. Eugenius appointed a commission under Blessed Albero de Chiny, Bishop of Verdun, to examine both them and her, and on receiving a favourable report he read and discussed the writings himself with his advisers, including St Bernard of Clairvaux, who wished him to approve the visions as genuine. The Pope then wrote to Hildegard expressing wonder and happiness at the favours granted her by Heaven, and warning her against pride ; authorising her to publish, with prudence, whatever the Holy Ghost told her to publish ; and exhorting her to live with her sisters in the place she had seen in vision in faithful observance of the Rule of St Benedict. St Hildegard wrote a long letter in reply full of parabolic allusions to the troubles of the times and warning the Pope against the ambitions of his own household.

The place to which Blessed Eugenius referred was the new home which Hildegard had chosen for her community, which had out-grown its accommodation at the Diessenberg. The migration was stoutly opposed by the monks of St Disibod's, whose abbey owed much of its importance to the neighbouring convent, with its relics of Blessed Jutta and the growing reputation of Hildegard. The abbot accused her of acting from pride, but she claimed that God had revealed to her that she should move her nuns and the place to which they should go. This was the Rupertsberg, an exposed and unfertile hill above the Rhine, near Bingen, which belonged in part to the chapter of Mainz and in part to Count Bernard of Hildesheim, from whom she obtained a grant of land. During the dispute with the monks of St Disibod's, Hildegard was reduced to a very bad state of weakness and ill-health. Abbot Conon, perhaps doubting the reality of her illness, visited her and, when he saw she was not " putting it on," he told her to get up and prepare to visit the Rupertsberg. Immediately she was cured and got ready to obey. This was enough for Conon, who withdrew his objections, but the strong feeling of his monks in the matter were by no means allayed, though the leader of the opposition, one Arnold, was won to Hilde-gard's side by being cured of a painful malady in her church. The move was made some time between 1147 and 1150, the nuns exchanging their convenient house on the vine-clad Diessenberg for a dilapidated church and unfinished buildings in a deserted spot. In 1155, relations between the two communities being still strained, the Archbishop of Mainz decreed that the nuns of St Rupert's were entirely independent of the monks of St Disibod's, but that the nuns must pay over a considerable sum of money to balance their material obligations, and the monks must provide chaplains for them. In spite of these handicaps and having no very wealthy patrons, the energy of St Hildegard was responsible for the building of a large and convenient monastery, "with water piped to all the offices," we are told, which housed a community of fifty nuns. For the recreation of these the versatility of Hildegard provided a large number of new hymns, canticles and anthems, of which she wrote both the words and the music, and a sort of morality play, or sacred cantata, called *Ordo Virtutum*, and for reading in the chapter-house and refectory she composed fifty allegorical homilies. Her Lives of St Disibod and St Rupert were claimed to be revelations (in common with a good deal else that was probably a purely natural production), gratuitously, for they bear the marks of local traditions. Among the diversions of her leisure hours—though it is hard to believe that St Hildegard ever had any leisure—is the so-called "unknown language," a sort of Esperanto, of which nine hundred words and a made-up alphabet have come down to us. These words seem to be simply assonant versions of Latin and German words with a liberal addition of final zeds. From the Rupertsberg St Hildegard conducted a voluminous correspondence, and nearly three hundred of her letters have been printed, though doubt has been thrown on the authenticity of some of them and of the letters she received. Except when writing to one or other of the numerous abbesses that consulted her, the letters are rather in the nature of homilies, prophecies, and allegorical treatises. They were addressed to popes and emperors, to kings (including Henry II of England, before he had slain Becket), to bishops and abbots. She wrote once to St Bernard and received a reply, to St Eberhard of Salzburg, and frequently to the Cistercian mystic, St Elizabeth of Schönau. In two letters to the clergy of Cologne and Trier she rates the carelessness and avarice of so many priests, and foretells, in what are for her unusually clear terms, the scourges that will follow, a prophecy in which many have seen a prevision of the Reformation. Her letters are very full of these prophecies and warnings and they soon made her notorious. On the one hand people of all kinds came from all parts to consult her ; on the other she was denounced as a fraud, a sorceress, a demoniac. Though her meaning was often wrapped up in difficult symbolism, she always made it quite clear when she was reproving, which she most frequently found occasion to do. Henry, Archbishop of Mainz, wrote rather brusquely requiring St Hildegard

232

to allow one of her nuns, Richardis, to become abbess of another monastery. She replied : " All the reasons given for the promotion of this young woman are worthless, before God. The spirit of this jealous God says : Weep and cry out, ye pastors, for you know not what you do, distributing sacred offices in your own interest and wasting them on perverse and Godless men. . . . As for yourself, arise !—for your days are numbered." He was in fact deposed and died soon after. To the Bishop of Speyer she wrote that his deeds were so evil that his soul was scarcely alive, and told the Emperor Conrad III to reform his life lest he have to blush for it. But she did not pretend to make these judgements on her own. " I am a poor earthen vessel and say these things not of myself but from the serene Light," she writes to St Elizabeth of Schönau. Nevertheless, such a disclaimer could not save her from criticism, and she had trouble even with some of her own nuns, high-born German girls in whom personal pride and vanity were still strong. " Some of them persist in regarding me with an unfavourable eye, pulling me to pieces with malicious tongues behind my back, saying that they cannot stand this talk about discipline that I keep on dinning into them, and that they won't let themselves be ruled by me."

In spite of all her activities and continual sickness the activities of St Hildegard were not confined to her convent, and between 1152 and 1162 she made numerous journeys in the Rhineland. She founded a daughter-house at Eibingen, near Rudesheim, and did not hesitate roundly to rebuke the monks and nuns of those monasteries whose discipline she saw to be relaxed ; indeed, her expeditions were rather in the nature of the progress of an " abbess visitor." At Cologne, Trier, and elsewhere, she addressed herself to selected representatives of the clergy, imparting to them the divine warnings she had received, and exhorted bishops and lay-folk with equal ease and straightforwardness. Probably the first of these journeys was the one she made to Ingelheim to meet Frederick Barbarossa, but what took place at that interview is not known. She also visited Metz, Würzburg, Ulm, Werden, Bamberg and other places, and with all this travelling, penetrating in spite of her weakness and the bad conditions into inaccessible spots to visit remote monasteries, she continued to write. Among other works she wrote an explanation of the Athanasian Creed, a commentary on the Rule of St Benedict for the monks of Huy (she held that his prohibition of flesh meat did not include that of birds), the answers to thirty-eight scriptural and theological questions put to her by the Cistercians of Villars in Brabant, and two books of medicine and natural history. One of these treats of plants, elements, trees, minerals, fishes, birds, quadrupeds, reptiles, and metals, and is distinguished by careful scientific observation ; the other treats of the human body, and the causes, symptoms, and treatment of its ailments. In it nearly all the modern methods of diagnosis are at least adumbrated, and she came very near to certain later discoveries, such as the circulation of the blood. She deals with normal and morbid psychology, refers to frenzy, insanity, dreads, obsessions, and idiocy, and says that " when headache, vapours, and giddiness attack a patient simultaneously they make him foolish and upset his reason. This makes many people think that he is possessed by an evil spirit, but that is not true." She was undoubtedly the most important medical writer of her time in Europe and held the place in the twelfth century that another Benedictine, Constantine Africanus of Monte Cassino, had held in the eleventh.

During the last year of her life St Hildegard was in great trouble on account of a young man who, having been at one time excommunicated, died and was buried in the cemetery at St Rupert's. The see of Mainz had recently undergone a schism, probably in the course of which the dead man had incurred censure, and the vicar general ordered that the body be removed. St Hildegard refused, on the grounds that the man had received the last sacraments and that she had been favoured with a vision justifying her action. Thereupon the church was put under an interdict. This meant that neither the holy Sacrifice nor the divine Office could be celebrated therein, and after some time Hildegard wrote to the chapter of Mainz a long letter about sacred music—" A half-forgotten memory of a primitive state which we have lost since Eden "—" symbol of the harmony which Satan has broken, which helps man to build a bridge of holiness between this world and the World of all Beauty and Music. Those therefore who, without a good reason, impose silence on churches in which singing in God's honour is wont to be heard, will not deserve to hear the glorious choir of angels that praises the Lord in Heaven." Apparently she was doubtful of the effect of her touching eloquence on the canons of Mainz, for at the same time she wrote very energetically to the Archbishop himself who was in Italy. He thereupon removed the interdict, but, in spite of a promise, he did not fulfil Hildegard's other request, to leave fighting and intriguing and come and govern his diocese. St Hildegard was now broken by infirmity and mortifications, she could not stand upright and had to be carried from place to place. But the broken instrument, in the phrase of her friend and chaplain, Martin Guibert, still gave out melody ; to the last she was at the disposition of everybody, giving advice to those that sought it, answering perplexing questions, writing, instructing her nuns, encouraging the sinners who came to her, never at rest. She survived her trouble with the chapter of Mainz a very little time, and died peacefully on September 17, 1179. Miracles, of which a number are recorded of her during her life, were multiplied at her tomb, and the process of her canonization was twice undertaken. It was never achieved, but she is named as a saint in the Roman Martyrology and her feast is kept on this day in several German dioceses.

The visions and revelations claimed by or for St Hildegard are among the best known in this class of phenomena, and her actualisation of ideas in symbols and images has provoked comparison both with Dante and William Blake. She thus describes the fall of the angels : " I saw a great star, most splendid and beautiful, and with it a great multitude of falling sparks which followed it southward. And they looked on Him upon His throne as it were something hostile, and turning from Him they sought rather the north. And suddenly they were all annihilated and turned into black coals . . . and cast into the abyss, so that I could see them no more." In the drawings which illustrate some of the MSS. these fallen angels are shown as black stars with points of white in the centre and a gold disc surrounded by white points in one of them, while above the horizon other stars still shine in golden light. In many of them " a prominent feature is a point or a group of points of light, which shimmer and move, usually in a wave-like manner, and are most often interpreted as stars or flaming eyes. . . . Often the lights give that impression of working, boiling, or fermenting, described by so many visionaries from Ezekiel onwards." " These visions which I saw," wrote St Hildegard, " I beheld neither in sleep nor dreaming nor in madness nor with my bodily eyes or ears, nor in hidden places ; but I saw them in full view and according to God's will, when I was wakeful and alert, with the eyes of the spirit and the inward ears. And how this was brought about is indeed hard for human flesh to search out." The visions recorded in the *Scivias* received the guarded approbation of Pope Eugenius III, but this and similar confirmations of private revelations impose no obligation of belief. The Church receives them only as probable, and even those most worthy of faith may be prudently rejected by individuals.

A great part of our information concerning the life of St Hildegard is derived from her own correspondence and writings, but there are also two or three formal biographies, as biography was understood in the Middle Ages. The most noteworthy is that by two monks, Godefride and Theodoric, printed in the *Acta Sanctorum*, September, vol. v. Another by Guibert of Gembloux was edited by Cardinal Pitra in his *Analecta Sacra*, vol. viii. Also there are remnants of an inquisition made in 1233 with a view to her canonisation, most of which has been published by the Bollandists. More-over, in recent times a considerable literature has grown up dealing with this remarkable mystic. See in particular J. May, *Die St Hildegard von Bingen* (1911) ; and for a fuller bibliography the *Dictionnaire de Théol. Cath.*, vol. vi, cc. 2468-2480. But now almost every aspect of St Hilde-garde's activities is being independently studied. Her work as a pioneer in science has attracted attention even in England, as may be noted in C. Singer, *Studies in the History and Method of Science* (Oxford, 1917). A number of monographs have appeared in Germany and France, dealing not only with her medical speculations, but also with her musical and artistic com-positions. The illustrations, for example, which adorn the " codex minor " of the *Scivias* have been reproduced by L. Baillet in *Monuments et Mémoires publiés par l'Académie des Inscriptions et Belles-lettres*, vol. xix (1911). A short popular account of St Hildegard from a Catholic point of view is provided in Miss F. M. Steel's *Life and Visions of St Hildegarde* (1914). A much needed critical text of Hildegard's *Opera Omnia* is understood to be in preparation under the editorship of Dom Huyhen, O.S.B.

ST PETER ARBUEZ, Mart.

A.D. 1485

One of the chief problems of Church and State in medieval Spain was how to deal with the Jews and the Mohammedans who were so numerous in the country : a problem complicated by the active hatred against them displayed by the common people, who shared neither the Christian sentiments of the more tolerant high eccle-siastics nor the material interest involved for the civil authorities. During the fourteenth century the Jews in particular had acquired great influence, not only the underground influence of finance but also the open power of high secular and even ecclesiastical offices. This had been attained, could be attained, only by profession of Christianity, a profession to a very considerable extent false, and when genuine often superficial and unreliable. The crypto-Jews moreover quite deliberately aimed at the overthrow of the Church in Spain and the destruction of the Gentile power. Two classes of these people who gave particular trouble and were especially dangerous were the Maranos and the Moriscos, Jews and Moors respectively who, having for one reason or another, good or bad, been converted to Christianity and received baptism, subsequently relapsed, either openly or secretly, into their former infidelity. In the year 1478 Pope Sixtus IV, at the urgent request of King Ferdi-nand of Aragon and Queen Isabella of Castile, issued a bull em-powering them to appoint a tribunal of learned and virtuous bishops to deal with Jewish and other apostates and sham converts. Thus was established the institution known in history as the Spanish Inquisition.* This is not the place to discuss its merits and demerits, but it may be noted in passing that, though primarily an ecclesiastical tribunal, it acted independently and often in defiance of the Holy See ; and that though it was undoubtedly often brutal, harsh, and cruel in its methods, yet its theoretical basis was reasonable and just. It was not concerned with *bona-fide* Jews and Mohammedans, and all who voluntarily confessed apostasy and promised amendment were reconciled, with a light penance.

A few years before the establishment of this Inquisition there was professed with the canons regular at Saragossa a certain Dom Peter Arbuez. He had been born at Epila in Aragon about the year 1442, son of the noble Antony Arbuez and his wife Sanchia Ruiz, and after doing his philosophy at Huesca he had graduated brilliantly in theology and canon law in the Spanish College at Bologna. His virtue and enthusiasm had turned him to the religious life, but the reputation of his learning and zeal caused him to be called from his cloister ten years after his profession. The organisation of the nascent Inquisition was in the hands of the Dominican friar Thomas Torquemada, and he, looking about for a provincial inquisitor for the kingdom of Aragon, selected Peter Arbuez, who took up his appointment in the year 1484. During the few months that he discharged this office Dom Peter preached and worked unwearyingly against the bogus Christians and apostates, and their characteristic vices of perjury, usury, and sexual immorality. His zeal made him many enemies, who traduced his character and started the legend of his cruelty, a legend familiar to many who have not otherwise heard of Peter Arbuez from the picture painted by Wilhelm von Kaulbach, in which the forty-four-year-old canon is represented as an aged and sadistic tyrant. Apart from the fact that in St Peter's day the Spanish Inquisition was still more or less in the control of the more humane spirit of Rome, he was responsible for no sentence of death, and only two arrests were made at his instance. But the Maranos were determined to get rid of him, and collected a large sum of money to recompense the murderers. St Peter was aware of what was going on, but refused to take any extraordinary precautions, even after an unsuccessful attempt had been made on his life in the building of the Inquisition. But on the night of September 14–15, 1485, three men, led by Juan de la Abadia against whose sister the Inquisition had pronounced a sentence, entered the cathedral of St Saviour at Saragossa and stabbed the canon as he knelt in

* In view of popular misconceptions it may be pointed out that this was long before the rise of Protestantism or of the Jesuits.

prayer. He died two days later, and was at once acclaimed throughout the land as a martyr for the Faith. St Peter Arbuez was beatified by Pope Alexander VII in 1664 and canonised by Pius IX in 1867.

A sufficient account of St Peter is given in the *Acta Sanctorum*, September, vol. v. We have no formal biography of early date, but a good deal of information is provided by the chronicles of the time. See also G. Cozza, *Della Vita Miracoli e Culto del martire S. Pietro de Arbues*, Rome, 1867.

SEPTEMBER 18

ST JOSEPH OF CUPERTINO, Conf.

A.D. 1633

JOSEPH DESA was born June 17, 1603, at Cupertino, a small village between Brindisi and Otranto, six miles from the coast of the gulf of Taranto. His parents were poor and unfortunate. Joseph himself was born in a shed at the back of the house, because his father, a carpenter, was unable to pay his debts and the home was being sold up. His childhood was unhappy. His widowed mother looked on him as a nuisance and a burden, and treated him with great severity. When he was seven he was troubled with running ulcers that would not heal, and he developed an extreme absent-mindedness and inertia. He would forget his meals, and when reminded of them say simply, " I forgot," and wander in an aimless way about the village so that he earned the nick-name of " Bocca aperta," the gaper. He had a hot temper, which made him more unpopular, but was exemplary and even precocious in his religious duties. When the time came for him to try and earn his own living, Joseph was bound apprentice to a shoemaker, which trade he applied himself to for some time, but without any success. When he was seventeen years of age he presented himself to be received amongst the Conventual Franciscans, but they refused to have him because of his ignorance. Then he went to the Capuchins at Martino, near Taranto, and they took him as a lay-brother ; but after eight months he was dismissed as unequal to the duties of the order : his clumsiness and preoccupation made him an apparently impossible subject, for he dropped piles of plates and dishes on the refectory floor, forgot to do things he was told, and could not be trusted even to make up the kitchen fire. Joseph then turned for help to a wealthy uncle, who curtly refused to aid an obvious good-for-nothing, and the young man returned home in despair and misery. His mother was not at all pleased to see him on her hands again and used her influence with her brother, a Conventual Franciscan, to have him accepted by the friars of his order at Grotella as a servant. He was given a tertiary habit and put to work in the stables. Now a change seems to have come over Joseph ; at any rate he was

239

more successful in his duties and performed the meanest offices of the house with the most perfect fidelity. He practised fasts and austerities, prayed continually, and slept only three hours every night. His humility, his sweetness, his love of mortification and penance, gained him so much regard that in a provincial chapter held at Altamura in 1625 it was resolved he should be admitted amongst the religious of the choir, that he might qualify himself for holy orders.

Joseph therefore began his novitiate, during which he ever sought to unite himself more closely to God by prayer and contemplation. He looked upon himself as a great sinner, and imagined it was through charity that the religious habit was given him. His patience made him bear in silence and with joy rebukes for faults which he had not committed, and he undertook without delay the most difficult duties enjoined him. So many virtues rendered him an object of admiration, but his lack of progress in studies was also remarked. Try as he would, the extent of his human accomplishments was to read badly and to write worse. He had no gift of eloquence or for exposition, the one text on which he had something to say being, " Blessed is the womb that bore thee." When he came up for examination for the diaconate the bishop opened the Gospels at random and his eye fell on that text : he asked Brother Joseph to expound it, which he did with brilliance. When it was a question of the priesthood, the first candidates were so satisfactory that the remainder, Joseph among them, were passed without examination. So he was ordained priest in 1628, and celebrated his first Mass with inexpressible sentiments of faith, of love, and respect. He chose a retired cell that was dark and inconvenient and would often go to pray to the most unfrequented oratories, that he might give himself up more freely to contemplation. He divested himself of everything that was allowed him by his rule, and he cried out, prostrate before his crucifix : " Behold me, O Lord, bereft of all earthly things : be thou my only good ; every other thing is a danger and a loss to my soul." After having received the priesthood he passed five years without tasting bread or wine, and the herbs he ate on Fridays were so distasteful that only himself could use them. His fast in Lent was so rigorous that he took no nourishment except on Thursdays and Sundays, and he spent the hours devoted to manual work in performing those simple household and routine duties which he knew were, humanly speaking, all he was fitted to undertake.

From the time of his ordination St Joseph's life was one long succession of ecstasies, miracles of healing, and supernatural happenings on a scale not parallelled in the reasonably authenticated life of any other saint. Anything that in any way could be particularly referred to God or the mysteries of religion was liable to ravish him from his senses and make him oblivious to what was going on around him ; the absent-mindedness and abstraction of his childhood now had an end and a purpose clearly seen. The sight of a lamb in the garden of the Capuchins at Fossombrone caused him to be lost in contemplation of the spotless Lamb of God and, it is said, be caught up into the air with the animal in his arms. At all times he had a command over beasts surpassing that of St Francis himself ; sheep were said to gather round him and listen to his prayers, a sparrow at a convent came and went at his word. Especially during Mass or the Divine Office he would be lifted off his feet in rapture, sometimes to a great height and for a long time. One Christmas Eve while the country people were singing carols in the church at Grotella he rose in the air with a great cry, flew on to the high altar, and remained there on his knees before the Blessed Sacrament for a quarter of an hour. During the seventeen years he remained at this friary over seventy occasions are recorded of his levitation, the most marvellous being when the friars were building a calvary. The middle cross of the group was thirty-six feet high and correspondingly heavy, defying the efforts of ten men to lift it. St Joseph is said to have flown seventy yards from the door of the house to the cross, picked it up in his arms " as if it were a straw," and deposited it in its place. This staggering feat is not attested by an eye-witness, and, in common with most of his earlier marvels, was recorded only after his death, when plenty of time had elapsed in which events could be exaggerated and legends arise. But, whatever their exact nature and extent, the daily life of St Joseph was surrounded by such disturbing phenomena that for thirty-five years he was not allowed to say Mass in public, to keep choir, to take his meals with his brethren, or to attend processions and other public functions. Sometimes when he was bereft of his senses they would try to bring him to by hitting him, burning his flesh or pricking it with needles, but nothing had any effect except, it is said, the voice of his superior. When he did come back to himself he would laughingly apologise for what he called his " fits of giddiness."

Levitation, the name given to the raising of the human body from the ground by no apparent physical force, is recorded in some form or other of over two hundred saints and holy persons (as well as of many others), and in their case is interpreted as a special mark of God's favour whereby it is made evident even to the physical senses that prayer is a raising of the heart and mind to God. St Joseph of

Cupertino, in both the extent and number of these experiences, provides the classical examples of levitation, for, if many of the earlier incidents are doubtful, some of those recorded in his later years are very well attested. For example, one of his biographers states that : " When in 1645 the Spanish ambassador to the papal court, the High Admiral of Castile, passed through [Assisi] he visited Joseph of Cupertino in his cell. After conversing with him he returned to the church and told his wife : ' I have seen and spoken with another St Francis.' As his wife then expressed a great desire to enjoy the same privilege, the father guardian gave Joseph an order to go down to the church and speak with her Excellency. To this he made answer : ' I will obey, but I do not know whether I shall be able to speak with her.' In point of fact no sooner had he entered the church than his eyes rested on a statue of Mary Immaculate which stood over the altar, and he at once flew about a dozen paces over the heads of those present to the foot of the statue. Then after paying homage there for some short space and uttering his customary shrill cry he flew back again and straightway returned to his cell, leaving the Admiral, his wife, and the large retinue which attended them, speechless with astonishment." This story is supported in two biographies by copious references to depositions in the process of canonisation of witnesses who are expressly stated to have been present. " Still more trustworthy," says a writer in the *Month* for May 1919, " is the evidence given of the saint's levitations at Osimo, where he spent the last six years of his life. There his fellow-religious saw him fly up seven or eight feet into the air to kiss the statue of the infant Jesus which stood over the altar, and they told how he carried off this wax image in his arms and floated about with it in his cell in every conceivable attitude. On one occasion during these last years of his life he caught up another friar in his flight and carried him some distance round the room, and this indeed he is stated to have done on several previous occasions. In the very last Mass which he celebrated, on the festival of the Assumption 1663, a month before his death, he was lifted up in a longer rapture than usual. For these facts we have the evidence of several eye-witnesses who made their depositions, as usual under oath, only four or five years later. It seems very difficult to believe that they could possibly be deceived as to the broad fact that the saint did float in the air, as they were convinced they had seen him do, under every possible variety of conditions and surroundings." Prosper Lambertini, afterwards Pope Benedict XIV, the supreme authority on evidence and procedure in canonisation causes, personally studied all the details of the case of St Joseph of Cupertino. The writer goes on : " When the cause came up for discussion before the Congregation of Rites [Lambertini] was ' promotor Fidei ' (popularly known as the Devil's Advocate), and his ' animadversions ' upon the evidence submitted are said to have been of a most searching character. None the less we must believe that these criticisms were answered to his own complete satisfaction, for not only was it he himself who, when pope, published in 1753 the decree of beatification, but in his great work, *De Servorum Dei Beatificatione*, etc., he speaks as follows : ' Whilst I discharged the office of promoter of the Faith the cause of the venerable servant of God, Joseph of Cupertino, came up for discussion in the Congregation of Sacred Rites, which after my retirement was brought to a favourable conclusion, and in this *eyewitnesses of unchallengeable integrity* gave evidence of the famous upliftings from the ground and prolonged flights of the aforesaid servant of God when rapt in ecstasy.' There can be no doubt that Benedict XIV, a critically-minded man, who knew the value of evidence and who had studied the original depositions as probably no one else had studied them, believed that the witnesses of St Joseph's levitations had really seen what they professed to have seen."

There were not wanting persons to whom these manifestations were a stone of offence, and when St Joseph attracted crowds about him as he travelled in the province of Bari, he was denounced as " one who runs about these provinces and as a new Messias draws crowds after him by the prodigies wrought on some few of the ignorant people, who are ready to believe anything." The vicar general carried the complaint to the inquisitors of Naples, and Joseph was ordered to appear. The heads of his accusation being examined, the inquisitors could find nothing worthy of censure, but did not discharge him. He said Mass at Naples in the church of St Gregory the Armenian, which belonged to a monastery of Benedictine religious. The holy Sacrifice being finished, he fell into an ecstasy, as many eyewitnesses testified in the process of canonisation. Then the inquisitors sent him to Rome to his minister general, who received him at first with harshness, but he became impressed by St Joseph's innocent and humble bearing and he took him to see the pope, Urban VIII. The saint went into ecstasy at the sight of the Vicar of Christ, and Urban declared that if Joseph should die before himself he would give evidence of the miracle to which he had been a witness. It was decided to send Joseph to Assisi, where again he was treated by his superiors with considerable severity, they at least pretending to regard him as a hypocrite. But his sanctity shone forth more and more, and persons of distinction expressed an ardent desire to see him. He arrived at Assisi in 1639, and remained there thirteen years. At first he suffered many trials, both interior and exterior. God seemed to have abandoned him; his religious exercises were accompanied with a spiritual dryness that afflicted him exceedingly and terrible temptations cast him into so deep a melancholy that he scarce dare lift up his eyes. His general, being informed, called him to Rome, and having kept him there three weeks he sent him back to his convent of Assisi. The saint on his way to Rome experienced a return of those heavenly consolations which had been withdrawn from him. At the name of God, of Jesus, or of Mary, he was as it were out of himself. He would often cry out : " O my God, fill all my heart ! O that my soul was freed from the chains of the body and united to Jesus Christ ! Jesus, Jesus, draw me to thyself; I am not able to live any longer on the earth." He would excite others to the love of God and say to them : "Love God ! He in whom this love reigns is rich although he does not perceive it." Reports of his sanctity and miracles spread over the borders of Italy, and distinguished people, such as the Admiral of Castile mentioned above, would call at Assisi to visit him. Among them was John Frederick, Duke of Brunswick and Hanover. This prince, who was a Lutheran, was so struck with what he had seen that he abjured his former tenets and embraced the Catholic faith. Joseph used to say to some scrupulous persons who came to consult him : " I like neither scruples nor melancholy ; let your intention be right and fear not," and he was always urging people to prayer. "Pray," he would say, "pray. If you are troubled by dryness or distractions, just say an Our Father. Then you make both vocal and mental prayer." When Cardinal Lauria asked him what souls in ecstasy saw during their raptures he replied : " They feel as though they were taken into a wonderful gallery, shining with never-ending beauty, where in a glass, with a single look, they apprehend the marvellous vision which God is pleased to show them." In the ordinary comings and goings of daily life he was so preoccupied with heavenly things that he would genuinely suppose a passing woman to be our Lady or St Catherine or St Clare, a strange man to be one of the Apostles, a fellow-friar to be St Francis or St Antony.

In 1653, for reasons which are not known, the Inquisition of Perugia was instructed to remove St Joseph from the care of his own order and put him in charge of Capuchins at a lonely friary among the hills of Pietrarossa, where he was to live in the strictest seclusion. " Have I got to go to prison then ? " he asked, and departed at once—leaving his hat, his cloak, his breviary, and his spectacles behind him. To prison, in effect, he had gone. He was not allowed to leave the convent enclosure, to speak to anyone but the friars, to write or to receive letters ; he was completely cut off from the world. Apart from wondering why he should be sundered from his fellow-Conventuals and treated like a criminal, this life must have been particularly satisfactory to St Joseph. But soon his whereabouts was discovered and pilgrims flocked to the place ; whereupon he was spirited away to lead the same sort of life with the Capuchins of Fossombrone. The rest of his life was spent like this. When in 1655 the chapter general of the Conventual Franciscans asked for the return of their saint to Assisi, Pope Alexander VII replied that one St Francis at Assisi was enough, but in 1657 he was allowed to go to the Conventual house at Osimo. Here the seclusion was, however, even more strict, and only selected religious were allowed to visit him in his cell. But all this time, and till the end, supernatural manifestations were his daily portion : he was in effect deserted by man but God was ever more clearly with him. He fell sick on August 10, 1663, and knew that his end was at hand ; on the feast of the Assumption he said Mass for the last time, being lifted off the ground in rapture as he celebrated. Then he took to his bed and received the last sacraments. Daily he cried : " Oh ! that my soul were freed from the shackles of my body to be reunited to Jesus Christ. Praise and thanksgiving be to God. The will of God be done. Jesus crucified, receive my heart and kindle in it the fire of Thy holy love." He died September 18 at the age of sixty years and three months. He had asked that his body be buried in some obscure place and there forgotten, but it was exposed in the church, and the whole town came to visit it with respect ; afterwards he was laid in the chapel of the Conception. The heroism of his virtues being proved and the truth of his miracles attested, he was beatified by Benedict XIV in 1753, and canonised by Clement XIII in 1767.

The austerities of a St Joseph of Cupertino are not suitable to persons engaged in the world ; they are even inconsistent with their obligations. But all are capable of disengaging their affections from inordinate passions and attachment to creatures, and of attaining to a pure and holy love of God, which may be made the principle of their thoughts and ordinary actions, and sanctify the whole circle of their lives. Of this all who have a heart are, through the divine grace, capable. In whatever circumstances we are placed we have opportunities of subduing our desires and subjecting our senses by frequent denials ; of watching over our hearts by self-examination, of purifying our affections by recollection and prayer, and of uniting our souls to God by continual acts of love. Thus may the gentleman, the farmer, the mechanic or the shopkeeper become a saint, and make the duties of his state an exercise of heroic virtue and so many steps to perfection and to eternal glory.

There is a printed "Summarium" prepared for the Congregation of Rites in 1688 and containing an abstract of the depositions of witnesses in the process of beatification. It is stated, however, that only two copies are now known to exist, and it does not seem to have been accessible to the Bollandists. In the *Acta Sanctorum*, therefore (September, vol. v), they contented themselves with translating from previously published biographies such as those of Pastrovicchi (1753), and Bernino (1722). The two Lives last named have been translated into French and other languages. A convenient version or adaptation of Pastrovicchi in English has been brought out by Father F. S. Laing (St Louis, 1918). The bull of canonization, a lengthy document, containing many biographical data, is printed in the later Italian Lives, and in the French translation of Bernino, 1856. In this the story of St Joseph's aerial flights, as recounted above, is told in detail and emphasized.

ST FERREOLUS, Mart.

c. A.D. 304 (?)

St Ferreolus was a tribune who lived at Vienne in Gaul, and was secretly a Christian. St Julian of Brioude, a native of that city, lodged in his house and made public profession of the Faith. When the persecution began under Diocletian and St Julian had been put to death, Crispin, governor of that part of Gaul, had St Ferreolus apprehended upon suspicion. Finding him refuse to offer sacrifice, he told him that, as he had the honour to serve the state as a military officer, it became him to set to others an example of obedience. The martyr answered : " I do not so much overrate honours and riches. If I may be allowed to live and to serve God, I am well satisfied. If even this seem too much, I am willing to resign my life itself rather than to abandon my religion." The judge commanded that he should be scourged, and then confined him in that inner pit of the prison into which the rest of the place drained. On the third day his chains fell off his hands and legs by the power of God, and, seeing a way out of the prison open and his guards asleep, he made his escape and went out of the city by the gate which led to Lyons. He swam over the river Rhône and got as far as the river Gêne which falls into the Rhône just above Vienne, when he fell again into the hands of the persecutors, who bound him and led him away to death. He was beheaded on the banks of the Rhône and the Christians of Vienne interred his body with great veneration near the same river.

A church was built over his burying-place, from whence his relics were removed by St Mamertus about the year 474 to a church built to shelter them within the city of Vienne.

On this same day is commemorated another ST FERREOLUS, a bishop of Limoges who died in 597 or thereabouts.

The " Acts " of St Ferreolus (printed in the *Acta Sanctorum*, September vol. v) are, as Père Delehaye states, " of little worth." But his martyrdom is authentic, and his *cultus*, to which both St Gregory of Tours and Venantius Fortunatus bear witness, very ancient. See the commentary on the *Hieronymianum* in the *Acta Sanctorum*, November, vol. ii, part 2, pp. 517–518.

ST METHODIUS, Bp. of Olympus, Mart.

c. A.D. 311

St Jerome states that this Methodius was bishop first of Olympus in Lycia and then of Tyre, and that he was crowned with martyrdom at Khalkis in Greece at the very end of the last persecution, under Maximian. These statements are reproduced in the Roman Martyrology, but it is practically certain that he was never bishop of Tyre ; Greek writers refer to him as bishop of Patara in Lycia. We have no particulars of his life or martyrdom and his fame rests on his writings, especially his detection and refutation of the errors of Origen, against whose teaching that man's risen body is not the same as his earthly body he wrote a treatise *On the Resurrection.* He wrote on Free Will against the Valentinians, and other works which caused St Jerome to refer often to him as " the most eloquent Methodius," and the Roman Martyrology to call him " most renowned for the brilliance of his preaching and his learning." Methodius himself, however, gave support to the error of Millenarianism *i.e.* Christ's temporal reign of a thousand years before the general resurrection, in his *Symposium.* The best-known of his works is this *Symposium* or Banquet of the Ten Virgins, written in imitation of the *Banquet* of Plato. As an imitation it is hardly a success (Alban Butler calls his style " diffusive, swelling, and full of epithets "), but as an ascetical treatise on virginity it was formerly famous. In it a matron called Gregorium is introduced to tell her friend Eubulus (the surname of St Methodius himself) the conversation of ten maidens at a festive meal in the garden of Arete (Virtue). A discourse is put into the mouth of each of these in commendation of virginity. The symposium ends with a hymn to our Lord as the Bridegroom of the Church, in which the maiden Thecla sings a series of alphabetical strophes and is answered by the others with a refrain. This forms one of the earliest of Christian hymns.

The slender data available concerning the life of St Methodius of Olympus have been collected in the *Acta Sanctorum*, September, vol. v. With regard to his literary work, research in modern times has brought to light a Slavonic text of several of his writings which has been turned to profit by N. Bonwetsch in his *Methodius von Olympus* (1891). See also Bardenhewer, *Altkirchliche Literatur*, 2nd Edition, 1913, vol. ii, pp. 334 *seq.*, and *Dictionnaire de Théol. cath.*, vol. x, cc. 1606–1614.

ST RICHARDIS, Empress

c. A.D. 895

When she was twenty-two years old Richardis, daughter of the Count of Alsace, was married to Charles the Fat, son of King Louis the German. Nineteen years later she accompanied him to Rome, to be crowned Emperor and Empress of the Holy Roman Empire by Pope John VIII on Christmas day 881. Hitherto they had lived together in amity but a few years later Charles, either because his suspicions were genuinely aroused or else in order to serve some unworthy purpose of his own, charged his wife with unfaithfulness. He named as her accomplice his chancellor, Luitward, who was bishop of Vercelli and a man greatly esteemed both for his abilities and his virtue. Richardis and Luitward appeared before the imperial assembly and solemnly denied the allegation ; the bishop purged himself by an oath and the Empress appealed to the judgement of God by claiming an ordeal, either by fire or (by proxy) of battle. It is said that the ordeal by fire was accepted and that St Richardis, with bare feet and wearing an inflammable smock, walked unharmed across burning embers. Luitward was nevertheless deprived of his chancellorship and, it not being decent after so public an exhibition that they should continue to live together, Richardis was allowed to separate from Charles. She went for a time to a nunnery at Hohenburg and then to the abbey of Andlau, which she had herself founded. Here she lived in peace until her death about the year 895, joining in the life of the nuns, interesting herself on their behalf with the Holy See, caring for the poor, and writing verses. When Pope St Leo IX visited Andlau in 1049, on his way from a council at Mainz, he ordered her relics to be disinterred, enshrined, and exposed for the veneration of the faithful. This *cultus* has continued and the feast of St Richardis is now observed in the dioceses of Strasburg and Saint-Dié.

There is no formal Life of St Richardis, but a few breviary lessons, pane-
gyrics, etc., have been brought together in the *Acta Sanctorum*, September,
vol. v. A biographical sketch by Deharbe, *Ste Richarde, son Abbaye de
Andlau*, etc., was published at Paris in 1874. See also the *Allgemeine Deutsche
Biographie*, vol. xxviii, pp. 420 *seq.*

BD. JOHN MASSIAS, Conf.

A.D. 1645

The lessons of his office state that the parents of Blessed John
Massias were John of Arca and Agnes Sanchez, representatives of
noble and ancient families, who "had been deprived of rank and
wealth by the various misfortunes of an unreliable world." He was
born at Ribera in Estramadura in 1585 and was brought up very
piously. When he was five he would rather be in church than
playing games, and he soon learned to say the rosary three times
every day, for the conversion of sinners, for the souls in Purgatory,
and for himself, a practice he kept up throughout his life. He was
left an orphan while still young, and was looked after by an uncle,
who made the boy earn his living as a shepherd. During the long
hours when there was nothing particular to do except keep his eyes
open John would say his rosary and meditate on the Christian
mysteries, and it sometimes appeared that the holy ones were there,
visible and talking to him, especially our Lady and St John the
Evangelist. He attributed to an instruction of the last named his
sudden decision to go to the Americas, as so many others of his
countrymen were then doing. He landed in Peru and got work on
a cattle-ranch, where he stopped for over two years and saved a
little money with which he made his way to Lima. Here he decided
to become a religious and, having given what was left of his savings
to his friends, he was accepted as a lay-brother by the Dominicans
of St Mary Magdalen's, a house of very strict observance. Brother
John's austerities exceeded the bounds of prudence, and his prior
had to insist on moderation : for he would content himself with one
hour of sleep, and that on his knees with his head on the bed, and
brought on himself a disease which required a painful and dangerous
operation. He was made porter and his lodge soon became the
meeting-place for the poor, the sick, and the wretched of the city ;
he begged alms with which to feed and physic them, and accompanied his ministrations with good advice and exhortations to good
life and the love of God. Those who were too shy to beg he sought
out in their homes, and to save time in begging from door to door he

trained the priory donkey to go round by itself and receive in its panniers food and clothing for his beloved poor. Many and remarkable were the miracles attributed to Blessed John Massias, and his death at the age of sixty was mourned by the whole city, the Archbishop of Lima and the Viceroy attending his funeral. He was beatified by Pope Gregory XVI in 1837.

On the occasion of the beatification in 1837 an Italian Life, *Vita de Beato Giovanni Massias* was published, without the name of the author, by the Dominicans in Rome. See also Procter, *Lives of Dominican Saints*, pp. 263–274. There is a fuller bibliography in Taurisano, *Catalogus Historicus O.P.*

SEPTEMBER 19

ST JANUARIUS, Bp. of Benevento, and his Companions, Martyrs

c. A.D. 305

ST JANUARIUS (Gennaro), a native some say of Naples, others of Benevento, was bishop of this latter city, when the persecution of Diocletian broke out. Sosius, deacon of Miseno, Proculus, deacon of Pozzuoli, and Eutyches and Acutius, eminent laymen, were imprisoned at Pozzuoli for the Faith by an order of Dracontius, governor of Campania, before whom they had confessed their faith. Sosius by his wisdom and sanctity had earned the intimate friendship of St Januarius, who for many years had found comfort in his counsel and conversation. Upon the news that this servant of God and several others were fallen into the hands of the persecutors, the bishop determined to make them a visit in order to comfort and encourage them ; in this act of charity no fear of torments or danger of his life could deter him, and martyrdom was his recompense. He did not escape the notice of the keepers, who gave information that someone from Benevento had visited the Christian prisoners. Timothy, who had succeeded Dracontius in the government of that district of Italy, gave orders that Januarius, whom he found to be the person, should be arrested and brought before him at Nola, which was accordingly done. Festus, the bishop's deacon, and Desiderius, a lector of his church, were also taken as they were making him a visit, and had a share in the interrogatories and torments which the good bishop underwent at Nola. Some time after the governor went to Pozzuoli, and these three confessors, loaded with heavy irons, were made to walk before his chariot to that town, where they were thrown into the same prison where the four martyrs already mentioned were detained. They had been condemned by an order from the Emperor to be torn in pieces by wild beasts, and were then lying in expectation of the execution of their sentence. The day after the arrival of St Januarius and his two companions all these champions of Christ were exposed to the beasts in the amphitheatre, but none of the savage animals could be provoked to touch them. The people were amazed and imputed their preservation to magic, and the martyrs were condemned to be beheaded. This sentence was executed near Pozzuoli, and the martyrs were buried near that town.

Some time after the Christian faith had become triumphant their relics were removed. The bodies of SS Proculus, Eutyches, and Acutius were placed in tombs at Pozzuoli ; those of SS Festus and Desiderius were translated to Benevento ; that of Sosius to Miseno, where it was afterward deposited in a church built in his honour. The city of Naples was so happy as to get possession of the relics of of St Januarius, which in the fifth century were brought from the little church of San Gennaro near the Solfatara. During the wars of the Normans they were removed, first to Benevento, and some time after to the abbey of Monte Vergine ; but in 1497 they were brought back to Naples, where he has long been honoured as principal patron. Among many miraculous deliverances which the city ascribes to the intercession of this saint none is looked upon as more remarkable than its preservation from the eruptions of Mount Vesuvius, which has often threatened the entire destruction of Naples. His intercession was sought on those occasions, and the divine mercy so wonderfully interposed and made the impending evils suddenly to cease, especially in 685, that the Greeks of southern Italy instituted a feast in honour of St Januarius, with two yearly solemn processions to return thanks to God.

No reliance can be placed upon the above particulars of the martyrdom of St Januarius ; all the recensions of his " acts " are late and untrustworthy ; nothing certain is known of him or of those who suffered with him. All the fame of Januarius rests upon that " standing miracle " (as Baronius called it), the liquefaction of the alleged relic of his blood which is preserved in the chapel of the Treasury of the cathedral-church of Naples, a happening of which there are records for the past four hundred years. The relic consists of a dark, solid, opaque mass which half fills the small glass phial in which it is contained, the phial itself being fixed in a metal reliquary. Eighteen times a year, in connection with the feast of the translation of the relics to Naples (Saturday before the first Sunday in May), the feast of the saint (September 19), and the anniversary of the averting of a threatened eruption of Vesuvius in 1631 (December 16), this relic is brought out and held by a priest in the presence of what is believed to be the martyr's head, exposed in a silver reliquary on the altar. Prayers are said by the people, especially as represented by a number of poor women who have a privileged position in the church and are known as the " aunts of St Januarius " (*zie di San Gennaro*). After a varying interval, from two minutes to an hour as a rule, the priest from time to time turning the reliquary upside down, the dark mass, hitherto solid and immovable, detaches itself from the sides of the glass, becomes liquid and reddish in colour, and sometimes froths, bubbles up, and increases in volume. This takes place not only in full view of the people but in close proximity to any accredited persons who may have been admitted to the sanctuary. The priest then announces, " The miracle has happened," *Te Deum* is sung, and the relic venerated by the congregation and clergy. Few, if any, alleged miracles have been examined more carefully, more often, or by people of more divergent views than this of the blood of St Januarius, and it may be safely affirmed that no expert inquirer, however rationalist in temper he may be, now denies that what is said to take place *does* take place. There is no trick, and there is as yet no completely satisfactory explanation (though many have been advanced, both by Catholics and others), except the explanation of miracle. But before a miracle may be certainly recognised all natural explanations must have been examined and found wanting, and all objections answered. Among the undoubted facts concerning this relic are the following :

1. The dark substance alleged to be the blood of St Januarius (which for more than 300 years has remained sealed up in a glass phial immovably set in a metal reliquary) does not always occupy the same volume. Sometimes the black and hard mass is seen almost completely to fill the phial, at other times there is a vacant space above it of more than a third of its bulk.

2. Concurrently with this variation in volume there is a variation in weight, which of late years has been tested in an accurate chemical balance. Taking the extremes which have been recorded, this variation has amounted to as much as 27 grammes.

3. The rapidity of the liquefaction seems to bear no ratio to the temperature of the atmosphere. Sometimes when the temperature has stood as high as 86° Fahrenheit, more than two hours have passed before any signs of liquefaction were observed. On the other hand, when the temperature has been 15° or even 20° lower than this, complete liquefaction has occurred in from 10 to 15 minutes.

4. The liquefaction does not always take place in the same way. Instances are recorded in which the liquefied contents seem almost to boil and are of a vivid crimson colour, while in other cases the colour is dull and the movement sluggish.

On the other hand, among the difficulties in the way of accepting the phenomenon as a miracle the following have been pointed out. The fact that a very large majority of all other blood-relics of which

similar behaviour seems to be true are found in the neighbourhood
of Naples ; and some of the relics, *e.g.* those of St John Baptist,
St Stephen, St Ursula, are almost certainly spurious. The relic
has seven times been known to liquefy while a jeweller was repairing
the reliquary, but often during the December exposition it has failed
to liquefy at all. The authenticity of the relic itself is extremely
problematical ; we have no record of the *cultus* of St Januarius
before the fifth century. Moreover there is the consideration, of
yet greater weight if the relic be not authentic, of the seeming pur-
poselessness of the marvel. Such a criticism may be levelled at
many other alleged miracles ; we cannot search the ways of God ;
and it is true that for centuries the liquefaction has been a standing
manifestation of His omnipotence for thousands of Neapolitans. But
it must also be remembered that marvels of this kind, so far from
being a help, are a definite hindrance to the faith of other people,
of different temperament but of no less good will : and these also
have souls to be saved.

Miracles recorded in holy Scripture are revealed facts, and an
object of faith. Other miracles are not considered in the same light,
neither does our faith in part rest upon them as upon the former,
though they illustrate and confirm it ; nor do they demand or admit
any higher assent than that which prudence requires and which is
due to the evidence of human authority, upon which they depend.
When such miracles are propounded, they are not to be rashly
admitted : the evidence of the fact and circumstances ought to be
examined to the bottom, and duly weighed ; where that fails it is
the part of prudence to suspend or refuse our assent. If it appears
doubtful whether an effect be natural or proceed from a supernatural
interposition, our assent ought to lean according to the greater weight
of probability, and God, who is author of all events natural and
supernatural, is always to be glorified. If human evidence set the
certainty of a miracle above the reach of any doubt, it must more
powerfully excite us to raise our minds to God in humble adoration,
love, and praise, and to honour Him in His saints, when by such
wonderful means He gives us tangible proofs of the glory to which
He exalts them and of the tenderness with which He watches over
their mortal remains, to raise them one day in a state of glorious
immortality.

The unsatisfactory " Acts " of St Januarius and companions are preserved to us in varying forms. The texts printed in the *Acta Sanctorum*,
September, vol. vi (but out of place, at the end of the volume), sufficiently
illustrate this diversity. On the other hand there can be no serious doubt
that a bishop named Januarius was really martyred somewhere near Naples,
and that he was venerated at an early date. Not only does the priest Uranius,

shortly after the year 431, allude to him in terms which imply that he was a great saint in heaven, on a footing with the famous St Martin of Tours, but a fifth-century representation of him in the so-called "catacomb of St Januarius " at Naples depicts him with a nimbus. His name also is entered on this day in the early calendars both of East and West. See the *Acta Sanctorum*, November, vol. ii, part 2, p. 517; and Pio Franchi de' Cavalieri, in *Studi e Testi*, vol. xxiv (1912), pp. 79–114.

The question of the liquefaction of the blood has of course been discussed again and again. For a vindication of the supernatural character of the prodigy, consult especially Taglialatela, *Memorie storico-critiche del Culto e del Sangue di S Gennaro* (Naples, 1893); Cavène, *Le célèbre miracle de S. Janvier à Naples et à Pouzzoles* (Paris, 1909); Alfano e Amitrano, *Il miracolo di S. Gennaro* (Napoli, 1924)—this last includes a vast bibliography of 1346 entries—and for English readers, Bishop E. P. Graham, *The Mystery of Naples* (St Louis, 1909); and Ian Grant, *The Testimony of Blood* (Lond., 1929). The point of view of those who question the miraculous nature of the liquefaction is set out in Isenkrahe, *Neapolitanische Blutwunder* (Regensburg, 1912) and in *The Month*, January, February and March, 1927 and February, 1930. The *Kirchliches Handlexikon* (edited by the present Bishop of Regensburg) states (vol. ii, col. 25), " a conclusive judgement in this matter can hardly be arrived at, but so far no natural explanation has been found."

SS. PELEUS AND HIS COMPANIONS, MARTS.

c. A.D. 310

The holy confessors who were condemned to the mines (*i.e.*, quarries) in Palestine during the course of the last general persecution built little oratories where they met for the divine service, which was their chief comfort under their sufferings. Firmilian, governor of Palestine, informed the Emperor Galerius of the liberty they had taken, and the tyrant sent an order that they should be sent, some to the mines in Cyprus, others to those in the Lebanon, and others to other places. Firmilian being in the meantime beheaded himself for his crimes, the officer upon whom the command devolved removed the servants of God to the new places of their banishment, according to the imperial rescript; but first he caused four of their number to be burnt alive. These were Peleus and Nilus, two Egyptian priests, Elias, also a priest, and an Egyptian layman of learning and reputation. These probably suffered at Phunon, near Petra, at the same time as St Tyrannio of Gaza and his companions. SS. Peleus and Nilus are mentioned (as bishops) in the Roman Martyrology again on February 20, with the martyrs at Tyre under Venturius in the year 304 and others.

Eusebius, *De Martyribus Palestinæ* (xiii, 3), is the main authority. See also B. Violet, *Die palästinischen Märtyrer des Eusebius von Cäsarea*, pp. 105–107.

ST EUSTOCHIUS, Bp. of Tours, Conf.

A.D. 461

Was descended from an illustrious family of Auvergne, and according to St Gregory of Tours, was "a man of outstanding holiness." He was raised to the see of Tours after the death of St Brice in 444, and strenuously defended in the Council of Angers the privileges of the Church, which were invaded by a law of Valentinian III. He had a principal share in drawing up the regulations made in that council concerning discipline. He increased the number of parishes in his diocese and the first building of churches at Brissac in Anjou, Iseure and Loches in Touraine, and other places is attributed to him. He also built in the city of Tours a church to shelter the relics of SS. Gervasius and Protasius, which St Martin had received from Italy. St Eustochius wrote a joint pastoral with the Bishops of Bourges and Le Mans denouncing those clergy who resorted to the civil courts. He died in 461 after ruling his see for seventeen years, and is named in the Roman Martyrology.

We know little of this bishop beyond what St Gregory of Tours tells us in his various writings. The passages are quoted in the *Acta Sanctorum*, September, vol. vi. See also Duchesne, *Fastes Épiscopaux*, vol. ii, p. 303.

ST SEQUANUS, Abbot and Conf.

c. A.D. 580

This holy monk, called in France St Seine, was born in the little town of Maymont in Burgundy. His parents gave him an excellent education, and permitted him to embrace an ecclesiastical state, to which he was inclined from his childhood. Having received the clerical tonsure from the hands of his pastor, he was for a time a solitary at Verrey-sous-Drée. He lived in a hut that he built himself from forest timber, and was said to break his fast every day only after having recited the whole Psalter. The sanctity of his life soon recommended him to the Bishop of Langres, who promoted him to the priesthood. The saint having suffered some persecution from the local clergy, who had envied his merit, he put himself under the direction of the holy abbot John, who governed the monastery of Réome, since called Moutier St Jean. Here he perfected himself in the study of the holy Scriptures, and in the practice of all religious virtues. After some time he built a monastery in the forest of Segestre, near the source of the river Seine, in the diocese of Langres. It was dedicated in honour of our Lady and the monks did much to civilise the people of the neighbourhood. A village which grew up around the abbey became known as Saint-Seine, after the founder, and the regular discipline which he established there rendered it famous and drew to it a number of disciples. God was pleased to honour him with the gift of miracles, which added new lustre to his sanctity. He died, according to the most probable opinion, on September 19, about the year 580. He is mentioned in the Martyrologies of Ado and Usuard under the name of St Sigon.

Under the form " depositio sancti Sigonis, presbyteri et confessoris," St Sequanus was commemorated already before the time of Ado in the *Hieronymianum ;* but he is called " Sequanus " by St Gregory of Tours, who mentions him at a still earlier date. There is an anonymous Life printed in the *Acta Sanctorum*, September, vol. vi, but its value as an historical source is very questionable.

ST GOERICUS, or ABBO, Bp. of Metz, Conf.

A.D. 647

During the seventh century there were two great saintly families in Aquitaine, Salvia and Ansbertina, and in the second of these was born St Goericus. He became an officer in the palace of Dagobert I and was a soldier of distinction, when he was suddenly smitten with blindness. After bearing his affliction with patience for a time he decided to make a pilgrimage to the church of St Stephen at Metz, of which city his relative St Arnulphus was bishop, in consequence of a vision which he believed he had had. He therefore set out with his two daughters, Precia and Victorina, was well received by Arnulphus, and, while praying in the church, his sight was restored. In thanksgiving Goericus built the church of St Peter Major and became a priest, and when St Arnulphus resigned his see in the year 627 he succeeded to it. St Goericus as a bishop followed the golden example of his predecessor, whom he would often visit in his retreat at Habendum (Remiremont) ; and when St Arnulphus died he translated his body with great pomp to his cathedral city, an occasion said to have been marked with miracles. St Goericus founded a nunnery at Epinal, of which his daughter Precia was first abbess, and three hundred years after his death his own relics were transferred to the same town.

A medieval Life of the usual unsatisfactory type is printed in the *Acta Sanctorum*, September, vol. vi. Goericus was in correspondence with Bishop Desiderius of Cahors (Migne, P. L., vol. 87, cc. 218 *seq.*). See also Duchesne, *Fastes Épiscopaux*, vol. iii, p. 56.

ST THEODORE, ABP. OF CANTERBURY, CONF.

A.D. 690

Theodore, sometimes called "the Philosopher," was a Greek, born at Tarsus in Cilicia (the birthplace of St Paul), the last early bishop of foreign birth to occupy the metropolitan throne of Canterbury and one of the greatest of its archbishops. After the death of St Deusdedit, sixth archbishop of Canterbury, in 664, Oswy, King of Northumbria, and Egbert, King of Kent, sent a virtuous and learned priest named Wighard to Rome that he might be consecrated bishop and duly confirmed to that see by the Pope himself. Wighard and most of those that attended him died in Italy of the plague, and St Vitalian, who then sat in St Peter's chair, chose Adrian, abbot of a monastery near Naples, to be raised to that dignity. This abbot was by birth an African, understood Greek and Latin perfectly, was thoroughly versed in theology and in the monastic and ecclesiastical discipline. But so great were his fears of the office to which he was called that the Pope was compelled by his entreaties to yield to his excuses. He insisted, however, that Adrian should find a person equal to the charge, and Adrian first named a monk called Andrew ; but he was judged incapable on account of his bodily infirmities, though otherwise a person extremely well qualified. Adrian then suggested another monk, Theodore of Tarsus, and he was accepted, but on condition that Adrian should accompany him to Britain, because he had already travelled twice through France and also to watch over Theodore lest he introduce into his church anything contrary to the Faith ("as the Greeks have a habit of doing," comments St Bede). Theodore was at that time sixty-six years old, well instructed in secular and sacred learning, and of exemplary life, and was not in holy orders. Being ordained subdeacon, he waited four months for his hair to grow, that it might be shaved in the form of a crown according to the Roman custom : from which it may be gathered that he had hitherto been a monk of the Eastern obedience and that his promotion involved what we should now call a "change of rite." At length Pope Vitalian consecrated him bishop on Sunday, March 26, 668, and recommended him to St Benedict Biscop, who was then a third time in Rome and whom the Pope obliged to return to England with SS Theodore and Adrian in order to be their guide and interpreter. They set out on May 27, went by sea to Marseilles, and from thence by land to Arles, where they were entertained by the archbishop, John, till Ebroin, mayor of the palace, had sent them permission to continue their journey.

St Theodore passed the winter at Paris with the bishop, Agilbert, who had formerly been bishop of Winchester, in England. From his conversation the new archbishop informed himself of the circumstances and necessities of the church of which he was going to take charge, and he also began to learn the English language. Egbert, King of Kent, hearing his new archbishop had arrived at Paris, sent one of the lords of his court to meet him, who, having obtained leave of Ebroin, took him to the port of Quentavic, now called Saint-Josse-sur-Mer; Theodore, falling sick, was obliged to stay there some time. As soon as he was able to travel he proceeded on his voyage, with St Benedict Biscop, and took possession of his see of Canterbury on Sunday, May 27, 669, a year to a day after leaving Rome. Adrian meanwhile was detained in France some time by Ebroin, who suspected that he was sent by the Emperor to the kings of England with some design against the Franks. He stayed a considerable time, first with St Emmo, Archbishop of Sens, and afterwards with St Faro, Bishop of Meaux. Ebroin being at last satisfied, he was permitted to follow St Theodore, by whom he was made abbot of SS. Peter and Paul's monastery (afterwards called St Augustine's) at Canterbury in succession to St Benedict Biscop, who resigned that abbacy in 671 to return to Rome. This Adrian was afterwards venerated as a saint.

St Theodore made a general visitation of all the churches of the English nation, taking with him the abbot Adrian. He was everywhere well received and heard with attention; and wherever he came he established sound morality, confirmed the discipline of the Catholic Church in the celebration of Easter, and introduced the Gregorian or Roman chant in the divine offices, till then known in few of the English churches except those of Kent. He regulated all other things belonging to the divine service, reformed abuses, and ordained bishops in all places where they were wanting. When he came into Northumbria he had to deal with the difficulties that had arisen between St Wilfrid and St Chad, both of whom laid claim to the see of York. St Theodore judged that Chad had been improperly consecrated, to which he replied that he had been ordained against his inclination, confessed himself unworthy of that dignity, and retired with joy to his monastery of Lastingham. But St Theodore made him bishop of the Mercians, or Lichfield, when that see became vacant by the death of Jaruman. St Wilfrid was confirmed as the true bishop of York, to ensure the support of whose pro-Roman policy against the Celtic elements in Northumbria was probably the principal reason for St Adrian's being sent to England with Theodore. He penetrated to the stronghold of Celtic influence at

Lindisfarne and there consecrated the church in honour of St Peter. During these journeys he is said to have ordered that every head of a household should each day say with his family the Our Father and the Creed in the vulgar tongue.

St Theodore was the first bishop whom the whole English church obeyed, the first metropolitan of all England, and his fame penetrated into the remotest corners of the land. Many students gathered round these two foreign prelates who knew Greek as well as Latin, for Theodore and Adrian themselves expounded the Scriptures and taught all the sciences, particularly astronomy and arithmetic (for calculating Easter), and to compose Latin verses. Many under them became as perfect in the Latin and Greek languages as they were in their own tongue. Britain had never been in so happy a condition as at this time since the English first set foot in the island. The kings were so brave, says Bede, that all the barbarous nations dreaded their power ; and men such good Christians that they aspired only after the joys of the kingdom of Heaven which had been but lately preached to them. All who desired to learn could find instructors, and it is hard to know whether to admire more the zeal and un-wearied labours of the pastors or the docility, humility, and ardour of the people, with whom to hear, to learn, and to practise seemed one and the same thing.

Theodore gave to the long vacant see of Rochester a bishop in the person of Putta, who was particularly skilled in the Roman chant, which he had learnt from the disciples of St Gregory him-self, and authorised the inclusion of all Wessex in the see of Win-chester. Then, in 673, he held the first national council of the English Church, at Hertford. There were present at this council, under the presidency of the primate, Bisi, Bishop of the East Angles, Putta of Rochester, Eleutherius of Wessex, Winfrid of the Mercians, and the proxies of St Wilfrid. St Theodore addressed them, saying : " I beseech you, most dear brethren, in the love and fear of our Redeemer, that we may all treat in common for our faith to the end that whatsoever has been decreed and defined by the holy and venerable Fathers may be inviolably observed by all." He then produced a book of ecclesiastical canons of which ten were marked as being of special importance to England. The first one was that Easter should everywhere be kept on the Sunday after the full moon which occurs on or next after March 21, in accordance with the Council of Nicæa and against the Celtic recalcitrants. Other canons restrained bishops with respect to one another and to monasteries, confined monks to the houses of their profession and clergy to their dioceses, and affirmed the Christian law of marriage. All these canons were approved, together with one that provided for an annual synod of the bishops, to meet every August 1 at Clovesho.* Another provincial council held by St Theodore, ten years later at Hatfield, was convened in order that he might safeguard the purity of the faith of his clergy from any taint of Monophysite errors. After discussing the theology of the mystery of the Incarnation the members of the council expressed their adherence to the first five œcumenical councils and their abhorrence of the heresies condemned thereat.

Two years previously, 678, " the year of the comet," trouble had arisen between Egfrid, King of the Northumbrians, and St Wilfrid, who had supported the king's wife, St Etheldreda, in her desire to retire to a convent. St Wilfrid's administration of his huge diocese had not been altogether well received, even by those who sympathised with his aims, and St Theodore took this to be a good opportunity to assert his metropolitan authority in the north. He therefore ordered that three suffragan sees should be carved out of the diocese of York, and in concert with King Egfrid proceeded to appoint bishops thereto. St Wilfrid objected and appealed to Rome, going off to conduct his case in person, while Theodore consecrated new bishops in the cathedral of York and still further divided the diocese. Pope St Agatho decided in favour of Wilfrid : that he was to be restored to his undivided see but that auxiliary bishops were to be given him to assist in its government. However, King Egfrid refused to accept the Pope's decision on the ground that it had been bought, and St Wilfrid went into exile, eventually to evangelise the South Saxons. St Theodore, so far as is known, did not attempt to stop Egfrid's high-handed action, and a few years later consecrated St Cuthbert as bishop of Lindisfarne in the cathedral at York. Any injustice that he may have been guilty of herein was atoned for in the closing years of his life, when with St Erconwald he met St Wilfrid in London, and it was agreed that he should again govern York but in its smaller extent ; St Theodore wrote to King Ethelred of Mercia and to King Aldfrid of Northumbria recommending St Wilfrid to them, and to St Elfleda, abbess of Whitby, and others who had opposed Wilfrid or were interested parties ; and he had the happiness of seeing his efforts successful.

* The identity of this place has never yet been discovered, but a number of these synods were held there. The first of which we have any authentic evidence was, however, sixty-nine years after the Council of Hertford, in 742 ; between that date and 825 six more are known of, and they are of considerable importance in the history of the early English Church.

Theodore had been a personal friend of Ethelred of Mercia ever since he had brought about peace between him and Egfrid in 679. In that year war broke out between the Northumbrians and the Mercians, and a battle was fought near the Trent, in which Elfwin, the young brother of Egfrid, was slain. At this news St Theodore, relying upon the divine assistance, immediately set out to try to extinguish the flame of a war which both kings were bent on carrying on with greater fury than before. The authority of the good bishop and the religious motives which he made use of disarmed them both, and Theodore was so happy as to make a firm and cordial peace between the two provinces upon no other condition than that of paying the usual tribute to King Egfrid for the loss of his brother. In the above-mentioned letter to Ethelred St Theodore asks him to come and visit him, that he may see his pleasant face and bless him once more before he dies.

St Theodore's great achievements were all in the sphere of active organisation and administration, and the only literary work that bears his name is a collection of disciplinary decisions and canons called the *Penitential of Theodore*, and this was his work only in part. In it is given a summary account of the discipline of the Western and Eastern churches, and we learn that in England in his day one year's canonical penance was imposed for fornication, three for adultery, and seven for murder, and that the " month's mind " for a person deceased signified not merely the requiem Mass celebrated a month after death, but constant prayer for the dead one's soul throughout that period. When a monk died his breast was anointed with chrism when he had been carried to the church, and a requiem was celebrated on the first, third, ninth, and thirtieth day, and at the year's end ; Mass was likewise offered for the laity and accompanied by fasting.

It is sometimes said that St Theodore of Canterbury organised the parochial system in England, but this is far from being true. The parish system in this country was one of very slow growth, over a long period of time and under several influences, and was not the work of any one man. What he did do was to find the Church in this country a missionary body, distressed by faction and with no particular cohesion, and to leave it, after twenty-one years' episcopate, a properly organised province of the Catholic Church, divided into dioceses which looked to Canterbury as their metropolitan see. The work he did remained for eight hundred and fifty years his monument, and is still the basis of the hierarchical organisation of the Protestant Church of England. He died on September 19, 690, and was buried in the abbey-church of SS. Peter and Paul at Canterbury, the Greek monk nigh to his first predecessor the Roman monk, Augustine. " To say all in a few words," says St Bede, " the English churches prospered more during the pontificate [of Theodore] than ever they had done before." This has not been forgotten, and his feast is to-day observed in seven of our English dioceses.

The main authority, of course, is Bede's Ecclesiastical History, which has been in many points elucidated by C. Plummer's valuable commentary ; and second to this Eddius's *Vita Wilfridi*. Much has been published in England of recent years bearing upon the period of St Theodore's activities, but, apart from some fresh archæological illustrations which they supply, such books as G. Forrest Browne's *Theodore and Wilfrith*, Sir Henry Howorth's *Golden Days of English Church History* and Canon Bright's chapters on *Early English Church History* are apt to exhibit a pronounced anti-Roman bias. As for Theodore's share in the " Penitential " attributed to him, the researches of Paul Fournier, culminating in his *Histoire des Collections canoniques en Occident* (1931–2), tend to render the Archbishop's personal connection with even that part of the code assigned him by Wassersleben and Stubbs extremely doubtful.

BD. MARY OF CERVELLIONE, Virg.

A.D. 1290

Is venerated as the first nun of the order of our Lady of Ransom (Mercedarians). She was the daughter of a Spanish nobleman of Barcelona, and is said to have been born to her childless parents at the prayers of St Peter Nolasco, who is credited with founding that order. A sermon by the Mercedarian Blessed Bernard Corbaria on the hardships and outrages suffered by Christian slaves at the hands of the Moors and Saracens inspired her to devote her life to their cause. In 1265 she joined a community of women who lived under the direction of Blessed Bernard and reinforced the work of the Mercedarians by their prayers. These were formed into a third order regular of our Lady of Ransom, and Blessed Mary of Cervellione was their first prioress. The assiduity of her prayers and her generosity in temporal good works caused her to be called *Maria de Socos*, Mary of Help, the name by which she is still commonly known in Spain, where she is venerated also as a patroness of seamen, especially those in danger of shipwreck. Blessed Mary died at Barcelona in 1290. Many miracles were claimed at her tomb and her *cultus* was confirmed by Pope Alexander VIII in 1690. The Roman Martyrology says that she is called Mary of Help " because of her present aid to them that call upon her."

A short Latin Life by Juan de Laes and Guillermo Vives was printed in the *Acta Sanctorum*, September, vol. vii, but its apocryphal character is now hardly disputed by serious investigators. The fact is that the story of Maria de Socos has got mixed up with the notorious forgeries which marked the attempts to create an imposing record for the early developments of the Mercedarian Order. See the January volume of this series, p. 395. It was in the folio *Vida de d. Maria de Corveilon*, by Estevan de Corbera (1639), that many of the impugned documents, together with that known as " de los sellos," first saw the light. The author of the Life, and other biographers who followed, may have been imposed upon, but it is only too plain that the *hechos maravillosas* attributed to Bd. Maria de Socos must be for the most part suspect.

BD. ALPHONSUS D'OROSCO, CONF.

A.D. 1591

The Protestant and nationalist sentiment which informs popular history in England has made of King Philip II of Spain a sinister figure, that of a wicked and unscrupulous tyrant. In his own country, on the contrary, he is regarded as a man of great wisdom and prudence, and more than half a saint. Both estimates are exaggerated, though that of the Spaniards is considerably nearer the truth. Philip was a fervent Catholic, and both by circumstances and choice the chief defender of the Faith and opponent of heresy in his time. It was his will that his court and his nobles should be fervently Catholic too, and in the task of maintaining a high standard of austerity and devotion among a sixteenth-century aristocracy no churchman was more enthusiastic or more effective than this Augustinian friar, Blessed Alphonsus d'Orosco. He was born at Oropesa in the diocese of Avila in the year 1500, and so early as six years of age made up his mind that he wanted to be a priest. He studied at Talavera and Toledo, and then went on to the University of Salamanca, where he attended the sermons of St Thomas of Villanova. By him he was attracted to the religious life and to the Hermits of St Augustine in particular, and when he was twenty-two he was clothed with the habit of that order.

For thirty years after his profession Friar Alphonsus was engaged in teaching, preaching, and the other activities of his state, and his success and shining goodness made him in great request as a confessor. He was four times prior of different houses, and then in 1554, the year in which Philip married Queen Mary of England, he was sent to take charge of the Augustinian priory in the royal city of Valladolid. Two years later the Emperor Charles V, who himself valued the direction of Blessed Alphonsus, transferred the

Spanish crown to his son Philip, and the friar was appointed court preacher. He at once began exercising his beneficent influence over the nobility, attracting them to his sermons by the quality both of his preaching and of his music, of which he was very fond. In 1561 King Philip definitely established his court at Madrid, declaring that city to be the *unica corte* and sole capital of Spain, and Blessed Alphonsus went along with the court. He had a cell in the friary of San Felipe el Real, where he lived a life of great austerity and simplicity, in sharp contrast with the official functions of the court in which of necessity he had to take part. While he was prior at Seville in his earlier days Blessed Alphonsus had had a vision of our Lady, in which she had told him that he was to use his pen for the glory of God and the salvation of souls. This he did thenceforth with great application. Every year he produced a work on the blessed Mother of God herself, and was the author of numerous mystical and other treatises which fill seven large volumes, and range him among the great Spanish mystics of the sixteenth century. At the order of his superiors he also wrote an account of his own religious experiences which, lest he should seem to lack in humility, he called his " Confessions." For thirty-five years he continued his good work in maintaining Christian life among the nobility and gentry and also among the lesser folk of the Spanish court ; they flocked to his sermons and his confessional, and read his writings, and when he died at the age of ninety-one followed his coffin to its burial with unfeigned lamenting. Blessed Alphonsus d'Orosco was beatified by Pope Leo XIII in 1882.

The literary quality of the Augustinian friar's writings as well as their devotional appeal have helped to make him well remembered. T. Cámara in 1882 brought out a volume dealing with his *Vida y Escritos*, which has been translated into German. See also J. Ag. Fariña, *Doctrina de Oración del B. Alfonso* (1927), and further a sketch in the *Katholik* of Mainz, 1882, vol. ii, pp. 375–411.

SEPTEMBER 20

ST EUSTACE AND HIS COMPANIONS, MARTS.

A.D. 118 (?)

ST EUSTACE (Eustachius) is among the most famous martyrs of the Church, venerated for many centuries in both East and West. He is one of the Fourteen Holy Helpers, a patron of hunting men, and at least since the ninth century has given his name to the titular church of a cardinal-deacon at Rome. But there is nothing that can be said of him with any sort of certainty. His quite unreliable seventh-century legend relates that he was a Roman general under Trajan, by name Placidus, and while out hunting one day he saw coming towards him a stag, between whose antlers appeared a figure of Christ on the cross (which incident was afterwards borrowed and incorporated in the legend of St Hubert), and a voice issuing therefrom calling him by name. This is said to have occurred at Guadagnolo, between Tivoli and Palestrina. Placidus was at once converted by the vision and received baptism with his whole family. His own name he changed to Eustachius, that of his wife Tatiana to Theopistis, and his sons to Agapitus and Theopistus. Eustace is said to have distinguished himself by his great liberality to the poor, and after various misfortunes he and his family were martyred by being confined in a brazen bull wherein they were roasted to death, for refusing to sacrifice after a victory of the imperial arms.

In the histories of the Christian martyrs we continually see integrity and faith triumphing over self-interest, passion, and death, and setting the whole world at defiance ; we see great men preferring the least duty of justice, truth, or religion to the favour or menaces of princes, readily quitting estates, friends, country, and life rather than consent to anything against conscience : and at the same time meek, humble, and modest in their sufferings, forgiving from the heart the most unjust and treacherous enemies and persecutors. Passion and revenge often make men eager and enthusiastic : and the lust for power, worldly honour, or wealth may prompt them to brave dangers ; but these passions leave them weak and unscrupulous, and often reduce them to the basest slavery, crimes, and

266

misery. Religion is the only basis on which true large-heartedness
and courage can stand. It enlightens the mind so as to set a man above
human events and to keep him in all changes and trials steady and
calm in himself ; it secures him against the errors and injustices of
the world, and is by its power the strongest spur to generous actions.
In affliction and suffering it is a source of unalterable peace and joy,
which spring from an assured confidence that God's will is always
most just and holy, and that He will be its protector and rewarder.
Does religion exert this powerful influence in us ? Does it appear in
our hearts, in our actions and conduct ? It is not enough to encounter
dangers with resolution ; we must with equal courage and perseverance set ourselves against the enticements of pleasure, innocent
dissipation, and easy-goingness, or we do not possess the virtue of
true fortitude.

Popular as was the legend of St Eustace—the number of different
recensions both in prose and verse prove this—even the historical existence
of the martyr must remain a matter of doubt. The cult is not early, nor
can its origins be clearly located. It probably came from the East ; but it
had been adopted in Rome before the first half of the eighth century.
The legend has been very thoroughly analysed by Père Delehaye in the
Bulletin de l'Académie royale de Belgique, classe des Lettres, 1919, pp. 175–
210. The attempt of A. H. Krappe, *La Leggenda di S. Eustachio* (1929), to
link it up with the Dioscuri is altogether futile. For St Eustace in art see
Künstle, *Ikonographie*, vol. ii, pp. 220–221 ; and for the folklore see Bächtold-Stäubli ; *Handwörterbuch d. deutsch. Aberglaubens.*

ST VINCENT MADELGARUS, Abbot and Conf.

A.D. 677

The feast of this saint, under the name of Madelgarus, is kept
in Artois and Hainault on the date of his death, July 14, but in
Flanders, as Vincent of Soignies, he is venerated on September 20.
He was born into the family of the Counts of Hainault at Strépy-
les-Binches in the year 615, and became the husband of St Waldetrudis (Vaudry). They had four children, all venerated as saints,
namely Landericus or Landry, Madelberta, Aldetrudis, and Dente-
linus. About 653 his wife became a nun, and Madelgarus took the
Benedictine habit and the name of Vincent in the monastery of
Hautmont, which he founded. He later established another abbey
at Soignies, where he died in 677.

His biography was written in the abbey of Hautmont in the
twelfth century, and in his *Légendes Hagiographiques* Père Delehaye
refers to it at some length *à propos* of deliberate plagiarisms in the

Lives of saints, as distinct from accidental coincidences. He says (Mrs. Crawford's trans.) : " The naïve hagiographers of the Middle Ages, compelled to supplement the paucity of primitive sources by more or less legitimate means, do not introduce us to any very embarrassing dilemmas. As a rule their methods are simple, and their secrets are easily surprised. The following, for example, shows the process by which the biographer of St Vincent Madelgarus honoured his patron with a literary composition of adequate dimensions.

" In the preface he begins by transcribing the prologue from the Life of St Erminus, to which he adds a phrase from Sulpicius Severus ; there follows a second introduction which reproduces, word for word, St Gregory of Tours's preface to the Life of St Patroclus. In order to describe the birth and early years of the saint, he accumulates reminiscences from the life of St Erminus, without speaking of others from members of St Vincent's own family, St Waldetrudis and St Aldegondis, while the history of his marriage is extracted literally from the *Vita Leobardi* by Gregory of Tours. Vincent's son Landry embraces the ecclesiastical state : this is taken from the Life of St Gallus by Gregory of Tours. The same author furnishes him with the greater part of a vision, which fills one of the chapters in the life of St Leobardus. St Vincent enters on the religious life and trains his followers : taken from the lives of SS. Martius and Quintianus by Gregory of Tours. He gives himself up to prayer and penance and practises all the religious virtues : taken from the life of St Bavo. Knowing himself to be on the point of death he confides his spiritual children to his son Landry : taken from the life of St Ursmar. He is buried within his monastery where he exercises his power on behalf of the faithful who invoke him : taken from the life of St Bavo. A blind cleric recovers his sight on his tomb : this miracle is appropriated in its entirety from Gregory of Tours, who relates it of St Martin. We must add, moreover, to our plagiarist's account six chapters from the Life of St Waldetrudis, which, it is true, served him as an historic source, but which he transcribes word for word, besides numerous other reminiscences which it would take too long to enumerate.

" The lives of saints filled with extracts from other lives of saints are exceedingly numerous, and some are nothing more than a mere hagiographic anthology. . . ."

One biography of the Saint was printed by the Bollandists in their third volume for July ; but a somewhat older version, possibly of the tenth century, has been edited by them in *Analecta Bollandiana*, vol. xii (1893), pp. 422–440. In this on p. 425 the dependence of the Life on other texts has been pointed out in detail.

BD. FRANCIS POSSADAS, Conf.

A.D. 1713

Was born at Cordova in 1644 and brought up by his parents to the idea that he should become a religious, in particular a Friar Preacher, a prospect that was more than attractive to him. But on the death of his father his mother married again, and his stepfather decided that the studies on which he was engaged were a waste of time. He therefore made Francis give them up and apprenticed him to a trade. His master at first treated him very roughly, but Francis won him over by patience and good temper and by sticking to his work, and eventually the master even helped him to get on with his studies in his spare time. When his stepfather also died, Francis had to devote himself to the care of his mother for a time, but in 1663 was able to enter the Dominican noviciate at the convent of Scala Cœli in Cordova. For a time his experience here was not happy. He was misunderstood by his fellows and made the butt of ridicule and petty persecution ; he persevered, was professed, and admitted to the priesthood at Saint-Lucar de Barmeja. Francis at once made his mark as a preacher and he was hailed as a second Vincent Ferrer. He gave missions all over the south-west of Spain, adding to the fatigues of preaching, hearing confessions, and travelling on foot voluntary mortifications of a most rigorous kind. His combination of example and precept won him a great influence over all with whom he came in contact, and in his native city he brought about a much-needed reform and improvement in public and private morals ; disorderly places of amusement shut up for lack of business. He was always at the service of the poor and learned from them an humility that made him avoid not only the offices of his order but also the bishoprics of Alghero in Sardinia and of Cadiz that were offered to him. Blessed Francis wrote several books—*The Triumph of Chastity*, Lives of St Dominic and other holy ones of his order, moral exhortations—and died at Scala Cœli after forty years of uninterrupted work for souls on September 20, 1713. He was beatified by Pope Pius VII a little over a hundred years later.

Following close upon the beatification in 1817, Father Vicenzo Sopena published in Rome a *Vita del B. Francesco de Posadas.* It contains amongst other things an interesting account of his levitations (pp. 42–45) when he was saying Mass, and of his own sensations in endeavouring to resist this lifting of his body into the air. See also Martinez-Vigil, *La Orden de Predicadores* (Madrid, 1884), pp. 352 *seq. ;* and a short notice in Procter, *Dominican Saints*, pp. 263–265. For a fuller bibliography consult Taurisano, *Catalogus Hagiographicus O.P.*

SEPTEMBER 21

ST MATTHEW, Apostle and Evangelist

FIRST CENTURY

ST MATTHEW is called by two evangelists Levi, and by St Mark "the son of Alpheus"; it is probable that Levi was his original name and that he took, or was given, that of Matthew ("the gift of Yahveh") when he became a follower of our Lord. But Alpheus his father was not he of the same name who was father of St James the Less. He seems to have been a Galilæan by birth, and was by profession a publican, or gatherer of taxes for the Romans, a profession which was infamous to the Jews, especially those of the Pharisees' party, for the publicans were regarded as enemies to the national freedom which God had given them, as defiled by their frequent dealings with the pagans, and as conspiring with the Romans to entail slavery upon the Jewish people. Moreover, they were in general so grasping and extortionate that they were no more popular among the Gentiles. The Jews abhorred them to the extent of refusing to marry into a family which had a publican among its members, banished them from communion in religious worship, and shunned them in all affairs of civil society and commerce. But it is certain that St Matthew was a Jew, as well as a publican, and he carried on business at Capharnaum.

The story of Matthew's call is told in his own gospel. Jesus had just confounded some of the Scribes by curing a man who was sick of the palsy, and passing on saw the despised publican in his customhouse. "And He saith to him, ' Follow me.' And he arose up and followed Him." Matthew was probably rich, had a lucrative post, was a prudent man, and perfectly understood what his compliance would cost him and what an exchange he made of wealth for poverty. But he left all his interests and relations to become our Lord's disciple and to embrace a spiritual commerce. We cannot suppose that he was before wholly unacquainted with our Saviour's person or doctrine, especially as his office was near Capharnaum, where Christ had resided for some time and had preached and wrought many miracles, by which no doubt Matthew was in some measure prepared to receive the impression which the call of Christ made upon him.

St Jerome says that a certain shiningness and air of majesty which appeared in the countenance of our divine Redeemer pierced his soul and strongly attracted him. But the great cause of his conversion was, as St Bede remarks, that " He who called him outwardly by His word at the same time moved him inwardly by the invisible instinct of His grace."

The calling of St Matthew happened in the second year of the public ministry of Christ, who adopted him into that holy family of the apostles, the spiritual princes and founders of His Church. It may be noted that whereas the other evangelists in describing the Apostles by pairs rank Matthew before St Thomas, he places that apostle before himself and in this list adds to his own name the epithet of " the publican." He followed our Lord throughout His earthly life, and after His ascension preached for several years in Judea and the neighbouring countries till the dispersion of the Apostles ; and a little before this dispersion, according to Eusebius, he wrote his gospel or short history of our blessed Redeemer, at the entreaty of the Jewish converts and in the Aramaic language which they spoke. We are not told that Christ gave any charge about committing to writing His history or doctrine, but it was, nevertheless, by special inspiration of the Holy Ghost that this work was undertaken and executed by each of the four evangelists, and the gospels are the most excellent part of the sacred writings. For in them Christ teaches us, not by His prophets but by His own mouth, the great lessons of faith and of eternal life ; and in the history of His life the perfect pattern of sanctity is set before our eyes for us to strive after.

It is said that St Matthew, after having made a great harvest of souls in Judea, went to preach the faith to the barbarous nations of the East. St Ambrose says that God opened to him the country of the Persians. Rufinus and Socrates tell us that he carried the gospel into Ethiopia, meaning probably the parts of Asia south of the Caspian Sea. St Paulinus mentions that he ended his course in Parthia, where Venantius Fortunatus relates that he suffered martyrdom ; but other authorities say he died a natural death. He is venerated by the Church as a martyr, though the time, place, and circumstances of his end are unknown. Portions of his relics are claimed by St Mary Major, the cathedral of Salerno, and other churches. The Fathers find a figure of the four evangelists in the four living animals mentioned by Ezechiel and in the Apocalypse of St John. The eagle is generally said to represent St John himself, who in the first lines of his gospel soars up to the contemplation of the eternal generation of the Word. The ox agrees to St Luke, who begins his gospel with the mention of the sacrificing priesthood. Some make the lion the symbol of St Matthew, who explains the royal dignity of Christ ; but others give it to St Mark, and the man to St Matthew, who begins his gospel with Christ's human generation.

The account of St Matthew furnished in the *Acta Sanctorum*, September, vol. vi, is largely taken up with the discussion of his alleged relics and their translations to Salerno and other places. How little trust can be placed in such traditions may be judged from the fact that four different churches in France have claimed to be in possession of the head of the Apostle. A long apocryphal narrative of his preaching and martyrdom has been edited by M. Bonnet, *Acta Apostolorum apocrypha* (1898), vol. ii, part 1, pp. 217–262, and there is another much shorter in the Bollandists. The Roman Martyrology describes his martyrdom as having taken place " in Æthiopia," but in the *Hieronymianum* he is said to have suffered " in Persia in the town of Tarrium." This according to von Gutschmid is a misreading for Tarsuana, which Ptolemy places in Caramania, the region east of the Persian Gulf. In contrast to the varying dates assigned to the other apostles, St Matthew's feast seems uniformly to have been kept in the West on this day (September 21). Already in the time of Bede, we find a homily of his assigned for this particular feast (see Morin in the *Revue Bénédictine*, vol. ix (1892), p. 325). On the symbols of the evangelist see *Dictionnaire d'Archéologie chrét.*, vol. v, cc. 845–852. To St Matthew, according to St Jerome and St Augustine, is allotted the figure of a man because his gospel begins with the genealogy of Christ, emphasising His human origin.

ST MAURA, Virg.

A.D. 850

She was nobly born at Troyes in Champagne in the year 827, and in her youth obtained of God by her prayers the conversion of her father, who had till then led a worldly life. After his happy death, Maura continued to live in dutiful obedience to her mother, Sedulia, and by the fervour of her example was the sanctification of her brother Eutropius, who became bishop of Troyes, and of the whole family. The greatest part of the revenues of their large estate was converted into the patrimony of the poor. The maiden's whole time was consecrated to prayer, to offices of obedience or charity in attending on her mother and serving the poor, or to her work, which was devoted to the service of the needy and of the Church : it was her delight in a spirit of religion to make sacred vestments, clean the lamps, and prepare wax candles and other things for the altar. As order in what we do leads a soul to God, according to the remark of St Augustine, she was regular in the distribution of her time and in all her actions. She spent almost the whole morning in the church, adoring God, praying to her divine Redeemer, and meditating on His sacred life and passion. Every Wednesday and Friday she fasted, allowing herself no other food than bread and water, and she sometimes walked barefoot to the monastery of Mantenay, two leagues from the town, to open the secrets of her soul to the holy abbot of that place, who was her spiritual director and without whose advice she did nothing. The profound respect with which she was penetrated for the word of God and whatever regarded the honour of His name is not easily to be expressed, and so wonderful was her gift of tears that she seemed never to fall upon her knees to pray but they streamed from her eyes. God performed miracles in her favour, but it was her care to conceal His gifts, because she dreaded human applause. In her last sickness she received the Extreme Unction and Viaticum with divine joy and love and, often reciting the Lord's Prayer, died as she pronounced the words, " Thy kingdom come," on September 21, 850, being twenty-three years old. The relics of St Maura are preserved in the churches of St Martin at Tours and of the village of Sainte-Maure, near Gournay, and she is the local patroness of cloth-fullers.

The *Acta Sanctorum*, September, vol. vi, print a short Life by St Prudentius, Bishop of Troyes, who died in 861. See also Em. Socard, *Ste Maure de Troyes et son tombeau* (1867).

BD. LAURENCE IMBERT, Titular Bp. of Capsa, and his Companions, the Martyrs of Corea

A.D. 1839

Corea, that mountainous peninsula between Manchuria and Japan, is probably the only country in the world to which Christianity was first introduced otherwise than by Christian missionaries. During the eighteenth century some Chinese Christian books were brought into the country, and a man who had read them joined the embassy from Seoul to Pekin in 1784, sought out Mgr. de Gouvea there, and from him received baptism. He returned to his own country and when, ten years later, a Chinese priest, James Tijou, came to Corea he found four thousand Christians awaiting him. He was their only pastor for seven years, and after he was killed or exiled in 1801 they were without a priest for thirty years. A letter is extant written by the Coreans to Pope Pius VII, imploring him to send them priests at once; their little flock had already given martyrs to the Church. In 1831 the vicariate apostolic of Corea was created, but the first vicar never reached there. His successor, Mgr. Laurence Joseph Mary Imbert, a member of the Paris Foreign Missions who had been in China for twelve years, entered the country in disguise at the end of 1837, having been preceded by BLESSED PETER PHILIBERT MAUBANT and BLESSED JAMES HONORÉ CHASTAN, priests of the same missionary society.

Christianity was now definitely proscribed in Corea, and for two years the missionaries went about their work with complete secrecy. Of its circumstances and difficulties Mgr. Imbert wrote : " I am overwhelmed with fatigue and in great danger. I get up at half-past two every morning. At three I call the people of the house to prayers, and at half-past I begin the duties of my ministry by baptising, if there are any converts, or by giving Confirmation. Then come Mass, communion, and thanksgiving. The fifteen to twenty people who have received the sacraments can thus get away before daybreak. During the day about as many come in, one by one, for confession, and do not go until the next morning after communion. I stay two days in each house, where I get the Christians together, and before it is light I go on to another. I suffer a great deal from hunger : for it is no easy matter in this cold and wet climate to get up at half-past two and then wait until noon for a meal which is poor, insufficient, and lacking in nourishment. After dinner I rest a little until I have to take my senior scholars in theology, and finally I hear confessions again until nightfall. At nine o'clock I go to bed —on a mat on the floor with a Tartary wool blanket ; there are no bedsteads or matresses in Corea. In spite of my weak body and poor health I have always led a hard and very busy life : but here I think I have reached the positive limit of work. You will well understand that, leading a life like this, we scarcely fear the sword-stroke that may at any time end it." By these heroic means the Christians in Corea were increased by a half, roughly from 6000 to 9000, in less than two years. What was going on soon became known, and a decree for their extermination was published. An example of the horrors that took place is provided by BLESSED AGATHA KIM, one of the seventy-six Coreans beatified with the three priests. She was asked if it were true that she practised the Christian religion. " I know Jesus and Mary," she replied, " but I know nothing else."—" If you are tortured you will give up this Jesus and Mary."—" If I have to die I will not." She was long and cruelly tormented and at last sentenced to death. A tall cross of wood was fixed to a cart and to this cross Blessed Agatha was hung by her arms and hair. The cart was driven off and at the top of a steep and very rough slope the oxen were pricked up and the cart sent lurching and jolting down, the woman swinging at every movement with all her weight on her hair and wrists. At the place of execution she was stripped naked, her head forced down on to a block, and there cut off. BLESSED JOHN RI wrote from prison : " Two or three months passed before the judge sent for me, and I became sad and anxious. The sins of my whole life, when I had so often offended God from sheer wickedness, seemed to weigh me down like a mountain, and I wondered to myself, ' What will be the end of all this ? ' But I never lost hope. On the tenth day of the twelfth moon I was brought before the judge and he ordered me to be bastinadoed. How could I have borne it by my own strength alone ? But the strength of God and the prayers of Mary and the saints and all our martyrs upheld me, so that I believe I scarcely suffered at all. I cannot repay such a mercy, and to offer my life is only just." To avert a general massacre and its attendant danger of apostasy, Mgr. Imbert allowed himself to be taken and recommended M. Maubant and M. Chastan to do the same. This they did, after writing letters to the Congregation of Propaganda at Rome explaining their action and giving an account of their charge. They were all three bastinadoed, then carried on chairs to the banks of the river which flows around Seoul, tied back to back to a post, and there beheaded. This was on September 21, 1839, but their feast is kept by the Paris Foreign Missions on the 26th. In the year 1904 the relics of eighty-one martyrs of Corea were translated to the episcopal church of the vicar apostolic at Seoul, and in 1925 Blessed Laurence and his companions were beatified by Pope Pius XI.

In C. Dallet, *L'Histoire de l'Eglise de Corée* (1874), especially vol. ii, pp. 118–185, the life and sufferings of these martyrs are recounted in detail. See also Launay, *Les Missionnaires français en Corée* (1895) ; and Kempf, *The Holiness of the Church in the Nineteenth Century* (Eng. Tr.), pp. 350–355.

SEPTEMBER 22

ST THOMAS OF VILLANOVA, Abp. of Valencia, Conf.

A.D. 1555

ST THOMAS, a glory of the church of Spain, was born at Fuentellana in Castile in 1488, but received his surname from Villanueva de los Infantes, a town where he was brought up about two miles from the place of his birth. His parents, Alonzo Tomas Garcia and Lucia Martinez Castellanos, were also originally of Villanueva ; the father was a miller and their state was not affluent, but it contented them and their prudent frugality enabled them liberally to assist the poor. Instead of selling that corn which was not necessary for the subsistence of the family, they made bread of it, which they bestowed on the needy, and they loaned money and stock on easy terms to the more struggling farmers. This charitable disposition was the most valuable part of their son's inheritance. At the age of sixteen he was sent to the University of Alcalá, which had been lately founded by Cardinal Ximenez, and he pursued his studies there with a success that drew all eyes upon him. By the regularity of his own conduct he encouraged many of his fellow-students in the practice of Christian perfection. He mortified his senses with great severities and his whole time was divided between prayer, study, and actions of charity. While still a student his father died, and Thomas resigned his share in his estate except so far as was necessary for him to finish his education ; his mother was thus enabled to continue her charities and to supply small dowries for poor girls of the village. He became master of arts and licentiate in theology and, after ten years at Alcalá, was made professor of philosophy in that city, being then twenty-six years old ; among those who attended his lectures was the famous Dominic Soto. At the end of two years he was offered the chair of philosophy in the University of Salamanca, but he declined the post as he had made up his mind to enter religion.

In 1516 Thomas joined the Augustinian friars at Salamanca, and his behaviour in the novitiate showed he had been long inured to austerities, to renouncing his own will, and to the exercise of contemplation. The simplicity of his behaviour in his whole conduct charmed his fellow-religious, and he seemed totally to forget that he had been a professor in a famous university. He was professed in the following year, and in 1518 was promoted to priestly orders and employed in preaching the word of God and in administering the sacrament of Penance. He acquitted himself with dignity and success, nor did he interrupt these employments or allow himself any relaxation in his monastic rule or austerities whilst he taught a course of divinity in his convent. His text-books were Peter Lombard and Aquinas, and students from the university soon sought permission to attend his lectures. He was exceptionally clear-headed, with a firm and solid judgement, but had always to cope with absent-mindedness and a poor memory. He was afterward successively prior at Salamanca, Burgos, and Valladolid, was twice provincial, of Andalusia and of Castile, and behaved himself in all these offices with a sweetness and zeal which edified and gained the hearts of his religious brethren, so that he governed them rather by the example of his holy life than by authority. He was always particularly solicitous for those friars who were sick, and when superior would often tell his religious that the infirmary was like the bush of Moses, where he who devotes himself to the sick will assuredly find God among the thorns with which he is surrounded. In 1533, while provincial of Castile, he sent the first band of Augustinians to the Americas, where they established their order as missionaries in Mexico. He fell into frequent raptures at his prayers, especially at Mass ; and though he endeavoured to hide such graces he was not able to do it : his face after the holy Sacrifice shone like that of Moses and as it were dazzled the eyes of those that beheld him. Preaching once in the cathedral-church at Burgos, reproving the vices and ingratitude of sinners, he held in his hand a crucifix and cried out from the bottom of his heart with a broken voice : " O Christians, look here ! "— and he was not able to go on, being ravished in an ecstasy. Once while addressing a community at the clothing of a novice he was rapt and speechless for a quarter of an hour. When he recovered himself he said : " Brethren, I beg your pardon. I have a weak heart and I feel ashamed of being so often overcome on these occasions. I will try to repair my fault." The Emperor chose him for one of his preachers and afterwards made him a counsellor, receiving his advice and sometimes writing to him when at a distance. This Emperor had signed an order for the execution of certain persons condemned for treason ; and neither the Archbishop of Toledo, nor his own son Philip, nor all the nobility of Spain were able to move him to mercy. At length St Thomas, at the request of Philip of Spain, went to him, and by discoursing some time with him prevailed upon the angry monarch to grant what he asked. When the princes and nobles expressed their surprise, the Emperor told them that when the Prior of the Austin Friars at Valladolid desired to obtain anything of him he rather commanded than asked it, so strongly did he incline him to what he pleased by showing that it was the will of the Almighty. " He is a true servant of God," said the prince, " and though he abides among mortals he is worthy of the honour due to those who wear the crown of immortality." When he was provincial he visited his convents with diligence and was particularly careful about four things. The first was the worship of God, that the divine service should be performed with the utmost reverence and attention ; that a moderate pause should be observed in the middle of each verse by those that sung in choir ; and that all things belonging to the altar should be kept with great neatness and cleanness. The second thing was assiduous reading of the holy Scriptures and spiritual books with meditation, without which he said it is impossible for devotion to last long. Thirdly, he was solicitous to settle all the religious in every convent in perfect concord and union, exhorting everyone to the most sincere and tender fraternal charity. Fourthly, he arranged that everyone should be employed according to his talents and in those offices for which he was fittest.

Whilst St Thomas was performing a visitation of his convents, he was nominated by the Emperor Charles V to the archbishopric of Granada, and commanded to go to Toledo. He obeyed ; but undertook the journey with no other object than that of declining the dignity, in which he succeeded according to his wish. When, some years later, in 1544, Don George of Austria, uncle to the Emperor, resigned the archbishopric of Valencia to pass to the bishopric of Liége, the Emperor, who was then in Flanders, thought of not offering St Thomas this see because he knew how grievous a trial it would be to him. He therefore, it is said, ordered his secretary to draw up a letter of nomination in favour of a certain religious of the Order of St Jerome. Afterwards, finding that the secretary had put down the name of Brother Thomas of Villanova, he asked the reason. The secretary answered that he thought he had heard this name, but would rectify the mistake. " By no means," said Charles. " This has happened by a particular providence of God. Let us therefore follow His will." So he signed the appointment for St Thomas and it was forthwith sent to Valladolid, where he was prior. The saint used all means possible to excuse himself. But Prince Philip, who was regent of Spain during his father's absence, was not easily to be put off, and the Archbishop of Toledo and others, fearing lest the nomination should be withdrawn, asked Brother Thomas's provincial to command him, in virtue of his religious obedience and under a threat of excommunication, to submit to the Emperor's will, which was done, and the saint accepted the see. Pope Paul III sent the bull for his consecration and it was performed at Valladolid by Cardinal Tavera de Pardo, Archbishop of Toledo. The saint set out very early next morning for Valencia. His mother, who had converted her house into a hospital for the use of the poor and sick, and resolved to spend the rest of her days in their service, had asked him to take Villanueva on the way ; but Thomas applied literally the words of the gospel, " a man shall leave his father and mother and shall cleave to his wife," and hastened direct to the see with which he was now wedded, convinced that his office obliged him to postpone all other considerations to that of going to the flock committed to his care. He travelled on foot in his monastic habit (which was very old) with the hat he had worn ever since his profession, accompanied by one religious of his order and two servants. Upon his arrival at Valencia he retired to an Augustinian friary outside the walls, where he spent several days in penance and prayer to beg the grace of God by which he might be enabled worthily to acquit himself of his charge. He took possession of his cathedral on the first day of the ensuing year, 1545, with the usual ceremonies and amidst the rejoicings and acclamations of the people. The chapter, in consideration of his poverty, made him a present of four thousand crowns towards furnishing his house, which he accepted in a humble manner and thanked them for their kindness, but he immediately sent the money to the great hospital with an order to lay it out in repairing the house and for the use of the poor patients. He explained to the canons that " our Lord will be better served and glorified by your money being spent on the poor in the hospital, who need it so much, than if it had been used by me. What does a poor friar like myself want with furniture ? " The first thing he did after the public ceremonies were over was to visit the prisons of his bishopric and, finding them too dark and inconvenient, he ordered them to be changed and improved.

It is often said that " Honours change manners," but St Thomas kept not only the same humility of heart but as much as possible the same exterior marks of contempt of himself and all vanity. He went almost as poorly dressed as before and even kept for some years the very habit which he brought from his monastery, which he sometimes mended himself as he had been wont to do in his convent. One of his canons, surprising him one day at this, said he wondered he could so employ his time which a tailor would save him for a trifle. The Archbishop replied that he was still a friar and that that trifle would feed some poor man ; but he asked the canon to tell nobody of what he saw him doing. Ordinarily he wore such clothes that his canons and domestics were ashamed of him. When he was pressed by them to put himself into a dress suitable to his dignity, his answer was : " Gentlemen, I am much obliged to you for the care you take of my person, but really I do not see how my dress as a religious interferes with my dignity as archbishop. You know well enough that my position and duties are quite independent of my clothes, and consist in taking care of the souls committed to me." The canons eventually induced him to cast away his woollen hat and wear one of silk. He used afterwards sometimes to show this hat and say merrily : " Behold my episcopal dignity. My masters the canons judged it necessary that I should wear this silk hat that I might be numbered among the archbishops." He discharged all the duties of a good pastor and visited the churches of his diocese, preaching everywhere in the towns and villages with such zeal and affection that the words which came from his mouth seemed so many flashes of lightning. His sermons were followed by a wonderful change in the lives of men in all places he visited, so that one might say he was a new apostle or prophet raised by God to reform the people. Having ended his visitation, he assembled a provincial council (the first for many years) wherein with the help of his fellow bishops he made ordinances to abolish the abuses he had taken notice of in his visitation of his clergy. To effect that of his own chapter cost him much difficulty and time. At all times he had recourse to the tabernacle to learn the will of God ; he often spent nights and days in his oratory and, perceiving that his servants were unwilling to disturb him at his devotions when persons came to consult him, he gave them strict instructions that as soon as anyone asked for him they should immediately call him, without making the visitor wait. When any affair of consequence was to be dealt with or any notorious sinner or public malefactor appeared deaf to all exhortations, St Thomas spent whole nights in prayer, and to render his prayers more efficacious he accompanied them with austerities and alms. Thus he obtained several conversions of obstinate sinners, especially of two wicked priests. One of these he had besought, in most tender and vehement words, to remember how dear a price his soul cost our Redeemer. Finding him not softened, he threw himself down before a crucifix, uncovered his back, and tore his body with a discipline, so that his garments were all stained with blood. Whereat the other began to weep penitently and cast himself at his feet, beseeching him to forbear, saying : " It is I that have sinned, and that deserve punishment."

His bishopric was worth eighteen thousand ducats per annum, two thousand of which were paid to Don George of Austria as a pension reserved to him upon his resignation ; twelve thousand the saint gave to the poor, not reserving one penny for the following year, and he allowed himself only four thousand to defray all the expenses of his household and office. There came to his door every day about five hundred poor people, and each of them received an alms, which was ordinarily a meal with a cup of wine and a piece of money. He took destitute orphans under his particular care, and for the eleven years that he was archbishop not one poor maiden was married who was not helped by his charity. He brought up the foundling infants in his diocese with the tenderness of a mother, often visited them, and gave good remuneration to those nurses who were particularly tender and diligent. To his porters, to make them more keen in finding children that were exposed by their parents, he gave a crown for every foundling they brought him. When in 1550 pirates had plundered a coast town in his diocese the Archbishop immediately sent four thousand ducats and cloth worth as much more to furnish the inhabitants with necessaries and to ransom the captives. Like many good men before and since, St Thomas was remonstrated with because a number of those whom he relieved were idle fellows who abused his kindness. " If," he replied, " there are vagabonds and work-shy people here it is for the governor and the prefect of police to deal with them : that is their duty. Mine is to assist and relieve those who come to my door." Nor was he only the support of the poor himself, but he encouraged the great lords and all that were rich to make their importance seen not in their luxury and display but by becoming the fathers and protectors of their vassals and by their liberality to the necessitous. He exhorted them to be richer in mercy and charity than they were in earthly possessions. " Answer me, O sinner," he would say, " what can you purchase with your money better or more necessary than the redemption of your sins ? " At other times : " If you desire that God should hear your prayers, hear the voice of the poor. If you desire that God should forestall your wants, prevent those of the indigent without waiting for them to ask you. Especially anticipate the necessities of those who are ashamed to beg ; to make these ask an alms is to make them buy it."

St Thomas was always averse from using the coercive weapons of the Church in bringing sinners to reason before methods of appeal and persuasion had been tried to the utmost. Of a theologian and canonist who objected to the Archbishop's delay in taking threatened strong measures to put down concubinage, he said : " He is without doubt a good man, but one of those fervent ones mentioned by St Paul as having zeal without knowledge. Is the good man aware of the care and pains I have taken to correct those against whom he fulminates ? . . . Let him enquire whether St Augustine and St John Chrysostom used anathemas and excommunication to stop the drunkenness and blasphemy which were so common among the people under their care. No ; for they were too wise and prudent. They did not think it right to exchange a little good for a great evil by inconsiderately using their authority and so exciting the aversion of those whose good will they wanted to gain in order to influence them for good." He invited a canon, in whom he had long tried in vain to procure an amendment of life, to come and stay in his own house under pretext of preparing to go on an errand to Rome for the Archbishop. Part of the preparation was to consist of a good confession. At the end of one, of two, of three months, the business for Rome was still not ready and all the time the canon was having unobtrusively put before him the fruits and benefits of penance. At the end of six months he left the saint's house a changed man, and his friends all supposing he had just returned from Rome. Another priest of irregular life upon being rebuked abused St Thomas to his face and left his presence in a rage. " Do not stop him," said the Archbishop to his chaplains, " it is my fault. My remonstrances were a little too rough." St Thomas wished to extend the same sort of methods to the *nuevos Cristianos* or *Moriscos*, Moors who were converted to Christianity but whose conversion was often unreal or who lapsed into apostasy and so were brought under the brutal jurisdiction of the Spanish Inquisition. He was never able to achieve much for them in his large diocese, but he induced the Emperor to provide a fund to support special priests for work among them and himself founded a college for the children of the newly converted. He also founded a college for poor scholars at his old university at Alcalá, and then, having scruples at having expended money outside his own diocese, he endowed another at Valencia. This last he named " Our Lady of the Temple " in memory of his having been clothed as an Augustinian on the feast of her Presentation and so to impress on religious how they should value their vocation. His material charity was equalled by his charity of judgement. Detraction he abhorred and he would always defend the cause of the absent. " Sir," he would say, " you do not look at this from a right point of view. You are wrong, because he may have had a good intention.

For myself, I believe that he had." Many examples are recorded of St Thomas's supernatural gifts, such as his power of healing the sick and of multiplying food, and numerous miracles were attributed to his intercession both before and after his death.

It is not known for certain why St Thomas did not attend the Council of Trent; he was represented thereat by the Bishop of Huesca, and most of the Castilian bishops consulted with him before they left. He impressed on them that it was at least as necessary for the Council to legislate for an internal reformation in the Church as against the Lutheran heresy, and made two interesting suggestions neither of which was in fact acted upon. One was that all benefices having the cure of souls should be filled by incumbents native of the place, so far as possible and providing they were well qualified, especially in rural districts ; the other was that the ancient canon which forbade the translation of a bishop from one see to another should be re-enforced. The idea of the union of a bishop with his see as with a bride was always present to the saint, and he lived in perpetual concern for the proper discharge of his own episcopal duties. " I was never so much afraid," he would say, " of being excluded from the number of the elect as since I have been a bishop." Several times he petitioned for leave to resign, and God was pleased at length to hear his prayer by calling him to Himself. He was seized by *angina pectoris* in August 1555, and began at once to prepare for the end by a general confession of his very least faults, which he made as if he had been the greatest of sinners. Then he received viaticum and, having commanded all the money then in his possession to be distributed among the poor in all the parishes of the city, he ordered all his goods to be given to the rector of his college, except the bed on which he lay ; he gave this bed to the gaoler for the use of prisoners, but borrowed it of him till such time as he should no longer require it. On September 8, the birthday of our Lady, the end was at hand. He ordered Mass to be said in his presence, and after the consecration recited the psalm *In te, Domine, speravi :* after the priest's communion he said that verse, " Into thy hands, O Lord, I commend my spirit," at which words he rendered his soul into the hands of God, in the sixty-seventh year of his age and the eleventh of his episcopal dignity. He was buried, according to his desire, in the church of the Austin friars at Valencia, was beatified by Paul V in 1618, and canonised by Alexander VII in 1658. St Thomas of Villanova was called in his lifetime " the Pattern of Bishops," " the Almsgiver," " the Father of the Poor," and nothing can be more vehement or more tender than his exhortation to divine love. " O wonderful beneficence ! " he cries out,

" God promises us Heaven for the recompense of His love. Is not His love itself the greatest reward, the most desirable, the most lovely, and the most sweet blessing ? Yet a further recompense, and so immense a recompense, waits upon it. O wonderful excess of goodness ! Thou givest thy love, and for this thy love thou bestowest on us Paradise. Such and so great a good is thy love that to obtain it all torments and fatigues ought joyfully to have been undergone. Yet thou bestowest it on us freely, and then givest Heaven for its reward. All-powerful Jesus, give me what thou commandest. For though to love thee be of all things the most sweet, yet it is above the reach and strength of nature. Nevertheless it is unpardonable if I do not love thee, for thou grantest thy love to all who desire and ask it. I cannot see without light : yet if I shut my eyes in the midst of the noon-day brightness, the fault is in me, not in the sun."

In setting out the history of St Thomas of Villanova (*Acta Sanctorum*, September, vol. v) the Bollandists have translated the Spanish Life of the Saint by Miguel Salon, who was a contemporary, and who, after a first biography published in 1588, utilised the materials furnished by the canonisation processes to produce a more complete work which appeared in 1620. They have also printed the memoir by his friend and fellow-Augustinian, Juan de Muñatones, Bishop of Segorbe and Albarracin. This had been prefixed to an edition of St Thomas of Villanova's sermons, etc., which Muñatones edited in 1581. Some other sources including a summary of the depositions in the Valencia and Castile processes were also available, and these are used in the Bollandist prolegomena and annotations. The whole is supplemented by a notice of the Saint's relics and miracles. Not much fresh biographical material seems to have added to our knowledge of the holy Archbishop of Valencia since the Bollandists published their account in 1755. There is a brief sketch by Quevedo y Villegas, which was translated into English through a French channel for the Oratorian series in 1847. There is also a German Life by Poesl (1860), and one in French by Dabert. The writings of St Thomas of Villanova, however, have been collected and more carefully edited and some of them have been translated into other languages.

ST MAURICE AND HIS COMPANIONS, MARTYRS
(THE THEBAN LEGION)
c. A.D. 287 (?)

A tribe of the Gauls called the Bagaudae having risen in revolt against Diocletian, the *Augustus* Maximian Herculius marched against them with an army, of which one unit was the Theban Legion. This had been recruited in Upper Egypt and was composed entirely of Christians. When he arrived at Octodurum

(Martigny), on the Rhone above the lake of Geneva, Maximian issued an order that the whole army should join in offering sacrifice to the gods for the success of their expedition. The Theban Legion hereupon withdrew itself, and encamped near Agaunum (now called St Maurice-en-Valais), and refused to take any part in these rites. Maximian repeatedly commanded them to obey their orders and be present at the sacrifices, and upon their constant and unanimous refusal he sentenced them to be decimated. Thus every tenth man was put to death, according as the lot fell, the rest exhorting one another all the while to perseverance. After the first decimation, a second was commanded, unless the soldiers obeyed the orders given ; but they cried out that they would rather suffer all penalties than do anything contrary to their religion. They were principally encouraged by three of their officers, Maurice, Exuperius, and Candidus, referred to respectively as the *primicerius*, the *campiductor*, and the *senator militum*. Maximian warned the remainder that it was of no use for them to trust to their numbers, for if they persisted in their disobedience not a man among them should escape death. The legion by the advice of their fearless leaders answered him by a respectful remonstrance : " We are your soldiers, but are also servants of the true God. We owe you military service and obedience ; but we cannot renounce Him who is our Creator and Master, and also yours even though you reject Him. In all things which are not against His law we most willingly obey you, as we have done hitherto. We readily oppose all your enemies, whoever they are ; but we cannot dip our hands into the blood of innocent persons. We have taken an oath to God before we took one to you : you can place no confidence in our second oath if we violate the first. You command us to punish the Christians ; behold, we are such. We confess God the Father, author of all things, and His Son, Jesus Christ. We have seen our companions slain without lamenting them, and we rejoice at their honour. Neither this nor any other provocation has tempted us to revolt. We have arms in our hands, but we do not resist because we would rather die innocent than live by any sin." This legion consisted of about six thousand six hundred men, who were all well armed, and might have sold their lives very dearly. But they had learned to give to God what is God's and to Cæsar what is Cæsar's, and they showed their courage more in dying than they had ever done in the most desperate battles. Maximian, having no hopes of overcoming their constancy, commanded the rest of his army to surround them and cut them to pieces. They made no resistance but, dropping their arms, suffered themselves to be butchered like sheep and without opening their mouths except to encourage one another. Not one out of so great a number failed in courage to the last, so that the ground was covered with their dead bodies, and streams of blood flowed on every side. Maximian gave the spoils of the slain to his soldiers for their booty, and they were sharing it out when a veteran named Victor refused to join in. At this the soldiers inquired if he was also a Christian. He answered that he was and would always continue one, upon which they fell upon him and slew him. Ursus and another Victor, two straggling soldiers of this legion, were found at Solothern and there killed, and according to local legends many others elsewhere, such as St Alexander at Bergamo, SS. Octavius, Adventor and Solutor at Turin, and St Gereon at Cologne. The Roman Martyrology mentions Vitalis and Innocent, as well as the above three and Victor, to-day, SS. Ursus and Victor on September 30, and St Antoninus at Piacenza, wrongly associated with the Theban Legion, on the same date. St Eucherius, speaking of their relics preserved at Agaunum in his time, says, " Many come from divers provinces devoutly to honour these saints, and offer presents of gold, silver and other things. I humbly present this monument of my pen, begging intercession for the pardon of my sins, and the perpetual protection of my patrons." He mentions many miracles to have been performed at their shrine and says of a certain woman who had been cured of a palsy by them : " Now she carries her own miracle about with her."

This St Eucherius is the principal witness for the story which has just been related. He was bishop of Lyons during the first half of the fifth century, and about the year 449 wrote down for Salvius, Bishop of Octodurum, an account of these martyrs of Agaunum, in whose honour a basilica had been built there towards the end of the previous century, in consequence of a vision of their place of burial vouchsafed to the then bishop, St Theodore. Eucherius says he had the story from St Isaac, Bishop of Geneva, who, Eucherius thought, was told it by Theodore, who presumably learned it from eyewitnesses. It will be noticed that, as related above, the legionaries in their manifesto speak of refusing to spill the blood of innocent Christians. This protest was probably composed by St Eucherius himself, who states that they were killed for refusing to undertake the massacre of Christians and does not mention the revolting Bagaudae ; the sixth century *acta* of the martyrs say they suffered for not sacrificing. St Maurice and his companions have been the subject of much discussion. That a whole legion was put to death is highly improbable ; Roman imperial generals were not incapable of such a wholesale slaughter, but the circumstances of the time and the lack of early evidence of an entirely satisfactory sort

are all against it. Alban Butler notes with pain that " the truth of
this history is attacked by some Protestant historians," but it has
been questioned by Catholic scholars as well, and some have even
gone so far as to reject the whole of it as a fabrication. But it seems
clear that the martyrdom at Agaunum of St Maurice and his companions is an historical fact : what was the number of men involved
is another matter ; in the course of a hundred and fifty years a
company could easily be exaggerated into a legion.

The church built at Agaunum by St Theodore of Octodurum
later became the centre of an abbey, which was the first in the West
to maintain the Divine Office continually by day and by night by
means of a cycle of choirs. This monastery came into the hands of
the Canons Regular in the ninth century, and is now an abbey-
nullius, whose abbot is also titular bishop of Bethlehem. Relics of
the martyrs are preserved here in a sixth century reliquary, but
veneration of the Theban Legion has spread with other relics far
beyond the borders of Switzerland. They are commemorated in
the liturgy of the whole Western Church, and St Maurice is patron
of Savoy and Sardinia and of several towns in other countries, as
well as of infantry soldiers, sword-smiths, and weavers and dyers.

In the martyrs we learn the character of true fortitude, of which
virtue many people have a very false idea. Real valour differs
infinitely from that rashness and contempt of danger which the
basest passions often inspire. It is founded on motives of duty and
virtue ; it does brave and great things and it bears injuries and
distress not for hope of reward, the desire of honour, or the fear of
punishment, but out of a consciousness of duty and to preserve
virtue entire. So infinitely more precious is the least part of integrity
than all the possessions of this world and so much does it outbalance
all trials that, rather than suffer it to be lost or impaired, the good
man is ready to venture all perils and behaves amidst them without
terror. This foundation of great and heroic performances, this just
and rational, considerate and sober, constant and uniform contempt
of danger and of death in all its shapes, is only derived from the
Christian principle. The characteristics of true virtue go along
with it, especially patience, humility, and gentleness. The Christian
hero obeys the precepts of loving his enemies, doing good to those
that persecute him, bearing wrong, and being ready to give his coat
also to him that would take away his cloak.

The text of St Eucherius which has suffered many interpolations will be
found in Ruinart and in the *Acta Sanctorum*, September, vol. vi ; but the
critical edition by B. Krusch in the *Monumenta Germaniæ, Script rerum
Meroving.*, vol. iii, pp. 32–41, is of first importance. On the whole question

of the martyrdom the volume of M. Besson, *Monasterium Acaunense* (Fribourg, 1913), is perhaps the most sober and reliable. He dissents from the extreme views of Krusch, though he is in some matters himself open to criticism (*cf.* the *Analecta Bollandiana*, xxxiii, pp. 243–245). The subject is also treated at great length by Dom H. Leclercq in the *Dictionnaire d'Archéologie chrét.*, vol. x (1932), cc. 2699–2729. The bibliography which he supplies extends to no less than four closely-printed columns, and shows impressively the interest which the controversy has excited. On St Maurice in art see Künstle, *Ikonographie*, vol. ii.

ST FELIX IV, POPE AND CONF.

A.D. 530

Upon his return from his visit to the Emperor at Constantinople in the year 526, Pope St John I was imprisoned by the Gothic king Theodoric at Ravenna, and died very shortly afterwards. When therefore Theodoric caused the cardinal priest Felix to be nominated as his successor, the clergy and people at Rome were relieved that the royal choice had fallen upon so blameless and otherwise suitable a person and that they could without hesitation proceed to elect him. The new Pope used his favour with the Arian court to promote the interests of the Catholic Church, and obtained from the queen-regent, Amalasuntha, a decree imposing a heavy fine on those who should disregard the ancient custom that a layman should cite a cleric only before the pope or his delegates. Fines levied for this offence were to be at the disposal of the Holy See for distribution among the poor. St Felix approved the writings of St Cæsarius of Arles on grace and free will against St Faustus of Riez, and suggested the assembling of the second Synod of Orange in 529. To the fathers of this council he sent a number of propositions about grace drawn from the works of St Augustine, and so led up to the condemnation of Semipelagianism by the council. This pope built the basilica of St Saturninus on the New Salarian Way, just within the walls, and Amalasuntha having given to him two ancient temples in the Roman Forum, Felix built on their site the basilica of SS. Cosmas and Damian; the mosaics to be seen to-day in the apse and on the triumphal arch of that church are those made at the direction of Felix IV.

After he had occupied the apostolic throne for four years St Felix became seriously ill and knew his death to be at hand. Fearing lest the political rivalry between Ravenna and Constantinople would cause dissension over the vacant see, he publicly nominated Boniface, archdeacon of the City, to succeed him and informed the ecclesiastical and civil authorities of what he had done. St Felix IV died about September 20 in the year 530, but only a small minority of the clergy of Rome accepted his nominee. The majority elected one Dioscorus, but as he died in three weeks the minority election of Boniface II was ratified. It is now an accepted principle of canon law that the pope cannot nominate his successor. St Felix IV was revered in his day as a man of great simplicity, humility, and kindness to the poor, and was noted for the large number of bishops, twenty-nine, that he consecrated during a short pontificate.

Though described in the Roman Martyrology as Felix IV, modern criticism of the lists of popes has decided that he is properly Felix III, a previous anti-pope having no right to figure in the numbering. A short account of his pontificate is given by the Bollandists under January 30. See also the *Liber Pontificalis* (Duchesne), vol. i, pp. 270 *seq.*; Grisar, *Geschichte Roms und der Päpste*, i, pp. 183 *seq.*, and 495 *seq.*

ST SALABERGA, MATRON AND ABBESS

c. A.D. 665

St Eustace of Luxeuil, travelling from Bavaria back to his monastery, was entertained in a household where one of the children, a small girl called Salaberga, was blind. When he was about to leave the holy abbot blessed all the members of the family, but when he came to Salaberga he took oil, blessed it, and anointed her sightless eyes. Then he prayed over her, and her sight was restored. When she grew up Salaberga was married to a young man, who, however, died two months after the wedding. She took this to be a sign that she was called to serve God in a monastery, but her parents thought otherwise and she married again, a nobleman called Blandinus. By him she had five children, of whom two, Beauduin and Anstrudis, are venerated as saints. Salaberga had endowed a convent at Poulangey, and when they had lived in happy wedlock for a number of years she and her husband agreed both to withdraw from the world. Blandinus became a hermit and is venerated as a saint in the diocese of Meaux. Salaberga went to Poulangey first, and then, by the advice of St Walbert, abbot of Luxeuil, founded a new monastery at Laon about the year 650. This abbey, dedicated in honour of St John the Baptist, was a very extensive establishment, having, it is said, seven churches. It had provision for both monks and nuns, and each community numbered several hundred, so that by means of a rotation of choirs the praise of God in the Divine Office was kept up continually both day and night. St Salaberga had a married brother named Bodo, and him she persuaded to become a monk, his wife joining the community at Laon. He was made bishop of Toul, and founded three monasteries, for men at Etival and Offonville and for women at Bonmoutier ; of this last his own daughter was the first abbess. St Bodo's feast is observed on the 11th of this month. During the last two years of her life St Salaberga suffered continually from very great pain which she bore with corresponding courage and patience ; after her death her daughter St Anstrudis took up the government of the community of St John's wherein she maintained a perfect discipline. St Salaberga was buried at the abbey, and St Bodo's body was later exhumed at Toul and brought to be laid beside that of his sister.

A Life, previously printed in the *Acta Sanctorum,* September, vol. vi, has been critically edited by B. Krusch in the *Monumenta Germaniæ, Scriptores rerum Meroving.,* vol. v, pp. 40–66. He shows that the correct form of the name is Sadalberga ; but, what is more important, that the Life, which professes to have been written by a contemporary, is really a compilation of the beginning of the ninth century. Certain references made to Sadalberga by Jonas, Abbot of Bobbio, in his Life of St Columban, are, however, more trustworthy.

ST EMMERAMUS, Bp. and Mart.

End of the Seventh Century

This holy missionary was a native of Poitiers, of an illustrious family, and in his youth made a generous sacrifice of great temporal advantages to consecrate himself to God in the ministry of the altar. He preached the gospel with indefatigable zeal and without respect of persons in all the towns and villages around Poitiers, of which city he is often stated to have been bishop ; but his name does not appear in the episcopal lists of that or any other see. He gave instruction in Christian doctrine both publicly and privately, provided relief for the corporal necessities of the poor, and, seeking out the most hardened sinners in their houses, he with sweetness and tender eloquence drew them away from their evil ways and led them by sincere and perfect penance into the paths of everlasting salvation. After having laboured thus several years in his own country, St Emmeramus was so touched with compassion for the unhappy state of so many thousands of idolaters in Germany and beyond the Danube that he went to preach the gospel in Bavaria. Theodo, who ruled in that country with the title of duke under King

Sigebert III, detained him a long time at Ratisbon, as he was later to try and detain St Corbinian, to minister to his subjects. Emmeramus refused to receive any favours or gifts from the duke, saying it was his only desire to preach Christ crucified. After having preached there three years and gained to God a number of infidels and sinners, he undertook a pilgrimage to Rome to venerate the relics of the apostles and martyrs, to consult the Supreme Pontiff, and to study. He set out on his journey south, but when he had been travelling for five days and reached Kleinhelfendorf, between Munich and Tirol, he was overtaken by, apparently, some representatives of Duke Theodo, who brutally mishandled him. The saint managed to reach Feldkirchen, but there died of the injuries he had received. He was buried at Ascheim and his body shortly afterwards translated to Ratisbon, where he is venerated as a lesser patron. It is not known that he was ever bishop of that city or founder of the great monastery there that bore his name.

The motive and circumstances of the murder of St Emmeramus are a mystery (the Roman Martyrology says oracularly that he " patiently suffered a most cruel death for Christ's sake that he might set others free "). Less than a century after, his Life was written by Aribo, Bishop of Freising, who gives an account of it that is a characteristic example of hagiographical invention, exaggeration, embroidery, or all three, for the sake of popular edification. We are told that before St Emmeramus left for Italy the daughter of Duke Theodo, Oda, confided to him that she was with child by a nobleman of her father's court, and she feared the Duke's anger both for herself and her lover. Emmeramus authorised her to state that he himself was the partner of her guilt. The pious Aribo expects the reader to admire the magnanimity and self-sacrifice of Emmeramus, but, quite apart from the fact that he was recommending a lie, and a lie that would cause great scandal, it is difficult to see what would be gained by it except protection for the guilty man. However, the lady Oda acted accordingly when her secret was discovered, and her brother Lantbert and his men set off in pursuit of Emmeramus. When they came up with him at Kleinhelfendorf they tied him to a ladder, tore out his eyes and tongue, cut off his members, and left him to die amid an outbreak of supernatural marvels. St Emmeramus was at once acclaimed a martyr by the people.

Much has been written about St Emmeram (perhaps more correctly spelt " Haimhrammus "). There are Lives by Bishop Arbeo (in two recensions), another by Meginfrid of Magdeburg, and a third by Arnold, who belonged to the monastery called by the name of the Saint himself. In the critical edition of Arbeo prepared for the *Monumenta Germaniæ, Script. rer.*

Meroving., vol. iv, pp. 452–520, Bruno Krusch has shown that the text printed by the Bollandists (in *Acta Sanctorum*, September, vol. vi) represents substantially Arbeo's genuine work and that it was written about the year 772. But even in its authentic form the data provided by Arbeo's Life are not trustworthy. See also A. Bigelmair, " Die Anfänge des Christentums in Bayern," in *Festgabe A. Knöpfler* (1907), and J. A. Endres in the *Römische Quartalschrift* for 1895 and 1903. The genuine tomb of the Saint is believed to have been discovered in 1894. On this see especially J. A. Endres, *Beiträge zur Geschichte des M. A. Regensburgs* (1924).

SEPTEMBER 23

ST LINUS, POPE AND MART.

c. A.D. 78

ST LINUS was the immediate successor of St Peter in the see of Rome, as St Irenæus, Eusebius, St Hippolytus, the Liberian catalogue, and other ancient records assure us. St Irenæus, who wrote in the second half of the second century, further identifies Pope Linus with the Linus of 2 Timothy iv, 21, and implies that he was appointed to his office before the death of St Peter, " after the holy Apostles had founded and set the Church in order " at Rome. The *Liber Pontificalis* (sixth century) says of St Linus that he was " an Italian by nation, of the Tuscan region [he is claimed by Volterra] ; his father was Herculanus. He sat in the episcopal chair eleven years, three months, twelve days. He lived in the time of Nero, from the consulship of Saturninus and Scipio [A.D. 50] to that of Capito and Rufus [A.D. 67]. He is crowned with martyrdom. In accordance with the precept of Blessed Peter he decreed that women should come into church with covered heads. He held two ordinations, making fifteen bishops and eighteen presbyters. He was buried beside the body of Blessed Peter at the Vatican on December 23." Several of these statements are of very doubtful authenticity, particularly that which refers to his martyrdom, for no persecution of Roman Christians is known to have taken place between that of Nero and that of Domitian in A.D. 94 ; moreover St Irenæus names only St Telesephorus as a martyr among the earliest popes. It is not impossible that he was called a martyr on account of sufferings and labours for the Church, and he is named among the martyrs in the canon of the Mass.

Very little is known of St Linus beyond his name. See the *Liber Pontificalis* (Ed. Duchesne), vol. i, p. 121 ; Grisar, *Geschichte Roms und der Päpste*, p. 220 ; Lightfoot, *St Clement of Rome*, vol. i, p. 201.

ST THECLA OF ICONIUM, Virg. and Mart.

First Century

Thecla, still referred to liturgically in the East as " Protomartyr among women and equal with the Apostles," was one of the most revered heroines of the earlier ages of the Church. St Methodius of Tyre in his *Banquet of the Ten Virgins* tells us that she was well versed in profane philosophy and in the various branches of literature, and he commends her eloquence and the ease, strength, sweetness, and modesty of her speech, having received her instruction in divine and evangelical knowledge from St Paul. The same father extols the vehemence of her love for Christ, which she exerted especially in the conflicts which she sustained with the zeal and courage of a martyr, and with a strength of body equal to the vigour of her mind. St Augustine, St Epiphanius, St Ambrose, and other fathers mention that St Paul by his preaching converted her to the faith, and that his discourses kindled in her a love of holy virginity. St Gregory of Nyssa says that she undertook the sacrifice of herself by giving death to the flesh, practising great austerities, extinguishing in herself all earthly affections, and subduing her passions by a life dead to the senses, so that nothing seemed to remain living in her but reason and spirit : the whole world seemed dead to her as she was to the world.

It is, however, by no means certain that this St Thecla ever existed ; there may have been a convert of St Paul of that name who devoted herself to the service of the Church, but if there was we know nothing about her. Her widespread and popular legend depends entirely on a romance composed at the end of the second century and known as the *Acts of Paul and Thecla*. St Jerome recognised this work as apocryphal, and Tertullian tells us that it was written by a presbyter of Asia who, on being convicted of having falsely used St Paul's name, and confessing that he had done it from love of Paul, was deposed from his office. In spite of this the book continued to be popular in the Church, and its incidents were referred to as authentic by a long succession of Fathers, of whom some are mentioned above. It relates how St Paul (who is described as " a little man, bald-headed, bow-legged, stoutly built, with eyebrows meeting, rather long-nosed, graceful "), preaching in the house of Onesiphorus at Iconium, attracts the attention of the maiden Thecla, who determines to put into practice his teaching on virginity. She therefore broke off her engagement to marry a certain Thamyris. Her parents were indignant, Thamyris sought to move her with flatteries and caresses, her servants entreated her with tears, her friends and neighbours argued with her, and the authority and threats of the civil magistrate were employed to bring her to change her mind. Thecla, strengthed by the arm of the Almighty, was proof against all this influence ; and, regarding these worldly friends as her most dangerous enemies, she took the first favourable opportunity of escaping out of their hands, and fled to St Paul to receive from him comfort and advice. She forsook father and mother and a house where she lived in plenty, she left her companions, friends, and home, desiring to possess only the treasure of the love and grace of God, and to find Jesus Christ who was all things to her. Thamyris thereupon laid an information against St Paul, who was sentenced by the magistrate to be scourged and cast out of the city for persuading maidens from marriage and wives from their husbands. Thecla was ordered to be burnt, but a storm from Heaven put out the fire and she escaped to Paul and accompanied him to Antioch. Here the Syriarch Alexander tried to abduct her in the street. In defending herself, Thecla tore off his cloak and rolled his crown in the dust, and he, furious at being made a public laughing-stock, haled her before the governor, and she was condemned to the beasts. For a time she was sheltered in the house of a certain Queen Tryphæna (an historical personage), whose dead daughter had told her in a dream to adopt Thecla, for the significant reason that "she may pray concerning me and that I may be transferred to the place of the just." When the time came for her execution she was exposed naked in the amphitheatre, but clothed with her innocence, so that this ignominy enhanced her glory and her crown. Her heart was undaunted in the midst of lions, bears, and tigers, and she waited without concern the onset of the furious beasts, whose roaring filled even the spectators with terror. But the lions, forgetting their ferocity and their hunger, walked gently up to the maiden and, laying themselves down at her feet, licked them as if it had been respectfully to kiss them, and the other beasts fought among themselves, so that the keepers had to turn others into the arena. Then Thecla saw a ditch full of water and was reminded thereby that she was not yet baptised. And she threw herself in, saying : " In the name of Jesus Christ I am baptised on my last day." The fierce seals that were in the water floated about dead, and when Thecla came out there was a cloud of fire round her, so that the animals could not touch her nor the people see her naked. Then Alexander suggested to the governor that goaded bulls should be tried, " and the governor, looking gloomy, said : ' Do as you like.' " But the fire consumed the ropes which bound Thecla to the bulls, and at this moment Queen Try-phæna fainted. Then the governor put a stop to the games, for Tryphæna was a kinswoman of the Cæsar,* and amid the applause of the multitude Thecla was released. Dressed as a boy she rejoined St Paul at Myra in Lycia and was by him commissioned to teach the word of God, which she did to her mother in Iconium, and then retired to live in a cave at Seleucia for seventy-two years. Then it was rumoured among the Greek physicians of the city that " this Thecla is a virgin, and serves Artemis, and from this she has power of healing," for many miracles were done by her ; and they were jealous and sent a band of young men to slay (or to ravish) her. And Thecla praying to the Lord, the rock opened to receive her, and so was taken to Him. But another account says that within the rock she found a passage and thence made her way to Rome, where she found that St Paul was dead. " And after staying there a brief space she rested in a glorious sleep ; and she is buried about two or three stadia from the tomb of her master, Paul."

That this story is a romance in at least its details is apparent on the face of it. It was written to a considerable extent in praise of virginity and to impress on its hearers the Christian teaching about chastity. But herein the text of the *Acts of Paul and Thecla* is somewhat extravagant, making St Paul teach that salvation is hardly possible without virginity, so that some commentators suppose it to have been written under the influence of the Encratites, an early Christian heretical sect which reprobated the use of wine, flesh-meat, and marriage. St Thecla did not actually give her blood for Christ ; her martyrdom consists in the reproaches she receievd from her lover and her mother, her trial at the stake, and her trial among the lions. These are the three torments referred to in the *Rituale Romanum* where, in the recommendation of a departing soul, occurs the prayer : " And as thou didst deliver the blessed virgin and martyr Thecla from three most cruel torments, so deign to deliver the soul of this thy servant and bring him to rejoice with thee in heavenly happiness." From the great church built over her alleged tomb at Meriamlik, near Seleucia, veneration for St Thecla spread over all Christendom. It was never strong in Rome, but had its chief western centres at Milan, Lyons, and Tarragona ; the cathedral of Milan is dedicated in her honour and she is named in the canon of the Ambrosian Mass.

On this same day is venerated another St Thecla, foundress of the collegiate-church of Chamalières in Auvergne during the ninth

---

* She was second cousin to the Emperor Caligula, and widow of a king of Thrace.

century, and celebrated for her devotion to the mother of God. Her relics are now in the church of Sainte-Marie-de-Royat. Several other martyred Theclas are named in the martyrologies during this month.

If we desire to please Christ we must imitate the saints in their love of purity, and in strict chastity according to the circumstances of our state. We must earnestly beg this virtue of God, praying Him to inspire us with His holy fear, to create in us an aborrence of all sin and dangerous occasions, to purify our affections, and to teach us to set the strictest guard upon all our senses. We must learn sincere humility of heart and live in an entire distrust of ourselves and fear of dangers : to forget our weakness or to presume upon our own resolution or strength is equally foolish and fatal. We must shun all occasions which may incite and fire our passions, especially imprudent friendships or dangerous intimacies. Even such as are begun in the spirit tend, unless carefully watched, to develop in a disorderly way. We must be always employed, always eager in some serious business, which must never leave us one moment idle. Prayer and work must be alternately called in, so that the Devil may always find our mind occupied. We must live in the habitual practice of denying our inclinations and mortifying our senses. If we give our appetites full liberty in things that are not forbidden, they will quickly master us, and seek things that are unlawful with too great violence to be restrained by us.

The Greek text of the Acts of Paul and Thecla was edited by Tischendorf in 1851 ; and again in Lipsius-Bonnet in their *Acta Apostolorum Apocrypha*, 1891, vol. i. The Syriac version was rendered accessible by W. Wright in 1871 and the Armenian by F. C. Conybeare in *The Apology and Acts of Apollonius and other Monuments of Early Christianity* (1894). See also Pirot, *Supplément au Dictionnaire de la Bible* (1926), vol. i, cc. 494–495. Sir W. M. Ramsay in his book, *The Church in the Roman Empire*, committed himself to the view that there was a real person of the name of Thecla who embraced the teaching of the Apostle St Paul.

ST ADAMNAN, or EUNAN, ABBOT OF IONA, CONF.

A.D. 704

Adamnan, whom St Bede calls " a good and wise man, remarkably learned in the holy Scriptures," was related to St Columba through his father Ronan, and was born about the year 624 at Drumhome in the county of Donegal. He embraced a monastic life with great humility and fervour in a monastery which had been founded there. Afterwards, following the steps of his holy kinsman

Columba, he left Ireland and retired to the monastery of Iona, of which he became fifth abbot in the year 679 at the age of fifty-five. On the death of Oswy, King of Northumbria, in 670 his son Aldfrid had had to fly from the usurper Egfrid, and had taken shelter at Iona, where he met Adamnan. When in 685, Aldfrid being then on his throne, someone was required to go on behalf of the Irish to the Northumbrians to negotiate for the release of some captives, it was therefore natural that St Adamnan should be chosen for the mission. He succeeded happily in this negotiation : he was favourably received by the English monarch, and obtained full satisfaction for the damage done to his countrymen in the foregoing year. While he was in England he visited the monasteries of Wearmouth, and was seen by the young Bede, who was then a boy of thirteen. The most important result of this visit was that, by the persuasion of St Ceolfrid, he laid aside the custom of his predecessors and conformed to the true time of celebrating Easter. Upon his return home he used his utmost endeavours to guide his monks at Iona and all those who were subject to that monastery into the road which he himself walked, but was not able. He therefore sailed into Ireland, his native country, and there preached and with modest exhortations explained the true time for observing Easter : by which means he brought many to a conformity with the Universal Church in that point of discipline. He also, says St Bede, would have persuaded the clergy to wear the Roman tonsure if his authority had been sufficient. After his failure to convert his monks from Celtic to Roman customs, St Adamnan spent a good deal of time away from his monastery and made two more long visits to Ireland. At the Council of Tara he was instrumental in persuading the assembly that women should not take part in warfare and that they and their children should be neither killed nor taken as prisoners ; this decision was called after him, Adamnan's Canon. All the time he was zealously propagating the observance of the true Easter, which was accepted nearly wherever he went, except where the influence of Columban monasteries was strong, and notably in his own Iona. After his last visit to Ireland, where he celebrated the feast according to the Catholic canons, he made a final fruitless attempt to overcome the opposition of his community ; " and it so happened that he departed this life before the next year came round, the divine Goodness so ordaining that, as he was a great lover of peace and unity, he should be received into everlasting life before he should be obliged, by the return of the time of Easter, to dispute yet more seriously with those who would not follow him." This was on September 23, 704.

St Adamnan, " a man of tears and penitence, devoted in prayer, diligent, mortified, and learned in God's holy scriptures," was after St Columba Iona's brightest light and most accomplished scholar. He himself refers to the writing-tablets, the pens and styles and ink-horns, in the monastic scriptorium, and of these he made full use himself. His own name is remembered for, more than anything, his Life of St Columba, one of the most important hagiographical documents in existence and the most complete biography of the Middle Ages. He wrote it in Latin at the request of his brethren. In the latter part of the seventh century a Frankish bishop called Arculfus went on pilgrimage to Jerusalem, and on the way back his ship was so driven by contrary winds that he was eventually cast up on the western coast of Britain (which, unless they were trying to make a port on the west coast of France, seems a very remarkable occurrence). Arculfus " after many accidents " found himself at Iona, where he was warmly received by Adamnan and gave a long account to the monks of all he had seen in the East. St Adamnan had this narrative written down, and so composed his other well-known work, *de Locis Sanctis,* " beneficial to many and particularly to those who, being far from those places where the patriarchs and apostles lived, know no more of them than they can learn by reading." This book was presented by Adamnan to King Aldfrid, " and through his bounty it came to be read by lesser persons " even to the present day.

Among the popular tales told of this saint is that, to provide wood for his monastery, he felled with his own hands enough oak trees on a neighbouring island to load twelve boats. He is also said one day to have been missing from choir, and when his brethren sought him they found him in ecstasy before a vision of the Holy Child. St Adamnan was very greatly venerated among the people of Scotland, and the common Scots baptismal name of Adam is a corruption of his own. His feast is still observed in the diocese of Argyll and the Isles. Throughout Ireland he is commemorated on this day as St Eunan, and celebrated at Raphoe as its first bishop. Tirconail was occupied by men of the Hi-Niall, to whom St Adamnan's mother Ronnat belonged, but it is not certainly established that this Eunan and Adamnan are one and the same. That he was ever bishop in Raphoe is unlikely.

Our most reliable information about Adamnan comes from Bede, *Eccles. Hist.* See Plummer's edition and notes. But, though of a more legendary character, Irish materials are also available at least in the form of casual anecdotes. C. Plummer's *Miscellanea Hagiographica Hibernica* supplies references to many of these. There is even a short Irish Life of St Adamnan of which a translation has been printed in the *Celtic Review*, vol. v (1908), pp. 97–107. The best text of Adamnan's *De Locis Sanctis*, is that of Geyer in the Vienna *Corpus Scriptorum*, vol. xxxix, while the *Life of St Columba* has been well edited by J. T. Fowler (1920). See also L. Gougaud, *Christianity in Celtic Lands* (1932), pp. 192–193, 259, etc. ; and J. F. Kenney, *The Sources for the early History of Ireland*, vol. i, 1929.

BD. HELEN DUGLIOLI, WIDOW

A.D. 1520

Blessed Helen Duglioli has been selected by popular acclamation from among the unknown numbers of those who have served God heroically " in the world " to be exalted at the altars of the Church. She was born at Bologna in 1472, and when she was about twenty years old married Benedict dal'Oglio. Husband and wife lived together for thirty years in amity and happiness, supporting and encouraging one another in the life of Christians, and when Benedict died, Helen shortly after followed him to the grave. The common people, who have an almost unerring instinct for detecting true holiness, knew she was a saint, and the continual *cultus* they had given her was confirmed by Pope Leo XII in 1828. Blessed Helen was a benefactress of the canons regular at Bologna, and her feast is celebrated in their church in that city.

See the *Acta Sanctorum*, September, vol. vi. The most important part of the notice there devoted to her consists of an extract from the *De Servorum Dei Beatificatione* of Prosper Lambertini (afterwards Pope Benedict XIV) written when he was Archbishop of Bologna. In this (Bk. ii, ch. 18), he quotes the tributes paid to Bd. Helen at Bologna as an almost typical case of a spontaneous and immemorial *cultus*, and refers to sundry local publications which bore witness to the devotion of the citizens. Among other evidence cited by the Bollandists it is curious to find a passage from the *Ragionamenti* of Pietro Aretino, of all people, a contemporary of the Beata, who refers satirically to the crowds of candles, pictures and *ex votos* deposted " alla sepoltura di santa Beata Lena dall' Olio a Bologna ".

SEPTEMBER 24

OUR LADY OF RANSOM

THE first entry in the Roman Martyrology to-day is, "The feast of blessed Mary the Virgin, called of Ransom, institutress of the Order for the Redemption of Captives under that title. Her Appearing is mentioned on August 10," and accordingly under that date we find, "The Appearing in Spain of blessed Mary . . ." etc. In the note to the account of St Peter Nolasco (vol. i, p. 395) we have referred to the difficulties surrounding the history of the foundation of this order (*vulgo* Mercedarians), particularly the unsatisfactory nature of the evidence for the apparitions of our Lady to St Peter and others. The date of the order's first foundation in Spain was August 10 (in 1218 or 1223 or 1228), but the feast commemorating this event, under the name of the Solemnity of the Coming-down of Our Lady of Ransom, was kept by the Mercedarians on the Sunday nearest to August 1. The feast was granted to Spain at large in 1680, to France in 1690, and extended to the whole Western Church, for its present date, in 1696. It was a project of Pope Benedict XIV's commission for the reform of the Roman Breviary to suppress this feast of our Lady of Ransom altogether, a project to which effect has been given in the new kalendar approved for the Benedictines in 1915.

The invocation of our Lady under this title for the conversion of England has nothing to do with the historical and liturgical aspects of the feast. Our Lady of Pity was an old name for her in this country, expressing a cognate idea to "ransom," and she may be regarded as interceding for our country's release from the bonds of false religious teaching, just as in the prayer of the Mass to-day we ask for the deliverance of the faithful people from the bonds of sin. "And so may we all have recourse to the blessed Mother of God. We may run to her protection, praying for help from Heaven, if yet more difficult times come upon the Church, if faith declines with the growing-cold of charity, if private and public conduct becomes corrupt, if danger threatens the Catholic name and civil society. So, at last, in the supreme trial of death, when no hope or help can be looked for elsewhere, we may lift up to her our weeping eyes and trembling hands, asking through her for forgiveness from her Son and endless happiness in Heaven " (Pope Pius XI).

See Holweck, *Calendarium Festorum Dei et Dei Matris* (1925), p. 327, who seems to accept the Mercedarian traditions a little too trustfully. Holweck also appeals to D. Perez Sanjulian, *Historia de la SS. Virgen Maria* (1912), vol. ii, p. 645.

ST GEREMARUS, or GERMER, Abbot and Conf.

c. A.D. 658

This saint was one of the numerous Frankish noblemen who, after marrying and following a secular career, left the world and became distinguished in the monastic or other ecclesiastical life of their time. He belonged to the territory of Beauvais, and was attached in his youth to the court of Dagobert I, where he met his wife Domana, who is herself venerated as a saint in the diocese of Evreux. Their two girl children predeceased them, and their boy being grown up they, under the influence of St Audoenus (Ouen), Bishop of Rouen, determined to embrace the religious life. Geremarus had already built a monastery near his birthplace, but he himself chose to receive the monastic habit at Pentale on the Seine, near Brionne. He was a model religious and became in time abbot of the house. But strictness and regularity which are admired in a subject are not always so popular in a superior, and some of the monks at Pentale were very discontented under their new father. They were themselves such bad religious and even bad men that it is said they attempted to take the life of St Geremarus by fastening a sharp knife point upwards in the boards of his bed under the blanket—though unless he were a heavy man or in the habit of throwing himself into his bed, such a device was not likely to inflict a mortal wound. Whether for this reason or because of his unpopularity and lack of success in improving discipline, the abbot resigned his office and went to live as a hermit in a cave on the banks of the river. Here he passed five contented years, communing with God, working with his hands, and ministering to his neighbours, until one day news was brought to him of the sudden death at the court of Clovis II of his only son, Amalbert. " O my God," he cried, " I thank thee that thou hast shown thy mercy towards me by calling my son to thy glory." He ordered that Amalbert should be buried at his monastery of St Pierre-aux-Bois at l'Isle, and with the young man's estate which now reverted to him he founded a monastery at Flay, on the river Epte between Beauvais and Rouen, which was afterwards called St Germer's. St Geremarus now abandoned the solitary life to direct the new monastery of which he was abbot for some three years, till his death.

The Life of St Geremarus printed in the *Acta Sanctorum* (September, vol. vi) is not the earliest. That which B. Krusch has edited for the *Monumenta Germaniæ, Scriptores rerum Meroving.* (vol. iv, pp. 626–633), is of older date, but Krusch shows that even this can only have been written a little before 851, and that as a source of history it is quite untrustworthy. That printed by the Bollandists was compiled in the eleventh century. There are other accounts such, for example, as that written by Guibert of Nogent, but all are legendary. J. Depoin in the *Congrès archéologique de la France*, 1906, pp. 392–406, has attempted, but unsuccessfully, to vindicate the historical chracter of the oldest Life.

ST GERARD SAGREDO, Bp. of Csanad, Mart.

A.D. 1046

St Gerard, the apostle of a large district in Hungary, was a Venetian, and born about the beginning of the eleventh century. He renounced at an early age the enjoyments of the world, forsaking family and estate to consecrate himself to the service of God in the Benedictine monastery of San Giorgio Maggiore at Venice, of which he became abbot. After some years he undertook a pilgrimage to the Holy Sepulchre at Jerusalem, and while passing through Hungary became known to the king, St Stephen, who was attracted by his sincere piety and with earnestness pleaded that God had inspired him to make that pilgrimage that he might assist by his labours the souls of so many in that country who were perishing in infidelity. Gerard, however, would not at first consent to stay at court, but built a little hermitage at Beel, where he passed seven years with one companion called Maurus, in fasting and prayer. The King, having settled the peacc of his kingdom, drew Gerard out of his solitude and made him tutor to his son, St Emeric, and Gerard began as well to preach the gospel with wonderful success. In 1035 St Stephen established the new episcopal see of Csanad, and appointed St Gerard to be its first bishop. He looked for nothing in this dignity but labours, crosses, and the hopes of martyrdom. The greater part of the people were infidels, and those who bore the name of Christians were ignorant, brutish, and savage. Two-thirds of the inhabitants of the city of Csanad itself were idolaters, yet the saint in less than a year made them all Christians. His labours were crowned with almost equal success in other parts of the diocese. He always so far as possible joined to the perfection of the episcopal state that of the solitary life, and he built small hermitages or cells near the towns in the different parts of his diocese. In these he used to take up his lodgings wherever he came in his travels, avoiding cities that he might occupy himself with prayer and contemplation, which gave him fresh vigour in the discharge of his pastoral functions.

The holy King Stephen seconded the zeal of the good bishop as long as he lived, but on his death in 1038 his nephew and successor Peter, a debauched and cruel prince, declared himself the persecutor of all Christians who opposed him, of whom St Gerard was one. He was expelled by his own subjects in 1042, and Aba Samú, another nobleman of savage disposition, was placed on the throne. This tyrant soon began to put to death all those noblemen whom he suspected not to have been in his interest. St Stephen had established a custom that the crown should be presented to the king by some bishop on all great festivals. Aba Samú gave notice to St Gerard to come to court to perform this ceremony. The saint refused to pay the usurper that compliment, and told him that if he persisted in his crimes God would soon put an end both to his reign and life. Another prelate gave him the crown ; but two years after the very persons who had placed him on the throne turned their arms against him, treated him as a rebel, and cut off his head. A definite revolt against Christianity had begun, and the claimant to the throne, Andrew, did little to discourage it ; it was even rumoured that he had bargained with the army to restore paganism. St Gerard set out to meet and remonstrate with him, and when celebrating Mass at a little place on the Danube called Giod he had prevision that he would on that day receive the crown of martyrdom. His party arrived at Buda and were going to cross the river when they were set upon by a party of soldiers under the command of Duke Vatha, the most obstinate upholder of idolatry and enemy of the memory of St Stephen. They attacked St Gerard with a shower of stones, overturned his conveyance, and dragged him to the ground. Whilst in their hands the saint raised himself on his knees and prayed with the protomartyr St Stephen : " Lord, lay not this sin to their charge. They know not what they do." He had scarcely spoken these words when he was run through the body with a lance ; the fierce insurgents then hauled him to the edge of the cliff called the Blocksberg, on which they were, and dashed his body headlong into the Danube below. It was September 24, 1046. The heroic death of St Gerard had a profound effect on Duke Andrew, and after his coronation as king he was energetic in support of the Faith. Gerard was declared a martyr by Pope St Gregory VII, and his remains were taken up and put in a rich shrine in the church of Csanad during the reign of St Ladislas. At length the republic of Venice by repeated entreaties obtained the greater part of his relics from the King of Hungary, and with great solemnity translated them to the church of our Lady of Murano, wherein he is venerated as the protomartyr of Venice, the place of his birth.

The good pastor refuses no labour and declines no danger for the good of souls. If the soil where his lot falls be barren, and he plants and waters without increase, he does not lose patience but redoubles his efforts in prayer and work. If he perseveres to the end, he can say to God : " Thou, O Lord, wilt not less reward my pains if I am found faithful to the end." Zeal and charity give him fresh vigour, and he weeps many tears for the souls which perish and for their contempt of the infinite and gracious Lord of all. Yet his courage is never damped nor does he ever repine or disquiet himself. He is not authorised to curse the fig-tree which produces no fruit, but continues to dig about it and to fertilize the earth to the end, repaying all injuries with kindness and prayers and never weary with renewing his endeavours. Impatience and lack of confidence in pastors never spring from zeal or charity, but from self-love, which seeks to please itself in the success of what it undertakes. The more deceitful this evil principle is, and the more difficult to be detected, the more carefully must it be watched against. Sourness, discouragement, vexation, and weariness of mind are sure signs that a mixture of this evil debases our intention. The pastor must draw on the treasures of God's patience, goodness, and long-suffering ; he must never abandon any sinner to whom God, the offended one, still offers mercy.

The most reliable source for the history of St Gerard is, it appears, the short biography printed in the *Acta Sanctorum*, September, vol. vi (pp. 722–724). Contrary to the opinion previously entertained, it is not an epitome of the longer Life which is found in Endlicher, *Rerum Hungar. Monumenta Arpadiana* (pp. 205–234), but dates from the twelfth, or even the end of the eleventh, century. This, at least, is the conclusion of R. F. Kaindl in the *Archiv f. Oesterreichische Geschichte*, vol. 91 (1902), pp. 1–58. The other biographies are later expansions of the first named, and not so trustworthy. St Gerard's story and episcopate have also been discussed recently by C. Juhász in *Studien und Mittheilungen O.S.B.*, 1929, pp. 139–145, and 1930, pp. 1–35.

BD. ROBERT OF KNARESBOROUGH, Hermit

A.D. 1218 (?)

Like his fellow-hermit and fellow-Yorkshireman Richard Rolle, Robert Flower, the " Holy Hermit of Knaresborough," enjoyed a considerable *cultus* in medieval England which was never confirmed or made public by canonisation. His name has not even been found in any kalendars, but the Trinitarian church at York was called St Robert's, and Matthew Paris mentions him with St Edmund Rich and St Elizabeth of Hungary as one of the holiest persons of his time. He was born about the year 1160 at York, of which city his father was twice mayor, and at one time aspired to be a priest. But he never proceeded beyond the subdiaconate, " for what cause God best knoweth," as Leland says. His brother was a Cistercian in Newminster Abbey at Morpeth and Robert followed him there, but four and a half months of novitiate was enough to demonstrate that his vocation was not to the cenobitical life. He was convinced that God was calling him to a dedicated life of some sort, and so, forgoing his patrimony as eldest son, he went to live in a cave adjoining a poor chapel called St Giles's below a cliff by the river Nidd, near Knaresborough. This cave was already occupied by a knight who, it is surmised, was hiding from the wrath of his king rather than seeking the love of God, for immediately on the death of Henry II (or Richard I) he deserted his cave and his companion and went home to his wife. Robert remained there till the offer of a cell and chapel of St Hilda at Rudfarlington enticed him further into the forest ; his life here was rudely interrupted by the burglary and destruction of his hermitage by robbers. So he moved a few miles away to Spofforth, under the protection of the Percys, but he was beginning to become known as a holy man, and to avoid the people who insisted on coming to see him he fled in desperation to the priory of Hedley, near Tadcaster. But Robert was no more successful as a Cluniac than as a Cistercian, and when he took the liberty openly to criticise their interpretation of the Rule of St Benedict the monks dismissed him. He now went back to Rudfarlington, where his patroness gave him a barn and other buildings, some land, and four hinds to help him work it, and all went well for a year till he attracted the attention of William d'Estuteville, Constable of Knaresborough. He suspected the hermit of giving shelter to thieves and outlaws and had his buildings pulled down about his ears. Robert fled back to St Giles's chapel where he had started from, but was pursued by the wrath of the Constable who found him there and intended to have him ejected. However, he changed his mind, according to the fifteenth-century poem about Robert because he had a dream in which three demons of most terrifying aspect threatened his life on account of his wrongs to the man of God.

D'Estuteville gave to Robert all the land between his cave and

Grimbald's Crag and also two horses, two oxen, and two cows, which he was to farm for his own sustenance and the relief of the poor. Robert was now well provided for and left in peace, except that people of all degrees came to visit him " for to be edified." Another brother, Walter, a prosperous burgess and mayor of York, urged him to go into a monastery—probably he thought a hermit brother, however holy, did not consort with his own dignity—but Robert replied in the words of the psalmist : " Hic habitabo, quoniam elegi eam." So Walter agreed to send workmen to build a chapel of the Holy Cross, ruins of which still remain beside the cave which the hermit enlarged by his own labour. Unhappily the place is now more associated with the crime of Eugene Aram in 1744–5 than with Robert Flower, for in it the body of the murdered Daniel Clarke was hidden. Several miracles of the hermit passed into the memory of the countryside and he was popularly esteemed to have waged long warfare with visible manifestations of the Devil ; he is also said to have had a vision of his mother, asking him to pray for her in Purgatory and afterwards assuring him that his prayers were efficacious. Robert had a disciple called Ivo who, after an early attempt to run away was spoiled by his breaking his leg, persevered in this solitary life and succeeded to Robert's hermitage after his death. From his master he learnt that a hermit's first duty, after his own sanctification, is to care for the poor and oppressed ; Robert sheltered all unfortunates, whether " deserving " or not, who came to him, and collected alms and worked hard on his land for the relief of the needy. He refused to pay tithes of corn and hay to the parson of Knaresborough, pointing out in rather forcible language that his land was already the patrimony of the poor.

When King John was staying at Knaresborough Castle he visited the hermit, and is said to have found him at prayer. When Sir Brian de l'Isle called him to the King's presence, Robert presented him with an ear of corn, saying : " If you are a king, make such a thing as this. There is but one king, God ! " John accepted the lesson in silence, but sycophantic (or kindly tactful) bystanders were quick to point out that Robert was mad. The king asked if there was anything he could give him, and the hermit replied there was nothing. But directly John was gone he regretted a missed opportunity and sent Ivo after him to plead for the poor ; a plow-land of the adjoining wood was granted. While he lay dying, monks came from Fountains Abbey, offering him the Cistercian habit, which he refused, warning Ivo what would happen after his death. And directly he was dead the monks again came, and wished to have his body for burial in their great minster. But Robert had said definitely that he was to be buried in his own chapel of Holy Cross, and soldiers were sent from the castle to guard the body until it was buried in the appointed place in the presence of crowds of weeping people, mourning the " devout, debonair and discreet man, than whom a milder could not be met." After the death of Ivo, Robert's hermitage came into the hands of the Trinitarian order, whose friars cared for his shrine and entertained the pilgrims there until the dissolution of the religious houses.

There has been, for some reason, a strange confusion between Robert of Knaresborough, who died perhaps as late as 1235, and Robert, Abbot of Newminster (†1139). Concerning the former all the material sources of information were indicated as far back as 1896 by A. F. Pollard in the *Dictionary of National Biography*, vol. xlviii, p. 362. Apart from manuscript materials and many references to printed books, Mr. Pollard there notes that a medieval metrical Life of Bd. Robert was edited for the Roxburghe Club in 1824, and also that his legend was printed in English in a little book by Thomas Gent called *British Piety Displayed*, (York 1733). See also Stanton's *Menology*, p. 210 ; and J. I. Cummins, *Legends, Saints and Shrines of Knaresborough* (1928).

ST PACIFICUS OF SAN SEVERINO, CONF.

A.D. 1721

In the year 1653 there was born to Antony Mary Divini and Mary Angela Bruni, at San Severino in the March of Ancona, a son, who was baptised under the names of Charles Antony. Soon after his confirmation, at three years of age according to the custom of the time, both his parents died, leaving him to the care of his maternal uncle, a harsh and disagreeable man. He used the boy simply as a servant about the house and treated him with something less than the consideration due to a servant, all of which Charles bore with patience and humility until, in his seventeenth year, he offered himself to the Friars Minor of the Observance. On Holy Innocents' day, 1670, he was clothed in their monastery at Forano and received the name of Pacificus. After an exemplary novitiate he was professed, and after the usual course of studies was ordained at the age of twenty-five. For the two following years he taught philosophy to the junior friars and then, representing to his superiors that preaching was a more suitable employment for him, he was sent out on mission work in the neighbouring villages and hamlets. His sweet and simple discourses were everywhere well received, and were strengthened in their effect by his ability to read the consciences of his penitents. He reminded one James Sconocchia at Cingoli that he had forgotten to confess two sins of profanity, and another penitent said that the friar had brought back to his memory occasions on which he had been unkind to his mother and had entertained unchaste thoughts. But the public apostolate of Brother Pacificus was destined to last only for six or seven years, for when he was thirty-five he was overtaken by both deafness and blindness and by a chronic ulceration of his legs which almost crippled him. He continued to live at Forano, passing his time in prayer, penance, and alms deeds, but having for a short time filled the offices of vicar and guardian of the friary of San Severino, he was in 1705 transferred to that house where, amid the friends and scenes of his childhood, he passed the rest of his life. On several occasions St Pacificus displayed the gifts of prophecy, as, for example, in 1717 when he foretold the victory of the Christian army under Prince Eugene of Savoy over the Turks at Belgrade. As though his natural bodily afflictions were not enough, he still further mortified himself with hair-shirt and discipline, and his superiors had to interfere to limit his fasts. At Mass he was often rapt in ecstasy, sometimes for several hours. During the month of July 1721 he received a visit from the Bishop of San Severino, and as he was leaving St Pacificus suddenly cried out : " My lord—Heaven, Heaven ! And I shall soon follow you." Within fifteen days the bishop was dead, and on the following September 24 St Pacificus died also. Miracles took place at his tomb, as they had done in his lifetime, and in 1752 his cause was begun ; Cardinal Henry of York was *ponente* and Mgr. (afterwards Cardinal) Erskine Promoter of the Faith. His beatification was decreed in 1785 and he was canonised by Pope Gregory XVI in 1839. His body is enshrined at San Severino.

The *Summarium du Virtutibus* printed for the use of the Congregation of Sacred Rites is the most authentic source of information. Several biographies have been published since the saint was canonised notably those of Melchiorri (1839), Bernardino da Gajoli (1898), and Diotallevi (1910). See also Léon, *Auréole Séraphique* (Eng. Trans.), vol. iii, pp. 224–229.

SEPTEMBER 25

ST FIRMINUS I, Bp. of Amiens, Mart.

c. A.D. 287 (?)

ACCORDING to his "acts," he was a native of Pampeluna, in Navarre, initiated in the Christian faith by St Honestus, a disciple of St Saturninus of Toulouse, and consecrated bishop at Toulouse when he was thirty-one years old by St Honoratus, successor to St Saturninus, in order to preach the gospel in the remoter parts of Gaul. He preached the faith in the countries of Albi, Agen, Auvergne, Anjou, and Beauvais, and being arrived at Amiens there chose his residence and founded a church of faithful disciples. He received the crown of martyrdom in that city, whether under the prefect Rictius Varus about the year 287, or in some other persecution from Decius in 250 to Diocletian in 303, is uncertain. Faustinian buried him in his field called Abladana, where his son Firminus II (who is honoured on September 1) built a church over his tomb, dedicated under the invocation of the Blessed Virgin, but now known as St Acheul's. St Salvius in the beginning of the seventh century translated his relics into the cathedral.

From the year 1186, when a relic was given to the city, the feast of St Firminus was celebrated in Pampeluna with the same honours as those of the Apostles, but it is very doubtful if Firminus of Pampeluna (said to have been martyred in the second century) and Firminus of Amiens were the same person. On the other hand it is possible that Firminus I and Firminus II were only one man; they are both unheard of before the eighth century, the first known bishop of Amiens being Eulogius in the middle of the fourth century. Firminus was probably simply a missionary bishop in Gaul.

Two texts are known which claim to represent the "Acts" of St Firminus. The Bollandists (September, vol. vii) print one entire with extracts from the other. See also Salmon, *Histoire de S. Firmin, martyr* (1861), and Duchesne, *Fastes Épiscopaux*, vol. iii, pp. 122–127.

ST AUNACHARIUS OR AUNARIUS, BP. OF AUXERRE, CONF.

A.D. 605

He was born of a family of the Orléanois distinguished alike for its nobility and virtue ; his brother was Austreinus, venerated as a saint in his diocese of Orléans, and his sister St Austregildis was the mother of St Lupus of Sens.   Aunacharius passed his youth at the court of King Gontramnus of Burgundy, but renounced the world and put himself under the direction of St Syagrius, Bishop of Autun.   By him he was ordained priest, and about the year 570 was elected to the see of Auxerre.   St Aunacharius was one of the most influential and respected bishops of his time in France in both civil and religious affairs.   When Pope Pelagius II wanted the help of the Franks against the Lombards, the Eastern Emperor having failed him, it was to the Bishop of Auxerre he wrote, imploring him to get the Frankish kings to come to the succour of the Roman Church.   But it was in ecclesiastical discipline that St Aunacharius was particularly active.   He attended the synod of Paris under St Germanus in the year 573, and those at Mâcon convened by order of Gontramnus in 582 and 585, which among other things forbade clerics to summon one another before the civil courts, established the right of bishops to interfere on behalf of widows, orphans, and freed slaves, and enforced Sunday observance and the payment of tithes.   Aunacharius, zealous for discipline in his own diocese, tireless in his vigilance over public morals, and anxious to instruct his people in everything that affected their lives as Christians, himself held two synods at Auxerre in which the above legislation was applied to his own church.   In the first of these forty-five canons were enacted, some of which throw interesting light on the manners and customs of the place and time, when superstitious survivals of paganism and abuse of Christian practices had not yet attained the harmless respectability of " folk-survivals."   People were forbidden, for example, to use churches for dancing and to sing ribald songs or give entertainments therein ; they were not to dress themselves up as stags or calves on New Year's Day or to exchange " evil gifts," or to make vows or oaths before " holy " bushes, trees, and wells, or to practise sympathetic magic, or to meet together in private houses to celebrate the vigils of feasts (*cf.*, the abuse of " wakes " in England and Ireland).   For the edification and encouragement of the faithful St Aunacharius caused biographies of his two distinguished predecessors St Amatus and St Germanus to be written, and he increased the revenues of his church in order that divine worship might be conducted with more order and decency. Secular clergy as well as monks were bound to assist at the Divine Office daily, and solemn litanies of intercession were to be carried out every day by each church and monastery in turn, by the larger ones once every month. St Aunacharius died on September 25, in the year 605, and was buried in his cathedral where his relics were afterwards enclosed in a golden shrine. This was pillaged by Huguenots in 1567, but some of the relics were saved by being hidden in a hole hollowed out of a pillar in the crypt.

There are two short Lives printed in the *Acta Sanctorum*, September, vol. vii, with the usual prolegomena. See also Cochard, *Les Saints d'Orléans*, pp. 272–277 and Duchesne, *Fastes Épiscopaux*, vol. ii, pp. 435–437.

ST FINBAR, BP. AND CONF.

c. A.D. 623

Finbar, or Barr, founder of the city and see of Cork, is said to have been the natural son of a royal lady and of a master-smith called Amergin, craftsman to Tighernach, chief of the Hi-Eachach Mumhan. He was baptised Lochan, but the monks who educated him at Kilmacahill in Kilkenny changed his name to *Fionnbarr*, Whitehead, because of his fair hair. Legends say that he went to Rome on pilgrimage with one of his preceptors, called MacCoirpre, and on his way back passed through Wales and visited St David in Pembrokeshire. As he had no means of getting to Ireland, David lent him one of his own boats, called *Horse* on account of the carving of her figurehead, and in the channel he sighted and signalled St Brendan the Navigator, voyaging eastward. St Finbar is fabled to have gone again to Rome, in company with St David and others, when Pope St Gregory the Great would have made him a bishop but was deterred by a vision in which he learned that Heaven had reserved this prerogative for itself. Accordingly when Finbar returned to Ireland our Lord brought a miraculous flow of oil from the ground, caught him up into Heaven, and there consecrated him bishop, anointing him with the oil which flowed round the feet of the onlookers ! After preaching in various parts of southern Ireland, where he founded a dozen churches, and living as a hermit on a small island in Gouganebarra, not far from his birthplace at Rathculleen, he established a monastery at Lough Eirc, low marshy ground on the south side of the mouth of the river Lee, the *corcagh-mor* from which the city of Cork takes its name. The monastery

soon attracted disciples and its school exerted an influence all over
the south of Ireland ; " to this house, as an abode of wisdom and
sacred storehouse of all Christian virtues, so many came through
zeal of leading a holy life that it changed a desert into a great city,
from the number of its cells and of the holy men inhabiting them."

Accounts of St Finbar are full of conflicting statements and
decorated with surprising wonders. There is a charming story that
when he was visited by St Laserian the two monks sat together
under a hazel bush, talking of the things of God. Presently Laserian
asked Finbar for a sign that God was with him. Finbar prayed, and
the spring catkins on the bush above them fell off, nuts formed,
grew, and ripened, and he gathered them in handfuls and poured
them into Laserian's lap. The death of St Finbar was the occasion
of a very unusual miracle, for when he was taken to God the sun
did not set for a fortnight ! It would appear that the saint visited
and preached in Scotland. There was formerly considerable devotion
to him there, and the island of Barra in the Western Isles, as well as
other places, has its name from him. Kintyre was apparently the
scene of his labours. He is said to have died at Cloyne, which
church was founded by his disciple, St Colman MacLenin, and his
body was taken for burial back to his church in Cork. The feast of
St Finbar is kept on this day throughout Ireland.

There are both Irish and Latin Lives of St Finbar. The primary Irish
text has been edited by C. Plummer in his *Bethada Náem nÉrenn*, with a
translation in vol. ii, pp. 11–21. The best Latin Life has also been edited by
Plummer, *Vitæ Sanctorum Hiberniæ*, vol. i, pp. 65–74. See further Caul-
field, *Life of St Fin Barre* (1864). Some other Latin materials, more or less
dependent upon these, will be found in the *Acta Sanctorum*, September,
vol. vii. See also Forbes, *Kalendars of Scottish Saints*, pp. 275–276 ; O'Hanlon, *Lives of Irish Saints*, vol. ix, pp. 547 *seq.* ; and J. F. Kenney, *Sources for
the early History of Ireland*, vol. i. *Cf.* W. D. Simpson, *The Origins of Christianity in Aberdeenshire*, 1925.

ST CEOLFRID, Abbot of Wearmouth, Conf.

A.D. 716

Ceolfrid (Geoffrey) was born in the year 642, probably in
Northumbria, and certainly of a good family. When he was eighteen
he became a monk in his kinsman Tunbert's monastery at Gilling,
but soon migrated to St Wilfrid's monastery at Ripon, where the
Rule of St Benedict had been introduced, and was ordained there.
Soon afterwards he went to Canterbury to visit the communities of
Christ Church and SS. Peter and Paul's, and then spent some time

with St Botulph at his newly founded monastery at Icanhoe in East Anglia (generally supposed to be Boston in Lincolnshire). He returned to Ripon " so well instructed that no one could be found more learned than he in either ecclesiastical or monastic traditions." He was made novice-master, and the fame of his virtues and learning presently reached the ears of St Benedict Biscop at Wearmouth. At St Benedict's request St Wilfrid released Ceolfrid from his obedience at Ripon, and he went to Wearmouth, where he was soon appointed prior. When the abbot left on a journey to Rome, Ceolfrid was put in sole charge, a responsibility that accorded ill with his personal preferences. Some of the monks complained of the strictness with which he administered the house, and in consequence of the dissension so caused St Ceolfrid went back for a time to Ripon. St Benedict induced him to return, and about the year 678 took him with him when he made his fourth visit to Rome.

About 683, having received a gift of land from King Egfrid, Benedict founded another monastery, dedicated in honour of St Paul, at Jarrow, on the Tyne six miles from Wearmouth. The two houses in effect were one abbey, under the rule of St Benedict Biscop, but it was necessary to have a local superior at the new foundation. Ceolfrid was therefore appointed deputy abbot of St Paul's, and given seventeen monks from St Peter's at Wearmouth as the nucleus of a community. While St Benedict was absent in Rome for the fifth time an epidemic ravaged Tyneside. In it perished St Easterwin, deputy-abbot of St Peter's and a great part of his community, and at Jarrow every single monk died except St Ceolfrid and a young *alumnus* who was being educated at the monastery. It is recorded that Ceolfrid could not bear to give up celebrating the Divine Office in choir, so he and the boy continued to sing it alone together until a new community was formed. In the year 690 St Benedict Biscop died, after having, with the agreement of the monks, nominated Ceolfrid as his successor. He governed the two monasteries from Wearmouth for twenty-six years from the death of the founder, but he would have regarded it as his greatest happiness on earth if he could have been as much forgotten by all and despised by everyone as he despised and tried to forget himself. He lived in his community as St Antony and St Hilarion lived on their mountains, in the most profound recollection and in the practice of the most austere penance. Nevertheless, St Ceolfrid was diligent and active in everything he took in hand, of a sharp wit, mature in judgement, and fervent in zeal. St Bede, who had the happiness to live under this great man, has left authentic testimonies of his learning, abilities, and sanctity. He was a great lover of sacred literature, and enriched the libraries of his two monasteries with a great number of good books, but removed those which could only serve to entertain curiosity. To how great a pitch he carried the sacred sciences in his monasteries St Bede himself is the foremost example. He says of St Ceolfrid that : " Whatever good works his predecessor had begun he with no less energy took pains to finish. Among the improvements of his own which time suggested to him and enabled him to carry out were the building of several new chapels and the increase of altar-vessels and church vestments." He exchanged a book with King Aldfrid for an estate of eight hides (about 950 acres, probably) of land, according to an arrangement made by St Benedict Biscop, but afterwards paid an additional price and received instead twenty hides in a more convenient situation for the monastery. St Ceolfrid obtained from Pope St Sergius I a renewal of the charter of exemption and other privileges granted by Pope St Agatho, and this was accepted in a synod of bishops at which King Aldfrid was present and concurred. About the year 710 the King of the Picts, Naitan or Nechtan, sent to Wearmouth desiring to be informed concerning the right time of celebrating Easter, and the true form of the clerical tonsure. The Abbot proved and recommended to him the Catholic custom of observing Easter and the Roman tonsure, called " St Peter's," by a letter which the king received it with great joy and satisfaction, and commanded both points to be received and observed throughout his dominions. This king likewise desired Ceolfrid to send him builders who might erect a stone church after the manner of the Romans, promising to dedicate it in honour of St Peter, and the Abbot complied also with this request. The long and detailed letter which St Ceolfrid sent to Naitan has been preserved for us by Bede, who, in fact, probably drew it up. It ends : " I admonish your wisdom, O King, that you endeavour to make the people, over whom the King of kings and Lord of lords has placed you, observe in all points those things which belong to the unity of the Catholic and Apostolic Church. For so it will come to pass that, after your temporal kingdom has passed away, the blessed Prince of the Apostles will open to you and yours the gate of the heavenly Kingdom where you will rest forever with the elect. May the grace of the eternal King keep you in safety, most beloved son in Christ, to reign long for the peace of us all."

In the year 716 Ceolfrid, finding himself old and infirm and no longer able to teach his subjects by word and example the perfect form of monastic observance, decided to resign his office and told his unwilling and protesting monks that they must elect somebody in his place. He himself was determined to end his days in Rome and, fearful that he would die before arriving there, as in fact happened, he set out only three days after his decision was made known. Early in the morning of Wednesday, May 4, after the six hundred monks had assisted at Mass and received Communion, they all assembled in St Peter's church at Wearmouth. St Ceolfrid, when he had lighted the incense and sung a prayer, gave his blessing to them all, standing at the altar-steps with the thurible in his hand. Then in the chapel of St Laurence he addressed them for the last time, urging them to keep charity with one another and lovingly to correct those who were in fault ; he forgave whatever wrongs might have been done him, and asked them all to pray for him and to pardon him if he had ever reprimanded them too harshly. They then went down to the shore where, amid tears and lamentation, he gave them the kiss of peace and prayed aloud for them, and went aboard a boat, preceded by ministers with lighted candles and a golden crucifix. Having crossed the river, he kissed the cross, mounted his horse, and departed.

Among the treasures which St Benedict Biscop had brought from Rome, or received from his friend St Adrian, was a copy of St Jerome's Vulgate, and of this precious manuscript St Ceolfrid had had three copies made. One was given to the library at Wearmouth, one to that at Jarrow, and the third he now took with him as a present to the Pope. But he was not destined to deliver it. During his journey in spite of his weakness and the rigours of travel he relaxed none of his old discipline. Every day he said the Divine Office, and the psalms of the psalter twice as well, and even when he had to be carried in a horse-litter he celebrated Mass, " except one day which was passed at sea and the three days immediately before his death." After travelling for just on fifteen weeks he reached Langres in Champagne, where he died on the day of his arrival, September 25, 716. He was buried the next day, amid the sorrow not only of his companions but also of the people of the place, " for it was almost impossible not to weep at the sight of part of his company continuing their journey without their holy father, whilst part returned home to relate his death and burial, and others again, lingered in grief at his grave among strangers speaking an unknown tongue."

The immediate fate of the Bible which St Ceolfrid was taking to St Gregory II is not known ; in all probability it never reached the Pope. But there is in the Bibliotheca Laurentiana at Florence a manuscript, known as Codex Amiatinus, which has been known since the sixteenth century as one of the finest books in the world and as probably the purest text of the Vulgate extant. It was given by a Lombard abbot called Peter to the monastery of St Saviour on Monte Amiata, near Siena, in the ninth century and remained there till 1786 when, on the dissolution of the abbey, it was taken to Florence. For a time it was accepted that this codex was written in southern Italy during the sixth century (and so was the oldest manuscript of the Vulgate), it having been found that the donor's inscription was partly written over, partly composed of, an older one. But the great archæologist De Rossi was not satisfied with the received reconstruction of the original dedication ; about 1885 he came to connect it with Ceolfrid. His conjectures were confirmed by the researches of the Cambridge exegete, Dr. F. J. E. Hort, and it is now established beyond doubt that Codex Amiatinus was written (not necessarily by an Englishman) in the abbey of Wearmouth at the beginning of the eighth century and is the very book which St Ceolfrid carried with him to give to Pope St Gregory II.

St Ceolfrid was buried in the church of the Three Twin Brothers, SS. Speusippus, Eleusippus, and Meleusippus, at Langres. Thence his relics were later translated to Wearmouth, and finally, during the Danish invasions, to Glastonbury. His feast-day is still kept, by a commemoration on this day, in the diocese of Langres, where he is known as St Cenfroy ; it is the only place where his memory is observed liturgically.

The example of all the saints shows us that virtue is not to be attained without serious endeavour and much pains. We must counteract our depraved inclinations, which have taken a wrong bent, that they may recover their due rectitude ; the seeds of all virtues must be planted in our hearts with such care that they may take root, spring up, prosper, and bring forth fruit every day more and more abundantly. The observances of piety, religion, and penance, and all the conditions upon which God has promised His graces to us, must be performed with fervour, constancy, and perseverance. The slothful and fainthearted think everything above their strength, though they are never weary in labouring for this wretched world. If they set about the business of their salvation in good earnest they will learn to do with ease and pleasure that which their indolence made them look upon as impossible, and they will quickly find that there is a delicious hidden manna in true virtue. Its possession is to the soul a spring of pure joy, far beyond the delights of the world and the filthy pleasures of sin, even if these latter were not mixed with the bitter draughts which always go with them.

Besides the account which Bede gives of Ceolfrid in his *Historia Abbatum*, we have also the anonymous original from which he largely drew his information. Both texts are printed at the conclusion of C. Plummer's edition of the *Ecclesiastical History*, vol. i, pp. 364–404. Little can be added to these sources and to the material collected in Plummer's notes. See also Stanton, *Menology*, pp. 457–459. A certain amount of further illustration, chiefly archæological, may be obtained from Sir Henry Howorth's *The Golden Days of Early English History*, vol. ii. Of the " Codex Amiatinus " an exact description is given in the new critical edition of the Vulgate, vol. i (Rome, 1926), pp. xx–xxvi. Dom Quentin, the responsible editor, definitely states that the codex was written at Wearmouth or at Jarrow. *Cf.* the *Dictionnaire d'Archéologie chrét*, article " Ceolfrid," vol. ii, cc. 3260–3267.

ST ALBERT, PATRIARCH OF JERUSALEM, CONF.

A.D. 1214

When the Latin kingdom of Jerusalem was set up in 1099 by the Crusaders, under Godfrey de Bouillon, the schismatical Greek prelates were driven from their principal sees and churches and replaced by bishops from the West, whose only subjects were in the ranks of the Crusaders themselves. Thus there came to be a Latin patriarch in Jerusalem, and it must be regretfully recorded that most of the prelates who held this office in crusading times were as equivocal in character as they were in position. When therefore the Patriarch Michael died in the year 1203 the canons regular of the Holy Sepulchre, supported by the King of Jerusalem, Amaury II de Lusignan, and the Latin Patriarch of Antioch, petitioned Pope Innocent III to send to succeed him a prelate whose holiness and abilities were well known even in Palestine. This was Albert, Bishop of Vercelli. He belonged to a very distinguished family of Parma, and after brilliant theological and legal studies had become a canon regular in the abbey of the Holy Cross at Mortara in Lombardy. When he was about thirty-five years old, namely in 1184, he was made bishop of Bobbio and almost at once translated to Vercelli. His diplomatic ability and trustworthiness caused him to be chosen as a mediator between Pope Clement III and Frederick Barbarossa, and he was a favourite of the last-named's successor, Henry IV, who made him a prince of the Empire and officially protected his see. By Innocent III he was made legate in the north of Italy, and in that capacity he brought about peace between Parma and Piacenza in 1199. Innocent did not want to spare him for Jerusalem, but approved the choice of the canons ; Albert for his part was moved to accept by consideration of the shocking state of the Latin kingdom and the prospect of persecution and even martyrdom that the office held out to him. The Pope invested him with the *pallium* and created him his legate in Palestine, and in 1205 St Albert set out in a Genoese vessel.

Already in 1187 the Saracens had retaken Jerusalem, and the see of the Latin patriarch had been united with that of Saint-Jean d'Acre (Ptolemais), where the Frankish king had set up his court. At Acre accordingly St Albert established himself, and set out to gain the respect and trust not only of Christians but of the Mohammedans as well, which his predecessors had conspicuously failed to do. As patriarch and legate he took a foremost part in the ecclesiastical and civil politics of the Levant, and over a period of nine years had to deal with a variety of matters which exercised his patience and prudence to the utmost. In the first place and continually he was faced with the almost impossible task of keeping the peace between the Frankish leaders and their followers, within the factions themselves, and between the invaders and the natives of the country. When the Count of Tripoli quarrelled with the Patriarch of Antioch, the Count shut the Patriarch up in a castle, and St Albert had to negotiate for his release. The nobles and military orders had to be persuaded to fulfil their first duties and go to the rescue of Christian prisoners in Alexandria, and Walter, Constable of Jerusalem, had to be reconciled to Hugh I of Cyprus. Leo II of Armenia had brought excommunication on himself by his opposition to the Templars, and there was this excommunication to be enforced or the King to be brought to submission. King Amaury II died before the arrival of St Albert, and his stepdaughter Mary of Montferrat was chosen to succeed him. The nobles asked the King of France to provide a husband for her, and Philip Augustus sent John of Brienne, who arrived in Palestine in 1209 when St Albert blessed their marriage and crowned them at Tyre. Mary died soon afterwards, whereupon St Albert had added to his other tasks that of keeping the Franks in their allegiance to King John, from whom they wished to withdraw it.

But Albert is best remembered, and justly, for a more purely religious work than any of these. About 1209 St Brocard, prior of the hermits living on Mount Carmel, asked him to embody the life they were leading in a rule for the observance of himself and his subjects. This St Albert did in a document of sixteen short and definite chapters. He provided for complete obedience to an elected superior ; for a separate dwelling for each hermit, with a common church ; for long fasts and perpetual abstinence from flesh-meat ; and daily silence from Vespers till after Terce. " Let each hermit remain in or near his cell, meditating day and night on the law of the Lord and persevering in prayer, unless engaged in some legitimate occupation." This rule was confirmed by Pope Honorius III in 1226 and mitigated by Innocent IV twenty years later. Whoever may have been the founder of the Carmelite Order, there is no doubt that St Albert of Jerusalem, an Augustinian canon, was its first legislator.

In 1213 Innocent III, deceived by the Templars' reports of his good dispositions, wrote to the Sultan asking for the peaceful surrender of Jerusalem, and at the same time summoned St Albert to the forthcoming council of the Lateran ; but he did not live to be present at that great assembly, which opened in November 1215. For twelve months he faithfully supported the Pope's hopeless efforts to get back Jerusalem, and then his life was suddenly and violently cut short. He had found it necessary to depose from his office the master of the Hospital of the Holy Ghost at Saint-Jean d'Acre, and the man was nursing his resentment. On the feast of the Exaltation of the Cross in 1214 St Albert officiated at a procession in the church of the Holy Cross at Acre, and in the course of it he was attacked and stabbed to death by the deposed Hospitaller. His feast was first introduced among the Carmelites in 1411. The anomaly to which the Bollandists draw attention by which he was not honoured liturgically in his own order no longer exists, for the canons regular of the Lateran now keep his feast as a double on April 8.

A short early Life of St Albert is printed with ample prolegomena in the *Acta Sanctorum*, April, vol. i. See also the *Analecta Ordinis Carmelitarum Discalceatorum*, 1926, etc., vol. iii, pp. 212 *seq. ;* and the *Dictionnaire de Théol. Cat.*, vol. i, cc. 662–663. Some other data are supplied by Father Benedict Zimmerman, *Monumenta Historica Carmelitarum* (1907), pp. 277–281. The Rule compiled by St Albert is also edited in this last-named work, pp. 20–114.

BD. VINCENT STRAMBI, Conf.

BISHOP OF MACERATA AND TOLENTINO

A.D. 1824

Blessed Vincent, whose feast has now been fixed by the Passionists for this date, is spoken of herein under January 10.

SEPTEMBER 26

SS. CYPRIAN AND JUSTINA, MARTYRS
NO DATE

THE legend of this St Cyprian, distinguished as "of Antioch," is a moral tale, probably utterly fabulous (if there ever were a martyred Cyprian and Justina on whom the story was built all trace of them has been lost), composed in order to impress on the listener or reader the powerlessness of the Devil and his angels in the face of Christian chastity defending itself with the might of the Cross. The tale has been worked up from various sources, and was known as least as early as the fourth century, for St Gregory Nazianzen identifies this Cyprian with the great St Cyprian of Carthage ; the poet Prudentius makes the same mistake. The story as told by Alban Butler is as follows :

Cyprian, surnamed "the Magician," was a native of Antioch whose parents had devoted him from his infancy to the Devil, and he was brought up in all the impious mysteries of idolatry, astrology, and black magic. In hopes of making great discoveries in these infernal arts, he left his native country when he was grown up and travelled to Athens, Mount Olympus in Macedonia, Argos, Phrygia, Memphis in Egypt, Chaldæa, and the Indies, places at that time famous for superstition and magical practices. When Cyprian had filled his head with all the extravagances of these schools of wickedness and delusion he stuck at no crimes, blasphemed Christ, and committed secret murders in order to offer the blood and inspect the bowels of children as decisive of future events ; nor did he scruple to use his arts to overcome the chastity of women. At that time there lived at Antioch a lady called Justina, whose beauty drew all eyes upon her. She was born of heathen parents but was brought over to the Christian faith by overhearing a deacon preaching, and her conversion was followed by that of her father and mother. A young pagan, Aglaïdes, fell deeply in love with her, and finding himself unable to win her to his will he applied to Cyprian for the assistance of his art. Cyprian was no less enamoured of the lady than his friend, and tried every secret with which he was acquainted to conquer her resolution. Justina, finding herself vigorously attacked, armed herself by prayer, watchfulness, and mortification against all his artifices and the power of his spells, suppliantly beseeching the Virgin Mary that she would succour a virgin in danger. Three times she overcame the assaults of demons sent by Cyprian by blowing in their faces and making the sign of the cross. Cyprian, finding himself worsted by a superior power, threatened his last emissary, who was the Devil himself, that he would abandon his service. The Devil, enraged to lose one by whom he had made so many conquests of other souls, assailed Cyprian with the utmost fury, and he was only repulsed by Cyprian himself making the sign of the cross. The soul of the penitent sinner was seized with a gloomy melancholy, which brought him almost to the brink of despair, at the sight of his past crimes. God inspired him in this perplexity to address himself to a holy priest named Eusebius, who had formerly been his school-fellow, and by the advice of this priest he was comforted and encouraged in his conversion. Cyprian, who in the trouble of his heart had been three days without eating, by the counsel of this director took some food, and on the following Sunday was conducted by him to the assembly of the Christians. These assemblies were then held very early in the morning, both to watch in prayer, and for fear of the heathen. So much was Cyprian struck by the reverence and devotion with which their act of divine worship was performed that he said of it : " I saw the choir of heavenly men —or of angels—singing to God, adding at the end of every verse in the psalms the Hebrew word Alleluia, so that they seemed not to be men."* Everyone present was astonished to see Cyprian introduced among them by a priest, and the bishop was scarce able to believe that his conversion was sincere. But Cyprian gave him a proof the next day by burning before his eyes all his magical books, giving his goods to the poor, and entering himself among the catechumens. After due instruction and preparation, he received the sacrament of Baptism from the hands of the bishop. Aglaïdes was likewise converted and baptised. Justina herself was so moved at these wonderful examples of the divine mercy that she cut off her hair as a sign that she dedicated her virginity to God, and disposed of her jewels and all her possessions to the poor. St Gregory Nazianzen describes the astonishing change that was wrought in Cyprian, his edifying

* In the course of a footnote Butler here tells a story which admirably illustrates an eighteenth-century deist's knowledge of and attitude towards Catholic worship. Lord Bolingbroke, being one day present at Mass in the chapel at Versailles and seeing the bishop elevate the host, was much impressed and whispered to his companion, the Marquess de———, " If I were king of France, I would always perform that ceremony myself " !

deportment, his gravity and love of God, and tells us that, out of humility, he asked to be employed as sweeper of the church. He was made door-keeper and then promoted to the priesthood, and, after the death of Anthimus the bishop, was placed in the episcopal chair of Antioch. [No known bishop of Antioch in Syria or Antioch in Pisidia was called either Cyprian or Anthimus]. When the persecution of Diocletian began, Cyprian was apprehended and carried before the governor of Phœnicia, who resided at Tyre. Justina had retired to Damascus, her native country, which city at that time was subject to the same authority and, falling into the hands of the persecutors, was presented to the same judge. She was inhumanly scourged, and Cyprian was torn with iron hooks. After this they were both sent in chains to Diocletian at Nicomedia who, upon reading the letter of the governor of Phœnicia, without more ado commanded their heads to be struck off. This sentence was executed upon the banks of the river Gallus, after a vain effort had been made to slay the martyrs by boiling them in a cauldron of pitch. Theoctistus, also a Christian, was beheaded with them for speaking to Cyprian as he was going to execution.

This legend was widely popular, as the many texts in Latin and Greek, not to speak of other languages, abundantly attest. Some part of the story was certainly known before the time of St Gregory Nazianzen, for the orator, preaching about the year 379, attributes to St Cyprian of Carthage a number of incidents which are taken from the legend of Cyprian of Antioch. None the less no shred of evidence can be produced to justify the belief that any such persons as Cyprian of Antioch, the quondam magician, and Justina the virgin martyr, ever existed. See on this especially Delehaye, " Cyprien d'Antioche et Cyprien de Carthage " in the *Analecta Bollandiana*, vol. xxxix (1921), pp. 314–332. Apart from the text of the legend, which may be read in the *Acta Sanctorum* (September, vol. vii), and elsewhere in other forms, the story has given rise to a considerable literature. See, for example, Th. Zahn, *Cyprian von Antiochien und die deutsche Faustsage* (1882) ; R. Reitzenstein, *Cyprian der Magier* in the Göttingen *Nachrichten*, 1917, pp. 38–79 ; and Rademacher, " *Griesch. Quellen zur Faustsage*" in the Vienna *Sitzungsberichte*, vol. 206 (1927). This legend was taken by Calderon as the theme for one of the most famous of his dramas, " El Magico Prodigioso," and passages from this were selected by Shelley in his " Scenes from Calderon."

ST EUSEBIUS, Pope and Conf.

A.D. 310

Eusebius was a Greek by birth, the son of a physician, and was elected in succession to Pope St Marcellus, whom he survived by only a few months. During the episcopate of his predecessor serious trouble had been caused in the Roman Church by the question of the treatment which was to be accorded to those who had lapsed from the Faith during the persecution of Diocletian. A party led by a certain Heraclius opposed itself to the Pope, who maintained the traditional discipline of the Church with regard to the *lapsi*. Whether the malcontents wanted this discipline made more or less strict is not certain : there was a tendency among the rigorists in this matter to become schismatic (*e.g.* the Novatianists), but in this case probably Heraclius represented a number of *lapsi* who wanted immediate restoration to communion without further penance. It is recorded in an inscription put by Pope St Damasus over the tomb of St Eusebius in the cemetery of Callistus that this dispute was prolonged into his pontificate and caused disorder and bitter strife in the Church at Rome : probably the repentant *lapsi* tried to force their way into the assemblies of the faithful. So great was the uproar that the Emperor Maxentius banished both Pope Eusebius and Heraclius from the city. The Pope went to Sicily where he died almost at once, and this exile following on his determined upholding of the canons caused him for a time to be venerated as a martyr, a title which St Damasus accords him. The body of St Eusebius was brought back to Rome by his successor St Miltiades, and buried in the cemetery of Callistus.

On this same day the Roman Martyrology mentions another St Eusebius, Bishop of Bologna, who is referred to by his friend St Ambrose in his treatise *On Virgins*.

See the *Acta Sanctorum*, September, vol. vii ; the *Liber Pontificalis* (ed. Duchesne), vol. i, p. 167 ; and J. Carini, *I lapsi e la deportazione in Sicilia del Papa S. Eusebio*, 1886.

ST COLMAN ELO, Abbot and Conf.

c. A.D. 610

There are dozens of saints of the name of Colman who have been or are still venerated in Ireland ; twelve are mentioned in kalendars in this month of September alone, and of them the most important one is St Colman Elo. He belonged to a family of Meath, but was born in Glenelly in Tyrone, about the year 557. He was educated by St Coeman, abbot of Annatrim on Slieve Bloom, and came under the influence of St Columcille, who was his maternal uncle. Colman visited him at Iona, and is said to have been delivered from the perils of the voyage by his uncle's prayers. About the year 590 land was given to him by the Prince of Meath at Lynally in Offally, where

he founded a monastery and so fulfilled the prophecy made by
St Macanisius sixty years earlier. He also founded a monastery at
Muckamore, and from the fact that he is sometimes referred to as
" Coarb of MacNisse," he is supposed to have been bishop in Kells
or Connor. Near the end of his life he made a pilgrimage to Clonard,
where he had a vision of St Finian, and on his return announced his
approaching death to his monks. Throughout his life his heart was
perfectly disengaged from all creatures and attracted to God by that
divine love from whence proceeded the ardour of his contemplation ;
so that his soul was constantly united to Him who was the centre of
his heart and his whole happiness. A number of miracles of a
familiar type are attributed to St Colman Elo, and he is said to have
foretold the death of Pope St Gregory the Great and to have had a
vision of his soul ascending to Heaven on March 11 in the year 604.

There is both an Irish and a Latin Life of St Colman Elo. The former
has been edited by C. Plummer in his *Bethada Náem nÉrenn* (Eng. trans. in
vol. ii, pp. 162–176) ; and the latter by the same scholar in the *Vitæ Sanctorum Hiberniæ*, vol. i, pp. 258–273. See also Canon E. Maguire, *St Barron*
(1923) ; and J. Ryan, *Irish Monasticism*, from which last we learn (p. 130)
that to Colman is attributed the authorship of the tract called " Aibgitir in
Chrábaid," the Alphabet of Devotion. He is also said to have been deprived
for a while of his memory in punishment of his pride of intellect, and then to
have recovered it again by a miracle.

ST NILUS THE YOUNGER, ABBOT OF GROTTAFERRATA, CONF.

A.D. 1004

Nilus was born of a Greek family (said to have been the Malena)
of Magna Græcia at Rossano in Calabria about the year 910, and was
baptised Nicholas. So far from being in his youth " fervent in
religious duties and in the practice of all virtues," as Alban Butler
avers, he was at least lukewarm and careless in his early life ; it has
even been questioned whether the lady with whom he lived, and
who bore him a daughter, was married to him. But when he was
thirty she and the child died, and this double bereavement, aided
by a serious sickness, recalled him to a sense of his responsibilities
and brought about a complete turning to God. At that time there
were a number of monasteries of monks of the Byzantine rite in
southern Italy, and Nicholas received the habit at one of them,
taking the name of Nilus. At different times he lived in several of
these monasteries, after being for a period a hermit, and became
abbot of St Adrian's, near San Demetrio Corone. The reputation of
his sanctity and learning was soon spread over the country and many

came to him for spiritual advice. In 976 the archbishop Theophy-lactus, Metropolitan of Reggio, with the lord of that territory, named Leo, many priests, and others went to see him, rather desiring to try his erudition and skill than to hear any lessons for their edification. The abbot knew their intention, but having saluted them courteously and made a short prayer with them, he put into the hands of Leo a book in which were contained certain theories concerning the small number of the elect, which seemed to the company too severe. But the saint undertook to prove them to be clearly founded on the principles laid down not only by St Basil, St John Chrysostom, St Ephrem, St Theodore the Studite, and other fathers, but by St Paul and the gospel itself, adding at the close of his discourse : "These statements seem dreadful, but they only condemn the irregularity of your lives. Unless you be altogether holy you will not escape everlasting torments." One of them then asked the abbot whether Solomon was damned or saved ? To which he replied : "What does it concern us to know whether he be saved or no ? But it is needful for you to reflect that Christ pronounces damnation against all persons who commit impurity." This he said knowing that the person who put the question was addicted to that vice. And he added : "I would rather know whether you will be damned or saved. As for Solomon, the holy Scripture makes no mention of his repentance, as it does of that of Manasses." Euphraxus, a vain and haughty nobleman, was sent as governor of Calabria from the imperial court at Constantinople. St Nilus made him no presents upon his arrival, as other prelates did, and so the governor sought every occasion of mortifying the servant of God. But shortly after, falling sick, he sent for Nilus and begged his pardon and prayers, and asked to receive the monastic habit from his hands. St Nilus refused a long time to give it him, saying : "Your baptismal vows are sufficient for you. Penance requires no new vows, but a sincere change of heart and life." Euphraxus was not satisfied and continued so urgent that the saint at length gave him the habit. The governor made all the slaves free, distributed his estate among the poor, and died three days later with holy resignation.

About the year 981 the Saracen incursions into south Italy com-pelled St Nilus to flee, and with sixty of his monks this representative of Eastern monachism threw himself upon the hospitality of the headquarters of Western monachism at Monte Cassino. They were received "as if St Antony had come from Alexandria, or their own great St Benedict from the dead," and after living in the house for a time and celebrating their Greek offices in the church, the Bene-dictine abbot, Aligern, bestowed upon the fugitives the monastery

and lands of Vallelucio. There they lived for fifteen years, and then
moved to Serperi, near Gaeta. When in the year 998 the Emperor
Otho III came to Rome to expel Philagathos, Bishop of Piacenza,
whom the senator Crescentius had set up as anti-pope against
Gregory V, St Nilus went to intercede with the Pope and Emperor
that the anti-pope might be treated with mildness. Philagathos
(" John XVI ") was a Calabrian like himself, and Nilus had tried
in vain to dissuade him from his schism and treason. The abbot
was received with great honour and listened to with respect, but he
was not able to do much to modify the cruelty with which the aged
anti-pope was treated. When a prelate was sent to make an explanation to Nilus, who had protested vigorously against the injuries
done to the helpless Philagathos, he pretended to be asleep in order
to avoid an argument about it. Some time after Otho paid a visit to
the *laura* of St Nilus ; he was surprised to see his monastery consisting of poor scattered huts, and said : " These men who live in
tents as strangers on earth are truly citizens of Heaven." Nilus
conducted the Emperor first to the church, and after praying there
entertained him in his cell. Otho pressed the saint to accept some
spot of ground in his dominions, promising to endow it. Nilus
thanked him and answered : " If my brethren are truly monks our
divine Master will not forsake them when I am gone." In taking
leave the Emperor said to him : " Ask what you please, as if you
were my son : I will give it you with joy and pleasure. Our Lord
sent His disciples forth without money or staff and with only one
garment, but when His passion drew near He told them to take
purse and scrip. So you went out in poverty in your younger days,
but now that old age is upon you and death near take this purse that
I offer you." St Nilus, deeply touched, laying his hand upon the
Emperor's breast, said : " The only thing I ask of you is that you
would save your soul. Though emperor, you must die and give an
account to God, like other men."

In 1004 Nilus set out to visit a Greek monastery south of
Tusculum and on the journey was taken ill among the Alban hills.
Here he had a vision of our Lady, in which he learned that this was
to be the abiding home of his monks. From Gregory, Count of
Tusculum, he got a grant of land on the lower slopes of Monte
Cavo and sent for his community to establish themselves there.
But before the work could be begun he was dead. It was carried
on by his successors, especially by St Bartholomew of Rossano, who
wrote the Life of his master and died in 1065 ; the monastery of
Grottaferrata (of which St Nilus is generally accounted the first
abbot as well as founder) has existed from that day to this, peopled

by Italo-Greek monks, who thus have maintained the Byzantine life and liturgy within a few miles of the heart, not merely of the Latin, but of the Catholic world.

A Life of serious value as a historical source, which was written in Greek by one of his disciples (probably Bartholomew, who at a later date became Abbot) is printed with a Latin translation in the *Acta Sanctorum*, September, vol. vii. This biography has more than once been translated into Italian, *e.g.* by G. Minasi, *San Nilo di Calabria* (1893), and more recently by A. Rocchi, *Vita di San Nilo abate, fondatore della Badia di Grottaferrata*, 1904. St Nilus was also a writer of liturgical poetry, and his compositions have been edited by Dom Sofronio Gassisi, *Poesie di S. Nilo juniore* (1906). On the question of Nilus' alleged marriage see U. Benigni in *Miscellanea di storiá e coltura ecclesiastica* (1905), pp. 494–496. His view is adverse to the existence of any legitimate union. For St Nilus in art see Künstle, *Ikonographie*, vol. ii.

ST JOHN OF MEDA, Conf.

A.D. 1159 (?)

There is considerable discussion about the origins of the penitential association of lay-people who were in the Middle Ages called *Humiliati*. In the earlier part of the twelfth century numbers of persons of good position in northern Italy, while still living " in the world," gave themselves up entirely to works of penance and charity. In the year 1134 some of the men, on the advice of St Bernard, gave up secular life all together and began community life at Milan. At this time there was a certain secular priest from Como, John of Meda, who had been a hermit at Rodenario and then joined the *Humiliati*. He belonged to the Oldrati of Milan, and was a welcome recruit for the new community. On his recommendation they chose to live under the Rule of St Benedict, which St John adapted to their needs, but they nevertheless called themselves " canons." Among the peculiar observances which St John introduced was the daily recitation of the Little Office of our Lady and the use of a special Divine Office, called simply the " Office of the Canons." St John founded several other houses of the order in Lombardy. St John died in 1159 and was canonised a few years later. About 1200 Pope Innocent III approved the *Humiliati*, both male and female, and in connection with them appeared the first " third order " of associated lay-people. But the order eventually went into a bad decline and was suppressed by the Holy See in 1571.

In the *Acta Sanctorum*, September, vol. vii, the Bollandists have published a short medieval Life, introducing it with lengthy prolegomena. It is much to be feared that this pretended biography and indeed the whole traditional early history of the Humiliati is no better than a romance. A review of the controversy is impossible here, but it has been excellently summarised, with abundant bibliographical references, by F. Vernet in the *Dictionnaire de Théol. Cath.*, vol. vi, cc. 307–321. It must suffice to mention the important work of L. Zanoni, *Gli Umiliate nei loro rapporti con l'Eresia* (1911) ; the earlier investigation of Tiraboschi, *Vetera Humiliatorum Monumenta* (1766–1768) ; and the perhaps hypercritical article of A. de Stefano, ' Le Origini dell' ordine degli Umiliati " in the *Rivista storico-critica delle scienze teologice*, vol. ii (1906), pp. 851–871.

BD. DALMATIUS MONER, Conf.

A.D. 1341

The life of this confessor of the order of Friars Preachers was passed in the obscurity of his cell and the quiet discharge of his ordinary duties ; he was concerned in no public affairs whether of an ecclesiastical or secular nature. He belonged by birth to the village of Santa-Columba de Farnez in Catalonia and was eventually sent to the University of Montpellier. Here he had to struggle hard lest he be drawn into the disorderly life led by so many of the students ; with the aid of grace he triumphed and, after finishing his studies, was accepted by the Dominicans at Gerona. Blessed Dalmatius was then twenty-five and after profession was employed for many years in teaching, and became master of the novices. To those prescribed by his rule he added voluntary mortifications, such as abstaining from drink for three weeks on end and sleeping on the bare ground, and he loved to pray out of doors in places where the beauty of nature spoke to him of the glory of God. It is said that one day, when Brother Dalmatius was missing and another friar was sent to find him, he was found to be literally caught up in ecstasy and held by the power of God on a level with the top of a tall tree. The lessons of his office say that he was familiarly known as " the brother who talks with the angels."

It was a great desire of Blessed Dalmatius to end his days at La Sainte Baume, where the legend of Provence says thirty years were spent by St Mary Magdalen, patroness of the Dominican Order, to whom he had an intense devotion. This was not to be, but he was allowed to hollow out for himself a cave in the friary grounds at Gerona and he lived in that uncomfortable place for four years, leaving it only to go to choir, chapter, and refectory. Blessed Dalmatius died on September 24, 1341, and his *cultus* was confirmed by Pope Innocent XIII in 1721. One of his teeth kept as a separate relic at Gerona is popularly reputed to have been the means of many miraculous cures, wherefore Blessed Dalmatius Moner is invoked against toothache and the mothers of the neighbourhood dedicate to him their teething and fretful babies.

The Bollandists, writing of Bl. Dalmatius in the *Acta Sanctorum*, September, vol. vi, were unable to procure the original Latin Life of this holy ascetic which they knew had been compiled by his contemporary and fellow-religious, the famous inquisitor, Nicholas Eymeric. They therefore reproduced in Latin the Spanish translation, or rather adaptation, of the original, which had been made by Francis Diego for his history of the Aragon province of the Friars Preachers. In the early years, however, of the present century a copy of Eymeric's Life was identified and it was edited by Père van Ortroy in the *Analecta Bollandiana*, vol. xxxi (1912), pp. 49–81. This memoir is extremely interesting because we have evidence that unlike most hagiographical documents it was written within ten years of the death of Bd. Dalmatius. All the other accounts of him which we possess seem to be derived from this. Three eye-witnesses of his levitations are cited, though the original Latin text does not fully justify the statement that he was "held by the power of God on a level with the top of a tall tree." He was, in fact, seen gently floating down from a height, which is not quite the same thing.

THE MARTYRS OF NORTH AMERICA

A.D. 1646–49

The feast of these martyrs, canonised in 1930, is kept to-day in North America. An account of them will be found under the date March 16 herein.

SEPTEMBER 27

SS. COSMAS AND DAMIAN, Martyrs

A.D. 303 (?)

COSMAS and Damian are the principal and best known of those saints venerated in the East as ἀνάργυροι, "moneyless ones," because they practised medicine without taking reward from their patients. Though some writers have professed to be able to extract from their very extravagant and historically worthless *acta* fragments of lost and authentic originals, it is the opinion of Père Delehaye that their " origin and true history will probably always evade research." Alban Butler summarises the core of their story thus :

Saints Cosmas and Damian were twin brothers, born in Arabia, who studied the sciences in Syria and became eminent for their skill in medicine. Being Christians, and full of that holy temper of charity in which the spirit of our divine religion consists, they practised their profession with great application and success, but never took any fee for their services. They lived at Ægeæ on the bay of Alexandretta in Cilicia, and were remarkable both for the love and respect which the people bore them on account of the good offices which they received from their charity, and for their zeal for the Christian faith, which they took every opportunity their profession gave them to propagate. When the persecution of Diocletian began to rage, it was impossible for persons of so distinguished a character to lie concealed. They were therefore apprehended by the order of Lysias, governor of Cilicia, and after various torments were beheaded for the faith. Their bodies were carried into Syria, and buried at Cyrrhus.

The legends pad out this simple story with numerous marvels. For example, before they were eventually beheaded they defied death by water, fire, and crucifixion. While they were hanging on the crosses the mob stoned them, but the missiles recoiled on the heads of the throwers ; in the same way the arrows of archers who were brought up to shoot at them turned in the air and scattered the bowmen (the same thing is recorded of St Christopher and others).

The three brothers of Cosmas and Damian, Anthimus, Leontius, and Euprepius are said to have suffered with them, and their names are mentioned in the Roman Martyrology. Many miracles of healing were ascribed to them after their death, the saints sometimes appearing to the sufferers in sleep and prescribing for them or curing them there and then, as was supposed to happen to pagan devotees in the temples of Æsculapius and Serapis. Among the distinguished people who attributed recovery from serious sickness to SS. Cosmas and Damian was the Emperor Justinian I, who out of regard for their relics honoured the city of Cyrrhus and, finding a ruinous church at Constantinople said to have been built in honour of the martyrs by Theodosius II in the early fifth century, rebuilt and adorned it. At an unknown date the bodies of these martyrs were brought to Rome, where relics of all five brothers are venerated in their basilica. SS. Cosmas and Damian are named in the canon of the Mass, and they are, with St Luke, the patrons of physicians and surgeons. By an error the Byzantine Christians honour three pairs of saints of this name. " It should be known," says the Synaxary of Constantinople, " that there are three groups of martyrs of the names of Cosmas and Damian : those of Arabia who were beheaded under Diocletian [October 17], those of Rome who were stoned under Carinus [July 1], and the sons of Theodota, who died peacefully [November 1]," but these are all actually the martyrs of Ægeæ.

The holy moneyless ones regarded it as a great happiness that their profession offered them opportunities of giving comfort and relief to the most distressed of their fellow-creatures. By exerting our charity toward all in acts of benevolence and beneficence, according to our abilities, and in treating enemies and persecutors with meekness and kindness we prove ourselves followers of Christ, animated with His spirit. In the imitation of the divine goodness according to our abilities, at least in the temper of our mind, consists that Christian perfection which, when founded in true charity, is the accomplishment of the law. Men engaged in professions instituted for the service of their neighbour may sanctify their industry if actuated by the motive of charity towards others, whilst they also have in view the justice which they owe to themselves and their family of procuring an honest and necessary living, which is itself often a strict obligation, and no less noble a virtue if it be founded in motives equally pure and perfect.

The many recensions of the " Passion " of these saints are catalogued in the *Bibliotheca Hagiographica Greca* and the *Latina*. The texts printed in the *Acta Sanctorum*, September, vol. vii, serve abundantly to illustrate their fabulous nature, though others have come to light in recent years. See with regard to the early *cultus* the references given in the commentary on the *Hieronymianum* in *Acta Sanctorum*, November, vol. ii, part 2, pp. 528–529 ; also Delehaye, *Les Légendes Hagiographiques* (Eng. trans.) ; *Les recueils antiques de miracles des saints ; Les Origines du culte des martyrs*, and other works. The data supplied in Deubner, *Kosmas und Damianus* deserve special notice.

ST JOHN MARK, Bp. AND CONF.

FIRST CENTURY

The " John, surnamed Mark," referred to in the Acts of the Apostles xii, 12, 25, has been conjecturally identified by many writers with St Mark the Evangelist. But in the martyrologies and liturgical tradition of both East and West they are regarded as being separate. The Roman Martyrology has to-day : " At Byblos in Phœnicia, St Mark the bishop, who by blessed Luke is also called John and who was the son of that blessed Mary whose memory is noted on June 29." That he became a bishop at Byblos or elsewhere is a tradition of the Greeks from whom the West acquired it. St John Mark's mother had a house at Jerusalem, whither St Peter went for shelter when he had escaped from prison by the ministry of an angel, so he may have been a native of the Holy City. He went on the first missionary journey of St Paul, with St Barnabas, whose cousin-german he was, but got no further than Perga, whence he returned to Jerusalem. This was of his own accord—perhaps his heart failed him—for when St Barnabas proposed that he should come on the second journey, St Paul vetoed the suggestion, because John Mark had " departed from them out of Pamphylia and not gone with them to the work." This caused a sharp disagreement between Paul and Barnabas, which ended in Paul taking Silas, and Barnabas and John Mark going off to preach in Cyprus. Later on St Paul was satisfied about and reconciled with John Mark, if that is whom he refers to in his letters to the Colossians and to Philemon as the Mark who was his fellow-labourer during his first imprisonment at Rome. From Rome this Mark apparently went to Ephesus, for St Paul writes in his second letter to Timothy : " Take Mark and bring him with thee, for he is profitable to me for the ministry."

It will be sufficient to refer to the discussion of the subject in the *Acta Sanctorum*, September, vol. vii ; and to what has been said in the April volume of this series, pp. 283–285.

333

ST ELZEAR, CONF., AND BD. DELPHINA, MATRON

A.D. 1323 AND 1358

St Elzear of Sabran, Baron of Ansouis in Provence, Count of Ariano in the kingdom of Naples, was born in 1285 at Saint-Jean de Robians, a castle belonging to his father in the diocese of Apt. Immediately after his birth his mother, whose great piety and charity to the poor had earned her the name of " the Good Countess," taking him in her arms offered him to God with great fervour, begging that he might never offend His divine majesty but might rather die in his infancy than live to be guilty of so terrible a crime. The lessons in virtue he received from his mother were perfected by his uncle, William of Sabran, Abbot of St Victor's at Marseilles, under whom he had his education in that monastery. The abbot had severely to reprove him for the austerities which he practised, calling him a self-murderer, yet secretly admiring so great fervour in a young noble. While he was still a child, Charles II, King of Sicily and Count of Provence, caused him to be affianced to Delphina of Glandèves, daughter and heiress to the lord of Puy-Michel. She had been left an orphan in her infancy and was brought up by her aunt, an abbess, under the guardianship of her uncles. When they were both about fifteen years old the marriage took place at Château-Pont-Michel. Elzear was twenty-three years old when he inherited his father's honours and estates, and he soon found it necessary to go into Italy to take possession of the lordship of Ariano. He found his Neapolitan vassals badly disposed towards him as a Frenchman, and it required all his tact and gentleness to satisfy them. Elzear opposed to their rebellion for three years no other arms than those of meekness and patience, which his friends reproachfully called indolence and cowardice. His cousin, the Prince of Taranto, one day told him that his conduct hurt the common cause of his country, and said : " Let me deal with these people for you. I will hang up half a thousand, and make the rest as pliant as a glove. It is fit to be a lamb among the good, but with the wicked you must play the lion. Such insolence must be curbed. Say your prayers for me, and I will give so many blows for you that this rabble will give you no more trouble." Elzear smilingly replied : " Would you have me begin my government with massacres and blood ? I will overcome these men by good. It is no great matter for a lion to tear lambs ; but for a lamb to pull a lion in pieces is another thing. Now, by God's assistance, you will shortly see this miracle." The effect verified the prediction. For the citizens of Ariano of their own accord abandoned their rebellion and with submission and respect invited the saint to take possession of his territory. Their lord explained the true motive why he bore so patiently these insults and injuries when he said : " If I receive any affront or feel impatience begin to arise in my breast, I turn all my thoughts towards Jesus Christ crucified and say to myself : Can what I suffer bear any comparison with what Jesus Christ was pleased to undergo for me ? " To mention one other instance. Among the papers which his father left, Elzear found the letters of a certain gentleman under his command, filled with calumnies against him and persuading his father to disinherit him as one fitter to be a monk than to bear arms. Delphina was indignant at reading such impudence and said she hoped her husband would deal with the man as he deserved. But Elzear reminded her that Christ commands us not to revenge but to forgive injuries, and to overcome hatred by charity : therefore he would destroy and never make mention of these letters. He did so, and when their writer came to wait upon him he affectionately greeted him and won his good-will. In his county of Ariano he settled a rigorous administration of justice and punished the least oppression in any of his officers. He visited malefactors who were condemned to die, and many who had been deaf to priests were moved by his tender words to sincere repentance. When their goods were confiscated to him he secretly restored them to their wives and children. While in Italy he took up arms on behalf of the Guelf party and with his followers helped to drive the Emperor Henry VII from Rome in 1312 ; then, after an absence of four years, he returned to Provence. In 1315 he and his wife, after receiving communion, pronounced publicly at the foot of the altar in the chapel of their castle mutual vows of perpetual continence. In the lives of this holy couple the world saw religious devotion in the midst of secular dignities, contemplation amid the noise of public life, and in conjugal friendship a holy rivalry in goodness and charity. St Elzear recited the Divine Office every day and communicated almost as often. " I do not think," he said one day to Delphina, " that any man on earth can enjoy a happiness equal to that which I have in holy Communion." And he wrote to her : " You want to hear often of me. Go then and visit our loving Lord Jesus in the Blessed Sacrament, and enter in spirit into His sacred heart. You will always find me there."

It is a dangerous mistake to imagine that one can be devout, merely by spending much time in prayer and that pious persons may fall into careless neglect of their temporal concerns. On the contrary, solid virtue is also able to do business and to despatch it well.

St Elzear was rendered by his piety faithful, prudent, and dexterous in the management of temporal affairs, both domestic and public : valiant in war, active in peace, faithful in every trust, and diligent in the care of his household for which he drew up the following regulations : Every one in my family shall daily hear Mass, whatever business they may have. If God be well served, nothing will be wanting. . . . . . Let no persons be idle. In the morning a little time shall be allowed for meditation, but away with those who are perpetually in the church to avoid doing their work. This they do, not because they love contemplation, but because they want to have their work done for them. . . . . . When a difference or quarrel arises, let the scriptural precept be observed that it be composed before the sun goes down. I know the impossibility of living among men and not having something to suffer. Scarcely a man is in tune with himself one whole day ; but not to be willing to bear with or pardon others is diabolical, and to love enemies and to render good for evil is the touchstone of the sons of God. . . . . I strictly command that no officer or servant under my jurisdiction or authority injure any man in goods, honour, or reputation, or oppress any poor person, or damage anyone under colour of doing my business. I do not want my castle to be a cloister or my people hermits. Let them be merry, and enjoy recreation at the right times, but not with a bad conscience or with danger of transgressing against God.

St Elzear himself set the example in everything which he prescribed to others, and Blessed Delphina concurred with her husband in all his views and was perfectly obedient to him. No coldness interrupted the harmony or damped the affections of this holy pair. The countess never forgot that the devotions of a married woman ought to be ordered in a different manner from those of a nun, that contemplation is the sister of action and that Martha and Mary must mutually help one another.

About 1317 Elzear returned to Naples, taking with him Delphina, who waited upon Queen Sanchia, wife of King Robert, the successor of Charles II, and the tutorship of their son Charles was entrusted to Elzear. This young prince was sprightly, understood too well his high position, was intractable, and had all the airs of the court. The count saw his pupil's dangerous inclinations but took no notice of them till he had won his affection and gained credit with him. When he saw a fit time he spoke gently to him about his defects, on the necessity of virtue to support the dignity of his high rank, and on the life to come. The young prince was so overcome that, flinging his arms about his neck, he exclaimed : " It is not yet too late to begin. What must I do ? " Elzear explained to him the virtues of piety, magnanimity, justice, and clemency, showing that a prince who fears God has always comfort and protection in Heaven though earth should fail him. " Only religion," he said, " can safeguard against the dangers of vanity, flatterers, and the strong incentives of the passions. Go to confession and communion every great festival. Love the poor, and God will love your house. When you are angry, speak not a word ; otherwise you undo yourself. More princes are ruined by their tongues and anger than by the sword. Hate flatterers as the plague ; if you do not banish them, they will ruin you. Honour good men and the prelates of the Church. . . ." Thus did St Elzear lead the young Duke of Calabria into more sober and fruitful ways, and when his father had occasion to go into Provence he left Charles as regent for Naples with Elzear as his chief councillor. The saint took this opportunity to entreat the Duke to declare him advocate for the poor and their agent at court. The Duke, laughing heartily, asked : " What kind of office do you beg ? You will have no competitors in this ambition. I admit your request and recommend to you all the poor of this kingdom." Elzear thanked him heartily and had a great bag of purple velvet made with which he passed through the streets, receiving in it all the requests and suits of the poor. Whilst the chief authority of the state was lodged in his hands many offered him presents, which he refused, pointing out to those who criticised his niceness that, " It is more safe and easy to refuse all presents than to discern which might be received without danger. And it is not easy for one who begins to take any afterwards to know where to stop, for these things are apt to create an appetite."

On the death of Charles of Calabria's first wife, King Robert sent St Elzear to Paris to ask for the hand of Mary of Valois for his son. Blessed Delphina was a little nervous for her husband amid the dangers of the French court, but he replied drily that since by the grace of God he had kept his virtue in Naples he was not likely to come to any harm at Paris. In fact, the danger that awaited him was quite other. After he had successfully carried through his commission he fell sick and it was the sickness of death. He at once made a general confession and he continued to confess almost every day of his illness, though he is said never to have offended God by any mortal sin. The history of Christ's passion was every day read to him, and in it he found great comfort amidst his pains. Receiving the holy Viaticum, he said with great joy : " This is my hope ; in this I desire to die," and on September 27, 1323, he died in the arms of Father Francis Mayronis, a Franciscan friar and distinguished Scotist theologian, who had been his confessor. His body, according to his orders, was carried to Apt, and there interred in the church of the Franciscans, Father Francis accompanying the body and preaching the funeral sermon. About the year 1309 St Elzear had assisted as godfather at the baptism of William of Grimoard, son of the Sieur de Grisac, a sickly child whose health was restored at the prayers of his sponsor. Fifty-three years later this William became pope as Urban V, and in 1369 he signed the decree of canonisation of his godfather Elzear, who is named in the Roman Martyrology on this day.

Blessed Delphina survived her husband about thirty-five years. She remained at the Neapolitan court till the death of King Robert, when Queen Sanchia put on the habit of a Poor Clare in a nunnery which she had founded at Naples. In this state she lived ten years with great fervour, learning from Delphina the exercises of a spiritual life. After her death Delphina returned into Provence and led the life of a recluse, first at Cabrières and then at Apt. She gave away the proceeds of her estates to the poor, and during her last years was afflicted with a painful illness which she bore with heroic patience. She died about the year 1358 and was buried with her husband. An old tradition says that both St Elzear and Blessed Delphina were members of the third order of St Francis, and they are therefore particularly venerated by the Franciscans; in their supplement to the Martyrology Blessed Delphina is named on December 9.

The manuscript materials collected and printed by the Bollandists in their vol. vii for September are of considerable interest. From these sources P. Girard has compiled a popular biography, *Saint Elzéar de Sabran et la B. Delphine de Signe* (1912). A liturgical office formerly in use for their feast day will be found in the *Archivum Franciscanum Historicum*, vol. x (1917), pp. 231–238.

SEPTEMBER 28

ST WENCESLAS, Prince of Bohemia, Mart.

A.D. 929

THE baptism of the ruler of Bohemia, Borivoj, and his wife St Ludmila (September 16) was not by any means followed by the conversion of all their subjects, and many of the powerful Czech families were strongly opposed to the new religion. Borivoj was succeeded by his sons Sphytihnev and Ratislav as joint rulers, but on the death of the first in 915 Ratislav governed the whole country. He married a nominally Christian woman, Drahomira, daughter of the prince of the Lutici, a Slav tribe from the north, and they had two sons, Wenceslas (Vaclav), born in 907 near Prague, and Boleslas. St Ludmila, who was still living, arranged that the education of the elder might be intrusted to her, and she undertook with the utmost care to form his heart to the love of God. In this task she was assisted by Paul, her chaplain, a man of sanctity and prudence, who taught the young prince the first rudiments of learning. He was later sent to a college at Budec where, under the direction of an excellent master, he made great progress in Latin and other exercises suitable to his rank and in all the virtues which make up the character of a Christian and a saint. He was yet young when his father was killed fighting against the Magyars, and his mother Drahomira assumed the title of regent and the government. Being no longer held in by any restraint, she proceeded against the Christians and published a severe order forbidding priests and others who professed it to teach or instruct children. She removed the Christian magistrates and put heathens in their places, and employed every means to wean Wenceslas from his faith, so that he could worship and receive his Christian friends only in secret. In these measures Drahomira was probably acting chiefly at the instigation of the non-Christian elements in the nobility, and these encouraged her jealousy of St Ludmila's influence over her son, and represented him as being more suitable for a cloister than for a throne. St Ludmila, afflicted at the public disorders and full of concern for the interest of religion, which she and her consort had established with so much difficulty, showed Wenceslas the necessity of his taking the reins of the government into his own hands, promising to assist him with her direction and advice. Fearing what might happen, two nobles went to Ludmila's castle at Tetin and there strangled her, so that, deprived of her support, Wenceslas did not undertake the government of his people till he came of age. He then issued a proclamation that he would support God's law and His Church, punish murder severely, and endeavour to rule with justice and mercy. His mother had been banished to Budec, so he recalled her to the court, and there is no evidence that for the future she ever opposed herself to Wenceslas.

When on one occasion a neighbouring tribe raided his land Wenceslas, wishing to maintain peace, sent to its chief, Rastislas, asking what provocation he had given him, and declaring that he was ready to accept any terms that were consistent with what he owed to God and his people. Rastislas insolently answered that the surrender of Bohemia was the only condition on which he would hear of peace, so Wenceslas marched against the invader. When the two armies were near one another, Wenceslas proposed that, to spare the blood of so many innocent persons, it was a just expedient to leave the issue to a single combat between himself and Rastislas. The two princes accordingly met at the head of both armies. Wenceslas, armed with a short sword and a shield, marched boldly towards his antagonist, who attempted to throw a javelin at him. But, as it is said, Rastislas saw two angels protecting the saint, whereupon he threw down his arms. At a meeting of rulers presided over by the Emperor Henry I the Fowler, St Wenceslas arrived late in the day and kept everybody waiting. Some of the princes took offence and the Emperor, saying he was probably at his prayers, suggested that no one should greet him when he did arrive. Nevertheless, Henry himself, who really respected his sanctity, received him with great honour, and at the end of the conference bade him ask whatever he pleased, and it should be granted him. The saint asked an arm of the body of St Vitus, and to shelter it he began the building of a great church at Prague, where now stands the cathedral. He also caused the body of St Ludmila to be translated to the church of St George, which had been built by his father in that city. The political policy of St Wenceslas was to cultivate friendly relations with Germany, and he preserved the unity of his country by acknowledging the Emperor as his over-lord and paying him a yearly tribute. This policy, and the severity with which he checked oppression and other disorders in the nobility, raised a party against him, especially among the non-Christians. For a time Wenceslas thought of abdicating in favour of his brother, Boleslas, and going into a monastery, but he was held back by his desire to finish the church of St Vitus ; this ambition, never fulfilled, was his undoing.

Boleslas allied himself with the discontented party, and a plot was laid to kill his brother, and himself to succeed him. St Wenceslas was invited to come to Stara Boleslav for the feast of its patron saints, Cosmas and Damian, in the year 929. On the evening of the festival, after the celebrations were over, Wenceslas was warned of his danger. He refused to take any notice, proposed to the assembly in the great hall the toast of " St Michael, whom we pray to guide us to peace and eternal joy," and, after he had said his office, went to bed. That night final details of the plot were settled. Early the next morning, as St Wenceslas made his way to Mass through a private passage from the castle, he met Boleslas and stopped to thank him for his hospitality. " Yesterday," was the reply, " I did my best to serve you fittingly, but this must be my service to-day," and he came at him with a sword. The brothers closed and struggled, three other conspirators ran in, and St Wenceslas was despatched, murmuring as he died at the church door, " Brother, may God forgive you." Drahomira, who was not privy to this crime, had the body taken into the church of Altbunzlau, and then fled with her daughter Pribyslava, fearing where next the hand of the unnatural Boleslas might fall. He, terrified at the reputation of many miracles wrought at the martyr's tomb, caused his body to be translated to the church of St Vitus, at Prague, three years after his death. At once Wenceslas was acclaimed by the people as a martyr who had given his life in upholding the faith against pagan opposition, and at least by the year 985 his feast was being observed in Bohemia. His tomb became a place of pilgrimage and at the beginning of the eleventh century St Wenceslas was already regarded as the national patron of the Czechs ; he is now the patron saint of Czechoslovakia. It must not be inferred from the existence of a vernacular Christmas carol that there was formerly a widespread popular devotion to this saint in England : the words of " Good King Wenceslas " were written by the nineteenth-century hymn-writer J. M. Neale to fit a thirteenth-century air (" *Tempus adest floridum* ").

The safety and happiness of government and of all society among men is founded upon religion. Without it princes usually become tyrants and people lawless. He who so far degrades human reason as to deny any other difference between virtue and vice than in the apprehension of men or who reduces virtue to an ideal beauty and an empty name is a most dangerous enemy to mankind. The general laws of nations and those of particular states are too weak restraints upon those who, in spite of nature itself, laugh the law of God out of doors. Unless religion bind a man in his conscience he will become so far the slave of his passions as to be ready, with the unnatural brother, Boleslas, to commit every advantageous villainy to which he is prompted, whenever he can do it with secrecy or impunity. It is not consistent with the goodness and justice of God to have created men without an interior law, and a law enforced by the strongest motives and the highest authority. Nor can His goodness and justice allow obedience to His law to go unrewarded, or disobedience and contempt to remain unpunished. This consideration alone leads us to the recognition of that just providence which reserves to the life to come the recompense of virtue and chastisement of vice which faith reveals to us ; this is the sacred bond of justice and civil society in the present life.

See what has already been said in connection with St Ludmila (September 16), p. 209 ; the sources for any biography of St Wenceslas are practically identical. In a contribution to the *Analecta Bollandiana*, vol. xlviii (1930), pp. 218–221, Père Paul Peeters reviews the more outstanding features of the literature produced in Czechoslovakia, and mostly written in the Czech language, to do honour to the millenary of St Wenceslas, celebrated in 1929. It is unfortunate, as he points out, that a good deal of this literature seems to be coloured by racial and political prepossessions. The slight, but judicious, Life of St Wenceslas, by Fr. Dvornik (1929), is said to have appeared both in French and in English as well as in Czech. The German biography by A. Naegle, *Der Heilige Wenzel, der Landespatron Böhmens* (1928), is representative of a point of view which is somewhat adverse to that of Dvornik.

ST EXUPERIUS, or SPIRE, Bp. of Toulouse, Conf.

c. A.D. 415

He was probably born at Arreau in the High Pyrenees, where a chapel dedicated in his honour is a place of pilgrimage, and succeeded to the see of Toulouse on the death of St Sylvius about the year 405. He completed the great church of St Saturninus (Sernin), begun by his predecessor, and translated thereto with great magnificence the relics of a number of saints, among them those of the titular, who was founder of the see. Generosity seems to have been the outstanding characteristic of this bishop. He sent gifts so far away as to the monks of Egypt and Palestine, thereby earning the thanks and commendation of St Jerome, who dedicated to him his commentary on Zacharias and wrote of him : " To relieve the hunger of the poor he suffers it himself, and condemns himself to the severest self-denial that he may be enabled to minister to their wants. The paleness of his face shows the rigour of his fasts. But his poverty makes him truly rich. So poor is he that he has to carry the Body of the Lord in an osier-basket and His Blood in a glass vessel. His charity knew no bounds. It sought for objects in the most distant parts, and the solitaries of Egypt felt its beneficial effects." At home as well as abroad there was ample scope for his benefactions, for in his time Gaul was overrun by the Vandals and the Suevi, though he was spared by death from seeing his cathedral city captured by the Gothic king Walla. St Exuperius wrote to Pope St Innocent I for instruction on several matters of discipline and enquiring about the canon of holy Scripture. In reply the Pope sent him a letter giving a list of the authentic books of the Bible as they were then received in the Church, and that list was exactly the same as they are to-day, including the deuterocanonical books. The place and year of the death of Exuperius are not known. St Paulinus of Nola referred to him as one of the most illustrious bishops of the Church in Gaul, and by the middle of the sixth century he was held in equal honour with St Saturninus in the church of Toulouse.

It seems curious that St Exuperius, whose fame had reached Rome and Palestine, finds no place in the *Hieronymianum*. What has been recorded concerning him is gathered up in the *Acta Sanctorum*, September, vol. vii ; and there is a very full notice in the *Dict. de Théol. cath.*, vol. v, cc. 2022–2027. See also Duchesne, *Fastes Épiscopaux*, vol. i, p. 307.

ST EUSTOCHIUM, Virg.

A.D. 420

Eustochium Julia, whose memory is rendered illustrious by the pen of St Jerome, was daughter of St Paula, whose life is related on January 26 ; its exterior events and circumstances conditioned those of Eustochium, who was the third of four daughters and the only one to share her mother's life till its end. St Paula upon the death of her husband Toxotius devoted herself wholly to God in a life of simplicity, poverty, mortification, and prayer. Eustochium, who was about twelve years old when her father died, shared all the views of her mother and rejoiced to consecrate the hours which so many spend in vain amusements to works of charity and religion. When St Jerome came to Rome from the East in the year 382 she, with St Paula, put herself under his spiritual direction, and its trend soon alarmed some of her friends and relatives. An uncle, Hymettius, and his wife Praetexta tried to dissuade the young girl from a life of austerity and attempted to entice her into participation in the pleasures of ordinary life. Their efforts were wasted, for before very long Eustochium had taken the veil of perpetual virginity. To commend her resolution and to instruct her in the obligations of that state St Jerome addressed to her on this occasion his famous letter called Concerning the Keeping of Virginity, which he wrote about the year 384. The venerable author, however, does not confine his letter to ascetic teaching but writes passages of satire which suggest it was intended for a wider public than one young girl; he is merciless in his criticism of the behaviour of certain virgins, widows, and priests.

Much of the formation of Eustochium had been at the hands of St Marcella, that "glory of the Roman ladies," but when St Paula decided to follow St Jerome to Palestine she elected to go with her mother. With other maidens who aspired to the religious life, they met St Jerome at Antioch, visited the Holy Places, Egypt, and the monks of the Nitrian desert, and finally settled down at Bethlehem. Three communities of women were established, in the direction of which Eustochium assisted St Paula, and St Jerome has left us an account of the simple devoted lives that were passed therein. When his sight began to fail, these two women, who had learnt Greek and Hebrew, helped in the work of the Vulgate translation of the Bible by collating his manuscripts for him; at their request he wrote commentaries on the epistles to Philemon, the Galatians, the Ephesians, and Titus, and dedicated some of his works to them, for, as he said, "these women were more capable of forming a judgement on them than most men." Other duties of St Eustochium were to sweep out the house, trim and fill the lamps, and cook.

In 403 St Paula was taken ill, and Eustochium spent long hours between waiting on her and praying for her in the cave of the Nativity. At her death on January 26, 404, Eustochium, "like a baby weaned from her nurse, could scarcely be drawn away from her mother. She kissed her eyes and clung to her face and caressed her whole body and would even have been buried with her." Paula was succeeded as abbess by her daughter, who found the communities not only destitute but much in debt. With the encouragement of St Jerome and her own quiet intrepidity she faced the situation and retrieved it, with the assistance of funds brought by her niece, another Paula, who had joined the Bethlehem maidens. Excited probably by the opposition of St Jerome, a band of Pelagian heretics burnt down her monastery in 417 and committed many outrages: of which he, St Eustochium, and the younger Paula informed Pope St Innocent I by letter. He wrote in strong terms to John, Bishop of Jerusalem, charging him to put a stop to such violence and adding that otherwise he should be obliged to have recourse to other means to see justice done to those that were injured. St Eustochium did not long survive this terrible shock. We have no account from St Jerome of her death as we have of that of her mother, but he wrote to St Augustine and St Alipius that " such a sorrow caused him to disdain the outrageous writings of the Pelagian Anianus." She died peacefully on September 28, 419, and was buried in the same tomb as St Paula in a grotto adjoining the spot in which our Lord was born. There their tomb may still be seen, but it has long been empty and the fate of their relics is not known.

St Jerome's letters and other writings furnish almost all that we know concerning St Eustochium. The material has been gathered up in the *Acta Sanctorum*, September, vol. vii. All the Lives of St Jerome tell us a good deal about Eustochium (see, *e.g.* Cavallera, *St Jérome, sa vie et son œuvre*, 1922), and she also figures prominently in Lagrange's delightful *Vie de S⁰ Paule*.

ST FAUSTUS, Bp. of Riez, Conf.

c. A.D. 493

References are often made to Faustus of Riez as a chief exponent and defender of the Semipelagian heresy, but in justice to his memory it should also be stated that his name appears in several martyrologies and that his feast is observed in several churches of southern France. He was born in the early years of the fifth century, his contemporaries St Avitus and St Sidonius Apollinaris say in Britain, but more likely in Brittany. He is said to have begun life as a barrister, but can hardly have gone far in that profession because he became a monk of Lérins before the founder of that house, St Honoratus, had left it in 426. He was ordained to the priesthood, and after ten or so uneventful years in the monastery he was elected abbot after St Maximus, who was promoted to the see of Riez. He was greatly respected by St Honoratus and St Sidonius, who says that his monastic observance and regularity were worthy of the Fathers of the Desert, and he had a great gift of extempore preaching. He zealously defended the rights of his monastery against the claims of Theodore, Bishop of Fréjus, and a synod had to meet at Arles to settle the questions at issue between them. As he had followed St Maximus as abbot, so he followed him as bishop, going to Riez after he had governed Lérins for about twenty-five years. In his panegyric on his predecessor, Faustus exclaimed : " Lérins has sent two successive bishops to Riez. Of the first she is proud ; for the second she blushes." She had no need to blush. Faustus was as good a bishop as he had been an abbot, and encouraged the opening of new monasteries throughout his diocese. He continued his former mortified life, adding thereto the manifold duties of the episcopate and an apostolic concern for the purity of the Faith, opposing himself vigorously to Arianism and the errors of him whom he called " that pestiferous teacher Pelagius."

A certain priest called Lucidus having been preaching the heretical doctrine which denies that God has a true will to save all men, asserting that salvation or damnation depends on His will alone, irrespective of the action of man's free will and his consequent merits or demerits, two synods met at Arles and Lyons in 475 to deal with him. St Faustus induced Lucidus to retract his errors, and the bishops asked him to write a treatise against this Predestinarian teaching, as " erroneous, blasphemous, heathen, fatalistic, and conducive to immorality." Faustus complied with two books, on free will and grace, in which he refuted as well Pelagianism as Predestinarianism. In these he had occasion to deal with certain false private views of St Augustine, and in so doing himself propounded the Semipelagian error that, though grace is necessary for the accomplishment of good works, it is not necessary for their initiation. St Faustus erred in good faith and in the holy company of St Hilary of Arles and St John Cassian, but, though he was vehemently attacked directly his books appeared, their errors were not finally condemned as heretical until the Council of Orange in 529. But his theological activity raised up for him an enemy of a cruder sort, in another quarter. Euric, King of the Arian Visigoths, was in occupation of a large part of Southern Gaul and was offended by the attacks of Faustus on Arianism. He was therefore driven from his see about 478 and had perforce to live in exile until the death of Euric some years later. He then returned and continued to direct his flock until his death at about the age of ninety. His memory was greatly revered by his people, who built a basilica in his honour. St Faustus was among the principal of the writers for whom the abbey of Lérins was famous, and some of his letters, discourses, and other works are yet extant.

The life and activities of Faustus of Riez occupy sixty pages of the *Acta Sanctorum*, September, vol. vii. There is also a monograph by A. Koch, *Der hl. Faustus von Riez* (1895). The edition of the works of Faustus prepared for the Vienna *Corpus Scriptorum* by A. Engelbrecht has met with somewhat damaging criticism from Dom Germain Morin in the *Revue Bénédictine*, vol. ix (1892), pp. 49–61, and vol. x (1893), pp. 62–78. See further F. Wörter, *Zur Dogmengeschichte des Semipelagianismus* (1899), pp. 47 *seq.* ; the *Dict. de Théolog. catholique*, vol. v, cc. 2101–2105 ; and Duchesne, *Fastes Épiscopaux*, i, p. 284.

ST ANNEMUNDUS, ABP. OF LYONS, MART.

A.D. 657

Annemundus gives the name Saint-Chamond to a town near Vienne and is principally remembered as the friend and patron of St Wilfrid of York when he was a young man. He belonged to a very distinguished Gallo-Roman family, his father Sigonius being prefect of Lyons. Annemundus was trained in the court of Dagobert I and was an adviser of Clovis II, at whose request he became godfather at baptism to the future Clotaire III. A few years after he was appointed to the see of Lyons there came to his episcopal city St Benedict Biscop, on his way to Rome for the first time, accompanied by St Wilfrid of York, who was then about twenty years old. Benedict hastened on towards Rome but Wilfrid lingered at Lyons, whose prelate, says St Bede, " was pleased with the youth's wise conversation, the grace of his appearance, the quickness of his behaviour, and the gravity of his thoughts. He therefore supplied Wilfrid and his friends with all they required so long as they stayed with him." Annemundus even offered to adopt the young Englishman, to give him his niece to wife, and a post of honour for his maintenance. Wilfrid thanked him for his so great kindness to a stranger, and explained that he was determined to serve God in the clerical state and was for that very reason travelling to Rome. Whereupon St Annemundus made provision for the rest of his journey, and pressed him to come back through Lyons when he returned to England. This Wilfrid did and stayed three years with the archbishop, by whom he was tonsured. He might have stayed on indefinitely and with very important results, for Annemundus is said to have had thoughts of Wilfrid as his successor, but for the untimely and tragic death of the archbishop. On September 28, 657, he was slain by soldiers at Chalon-sur-Saône. Wilfrid was present and offered to die with him, but when the executioners heard that he was a foreigner and an Englishman they let him go. Eddius, the biographer of St Wilfrid, lays the assassination of St Annemundus (and of nine other French bishops) at the door of the queen-regent, St Bathildis, and his statement has been copied by St Bede. But it is very improbable that she was guilty of this crime, which French writers attribute to the political ambitions of the notorious Ebroin, afterwards mayor of the palace to Clotaire III. St Wilfrid helped to bury the body of St Annemundus at Saint-Nizier, where he was at once venerated as a martyr, and departed to his own country. Eddius calls St Annemundus *Dalfinus*, by confusion with his brother Count Dalfinus, and St Bede refers to him by this name.

A brief " Passion " of St Annemundus is printed in the *Acta Sanctorum*, September, vol. vii, with the usual prolegomena ; but the principal authorities are Eddius and Bede. See Plummer's edition of the latter and his notes ; also Duchesne, *Fastes Épiscopaux*, vol. i, p. 170 ; and *Mon. Germ. Script. rer. Meroving.*, vol. vi, pp. 197 seq.

ST LIOBA, Virg. and Abbess

c. A.D. 779

The active participation of nuns and religious sisters in the work of the foreign missions has so greatly developed and extended in our own time that we have come to regard it as a modern innovation altogether. It is, of course, nothing of the sort and, allowing for a certain difference of method consequent on the development of " unenclosed active congregations," we find just the same sort of thing happening during the evangelisation of barbarians in Europe during the Dark Ages. An outstanding example is the request of St Boniface that took SS. Lioba, Thecla, Walburga and others from their quiet abbey at Wimborne to the wilds of heathen Germany. Lioba was of a good Wessex family, and Ebba, her mother, was nearly related to St Boniface. She had been long barren and had no prospect of issue, when Lioba was born, and she offered her to God from her birth and trained her up in indifference to the world. By her direction Lioba was placed while young in the great monastery of Wimborne in Dorsetshire, under the care of the abbess St Tetta, a person eminent for her extraordinary prudence and sanctity. The girl had been baptised Truthgeba but came to be called Liobgetha, abbreviated to Lioba, " the dear one," a name which was fitting to one so precious in the eyes of God and man and which has been used of her ever since. When she came to the requisite age Lioba elected to remain in the monastery, wherein she was duly professed and made progress in virtue and knowledge. Her innocence and single-mindedness were an example even to her seniors, and reading and books were her delight.

In the year 722 St Boniface was consecrated bishop by Pope

St Gregory II and sent to preach the gospel in Saxony, Thuringia, and Hesse. He was a native of Crediton, not very far from Wimborne, and when accounts of his labours and successes reached the nuns there his young relative Lioba made bold to write to him, in the following terms :

"To the most reverend Boniface, bearer of the highest dignity and well-beloved in Christ, Liobgetha, to whom he is related by blood, the least of Christ's handmaids, sends greetings for eternal salvation.

"I beg you of your kindness to remember your early friendship in the west country with my father, Tinne, who died eight years ago and from whose soul, therefore, I ask you not to withhold your prayers to God. I also commend to your memory my mother Ebba, who still lives, but painfully, long weighed down by infirmity ; she is, as you know, related to you. I am the only child of my parents and, unworthy though I be, I should like to look on you as my brother, for I can trust you more than anyone else. I venture to send you this little gift [the letter itself ?] not because it is worth your consideration but simply so that you may have something to remind you of my humble self, and so not forget me when you are so far away ; may it draw tighter the bond of true love between us for ever. I beseech you, dear brother, help me with the shield of your prayers in my conflict against the attacks of the hidden enemy. I would ask you, too, if you would be so good as to correct this unlearned letter and not to refuse to send me a few kind words, which I eagerly look forward to as a token of your good will. I have tried to compose the subscribed lines according to the rules of verse, as an exercise for my very poor skill in poetry, wherein also I have need of your guidance. I have learned this art from Edburga, who is ever in mind of God's holy law.

"Farewell ! May you live long and happily, and pray for me always.

> "Arbiter omnipotens, solus qui cuncta creavit
> in regno Patris semper qui lumine fulget
> qua iugiter flagrans, sic regnat gloria Christi,
> illæsum servet semper te iure perenni."

(May the Almighty Judge, who alone has created all there is, who for ever shines with light in the kingdom of the Father, where also the burning glory of Christ reigns perpetually, keep you for ever in safety by His never-failing law.)

St Boniface was not unmoved by so touching an appeal, and entered into a correspondence of which the upshot was that in 748 he asked St Tetta that St Lioba might be sent to him with certain companions, in order to settle some monasteries as centres of religion for women in the infant church of Germany. Tetta accordingly sent out some thirty nuns, including SS. Lioba, Thecla (afterwards abbess of Kitzingen), and Walburga (afterwards abbess of Heidenheim), who joined St Boniface at Mainz. He settled St Lioba and her little colony in a monastery which he gave her, and which was called Bischofsheim, that is, Bishop's House, which suggests that he may have given up his own residence to the nuns. Under Lioba's care this nunnery became in a short time very numerous, and out of it she peopled other houses which she founded in Germany.

Rudolf, a monk of Fulda, who within sixty years of St Lioba's death wrote an account of her from the testimonies of four of her nuns, says that nearly all the convents of that part of Germany asked for a nun trained at Bischofsheim to guide them. The saint herself was so wrapped up in her work that she seemed to have forgotten Wessex and her own folk. Her beauty was remarkable; she had a face " like an angel," always pleasant and smiling, but rarely laughing outright. No one ever saw her in a bad temper or heard her speak an uncharitable word, and her patience and intelligence were as large as her kindness. How her nuns regarded her is shown by the way they referred to her drinking vessel : it was always *Dilectae parvus*, "the darling's little cup," and its small size witnessed to her own abstemiousness in a community which kept to St Benedict's provision of two meals a day, at the sixth and ninth hours, each of two dishes with some fruit or young vegetables. All the nuns engaged in manual work, whether in bakehouse, brewhouse, household duties, or otherwise, and at the same time had what to-day would be called "higher education"; all had to know Latin, and their scriptorium was kept busy. St Lioba would allow no imprudent austerities, such as deprivation of sleep, and insisted on the observance of the midday rest prescribed by the Rule. She herself spent this hour lying down, while one of the novices read to her from the Bible, and if it appeared that Mother Abbess had gone to sleep and the reader became careless, she would soon find herself corrected for a mispronunciation or a false quantity. Afterwards Lioba would devote two hours to private talk with any of the sisters who wished to see her. All this activity subserved the main business of public prayer and worship of Almighty God, and the spiritual support of the missionary monks who worked in the land around them. A letter is extant from St Boniface to the " reverend and most dear sisters Lioba, Thecla, Cynehild, and those who dwell with them," asking for the continuance of their prayers. St Lioba's fame was widespread ; her neighbours came to her in peril of fire and tempest and sickness, and men of affairs in Church and State asked her counsel.

St Boniface, before his mission into Friesland and his marytrdom, took a moving farewell of Lioba and recommended her in the most earnest manner to St Lullus, a monk of Malmesbury and his episcopal successor, and to his monks at Fulda, entreating them to care for her with respect and honour, and declaring it his desire that after her death she should be buried by his bones, that both their bodies might wait the resurrection and be raised together in glory to meet the Lord and be for ever united in the kingdom of His love. After St Boniface's martyrdom she made frequent visits to his tomb at the abbey of Fulda, and she was allowed by a special privilege to enter the abbey with a senior nun and assist at the divine service and conferences, after which she went back to her own nunnery. When she was grown very old, and had been abbess at Bischofsheim for twenty-eight years, by the advice of St Lullus she settled all the nunneries under her care and, resigning their government, came to reside at the convent of Schönersheim, four miles from Mainz. Her friend St Hildegardis, Charlemagne's queen, invited her so earnestly to the court at Aix-la-Chapelle that she could not refuse to go, but had to insist on being allowed to return to her solitude. Taking leave of the queen, embracing and kissing her, she said : " Farewell, precious part of my soul ! May Christ our Creator and Redeemer grant that we may see each other without confusion of face in the day of Judgement, for in this life we shall never more see each other." And so it was. For St Lioba died a very short while after and was buried in the abbey-church of Fulda, not in the tomb of St Boniface, for the monks feared to disturb his relics, but on the north side of the high altar. She is named in the Roman Martyrology, and her feast is kept at several places in Germany.

There is a biography, said to have been compiled by Rudolf, a monk of Fulda, before 838, which has been printed by Mabillon and the Bollandists (September, vol. vii) ; and, as pointed out above, a good deal of reliable information comes to us through the correspondence of St Boniface and of Lull. This has been edited in modern times by Jaffé, and still more recently in the *Monumenta Germaniæ*, first by Dümmler and again by Tangl. See also H. Timerding, *Die christliche Frühzeit Deutschlands*, ii, *Die angelsächsische Mission*, 1929 ; L. Eckenstein, *Woman under Monasticism*, ch. iv ; and C. Plummer ; Bede, ii, p. 150.

BD. LAURENCE OF RIPAFRATTA, Conf.

A.D. 1457

The so-called Great Schism of the West, during which the papacy underwent a "Babylonian captivity" at Avignon, was inevitably a time of great trial and difficulty for all Catholic institutions, and among them the Order of Preachers went through a period of relaxation of its earlier fervour. In Italy and other places this was aggravated by outbreaks of plague which depopulated the houses of the order, but there also God raised up Blessed Raymund of Capua to lead a movement of reform. Among those who supported him was Blessed John Dominic, Archbishop of Ragusa and Cardinal, who discovered the abilities and virtues of Friar Laurence of Ripafratta. He had entered the order at Pisa about 1379, when he was already a deacon, and after studying the Scriptures and preaching for some twenty years he was appointed by Blessed John Dominic to be master of novices in the priory of Cortona. It was an office for which Blessed Laurence was peculiarly well qualified. He was a champion of rigorous observance but understood how properly to make use of the adaptability of the constitutions of his order; and he knew that if once the hearts of his novices were fired with the love of God respect for and obedience to the least provisions of their rule would follow. Among those who made their novitiate under his direction were St Antoninus, one of the greatest moral theologians and preachers of the Middle Ages, Fra Angelico, and his supposed brother, Benedict of Mugello. Blessed Laurence encouraged these last two to paint, seeing that preaching may be done as well by pictures as by word of mouth, and in one respect more advantageously : " The most persuasive tongue becomes silent in death, but your heavenly pictures will go on speaking of religion and virtue throughout the ages."

For his Biblical knowledge Blessed Laurence was, like St Antony of Padua, called the " Ark of the Testament," and he used his learning in preaching up and down Etruria with such effect that St Antoninus referred to him as another St Paul. When he was made vicar general of the priories that had taken up the reform he went to live at Pistoia, where almost at once there was a sharp outbreak of plague. Laurence immediately turned from his administrative duties to give himself to the service of the sufferers, both in that city and Fabriano, and, as always, many who were deaf to the appeals of the preacher were moved to penitence by the example of priests moving fearlessly among the infected to minister to their souls and bodies. In 1446

St Antoninus was called to the see of Florence, a responsibility he was most unwilling to take up ; but, when the wishes of Pope Eugenius IV and of the magistrates of the city failed to move him, he listened to Blessed Laurence and accepted the dignity, wherein he was always sustained by the counsel of his friend. After the death of Blessed Laurence at the age of ninety-eight St Antoninus wrote to the Dominicans of Pistoia, condoling them on their loss and eulogising the memory of their leader. "How many souls have been snatched from Hell by his words and example and led from depravity to a high perfection ; how many enemies he reconciled and what disagreements he adjusted; to how many scandals did he put an end ! I weep also for my own loss, for never again shall I receive those tender letters of his wherewith he used to stir up my fervour in the duties of this pastoral office." His tomb was the scene of many miracles, and in 1851 Pope Pius IX confirmed his *cultus* in the Order of Preachers and as minor patron of the city of Pistoia.

Apart from the documents presented to the Congregation of Rites for the confirmation of *cultus*, see V. Marchese, *Cenni storici del b. Lorenzo di Ripafratta* (Florence, 1851) ; a short Life by M. de Waresquiel (Paris, 1907), and Procter, *Dominican Saints*, pp. 38–41.

BD. BERNARDINO OF FELTRE, CONF.

A.D. 1494

The fifteenth century in Italy was a peroid of incessant warfare and internal disorder ; not the defence of a united nation against unjust aggression, but the outcome of commercial rivalry and political disputes between neighbouring states, the quarrels of princes carried on to a great extent by hired mercenaries, who cared nothing for the goodness or badness of their cause and who would always rather plunder than fight, and fight than work honestly. The people of the peninsula were at the mercy of tyrants and demagogues, demoralised by fighting and political uncertainty, weakened by the refinement of the Renaissance, divided by factions and parties whose differences penetrated into the Church and enfeebled her influence ; a lively faith tended to degenerate into superstition and morality became more and more corrupt. Of the saints whom this state of things did not fail to bring forth to cope with it, many were members of the Franciscan order in one or other of its branches, and foremost among them Blessed Bernardino

Tomitani, called " of Feltre," preacher and practical economist. His coming had been foretold by another Bernardino, of Siena, who, preaching at Perugia, had said : " After me will come another Bernardino, dressed in this same habit, who will do great things. Many, I know, will not listen to him, but do you believe his words and conform to his teaching." And at Florence in 1442 : " Within fourteen years another Bernardino will come, O Florentines, who will do great things. Accept his words and do what he tells you, for he will be the trumpet of Heaven and the organ of the Holy Ghost."

He was born in 1439, at Feltre in Venezia of the noble family of Tomitani (though some have claimed for him a more humble origin at Tome), the eldest of ten children, and received at baptism the name of Martin. The trouble which Donato Tomitani and Corona Rombaldoni took over the upbringing of their family is shown by the fact that, besides Martin, one boy and three girls became religious. Martin was the studious one of the family. When he was twelve he could write Latin verse, and his mother had to force him to play games for the good of his health. At about the same age he cut off his luxuriant hair, saying he would rather use a pen than a comb. Three years later, in 1454, when a peace was made between the Venetians, the Milanese, and the Neapolitans, Martin was chosen to pronounce a public eulogy of peace before the magistrates and burgesses of Feltre. Pleased with his success, his father got him admitted into the local college of notaries, and after two years sent him to the University of Padua where he plunged ardently into the study of philosophy and law, and began that acquaintance with the fashionable thought of his time which was afterwards valuable to him as a preacher. The sudden death of two of his professors at Padua had a profound effect on the young student, and soon after he came under the influence of the Franciscan St James della Marca, who preached the Lent at Padua in 1456. In May of the same year Martin was clothed as a novice among the Friars Minor of the Observance, and took the name of Bernardino, after him of Siena who had just been canonised. " We have to-day," said St James, " enrolled in the militia of Jesus Christ a soldier who will shed a lustre over our order and contribute mightily to the glory of God and the confusion of Satan." During his novitiate the young friar was terribly tried by temptations, but he surmounted all difficulties and after his profession was sent to Venice, Mantua and Verona to finish his studies. Among the delights and interests which he cut himself off from was music. " Above all," he wrote, " music is not suitable for those consecrated to God. Those chants which please the hearers by the harmony of the voices are not pleasing to the

Lord. I should not wish to listen to a *Kyrie* in [figured] music, but I gladly hear it sung in plain chant. In all our monasteries of the Observance [figured] music is forbidden; we regard it as scandalous to do anything like a concerted piece." Friar Bernardino was ordained priest in 1463, and for six more years continued quietly in study and prayer, under the direction of the Venerable Sixtus of Milan.

Hitherto Friar Bernardino had done no public preaching, and when in 1469 a chapter at Venice appointed him a preacher he was much troubled. He was nervous, lacked confidence in himself, and seemed physically ill-equipped, for he was very short in stature. This was sufficiently noticeable to earn him the nickname of *Parvulus* from Pope Innocent VIII, and he used to sign himself " piccolino e poverello." He therefore consulted his director, Sixtus of Milan, pointing out his lack of experience, his ignorance, his disabilities. Sixtus bade him kneel down, and signing him on the lips with the cross said : " God will take away all hindrance from your tongue to show you that the gift of preaching is from Him alone. Fear no more, my son ! You will learn more from your crucifix than from books." Bernardino felt no more doubt or hesitation ; God had spoken through the holy friar Sixtus. Nevertheless when he first went into the pulpit before a large congregation at Mantua on the feast of his patron, he was seized with panic ; he forgot everything, what he wanted to say, how he wanted to say it, all his carefully prepared points and periods. But he remembered his love and admiration for the virtues of St Bernardino of Siena, and he spoke of those, spontaneously, easily, and compellingly. He never again tried to preach a sermon prepared in detail, but trusted to his heart made virtuous by prayer. " Prayer," he said, " is a better preparation than study : it is both more efficacious and quicker." Blessed Bernardino preached up and down Italy for twenty-five years, in Lombardy, Venezia, Tuscany, Rome and the Papal States, Genoa, Naples, and even Sardinia. Crowds acclaimed him ; the wise and holy, popes, bishops, and other great preachers such as Blessed Cherubino of Spoleto and Michael of Carcano, praised him ; the wicked raged against him ; all proclaimed his power. Churches were too small to hold the crowds who wanted to hear him. At Florence and Pavia his congregations covered the main square, and all could hear ; at Padua and Feltre people from afar booked up all the lodgings throughout his stay ; three thousand people followed him through the night from Crema that they might hear him again the next day at Lodi. It has been estimated that Blessed Bernardino preached over three thousand six hundred times, but only a few

extracts from his sermons and a conference he gave to the Benedictines of Florence are extant.* From these it can be judged that he
spoke simply, with liveliness, and without any oratorical flourishes.
He even eschewed quotations in Latin, because, as he said : " Osten-
tation never does any good. A sermon of which the thread is often
broken by quotations does not ' get across,' it moves the soul of
nobody."

Bernardino was sent to minister to a society that was in great
part selfish, proud, and depraved ; he opposed to its vices charity,
humility, and austerity. He never forgot he was a Friar Minor :
he washed the feet of visitors when he was at home, refused the
hospitality of the rich, and lodged in lowly places when abroad.
But a good example alone is rarely enough ; he had to inveigh
plainly and often against the evils he saw around him. " When
he attacks vice," wrote Jerome of Ravenna, " he does not speak—
he thunders and lightens." Twice this slightly built little man broke
a blood-vessel in the fury of his denunciation of public scandals.
" He has a heavy hand and he does not know how to flatter," said
Cardinal d'Agria. Naturally he made enemies for himself, and
several attempts were made on his life, but he pursued his way
unperturbed. He got the disorders of carnival time controlled and
public gambling establishments suppressed in several cities ; the
races at Brescia on the feast of the Assumption were abolished because of their abuses ; in many places vicious images and books
were destroyed by the public authorities ; and, of course, he had
continually to attack the extravagances of female dress. Like
St Bernardino of Siena before him and Savonarola contemporane-
ously he finished each mission by having a public bonfire of cards,
dice, obscene books and pictures, useless finery, false hair, superstitious philtres, badges of factions, and other vanities. This he
called the " burning of the Devil's stronghold," and it was designed
not so much to be a practical removal of occasions of sin as to be a
gesture forcibly to strike the imagination of the public. At his appeal
civil authorities enacted or repealed laws. Men and women were
separated in the public gaols ; the Married Women's Property Act
was anticipated and husbands were prevented from wasting the
goods of their wives ; the senates of Venice and Vicenza ceased to
grant immunity to transgressors who should bring the heads of out-
lawed relatives. Blessed Bernardino was no respecter of persons
when it was a question of the moral law. He reproved the Prince

* Blessed Bernardino has often been credited with the authorship of
Anima Christi, but this prayer was written at least ninety years before he
was born.

of Mantua, a liberal patron of the Friars Minor, for not restraining
the rapacity and oppression of his courtiers ; he preached at Milan
in defiance of the duke, Galeazzo Visconti ; he denounced the Oddi
and the Baglioni, heads of the factions in Perugia ; and when
Ferdinand I of Naples, worked on by the Jews, ordered him to come
from Aquila to answer before the courts, Bernardino refused to give
an account of his words unless commanded by his own superiors.
The wiser princes trusted and admired him, and when it served their
purpose made use of his services as a peacemaker. At Brescia, at
Narni, at Faenza, and other places he healed public strife and brought
tranquillity for a time, and Pope Innocent VIII sent him on a
mission of pacification into Umbria. But the feuds of one town
defied all his efforts. Three times, in 1484, in 1488, and again in
1493, the year before he died, he went to Perugia to try and compose its dissensions ; and each time he failed. As a contribution
towards making peace lasting he encouraged the formation of associations of Tertiaries, who were under obligation not to take up
arms. Unlike many lesser preachers and moralists in his time
Blessed Bernardino did not allow his personal successes and consciousness of ecclesiastical abuses to lead him into an independent
attitude towards the church authorities. When the Holy See offered
him faculties to absolve from sins reserved to the bishops, he replied :
" The bishops are the ordinary shepherds of the clergy and the
people, and I would rather depend on them in all those circumstances where the law of the Church requires it." " If you have
the virtue of obedience," he told the monks of Florence, " you have
all the other virtues. What you do from self-will is a wisp of straw ;
the same done under obedience is a rod of gold."

From time to time we hear much of the hardships which the
Jews suffered at the hands of Christians in the Middle Ages, and it
cannot be denied that many and grave injustices were perpetrated
against them. On the other hand the problem of how to deal with
the " anti-social " activities of the Jews was a real one, and most
inadequately met by the device of so far as possible isolating them
from the life of their Christian surroundings. Blessed Bernardino
of Feltre was, throughout his career, in conflict with the Jews, not
as Jews but as the cause and occasion of some of the worst of the
abuses which it was his business to combat. He spoke of them at
Crema thus : " The Jews must not be harmed either in their persons
or their property or in any way whatsoever. Justice and charity
must be extended even to them, for they are of the same nature as
ourselves. I say this everywhere and I repeat it here at Crema in
order that it may be acted upon, because good order, the Sovereign

Pontiffs, and Christian charity alike require it. But it is not less true that canon law expressly forbids too frequent dealings, too great familiarity with them. . . . To-day no one has any scruples in this matter, and I cannot be silent about it. Jewish usurers exceed all bounds ; they ruin the poor and get fat at their expense. I, who live on alms and myself eat the bread of poverty, cannot be a dumb dog before such outrageous injustice. The poor feed me and I cannot hold my tongue when I see them robbed. Dogs bark to protect their masters, and I must bark in the cause of Christ." The lending of money at usury, with huge rates of interest, to which Blessed Bernardino refers above, was the chief (but not the only) complaint against the Jews, who had thus succeeded in making themselves hated by the poor and necessary to the rich.* A century earlier a bishop of London, Michael of Northburg, had left a thousand silver marks to be lent to the needy without interest on the security of deposited articles, and among several experiments of the sort this was the first true *mons pietatis*.† In 1462 the Franciscan Barnabas of Terni founded at Perugia a " pawnship " which should make small loans to the poor upon pledged objects at a low rate of interest. It was immediately successful, and in the following year another was established, at Orvieto, and the institution soon spread to the Marches, the Papal States, Tuscany, and elsewhere. The scheme was taken up, organised, and perfected by Blessed Bernardino. In 1484 he opened a *mons pietatis* at Mantua (it soon succumbed under the influence of the Jews), and was responsible for twenty more during the following eight years. The details of the organisation varied, but they were generally administered by mixed committees of friars and laymen representative of different trades, and some were municipally controlled. The initial capital fund was obtained in part from voluntary subscriptions and in part by loans from the Jews themselves ; all profits were added to capital and applied to the reduction of rates of interest. It was natural that Blessed Bernardino should be fiercely attacked by the Jews and Lombards, who succeeded in getting some of his *montes pietatis* closed ; but a more serious and no less inevitable opposition came from some canonists and moral theologians who insisted that the

* The Jews were not the only offenders. There were, for example, also the Lombard bankers and the *Caorcini* (from Cavour in Piedmont). Blessed Bernardino was a child of his age and believed the charges brought against the Jews of Trent in 1475 in respect of Little St Simon. See an account of him herein under March 24.

† *Monte di pietà, mont-de-piété.* Literally a " heap of money of piety," *mons* signifying an accumulation of wealth, capital, and *pietatis* that it was not a commercial concern.

interest charged was usurious within the meaning of canon law and therefore sinful. They wished the loans to be free. This would have meant that the *montes* could not be self-supporting, and Blessed Bernardino stood firmly for the charging of small interest. The controversy was fierce and was never settled in his time. But the fifth General Council of the Lateran decreed in 1515 that *montes pietatis* were lawful and worthy of all encouragement, and thereafter they became common throughout Western Europe, always excepting the British Isles. His struggle for these institutions is the work for which Blessed Bernardino of Feltre is best remembered, and he is often represented in art with a little green hill of three mounds, each surmounted by a cross, with the legend *curam illius habe* : a more pleasing and good-omened device than the three bezants borrowed by English pawnbrokers from the arms of Lombardy—though this was the badge of Savonarola's *mons pietatis* at Florence.

Blessed Bernardino worked up to the last. Early in 1494 he told the Florentines he would never see them again, and when he arrived in Siena he heard a report of his own death. " I'm always dying, if one can believe all one hears," he observed. " But the day will come, and come soon, when it will be true." He welcomed Cardinal Francis Piccolomini (afterwards Pope Pius III), who wished to be his penitent : " We are both of us little men (*piccolomini*)," was his remark to his Eminence. At the end of August he dragged himself to Pavia to preach, and warned the city that he could " hear the French shoeing their horses for the invasion of Italy "—which within a few months King Charles VIII did. But Blessed Bernardino did not live to see it, for he died at Pavia on September 28 following. He was beatified by Pope Benedict XIII in 1728.

Materials for the Life of this holy Franciscan seem to be fairly abundant as Father Suyskens pointed out nearly two centuries ago in the long notice of one hundred folio pages accorded to him in the *Acta Sanctorum*, September, vol. vii. The most complete modern biography seems to be that of Father L. Besse, *Le bienheureux Bernardin de Feltre et son œuvre*, in 2 volumes (Tours, 1902). But even here an important manuscript source seems to have been but little used, to wit, the journal of Father Francis da Feltre, who for twelve years acted as the great preacher's secretary (see the *Analecta Bollandiana*, vol. xxii 1903, pp. 118–119). Other documents have since been brought to light, for example, a number of letters concerning Fra Bernardino's preaching in Reggio (Emilia), which are now printed in the *Archivum Franciscanum Historicum*, xix (1926), pp. 226–246. A conveniently brief account of Bd. Bernardino is that of E. Flournoy in the series *Les Saints*. See also Léon, *Auréole Séraphique* (Eng. Trans.), vol. iii, pp. 243–266.

BD. SIMON DE ROJAS OR ROXAS, CONF.

A.D. 1624

From being an exemplary friar of the Trinitarian order, Blessed Simon was called to the court of Philip III, King of Spain. Here he was chosen to be confessor to the King's wife, Isabella of Bourbon. When an epidemic of plague broke out at Madrid, Blessed Simon prepared to go to the help of the sufferers, but the King forbade him, fearing that infection might be brought to the court. " Sick-beds are more fitting places for me than royal palaces," replied the friar, " and if I must give up one I will give up the court." Like Blessed Alphonsus d'Orosco, his fellow-chaplain, Simon de Rojas exercised a strong influence in the royal entourage and contributed much to the high standard of religion and morality maintained therein. He was a great missionary, founded a confraternity of the *Ave Maria*, and wrote an office for the feast of the Holy Name of Mary, to which his order had a special devotion. Blessed Simon died ten days after the then date of this feast in 1624, and was beatified by Pope Clement XIII in 1766.

A copy of the printed *Summarium*, presented in the Beatification process, is preserved in the Bibliothêque Nationale at Paris. Several references to this process occur in the great work of Benedict XIV, *De Beatificatione*, etc., bk. ii. When Bd. Simon was beatified in 1766, there was published in Rome a *Compendio della Vita del. B. Simone de Roxas* (1767). See also P. Deslandres, *L'Ordre des Trinitaires* (1903), vol. i, p. 618, etc.

SEPTEMBER **29**

THE DEDICATION OF ST MICHAEL THE ARCHANGEL

THIS festival has been kept with great solemnity at the end of
September ever since the sixth century at least. The Roman
Martyrology implies that the dedication of the famous church
of St Michael on Mount Gargano (see May 8) gave occasion to the
institution of this feast in the West, but it would appear that it
really celebrates the dedication of a basilica in honour of St Michael
and all Angels on the Salarian Way six miles north of Rome, before
the sixth century. In the East where he was regarded as having care
of the sick (rather than, as to-day, captain of the heavenly host and
protector of soldiers) veneration of this archangel began yet earlier
and certain healing waters were named after him, as at Khairotopa
and Colossæ. Sozomen tells us that Constantine the Great built a
church in his honour, called the Michaelion, at Sosthenion, some
way from Constantinople, and that in it the sick were often cured
and other wonders wrought through the intercession of St Michael.
He assures us that he had often experienced such relief here himself ; and he mentions the miraculous cures of Aquilinus, an eminent
lawyer, and of Probianus, a physician, in the same place. Four
churches in honour of St Michael stood in the city of Constantinople
itself, including a famous one at the Baths of Arcadius, and their
number was afterwards increased to fifteen, which were built by
several emperors.

Though only St Michael be mentioned in the title of this festival,
it appears from the prayers of the Mass that all the good angels are
its object, together with this glorious prince and tutelary angel of
the Church. On it we are called upon in a particular manner to
give thanks to God for the glory which the angels enjoy and to
rejoice in their happiness. Secondly, to thank Him for His mercy
to us in constituting such beings to minister to our salvation by
aiding us. Thirdly, to join them in adoring and praising God with
all possible ardour, desiring and praying that we may do his will on
earth with the utmost fidelity and purity of affection, as it is done by
these blessed spirits in Heaven : that we may sanctify our souls
in imitation of the angels to whom we are associated. Lastly, we

are invited to honour them and implore their intercession and succour.

Honour being no more than a testimony which we bear to another's excellence, who can deny it to be due to the most sublime, perfect, holy, and glorious heavenly spirits ? Abraham fell down before the angels whom he received in his tent. Daniel did the same before one whom he saw upon the Tigris. God commanded the Israelites to fear and respect the angel whom He sent to be their conductor into the promised land. The first consideration for which the angels claim our respect is the excellence of their nature, in which they are essentially of an order superior to men, being pure spirits, exempt from the weaknesses of our earthly frame and endued with more noble faculties and qualities suited to the perfection and simplicity of their unbodied and uncompounded being. Secondly, the gifts of grace and glory are proportioned in them to the superiority of their nature ; and the Scriptures speak of angels as absolutely above men, though some particular saints may, for aught we know, enjoy a greater felicity than many angels, and our Lady is exalted in glory above all the heavenly spirits. Nor has any order of the highest spirits an honour or dignity equal to that which is conferred on mankind by the mystery of the Incarnation, in which the Son of God took not the nature of angels but assumed that of men, and as man is constituted by His Father lord of all creatures. However the blessed angels are creatures perfectly holy who without either division or interruption obey, love, and glorify God with all their powers. They are always employed in the contemplation of His infinite goodness and other perfections, swallowed up in the ocean of His love, and they never cease crying with all their might : " Holy, Holy, Holy, the Lord God of hosts ! all the earth is full of His glory." They cease not day or night saying : " Holy, Holy, Holy, Lord God Almighty, who was and who is and who is to come." In profound annihilation of themselves they give all honour and glory to Him alone, and professing their crowns to be entirely His gifts they cast them at His feet and sing : " The Lamb that was slain is worthy to receive power and divinity and wisdom and strength and honour and glory and benediction." Burning with love and the desire to praise more and more perfectly His goodness and greatness, they continually repeat their hymns with new jubilation. The psalmist, who felt in some degree the strength of this impulse in his own breast, knew no stronger motive to invite them to love and praise God with all their powers than their own desire so to do. And he cries out to them : " Bless the Lord, all ye His angels ; you that are mighty in strength and execute His word, hearkening to the voice of His orders. Bless the Lord, all ye His hosts; you ministers of His that do His will."

Not from any want of power but from His infinite goodness and wisdom God employs superior spirits in various dispensations of His providence concerning men, and therein they employ zeal for the divine honour, fidelity in executing His will, and affection and charity for us. Upon many occasions Abraham, Jacob, Moses, and other patriarchs and prophets were favoured with visions of these holy spirits. They brought many blessings from God, sometimes to the Church in general, sometimes to His faithful servants in particular, and they averted many evils. An angel sent by God relieved and comforted Agar in her despair. Other angels delivered Lot from the burning of Sodom, the three children from the flames, Daniel from the lions, St Peter from his chains, and the Apostles out of their dungeon. God gave His law to the Jews by an angel who was His ambassador. By angels He showed to St John the future state of His Church, and many visions to Daniel and other prophets. They were His messengers in the execution of the principal mysteries relating to the incarnation, birth, flight, temptation, and agony of Christ. An angel conducted the Israelites into the land of promise. The apostle Jude mentions a contest which St Michael had with the Devil about the burial of the body of Moses, in which he used no curse, no harsh or reproachful word, but to repress the malicious fiend only said: "The Lord command thee." St John describes a great battle of St Michael and the good angels with the Devil and his spirits which seems by the context not to belong properly to the expulsion of these latter out of Heaven when they sinned but to some efforts of the demons when they were vanquished by Christ in the mystery of our redemption. Angels carried the soul of Lazarus into the place of rest, and their host will descend with Christ at the last day and assemble men before his tribunal. The holy Scriptures assure us that the angels are the ministers of God, appointed to execute His orders and to do His will, and He promises their ministry and help to all that serve Him.

That the good angels intercede with God for us and that their patronage may be invoked is an article of the Catholic faith. Jacob entreated with the angel with whom he had wrestled that he would give him his blessing, and on his death-bed he prayed the angel who had conducted and protected him to bless his grandchildren, Ephraim and Manasses. The prophet Daniel was told in his visions how vigorously the guardian angel of Persia interposed in favour of that country, and what good offices Michael and other angels did for the Jews in removing obstacles which retarded their return from the captivity. The same prophet, speaking of the cruel persecution of Antiochus, says : " At that time shall Michael rise up, the great prince who standeth for the children of thy people." This implies that Michael would support the Machabees and other defenders of God's people, and " standing " for them must mean principally by praying for them, as it is said of the priests and Levites in Deuteronomy x, 8. Other books of the holy Scripture mention visible succour of angels which the Jews experienced, in their deliverance from the slavery of Egypt and the passage to Canaan ; and also many among the patriarchs, several among the judges of the Jewish nation, and others. The Church has always invoked and paid a religious honour to the holy angels. Origen teaches that they assist us in our devotions and join their supplications to ours. " The angel of the Christian," says he, " offers his prayers to God through the only high priest, himself also praying for him who is committed to his charge." He tells us that the angels carry our prayers to God and bring back His blessings to us, but that Christians do not call upon and worship them as they do God. He addresses a prayer to the angel of a person who is going to be baptised, asking that he would instruct him. The martyr Nemesianus and his companions, writing to St Cyprian, say : " Let us assist one another by our prayers, and beg that we may have God and Christ and the angels on our side in all our actions." St Gregory Nazianzen writes : " The angelical powers are a succour to us in all good." He prays the good angels to receive his soul at the hour of death, and threatens the Devil with the sign of the cross if he should approach him. St Ephrem says of Heaven that it is " where all the angels and saints of God reign, praying the Lord for us," and he repeats that the angels with joy offer our prayers to God. If we desire to live for ever in the company of the holy angels we must learn to converse with God by prayer and contemplation, and to walk in His presence, withdrawing our minds as much as we can from a vain distracting world ; worshipping and loving God, rejoicing in Him, bending our wills cheerfully under His, and striving with our whole strength to obey His law.

As a fuller note appears in connection with St Michael on May 8 in this series, it will be sufficient here to give a reference to the *Acta Sanctorum*, September, vol. viii ; Kellner, *Heortology* (Eng. Trans.), pp. 328–333 ; Duchesne, *Christian Worship* (Eng. Trans.), p. 276, and, for St Michael and the angels in art, to Künstle, *Ikonographie*, vol. i, pp. 239–264.

SS. RHIPSIME, GAIANA, AND THEIR COMPANIONS, VIRGINS AND MARTYRS

c. A.D. 290

Although these maidens, apparently the protomartyrs of the Armenian church, are mentioned in the Roman Martyrology on this date as suffering under King Tiridates, nothing at all is known of their history or the circumstances of their passion. They are referred to in the legend of St Gregory the Illuminator, and may be assumed to have been put to death during the persecution which preceded the baptism of Tiridates and his family by Gregory, but their Armenian *acta* is a romance of the most barefaced kind. These legends tell us that Rhipsime was a maiden of noble birth, one of a community of consecrated virgins at Rome presided over by Gaiana. The Emperor, Diocletian, having made up his mind to marry, sent a painter around Rome to paint the portraits of all those ladies who seemed to him eligible, and he did his work with such thoroughness that he penetrated into the house of Gaiana and made likenesses of some of her Christian maidens. When Diocletian examined the portraits his choice fell on Rhipsime, and she was informed of the honour that had befallen her. It was not at all to her liking, and Gaiana was so afraid of what the Emperor might do that she summoned her charges at once from Rome, went aboard ship, and proceeded to Alexandria. From thence they made their way through the Holy Land to Armenia, where they settled down at the royal capital, Varlarshapat, and earned their living by weaving. The great beauty of Rhipsime soon attracted attention, but the noise of it apparently reached back to Rome before it came to the ears of King Tiridates, for Diocletian wrote asking him to kill Gaiana and send Rhipsime back—unless he would like to keep her for himself. Tiridates thereupon sent a deputation to fetch her to his palace with great magnificence, but when it arrived at the convent Rhipsime prayed for deliverance, and so fierce a thunderstorm at once broke out that the horses of the courtiers and their riders were scattered in confusion. When Tiridates heard this and that the girl refused to come he ordered her to be brought by force, and when she was led into his presence he was so attracted by her beauty that he at once tried to embrace her. Rhipsime not only resisted but threw the King ignominiously to the floor, so that in a rage he ordered her to prison. But she escaped and returned to her companions during the night.

At morning when they found her gone the King sent soldiers

after her with orders that she was to die, and all the other maidens with her. St Rhipsime was roasted alive and torn limb from limb, and St Gaiana and the others to the number of thirty-five likewise were brutally slain. St Mariamne was dragged to death from a bed of sickness, but one, St Nino, escaped and became the apostle of Georgia in the Caucasus. This massacre took place on October 5, on which date the martyrs are named in the Armenian menology. A week later retribution overtook the brutal Tiridates who, as he was setting out to hunt, was turned into a wild boar! He was brought back to nature by St Gregory the Illuminator, who had been confined in a pit for fifteen years. These martyrs figured in the fabulous vision of St Gregory at Etshmiadzin, and around the great church there are three smaller churches on the alleged site of the martyrdom of St Rhipsime, of St Gaiana, and of the others.

Extravagant as the legend is, there can be no question that the *cultus* of these martyrs meets us at an early date in Armenia, and that it was very widely diffused. We find Rhipsime mentioned in Egypt under the Coptic form "Arepsima" (see *Analecta Bollandiana*, xlv, 157 and 395), as well as in Arabic texts and in the Syriac martyrology of Rabban Sliba. From the testimony of the Armenian historians Faustus and Lazarus, it seems safe to state that the martyrs were venerated before the middle of the fifth century. See Tournebize, *Histoire politique et religieuse d'Arménie*, pp. 452 seq. and *passim*. One Greek version of their "Acts," attributed to Agathangelus, is printed in the *Acta Sanctorum*, September, vol. viii, associated with those of St Gregory the Illuminator on September 30. *Cf.* also S. Weber, *Die katholische Kirche in Armenien* (1903), p. 117, etc.

ST THEODOTA, Mart.

c. A.D. 318

This Theodota suffered at Philippopolis in Thrace during the persecution raised by the *Augustus* Licinius when he openly professed paganism and went to war with Constantine the Great. Her "acts" are full of exaggeration and embroidery. According to them, Agrippa the prefect at a festival of Apollo commanded that the whole city should offer sacrifice with him. Theodota, who had been formerly a harlot, was accused of refusing to conform and, being called upon by the president, answered him that she had indeed been a grievous sinner, but could not add sin to sin nor defile herself with a sacrilegious sacrifice. Her constancy encouraged seven hundred and fifty people to step forward and, professing themselves Christians, to refuse to join in the sacrifice. Theodota was cast into prison where she lay twenty days, all which time she employed in prayer. Being brought to the bar again she burst into tears and prayed aloud that Christ would pardon the crimes of her past life, and arm her with strength that she might be enabled to bear with constancy the torments she was going to suffer. In her answers to the judge she confessed that she had been a harlot but that she had become a Christian, though unworthy to bear that sacred name. Agrippa commanded her to be scourged. Those that stood near exhorted her to free herself from torments by obeying the president : for one moment would suffice. But Theodota remained constant, and cried under the lashes : " I will never abandon the true God nor sacrifice to lifeless statues." The president then ordered her to be put on the rack and her body to be torn with an iron comb. Under these tortures she earnestly prayed to Christ, and said : " I worship you, O Christ, and thank you, because you have made me worthy to suffer this for your name." The judge, enraged at her resolution and patience, cried to the executioner : " Tear her flesh again with the comb ; then pour vinegar and salt into her wounds." But she only said : " I fear your torments so little that I ask you to increase them to the utmost, that I may find mercy and attain to the greater crown." Agrippa next commanded the executioners to pull out her teeth, which they did violently, one by one, with pincers. The judge at length condemned her to be stoned to death. She was led out of the city and during her martyrdom prayed : " O Christ, who showed favour to Rahab the harlot and received the good thief, turn not your mercy from me." In this manner she died and her soul ascended triumphant to Heaven.

This extravagant legend has not been included by the Bollandists in the *Acta Sanctorum*. The Syriac text was first published by Assemani in his *Acta Sanctorum Orientalium et Occidentalium*, vol. ii, pp. 210–226, and since then by other scholars. Mrs. A. Smith Lewis, in *Studia Sinaitica*, vol. x, has printed some better readings of the text.

BD. RICHARD ROLLE, Hermit

A.D. 1349

The authority for the attribution of the title Blessed to Richard Rolle of Hampole is no more than that given by a very considerable popular *cultus* in the past, which has never yet been confirmed by the competent authority. After his death the honour in which he was held and the miracles reported at his tomb caused preparations for his canonisation to be made, but the cause was never prosecuted. The Breviary of the Church of York had an office prepared for his

feast, to which this warning was attached : " The Office of Saint
Richard, hermit, after he shall be canonised by the Church, because
in the meantime it is not allowed to sing the canonical hours for
him in public, nor to solemnise his feast. Nevertheless, having
evidence of the extreme sanctity of his life, we may venerate him
and in our private devotions seek his intercessions, and commend
ourselves to his prayers." The Matins lessons of this office are the
principal source for the life of Richard, in whom more interest has
been taken in recent years than in any other English uncanonised
saint on account of the unique position which he holds among
English mystical writers.

Richard was born about the year 1300 at Thornton in Yorkshire,
traditionally identified as Thornton-le-Dale in the North Riding.
With the help of Master Thomas Neville, afterwards Archdeacon
of Durham, his parents sent him to Oxford, which he left in his
nineteenth year. The *officium* tells us that he went home, begged
two of his sister's gowns, and made out of them so well as he was
able a habit which roughly resembled that of a hermit. His sister
thought he was mad and told him so, and he fled away lest his
friends should prevent him, for he was acting without his father's
knowledge and against his wish. On the vigil of our Lady's Assumption he turned up in the church of a neighbouring parish (Topcliffe ?)
at Vespers, and knelt down at the bench reserved to the squire,
John of Dalton. He was recognised by the squire's sons, who had
been with him at Oxford. Next day he was in church again and,
vested in a surplice, assisted at the singing of Matins and Mass.
After the gospel he came and asked the celebrant's blessing, and
went into the pulpit and " gave the people a sermon of wonderful
edification, insomuch that the crowd that heard it was moved to
tears, and they all said that they had never before heard a sermon
of such virtue and power." After Mass John of Dalton asked
Richard to dinner, and when he had convinced himself of the youth's
good faith and honesty of purpose he offered him a suitable place
to live in and gave him proper clothes, food, and all else that he
required. " Then he began with all diligence by day and night to
seek how to perfect his life and to take every opportunity to advance
in contemplation and to be fervent in divine love."

On the face of it there are certain features in this narrative appro-
priate to a more primitive age of Christianity than England in the
fourteenth century, and there is reason to think that the pious author
of the *officium* has somewhat " telescoped " events, with the usual
object of making his story more edifying to the faithful. In his own
works Richard Rolle refers to his youth as having been unclean and

sinful, which, even after allowing for the self-depreciation of holiness, does not accord with the tone of the *officium*. Moreover, there is evidence to prove that from about the year 1320 to 1326 he was a member of the Sorbonne in Paris. It is possible therefore that when his sudden appearance in a Yorkshire parish church and subsequent events took place he was not a youth fresh from Oxford but an experienced man of twenty-seven or twenty-eight ; not, as is usually supposed, a relatively unlearned layman, but a trained priest, perhaps even a doctor of theology. " He was first a Doctor, and then leaving the world became an Eremite," wrote a Catholic priest who published an English Martyrology in the year 1608, and for some years he continued his eremetical life on the Daltons' estate. Writers on mysticism have described from his own writings his progress in contemplation, and brought it into accord with the now classical scheme of the purgative, illuminative, and unitive ways, though the terms which he uses, *dulcor, canor,* and *calor* or *fervor* do not corre- spond with these stages. The last is undoubtedly the state of pas- sive contemplation or mystical union where, as he says, the soul " ascends not into another degree, but as it were confirmed in grace, so far as mortal can be, she rests." " I did not think anything like it or anything so holy could be received in this life." But Richard claims no direct revelations or visions such as are apparently granted to so many of the mystics, and his spiritual experiences were, so far as we know, unaccompanied by any unusual physical phenomena. His seeing the Devil in a certain woman who tempted him seems to be a figure of speech, as perhaps were the demons who left the death-bed of Dame Dalton only to infest his own cell.

Richard himself tells us something of his early difficulties and discouragements. " Rotten rags hardly covered me, and in my nakedness I was annoyed with the bites of the flies which no com- fortable covering prevented from walking over me, and my skin became rough with ingrained dirt ; and yet in warm weather I was tormented by the heat, among men who were enjoying all the shade that they desired ; and my teeth chattered with the cold while they were indulging in rich adornments and rejoicing in superfluities— although nevertheless they loved not the Giver of these things." " Indeed, I have so weakened my body and suffer so from headaches in consequence that I cannot stand, so bad are they, unless I am strengthened by wholesome food." Later in life he wrote from experience, " It behoves him truly to be strong that will manfully use the love of God. The flesh being enfeebled with great disease oft-times a man cannot pray, and then much more he cannot lift himself to high things with hot desire. I would rather therefore that man failed for the greatness of love than for too much fasting. . . ." For many years he was troubled by mischief-making tongues, and learned that this too was a mortification to be turned to good account. " This have I known, that the more men have raved against me with words of backbiting, so much the more I have grown in spiritual profit. Forsooth, the worst backbiters I have had are those which I trusted before as faithful friends. Yet I ceased not for their words from those things that were profitable to my soul. . . ." At first Richard lived in the Daltons' house, but afterwards removed to a hermitage at some distance on their estate. But its proximity drew down ill-natured criticism ; " my detractors say that I am led astray by the pleasures in which the rich delight, and am unworthy of God." He provoked the resentment of some of the clergy including, it would seem, his own bishop, for he did not hesitate to attack those who lived evilly or were worldly and particularly those who discharged their duties mechanically and did not encourage those who were sincerely concerned for the good of souls. After the death of Dame Dalton, Richard " for most urgent and practical reasons " went to live in the district of Richmondshire, where one Maundy Thursday he was summoned to Dame Margaret Kirkby, a recluse and dear friend, who had been seriously ill for a fortnight and quite speechless. " And as she sat by the window of her dwelling and they were eating together, it befell at the end of the meal that the recluse desired to sleep and, so oppressed by sleep, she drooped her head at the window where Richard leaned. And after she had slept thus for a short time, leaning slightly upon Richard, suddenly a violent convulsion seized her. . . . She awoke from sleep, the power of speech was restored to her, and she burst forth, ' Gloria tibi Domine.' And Blessed Richard finished the verse which she had begun, saying, ' Qui natus es de Virgine,' with the rest of the Compline hymn. Then said he to her, ' Now your speech is come back to you, use it as a woman whose speech is for good.' " From time to time Richard visited various places in Yorkshire, " so that dwelling in many places he might benefit many unto salvation . . . for it is not ill for hermits to leave cells for a reasonable cause, and afterwards, if it accord, to turn again to the same," and eventually settled at Hampole, on the Wakefield road four miles from Doncaster, where he had a cell near the priory of Cistercian nuns. Whether he was their accredited chaplain or simply an unofficial adviser and friend is not known.

Some think that Richard Rolle's best-known work, *Incendium Amoris*, was written here, the book in which " I here stir all manner of folk to love, and am busy to show the hottest and supernatural desire of love." But it is more likely that he was now writing only, or mostly, in English. He had already translated and commented on the Psalms for Margaret Kirkby (a chained copy was kept at Hampole Priory) and written a little book in English for a Benedictine nun at Yedingham, and he now wrote for one of the Hampole nuns the *Commandment of Love to God*, a fruit of the experience of middle age and one of the most moving of all his works. Any further details of his life we do not know, but it is abundantly clear from his own writings that he had reached those heights of contemplation and joyful resignation to God's will that are hardly attainable without an exercise of virtue not less than heroic. " As death slays all living things in this world, so perfect love slays in a man's soul all earthly desires and covetousness. And as Hell spares nought to dead men but torments all that come thereto, so a man that is in this degree of love not only forsakes the wretched solace of this life but also he desires to suffer pains for God's love." Richard Rolle died at Hampole on September 29, 1349 ; the circumstances are not known but it is extremely likely that he was a victim of the Black Death which raged in Yorkshire in that year. The sort of man which Richard was, as seen in his written works, is no less attractive than the works themselves : he was the opposite of all those qualities which ignorance and prejudice attribute to those who choose to be hermits and seek God alone rather than in company. " The holy lover of God shows himself neither too merry nor full heavy in this habitation of exile, but he has cheerfulness with maturity. Some, indeed, reprove laughter and some praise it. Laughter therefore which is from lightness and vanity of mind is to be reproved, but that truly which is of gladness of conscience and spiritual mirth is to be praised ; the which is only in the righteous, and it is called mirth in the love of God. Wherefore if we be glad and merry the wicked call us wanton ; and if we be heavy, hypocrites."

Though Richard Rolle's claim to saintship has not been authoritatively recognised, his life and works have attracted much attention in England of late years. Miss Hope Emily Allen has of all other investigators rendered the greatest service to students in her book, *Writings ascribed to Richard Rolle and Materials for his Biography* (1927). But see also F. Comper, *Life and Lyrics of Richard Rolle* (1928) ; R. M. Woolley, *Richard Rolle of Hampole* (1919) ; C. Horstman, *English Works of Richard Rolle*, 2 vols. (1896)—an uncritical compilation ; M. Deanesley, the *Incendium Amoris* (1926) ; and finally a French translation of sundry works by Dom Noetinger, in his *Mystiques Anglais* (1928). See also Stanton's *Menology*, pp. 462–464, and G. C. Heseltine, *Selected Works of Richard Rolle* (1930) with bibliography.

BD. CHARLES OF BLOIS, DUKE OF BRITTANY, CONF.

A.D. 1364

This royal saint has a particular interest for English people as he had the misfortune to spend nine years in our country—as a prisoner in the Tower of London. He was born about the year 1316, the son of Louis de Châtillon, Count of Blois, and Margaret, the sister of the King of France, Philip VI, and as a young man showed himself both virtuous and brave and unusually worthy of his high rank. In 1341 he married Joan of Brittany, and by this marriage himself claimed the dukedom of Brittany. His claim was disputed by his uncle, John de Montfort, and he was immediately involved in warfare that continued to the end of his life. Blessed Charles did all in his power to allay the stress of war for his subjects, and is said to have offered to settle the succession by single combat in his own person. The first thing he did after the capture of Nantes was to provide for the poor and suffering, and he showed the same solicitude at Rennes, Guingamp, and elsewhere. To pray for his cause and the souls of those who were slain he founded religious houses, himself wore a hair-shirt and recited the office every day, and in general behaved so that the less devout of his followers complained that he was more fit to be a monk than a soldier. He went on pilgrimage barefooted to the shrine of St Yves at Tréguier, and when he held up the siege of Hennebon that his troops might assist at Mass one of his officers was moved to protest. " My lord," retorted Charles, " we can always have towns and castles. If they are taken away from us, God will help us to get them back again. But we cannot afford to miss Mass." And Charles was, in fact, as good a soldier as he was a Christian, but the weight of arms against him was too heavy. He had the support of the French King, but his rival John was helped by Edward III of England, who for his own reasons had announced his intention of winning back his " lawful inheritance of France." For four years Blessed Charles was able to keep his enemies at bay, but 1346 was a year of piled-up misfortune. France was beaten by England at Creçy, Poitiers was sacked, and Poitou captured ; then Charles faced his rival in a great battle at La Roche Derrien, not far from Tréguier, was defeated, captured, and shipped across to England.

He was housed in the Tower and a hundred thousand gold florins were asked for his ransom. The money was collected and sent off, but it went to the bottom of the sea with the ship that carried it, and it was nine years before Blessed Charles regained his liberty.

Like many prisoners in the Tower before and since his time he sanctified his confinement by patience and prayer and earned the ungrudging admiration of his gaolers. He pursued his struggle against John de Montfort for another nine years with varying fortunes but with ever growing respect and admiration from his people. At one time it was even thought that the pilgrimage of *Bonne Nouvelle* at Rennes commemorated one of his battles with Montfort, but this has been shown not to be so. The last engagement took place at Auray on September 29, 1364. Blessed Charles received the sacraments before the battle, and was killed on the field by an Englishman. Numerous and remarkable miracles were reported at his tomb, and in 1368 Blessed Urban V ordered his process to be begun. A few years later it was broken off by Gregory XI, and this has been attributed to the opposition of Duke John IV, whose prestige in Brittany might suffer were his late rival to be canonised. But the people continued to venerate Blessed Charles nevertheless, his feast was celebrated in some places, and finally in 1904 this ancient *cultus* was confirmed by Pope Pius X.

Among the " Prætermissi " of September 29 in the *Acta Sanctorum*, the Bollandists make mention of Charles of Blois and refer to Benedict XIV's great work *De Beatificatione*, etc., bk. ii, ch. 8. In this, curiously enough, an apostolic letter of Pope Urban V is quoted strictly *prohibiting* the cult of Charles. Extracts from the process which had been begun were printed by A. Duchesne, *Histoire de la Maison de Chantillon* (1621), pp. 126–131, and by Lobineau, *Histoire de Bretagne* (1744), vol. ii, pp. 540–570. See also R. Porcher, " Vie du B. Charles de Blois " in *Le Loir-et-Cher historique*, vol. x and xiv ; and F. B. Plaine, in *Revue des Questions historiques*, vol. xi (1872), pp. 41–90.

SEPTEMBER 30

ST JEROME, Conf. and Doctor of the Church

A.D. 420

JEROME (EUSEBIUS HIERONYMUS SOPHRONIUS), the father of the Church most learned in the sacred Scriptures, was born about the year 342 at Stridonium, a small town upon the confines of Pannonia, Dalmatia, and Italy, near Aquileia. His father, called Eusebius, was descended from a good family and had a large estate ; he took great care to have his son instructed in religion and in the first principles of letters at home and afterwards sent him to Rome. St Jerome had there for tutor the famous pagan grammarian Donatus and perhaps also Victorinus the Christian rhetorician. In this city he became master of the Latin and Greek tongues (his native language was the Illyrican), read the best writers in both languages with great application, and made such progress in oratory, that he for some time pleaded at the bar ; but being left without a guide, under the discipline of a heathen master in a school where an exterior regard for decency in morals was all that was aimed at, he forgot the true piety which had been instilled into him in his childhood, did not sufficiently restrain his passions, and was full of worldly ideas. His experience confirms the truth that though the advantages of emulation and mutual communication in studies are great with regard to learning, these must never be purchased with danger to virtue. Jerome went out of this school free indeed from gross vices, but unhappily a stranger to a Christian spirit and enslaved to vanity and other weaknesses, as he afterward confessed and bitterly lamented. On the other hand he was baptised at Rome (he was a catechumen till he was at least eighteen) and he himself tells us that " it was my custom on Sundays to visit, with friends of my own age and tastes, the tombs of the martyrs and apostles, going down into those subterranean galleries whose walls on either side preserve the relics of the dead." After some three years in Rome he determined to travel in order to improve his studies and, with his friend Bonosus, he went to Trier, then an imperial city. Here it was that the religious spirit with which he was so deeply imbued was awakened, and his heart was entirely converted to God so that, renouncing the vanity of his former pursuits and the irregularities of his life, he made a resolution to devote himself wholly to the divine service. From this time his ardour for virtue far surpassed that with which he had before applied himself to profane sciences, and he turned the course of his studies into a new channel. Being intent on enriching his library he copied at Trier St Hilary's book on Synods, and his commentaries on the Psalms and, having collected whatever he could meet with in Gaul to augment his literary treasures, he went, after a brief return to Rome when probably he was baptised by Pope Liberius, to Aquileia, where at that time flourished many eminent and learned men. St Valerian, the bishop, had entirely cleared that church of Arianism, with which it had been infected under his predecessor, and had drawn thither so many virtuous men, that the clergy of Aquileia were famous over all the Western Church. With many of these St Jerome became very friendly and their names appear often in his writings. Among these were St Chromatius, who was then priest and who succeeded St Valerian ; to him Jerome afterwards dedicated several of his works ; his two brothers, Jovinianus the archdeacon and Eusebius, deacon ; St Heliodorus and his nephew Nepotian ; and, above all, Rufinus, first the bosom friend and then the bitter opponent of Jerome. Already he was beginning to make enemies and provoke strong opposition, and after some years at Aquileia he was convinced that neither his own country nor Rome were fit places for a life of perfect solitude, at which he aimed. He resolved therefore to withdraw into some distant country. Bonosus, his countryman and foster-brother, who had been the companion of his studies and travels from his infancy, retired into a desert island on the coast of Dalmatia and there led a monastic life. Evagrius, a celebrated priest of Antioch, happened at that time to come into the West upon the affairs of his church, and he, meeting St Jerome at Aquileia, turned his mind towards the East. With his friends Innocent, Heliodorus and Hylas (a freed slave of St Melania) he determined to go thither.

St Jerome arrived in Antioch about the year 373 and made some stay in that city to attend the lectures of Apollinaris of Laodicea who had not yet openly broached the heresy into which he subsequently fell. Then, inspired by meeting a monk called Malchus, he himself with his companions left the city for the desert of Chalcis, a barren land about fifty miles south-east of Antioch. Innocent and Hylas soon died in this desert, and Heliodorus left it to return into the West ; but Jerome spent there four years in studies and the exercises of piety. In this lonely habitation he had many attacks of sickness but suffered a much more severe affliction from violent temptations to impurity. " In the remotest part of a wild and stony desert," he wrote years afterwards to St Eustochium, " burnt up with the heat of the scorching sun so that it frightens even the monks that inhabit it, I seemed to myself to be in the midst of the delights and crowds of Rome. . . . . In this exile and prison to which for the fear of Hell I had voluntarily condemned myself, with no other company but scorpions and wild beasts, I many times imagined myself witnessing the dancing of the Roman maidens as if I had been in the midst of them. My face was pallid with fasting, yet my will felt the assaults of desire : in my cold body and in my parched-up flesh, which seemed dead before its death, passion was able to live. Alone with this enemy, I threw myself in spirit at the feet of Jesus, watering them with my tears, and I tamed my flesh by fasting whole weeks. I am not ashamed to disclose my temptations, but I grieve that I am not now what I then was. I often joined night to day crying and beating my breast till calm returned." Thus does God allow His servants to be from time to time severely tried ; but the ordinary life of St Jerome was doubtless quiet, regular, and undisturbed. To forestall and ward off the insurgence of the flesh he added to his corporal austerities a new study, which he hoped would fix his rambling imagination and give him the victory over himself. This was to learn Hebrew. " When my soul was on fire with bad thoughts," says he, writing to the monk Rusticus in 411, " as a last resource I became a scholar to a monk who had been a Jew, to learn of him the Hebrew alphabet ; and, from the judicious rules of Quintilian, the copious flowing eloquence of Cicero, the grave style of Fronto, and the smoothness of Pliny, I turned to this language of hissing and broken-winded words. What labour it cost me, what difficulties I went through, how often I despaired and left off, and how I began again to learn, both I myself who felt the burden can witness, and they also who lived with me. And I thank our Lord, that I now gather such sweet fruit from the bitter sowing of those studies." However, he still continued to read the pagan classics with eagerness and pleasure, until an event which turned him from them, at any rate for a time. In a letter to Eustochium he relates that, being seized with sickness in the desert, in the heat of the fever he fell into a delirium in which he seemed to himself arraigned before the tribunal of Christ. Being asked who he was he answered that he was a Christian. " Thou liest," said the judge, " thou art a Ciceronian : for where thy treasure is, there is thy heart also."

The church of Antioch was at this time disturbed by doctrinal and disciplinary disputes. The monks of the desert of Chalcis vehemently took sides in these disputes and wanted St Jerome to do

the same and to pronounce on the matters at issue. He preferred
to stand aloof and be left to himself, but he wrote two letters to
consult St Damasus, who had been raised to the papal throne
at Rome in 366, what course he ought to steer. In the first he
says : " I am joined in communion with your holiness, that is,
with the chair of Peter ; upon that rock I know the Church is
built. Whoever eats the Lamb outside of that house is a profane
person. Whoever is not in the ark shall perish in the flood. I do not
know Vitalis ; I disown Meletius ; Paulinus* is a stranger to me.
Whoever gathers not with you, scatters ; he who is not Christ's
belongs to Antichrist. . . . Order me, if you please, what I should
do." Not receiving a speedy answer he soon after sent another
letter to Damasus on the same subject, in which he implores his
Holiness to answer his difficulties and not despise a soul for which
Jesus Christ died. " On one side the Arian fury rages, supported
by the secular power ; on the other side, the Church [at Antioch]
being divided into three parts, each would needs draw me to itself.
All the time I cease not to cry out : ' Whoever is united to the chair
of Peter, he is mine.' " The answer of Damasus is not extant : but
it is certain that he and all the West acknowledged Paulinus as bishop
of Antioch, and St Jerome received from his hands the holy order
of priesthood when he finally left the desert of Chalcis ; Jerome had
no wish to be ordained (he never celebrated the holy Sacrifice), and
he only consented on the condition that he should not be obliged to
serve that or any other church by his ministry : his vocation was
to be a monk or recluse. Soon after, about the year 380, he went to
Constantinople, there to study the holy Scriptures under St Gregory
Nazianzen, who was then bishop of that city. In several parts of his
works Jerome mentions with satisfaction and gratitude the honour and
happiness of having had so great a master in expounding the divine
writings. Upon St Gregory's leaving Constantinople in 382, St
Jerome went to Rome with Paulinus of Antioch and St Epiphanius to
attend a council which St Damasus held about the schism of Antioch
and other matters. Of this gathering Jerome was appointed secretary,
and acquitted himself so well that, when the council was over, Pope
Damasus detained him and employed him as his secretary in writing
his letters, in answering the consultations of bishops, and in other
important affairs of the Church. Jerome, indeed, claimed that he
spoke through the mouth of Damasus. At the Pope's request he
made a revision, in accordance with the Greek text, of the Latin
New Testament, which had been disfigured by " false transcription,
by clumsy correction, and by careless interpolations," and a first

* Rival claimants to the see of Antioch.

revision of the Latin Psalter. Side by side with this official activity
he was engaged in fostering and directing the marvellous flowering
of Christian asceticism which was taking place among some of the
noble ladies of Rome. Among them are several of the most famous
names of Christian antiquity : such were St Marcella, who is
referred to herein under January 31, with her sister St Asella and
their mother, St Albina ; St Lea ; St Melania the Elder, the first
one of them to go to the Holy Land ; St Fabiola (December 27) ;
and St Paula (January 26) with her daughters St Blesilla and
St Eustochium (September 28). The instruction and care of these
and other chosen souls did not so engross his time and attention but
that he was always at hand faithfully to discharge the duties imposed
on him by the pope ; but when St Damasus died in 384, and
his protection was consequently withdrawn from his secretary,
St Jerome found himself in a very difficult position. In the preceding
two years, while impressing all Rome by his personal holiness,
learning, and honesty, he had also contrived to get himself widely
disliked : on the one hand by pagans and men of evil life whom he
had fiercely condemned and on the other by people of good will who
were offended by the saint's harsh outspokenness and sarcastic wit.
When he wrote in defence of the fashionable young widow, Blesilla,
who had suddenly renounced the world, he was witheringly satirical
of pagan society and worldly life, and opposed to her lowliness the
the conduct of those who " paint their cheeks with rouge and their
eyelids with antimony ; whose plastered faces, too white for those
of human beings, look like idols, and if in a moment of forgetfulness
they shed a tear it makes a furrow where it rolls down the painted
cheek ; they to whom years do not bring the gravity of age, who
load their heads with other people's hair, enamel a lost youth upon
the wrinkles of age, and affect a maidenly timidity in the midst of a
troop of grandchildren." In the letter on virginity which he wrote
to St Eustochium he was no less scathing at the expense of Christian
society, and made a particular attack on certain of the clergy. " All
their anxiety is about their clothes. . . . You would take them for
bridegrooms rather than for clerics ; all they think about is to know
the names and houses and doings of rich ladies " ; and he proceeds
to describe a particular individual, who hates fasting, looks forward
to the smell of his meals, and has a barbarous and froward tongue.
Jerome wrote to St Marcella of a certain man who wrongly supposed
that he was an object of attack : " I amuse myself by laughing at
the grubs, the owls, and the crocodiles, and he takes all that I say
to himself. . . . Let me give him some advice. If he will only
conceal his nose and keep his tongue still he may be taken to be both

handsome and learned." It cannot be matter of surprise that, however justified his indignation was, his manner of expressing it aroused resentment. His own reputation was attacked with similar vigour ; even his simplicity, his walk and smile, the expression of his countenance were found fault with. Neither did the severe virtue of the ladies that were under his direction nor the reservedness of his own behaviour protect him from calumny : scandalous gossip was circulated about his relations with St Paula. He was properly indignant and decided to return to the East, there to seek a quiet retreat. He embarked at Porto in the month of August, 385, with his young brother Paulinian, a priest called Vincent, and some others. Before he left he wrote a fine *apologia*, in the form of a letter to St Asella. " Salute Paula and Eustochium," it concluded, " mine in Christ whether the world wills it or no . . . say to them, we shall all stand before the judgement seat of Christ, and there it shall be seen in what spirit each has lived." Landing at Cyprus, he was received with great joy by St Epiphanius, and at Antioch he visited the bishop Paulinus ; it was probably here, nine months after leaving Rome, that he was joined by Paula, Eustochium, and the other Roman religious women who had resolved to exile themselves with him in the Holy Land. Soon after arriving at Bethlehem they went to Egypt to visit the holy places there and to consult with the monks of Nitria, as well as with Didymus, a famous blind teacher in the school of Alexandria.

With what remained of Jerome's own patrimony and with the help of Paula's generosity a monastery for men was built near the basilica of the Nativity at Bethlehem, together with buildings for three communities of women. St Jerome himself lived and worked in a large cave near to our Saviour's birthplace, and opened a free school, as well as a hospice, " so that," as St Paula said, " should Mary and Joseph again visit Bethlehem there would be a place for them to lodge in." Here at last were some years of peace. " The illustrious Gauls congregate here, and no sooner has the Briton, so remote from our world, made some progress in religion than he leaves his early-setting sun to seek a land which he knows only by reputation and from the Scriptures. And what of the Armenians, the Persians, the peoples of India and Ethiopia, of Egypt, of Pontus, Cappadocia, Syria and Mesopotamia ? . . . They throng here and set us the example of every virtue. The languages differ but the religion is the same ; there are as many different choirs singing the psalms as there are nations. . . . Here bread, and herbs grown with our own hands, and milk, country fare, afford us plain and healthy food. In summer the trees give us shade. In autumn the

379

air is cool and the fallen leaves restful. In spring our psalmody is sweeter for the singing of the birds. We do not lack wood when winter snow and cold are upon us. Let Rome keep its crowds, let its arenas run with blood, its circuses go mad, its theatres wallow in sensuality and, not to forget our friends, let the senate of ladies receive their daily visits." But Jerome could not stand aside and be mute when Christian truth was threatened. He had, whilst he resided at Rome in the time of Pope Damasus, composed his book against Helvidius on the perpetual virginity of the Blessed Virgin Mary, Helvidius having maintained that Mary did not remain always a virgin but had other children, by St Joseph, after the birth of Christ. This and certain associated errors were again put forward by one Jovinian, who had been a monk. St Paula's son-in-law, St Pammachius, and other noble laymen were scandalised at his new doctrines, and, having met with a writing of Jovinian in which these errors were contained, carried it to Pope St Siricius, who condemned the same, as did St Ambrose. The heretical writings having been sent by Pammachius to St Jerome also, he in 393 wrote two books against Jovinian. In the first he shows the merit and excellence of virginity embraced for the sake of virtue, which had been denied by Jovinian, and in the second confutes his other errors. This treatise was written in Jerome's characteristically strong style and certain expressions in it seemed to some persons in Rome harsh and derogatory from the honour due to matrimony ; St Pammachius informed St Jerome of the offence which he and many others took at them. Thereupon Jerome wrote his Apology to Pammachius, sometimes called his third book against Jovinian, in which he shows, from his own book, that he commended marriage as honourable and holy, and protests that he condemns not even second or third marriages. A few years later he had to turn his attention to Vigilantius—Dormantius, sleepy, he calls him—a Gascon priest who both decried celibacy and condemned the veneration of relics, calling those who paid it idolaters and worshippers of ashes. St Jerome in his answer said : "We do not worship the relics of the martyrs ; but we honour them that we may worship Him whose martyrs they are. We honour the servants that the respect which is paid to them may be reflected back on the Lord." He vindicates the honour paid to martyrs from idolatry because no Christian ever adored them as gods, and in order to show that the saints pray for us he says : "If the apostles and martyrs while still living upon earth can pray for other men, how much more may they do it after their victories ? Have they less power now they are with Jesus Christ ? " He defends the monastic state, and says that a monk seeks his own security by flying occasions

and dangers because he mistrusts his own weakness and knows that
there is no safety if a man sleeps near a serpent. St Jerome often
speaks of the saints in Heaven praying for us. Thus he entreated
Heliodorus to pray for him when he should be in glory, and told
St Paula, upon the death of her daughter Blesilla : " She now prays
to the Lord for you, and obtains for me the pardon of my sins." But
the general tone of his reply to Vigilantius is even more vehement
than that to Jovinian. From 395 to 400 St Jerome was engaged in a
war against Origenism, which unhappily involved a breach of his
twenty-five years friendship with Rufinus. Years before he had
written to him the doubtful statement that " friendship which can
perish has never been a true one," as Shakespeare would write twelve
hundred years later :

> . . . . . Love is not love
> Which alters when it alteration finds
> Or bends with the remover to remove ;

and now his affection for Rufinus was to succumb to his zeal for
truth. Few writers made more use of Origen's works and no one
seemed a greater admirer of his erudition than St Jerome ; but
finding in the East that several monks and others had been seduced
into grievous errors by the authority of his name and some of his
writings he joined St Epiphanius in warmly opposing the spreading
evil. But Rufinus, who then lived in a monastery at Jerusalem,
translated many of Origen's works into Latin and was an enthusiastic
upholder of his authority : though it does not appear that he had
any intention of upholding those heresies which are undoubtedly
contained, at least materially, in Origen's writings. St Augustine
was not the least of the good men who were distressed by the resulting quarrel, which, however, he the more easily understood because
he himself became involved in a long controversy with St Jerome
arising out of the exegesis of the second chapter of St Paul's epistle
to the Galatians. By his first letters he had unintentionally provoked
Jerome, and he had to use considerable charitable tact to soothe his
easily wounded susceptibilities. St Jerome wrote in 416 : " I never
spared heretics and have always done my utmost that the enemies of
the Church should be also my enemies " ; but it seems that occasionally he unwarrantably assumed that those who differed from himself
were necessarily the Church's enemies. He was no admirer of
moderation whether in virtue or against evil. He was swift to anger
but also swift to remorse, even more severe on his own shortcomings
than on those of others. There is a story told that Pope Sixtus V,
looking at a picture of the saint which represented him in the act of

striking his breast with a stone, said : " You do well to carry that stone, for without it the Church would never have canonised you."

But his denunciations and controversies, necessary as most of them were, are the less important part of his activities : nothing has rendered the name of St Jerome so famous as his critical labours on the holy Scriptures. For this the Church acknowledges him to have been raised by God through a special providence, and she styles him the greatest of all her doctors in expounding the divine word. Pope Clement VIII did not scruple to call him a man divinely assisted in translating the holy Scriptures. He was furnished with the greatest helps for such an undertaking, living many years upon the spot where the remains of ancient places, names, customs which were still recent, and other circumstances set before his eyes a clearer representation of many things recorded in holy writ than it is possible to have at a greater distance of place and time. Greek and Chaldaic were then living languages, and Hebrew, though it had ceased to be such from the time of the captivity, was not less understood and spoken among the doctors of the law. It was thought that he could not be further instructed in the knowledge of Hebrew, but this was not his own judgement of the matter and he applied again to a famous Jewish master, called Bar Ananias, who for a sum of money came to teach him in the night-time, lest the Jews should know it. Above other conditions it is necessary that an interpreter of the holy Scriptures be a man of prayer and sincere piety. This alone can obtain light and help from Heaven, give to the mind a turn and temper which are necessary for being admitted into the sanctuary of the divine wisdom, and furnish the key. Jerome was prepared by a great purity of heart and a life spent in penance and contemplation before he was called by God to this important undertaking. We have seen that while in Rome under Pope St Damasus he had revised the New Testament and the Psalms in the Old Latin version. His new translation from the Hebrew of most of the books of the Old Testament was the work of his years of retreat at Bethlehem, which he undertook at the earnest entreaties of many devout and illustrious friends, and in view of the preference of the original to any version however venerable, and the necessity of answering the Jews, who in all disputations would allow no other. He did not translate the books in order, but began by the books of Kings, and took the rest in hand at different times. When he found that the book of Tobias and part of the book of Daniel were first written in Chaldaic he set himself to master that language : several times he was tempted to abandon this task in despair, but his vitality and determination kept him to it. The only parts of the Latin Bible called the Vulgate which were not either translated or worked over by St Jerome are the books of Wisdom, Ecclesiasticus, Baruch, and the two books of Machabees. The Psalms he revised again, with the aid of Origen's *Hexapla* and the Hebrew text, and this is the version included in the Vulgate and used in the Divine Office. The first revision, called the Roman Psalter, is still used for the invitatory psalm at Matins and throughout the Missal, and for the Divine Office in St Peter's at Rome, St Mark's at Venice, and in the Milanese rite. St Jerome's Vulgate was declared by the Council of Trent to be the authentic or authoritative Latin biblical text of the Catholic Church, without thereby implying any preference of this version above the original text or above versions in other languages. In 1907 Pope Pius X entrusted to the Benedictine Order the duty of restoring so far as possible St Jerome's text of the Vulgate, which during fifteen centuries of use has become considerably modified and corrupted. The version of the Bible ordinarily used by English-speaking Catholics is the translation of the Vulgate made at Rheims and Douay towards the end of the sixteenth century, as revised by Bishop Challoner in the eighteenth.

In the year 404 a great blow fell on St Jerome in the death of St Paula and a few years later in the sacking of Rome by Alaric ; many refugees fled into the East, and he wrote of them : " Who would have believed that the daughters of that mighty city would one day be wandering as servants and slaves on the shores of Egypt and Africa ? That Bethlehem would daily receive noble Romans, distinguished ladies brought up in wealth and now reduced to beggary ? I cannot help them all, but I grieve and weep with them, and, completely given up to the duties which charity imposes on me, I have put aside my commentary on Ezekiel and almost all study. For to-day we must translate the words of the Scriptures into deeds, and instead of speaking saintly words we must act them." Again towards the end of his life he was obliged to interrupt his studies by an incursion of barbarians, who penetrated through Egypt into Palestine, and some time after by the violence and persecution of the Pelagians who, after the Council of Diospolis, relying on the protection of John, Bishop of Jerusalem, sent a troop of ruffians to Bethlehem to assault the holy monks and nuns who lived there under the direction of St Jerome, who had opposed them. Some were beaten, and a deacon was killed by them, and they set fire to the monasteries. In the following year St Eustochium died and Jerome himself soon followed her : worn out with penance and work, his sight and voice failing, his body like a shadow, he died peacefully on September 30, 420. He was buried under the church of the Nativity close to Paula and Eustochium, but his body was translated in the thirteenth century and now lies somewhere in the Sistine chapel of St Mary Major's at Rome. He is often represented in art habited as a cardinal, because of the services he discharged for Pope St Damasus, and also with a lion from whose paw he was said to have drawn a thorn. This story has been transferred to him from the legend of St Gerasimus, but a lion is a far from inapt emblem of this fearless and fierce defender of the faith.

It is only by meditation on the Bible that its inexhaustible riches, concealed in every word, can be understood. We must also bring with us that spirit of prayer and that docility by which so many holy doctors have been rendered faithful interpreters of the word of God. The tradition of the Church must be our direction. Without an humble submission to this light we are sure to be led astray, and the most learned men who do not stick close to this rule (as experience and authority both teach us) tread in the steps of those whose study of the Scriptures has hurt the Church instead of serving her. The orthodox faith does not depend upon the Scriptures considered in themselves, but as explained by Catholic tradition. As the solid interpretation of the Bible is founded on the genuine and literal sense, to give this its fullest extent and force the aid of sober criticism must be called in, in which, among the Latin fathers, no one equals St Jerome. His example shows that criticism was not neglected by the Fathers in interpreting and vindicating the holy Scriptures : but they were chiefly solicitous in applying the types, figures, and prophecies, in setting forth Christ, and in bringing men to Him.

During the last few years much advance has been made in the study of the life of St Jerome. Of special value is the volume *Miscellanea Geronimiana* which was published at Rome in 1920 to do honour to the fifteenth centenary of his death. In this a number of eminent scholars, including such names as Duchesne, Batiffol, Lanzoni, Zeiller and Bulic, contribute studies on moot points of particular interest in connection with the saint. Then in 1922 appeared the best modern Life, that of Père F. Cavallera, *Saint Jerome, sa Vie et son Œuvre* (Paris, 2 vols.), though the criticisms of Père Peeters in *Analecta Bollandiana*, vol. xlii, pp. 180–184, claim careful attention. At an earlier date we have the discovery by Dom Germain Morin of Jerome's *Commentarioli* and *Tractatus* on the Psalms, with other finds (see his *Études, Textes, Découvertes*, pp. 17–25). Further a very full article on St Jerome by Dom H. Leclercq figures in the *Dict. d'Archéol. chrét.*, vol. vii, cc. 2235–2304 ; and another by J. Forget in the *Dict. de Théol. cath.*, vol. viii (1924), cc. 894–983. In the eighteenth century we have the painstaking labours of Vallarsi, and of the Bollandists (September, vol. viii). The early accounts of St Jerome, with the exception perhaps of the chronicle of Marcellinus (edited by Mommsen in the *Monumenta Germanie, Auct. antiquissimi*, ii, pp. 47 *seq.*), do not offer much of value. Jerome's correspondence and works must always remain the principal source for a study of his life.

ST GREGORY THE ILLUMINATOR, Bp. of Ashtishat. Conf.

c. A.D. 330

The Christian faith was first preached in Armenia during the second or third century, probably by missionaries from Syria and Persia, but the local beliefs concerning this first evangelisation are different and contradictory. These worthless legends give the credit for it to the apostles SS. Bartholomew and Thaddeus, and together with Thaddeus have appropriated the story of King Abgar the Black and the likeness of our Lord, which really belongs to Edessa and St Addai (August 5). Nevertheless, the Armenians also venerate St Gregory of Ashtishat as the apostle who brought the light of the Gospel to their country, whence he is named " the Illuminator " and regarded as their principal national saint and patron. He was born in the third century, at a time when the Persians had invaded Armenia, practically destroyed the infant church there, and imposed their own Mazdæism on the conquered people. His origin and even nationality are uncertain. According to unreliable Armenian tradition he was a son of that Parthian Anak who about the year 235 murdered King Khosrov I of Armenia. When the dying Khosrov ordered the extermination of Anak's family, the baby Gregory was smuggled away by a merchant of Valarshapat to Cæsarea in Cappadocia. Here certainly he was baptised and brought up a Christian, and in due course married and had two sons, St Aristakes and St Vardanes. In 261 Tiridates, a son of King Khosrov, who had been in exile among the Romans, returned with an army to his country and drove out the Persians. Gregory was given a place at the court of Tiridates (an unlikely thing if he were really a son of his father's murderer), but soon incurred the displeasure of the King by the encouragement he gave to the remaining Armenian Christians and by his zeal in making converts. Active persecution began, SS. Rhipsime, Gaiana, and others were put to death, and Gregory himself suffered greatly. But eventually he triumphed. Tiridates himself was converted (he is venerated as a saint), and while Christians in the Empire were suffering under the persecution of Diocletian, Christianity was proclaimed the official religion of Armenia, which thus became the first Christian state in the world's history. Somewhere about the year 302 St Gregory went to Cæsarea and there was consecrated bishop by the metropolitan Leontius. He established his see at Ashtishat and then set himself with the aid of Greek and Syrian missionaries to organise his church, instruct the new converts, and win over waverers. To recruit a native clergy he took a number of youths, instructed them in the holy Scriptures and Christian morality, and taught them Greek and Syriac. These entered into their studies with eagerness, gladly repudiating the barbarous customs of their parents, and the rough neophytes soon became gentle and spiritual, attentive to the word of God and the writings of the prophets and the apostles, and inheritors of the gospel and grace of Christ by obedience to his commandments. " Invincibly did our Illuminator carry the life-giving name of Jesus from end to end of the land, in all seasons and weathers, untiring and earnest in the duties of an evangelist, repelling adversaries, preaching before chieftains and nobles, and enlightening every soul which by the new birth of baptism was made a child of God. To show forth the glory of Christ he rescued prisoners and captives and those oppressed by tyrants ; he destroyed unjust contracts and liabilities ; he comforted by his words many who were afflicted or living in fear, putting before them the hope of the glory of God and planting our Lord Jesus Christ in their souls so that they became truly glad." Gregory, as head of the Armenian church, sent his son St Aristakes to represent him at the first œcumenical council at Nicæa, and when Gregory read the *acta* of that assembly he is said to have exclaimed : " As for us, we praise Him who was before time, worshipping the Holy Trinity and the one Godhead of the Father, the Son, and the Holy Ghost, now and throughout all ages." Whether or no St Gregory actually made use of these words, they are still repeated by the celebrant in the Armenian Liturgy when the deacon has recited the conciliar anathema after the creed. Shortly after Gregory consecrated Aristakes to succeed him, and himself retired to a hermitage on Mount Manyea in the province of Taron. In the following year he was found dead by a shepherd and was buried at Thortan.

Some of the above few particulars of this saint are at the best only probable, but if authentic information is scarce legends are not wanting, which are set out at length in a Life written by one who called himself Agathangelos and averred that he was secretary to King Tiridates. Actually it was not composed earlier than the second half of the fifth century. According to this work, which is still accepted by the majority of pious Armenians, Gregory first got into trouble with Tiridates for refusing to lay a garland of flowers on the image of the goddess Anahit in her temple at Ashtishat. When he could by no means persuade him to this act of worship, Tiridates had him tortured in twelve different ways, ways of a cruel ingenuity differing considerably from those usually recorded of martyrs under the Romans. Gregory was then thrown into a noisome pit, stinking with corpses, filth, and vermin, where he was left and forgotten for fifteen years. But he was kept alive by the ministrations of a kindly widow. After the martyrdom of St Rhipsime (September 29), King Tiridates was possessed by a devil and turned into a wild boar, roaming about the woods with others of his kind, and it was revealed in a vision to his sister that he would be restored to his natural shape only by the prayers of Gregory. Whereupon the pit was searched, he was found and released from confinement, and at once healed the King who in repentance and gratitude was baptised with his wife and sister. Gregory then fasted without food, prayed, and preached for seventy days, and had a vision at Valarshapat near Mount Ararat in which our Lord came down from Heaven and showed him that He wanted the chief cathedral-church of Armenia to be built there where he was. Which was done and the place called Etshmiadzin, which means " the Only-begotten has descended "; but the story of the vision was really invented to bolster up the claim of the Armenian church to be independent of Cæsarea. So great was Gregory's apostolic vigour that, though the false gods had to be opposed by force of arms, he baptised four million people in seven days! Each of these marvels, namely, the Twelve Torments, the Casting into the Pit, the Release from the Pit, and the Vision, is commemorated by a separate feast among the Armenians, who keep other feasts of St Gregory as well. He is sometimes erroneously venerated as a martyr, *e.g.* among the Greeks, who claim to have translated his relics to Constantinople at the end of the fifth century ; some of them found their way to Naples where they are still treasured and the saint is held in great honour.

Those who are not specialists in Oriental languages have to be content, in the case of Armenian and Georgian saints, to consult second-hand sources. Even the Bollandists in the eighteenth century (*Acta Sanctorum*, September, vol. viii) had to do the best they could with the aid of a Greek version or abridgement of the unreliable and often fabulous Armenian narrative attributed to Agathangelus. The genuine Armenian Agathangelus, if he ever existed, cannot be traced, but we seem to possess an Arabic version of an earlier stage in the development of the pseudo-Agathangelus. This is in a letter of the Arabian bishop George to the priest Joshua. See von Ryssel, *Ein Brief Georgs an den Presb. Joshua* (1883) ; A. von Gutschmid, *Kleine Schriften*, vol. iii (1892), pp. 339–420 ; Gelzer in the *Berichte* of the sächsischen Gesellschaft, Phil. Histor. 1895, pp. 109–174 ; Peeters in the *Analecta Bollandiana*, vol. xxvi (1907), pp. 117–120 and vol. l (1932), pp. 3–58. All these are agreed that the Rhipsime section of the story is pure fable. For fuller details concerning St Gregory's reputed activities consult Weber, *Katholische Kirche in Armenien*, pp. 115, etc., and Tournebize, *Histoire politique*, etc., pp. 423 seq.

ST HONORIUS, ABP. OF CANTERBURY, CONF.

A.D. 653

This apostolic man was a Roman by birth, and a monk by profession. St Gregory the Great, from the experience which he had of his virtue and skill in sacred learning, made choice of him for one of the missionaries which he sent to convert the English to the faith, though whether he was of St Augustine's orginal company or came over with the second band in 601 is not known. Upon the death of St Justus about the year 627 St Honorius was chosen archbishop of Canterbury. He was consecrated at Lincoln by St Paulinus, Bishop of York, and received the *pallium* sent from Rome by Pope Honorius I together with a letter, in which his Holiness ordained that whenever either the see of Canterbury or York should become vacant, the other bishop should ordain the person that should be duly elected, " because of the long distance of sea and land that lies between us and you." And to confirm this delegation of the patriarchal power of consecrating all bishops under him, a *pallium* was sent also to the Bishop of York. The new archbishop saw with joy the faith of Christ extending daily in many different parts of this island and the spirit of the gospel taking deep root in the hearts of many chosen servants of God. His care in filling all places with pastors truly dead to worldly interests or views, and his own zeal and shining example, contributed exceedingly, with the divine blessing, to so great an increase throughout a long episcopate of some twenty-five years. One of the first and most important of his acts was to consecrate the Burgundian St Felix as bishop of Dunwich and send him on his mission to convert the East Angles. After King Edwin was slain in battle at Hatfield Chase and Cadwallon of Wales, " more cruel than any pagan," says St Bede, " and resolved to cut off every Englishman in Britain," ravaged Northumbria, St Paulinus fled with Queen Ethelburga and was given shelter by St Honorius, who appointed him to the vacant see of Rochester. When Paulinus died there in 644 Honorius consecrated in his place St Ithamar, a man of Kent " but not inferior to his predecessors in learning and behaviour," and made several other Englishmen bishops. St Honorius died on September 30, 653, and was buried in the abbey-church of SS. Peter and Paul at Canterbury. He is named in the Roman Martyrology and commemorated liturgically in the dioceses of Southwark and Nottingham.

For all this see Bede, *Eccles. Hist.*, bks. ii and iii, with Plummer's notes ; and *cf.* Stanton's *Menology*, pp. 466–467.

ST SIMON OF CRESPY, Conf.

c. A.D. 1080

Simon, Count of Crespy in Valois, was descended from Charlemagne and a relative of Matilda, wife of William the Conqueror, in whose court he was brought up. He was favoured by William and fought against Philip I of France to keep the Vexin for Normandy, but he desired to be a monk, moved thereto, it is said, by the sight of the decomposing body of his father which he was taking from Montdidier to be buried at Crespy. There is a story told of his persuading his *fiancée* to be a nun, and of a romantic flight from their respective homes just before the wedding. Simon's intention was frustrated for a time by King William, who wished him to marry his daughter Adela. He was afraid directly to refuse his powerful benefactor, and went off to Rome on the pretext of finding out if the projected marriage were lawful, as the lady was his kinswoman. On the way he went to the abbey of Saint-Claude at Condat in the Jura, and there received the habit. Like other royal monks he was called on by his superiors and relatives to use his influence to bring about reconciliations and restorations of rights. St Hugh of Cluny sent him to the King of France to recover lands that had been taken from his monastery, and he intervened in the troubles between William the Conqueror and his sons. When Pope St Gregory VII, in view of his conflict with the Emperor, determined to come to terms with Robert Guiscard and his Normans in Italy, he sent for St Simon to help him in the negotiations. These were brought to a successful conclusion at Aquino in 1080, and the Pope kept Simon by his side. He died in Rome shortly afterwards, receiving the last sacraments from the hands of St Gregory himself. The feast of St Simon is kept in several French dioceses.

Many of Simon's contemporaries have sung his praises. Bd. Urban II (Otto de Lagery) compiled a eulogistic epitaph for his tomb, and Guibert de Nogent, who denounced so uncompromisingly the corruption of the age, wrote enthusiastically of the good example set by Simon. These and many other testimonies have been collected in the *Acta Sanctorum*, September, vol. viii, together with a separate biography, anonymous but written not long after his death. See also Corblet, *Hagiographie d'Amiens*, vol. iii, pp. 291–319.

INDEX TO VOLUME IX

(The numbers in brackets indicate date of death.)

E

Eanswida, St (c. 640), 153.
Edith of Wilton, St (984), 210.
Eleutherius, St (6th cent.), 67.
Elzear, St (1323), 334.
Emmeramus, St (7th cent.), 290.
Eulogius, St (607), 160.
Eunan, see Adamnan.
Euphemia, St (c. 307), 205.
Eusebius, St, pope (310), 323.
Eusebius and others, SS. (362), 86.
Eustace, St (118), 266.
Eustochium, St (420), 343.
Eustochius, St (461), 256.
Exaltation of the Cross (629), 166.
Exuperius, St (c. 415), 342.

F

Faustus of Riez, St (c. 493), 345.
Felix IV, St (530), 288.
Ferreolus, St (c. 304), 246.
Finbar, St (c. 623), 312.
Finnian of Moville, St (c. 575), 127.
Firminus I, St (c. 287), 310.
Firminus II, St (4th cent.), 5.
Flower, see Robert.
Francis of Camporosso, Bd. (1866), 218.
Francis Possadas, Bd. (1713), 269.
Franco, see Apollinaris.

G

Gentilis, Bd. (1340), 64.
Gerard Sagredo, St (1046), 303.
Geremarus or Germer, St (c. 658), 302.
Ghebre, see Michael.
Giles, St (c. 712), 1.
Goericus, St (647), 257.
Gorgonius and others, SS. (304), 93.
Gregory the Illuminator, St (c. 330), 385.
Grimonia, St (4th cent.), 73.
Guala Romanoni, Bd. (1244), 39.
Guy or Guido, St (c. 1012), 154.

H

Helen Duglioli, Bd. (1520), 300.
Hilarus, St (468), 126.
Hildegard, St (1179), 229.
Holy Cross Day, 166.
Honorius, St (653), 388.
Hyacinth, St (c. 257), 139.

I

Ida of Herzfeld, St (c. 813), 48.
Imbert, see Laurence.
Isaac the Great, St (c. 440), 94.
Ixida, see Antony.

J

Januarius, St (c. 305), 251.
Jerome, St (420), 374.
Joan Soderini, Bd. (1367), 11.
John Duckett, Bd. (1644), 78.
John the Dwarf, St (5th cent.), 178.
John-Gabriel Perboyre, Bd. (1840), 147.
John Mark, St (1st cent.), 333.
John-Mary du Lau, Bd. (1792), 28.
John Massias, Bd. (1645), 249.
John of Meda, St (1159), 328.
John of Nicomedia, St (303), 73.
John of Perugia, Bd. (1231), 38.
Joseph of Cupertino, St (1633), 239.
Justina, St (n.d.), 321.

K

Kieran, St (556), 96.

L

Laetus, St (c. 484), 66.
Lambert, St (c. 700), 224.
Laurence Imbert, Bd. (1839), 273.
Laurence Justinian, St (1455), 54.
Laurence of Ripafratta, Bd. (1457), 352.
Leu, see Lupus.
Linus, St (c. 78), 293.

The Mayflower Press, Plymouth. William Brendon & Son, Ltd.